Storytelling and the Future of Organizations

An Antenarrative Handbook

Edited by David M. Boje

Routledge
Taylor & Francis Group
New York   London

First published 2011
by Routledge
270 Madison Avenue, New York, NY 10016

Simultaneously published in the UK
by Routledge
2 Park Square, Milton Park, Abingdon, Oxon OX14 4RN

Routledge is an imprint of the Taylor & Francis Group, an informa business

Typeset in Sabon by IBT Global.
Printed and bound in the United States of America on acid-free paper by IBT Global.

Library of Congress Cataloging-in-Publication Data

Storytelling and the future of organizations : an antenarrative handbook / edited by David Boje.
   p. cm. — (Routledge studies in management, organizations, and society ; 11)
   Includes bibliographical references and index.
 1. Organization—Research.   2. Storytelling.   I. Boje, David M.
   HD30.4.S753 2011
   302.3'5—dc22
   2010031061

ISBN13: 978-0-415-87391-8 (hbk)

Contents

PART II
Organization and Writing Antenarratives

PART III
Antenarratives and Organization Change

PART IV
National and Globalizing Antenarratives: National and Globalizing Antenarratives

Figures

Tables

Acknowledgements

I would like to acknowledge the influence of my wife Grace Ann Rosile on the antenarrative ideas. She always sees far ahead into my future the antenarrative I am about to unfold, step by step, in my life.

I also want to acknowledge the authors of this book, who have worked with me since 2001 when I invented the term 'antenarrative' as a way to get at a kind of storytelling that has not solidified or cohered into a dominant narrative of the past. Each of the authors has done work in antenarrative that they now bring forward in this book.

The work of Stacy Noto of Routledge and Michael Watters of Integrated Book technology Global in getting the copy edits, proofs, and permissions together has been a great experience. Stacy and Michael have raised the quality of our writing. They were encouraging and easy to work with. I personally found the Routledge crew to be awesome.

Antenarratives shape the future of storytelling organizations. The work of the authors and the Routledge crew is allowing our collective work to play with visions of the future that have not yet fossilized into retrospective narratives. The antenarratives in this book are dialogically co-generative, shaping some future that is around the corner, out of view, on what I would call a Now Spiral. The Now Spiral has a sort of shape, but the rings of the spiral are uneven, and unpredictable.

Each of the chapters the wonderful authors have provided makes connections between the loops of the spiral, between its circuits, moving back and forward, and in-between the twirls. Ours is not a linear projection, not a prediction of some cyclic antenarrative ready to repeat. There is plenty of that in the management and organization writing. We have chosen to move together, this group of antenarrating authors, along a course, whose future we cannot chart. We are aware that with each Now, and the iterative, next Now, we get a glimpse for something we are shaping and that is shaping our storytelling. I acknowledge all my companions on this Now Spiral, and appreciate them immensely for our expedition.

David M. Boje November 12, 2010

Introduction to Agential Antenarratives That Shape the Future of Organizations

David M. Boje

INTRODUCTION TO AGENTIAL ANTENARRATIVE THEORY

Antenarrative is a word and concept I invented (Boje, 2001a) and has been studied by other authors such as Barge (2004), Collins and Rainwater (2005), Dalcher and Drevin (2003), Vickers (2005), and Yolles (2007), and those writing chapters in this handbook. 'Ante' refers to "a bet" and "a before." Therefore, antenarrative is a bet on the future and it's before narrative cohesion fossilizes the past. It is a bet that in this chapter, I will assert is 'agential.' Here is a more precise definition:

> *Antenarrative* is defined as a bet on the future pattern, in (more or less) authentic scenario of event-space. It is also a before narrative that serves as a hypothesis of the trajectory of unfolding events that avoids the pitfalls of premature narrative closure (Boje, 2001a, 2007b, 2008). Antenarratives involve a form of repackaging—where new characteristics are recognized and old characteristics are minimized. This morphological analysis of antenarratives uncovers forms of dissimulation and simulation that mask situational reality. Antenarratives morph and coalesce in storytelling networks. Antenarrative is a prospective sensemaking (looking forward), and is in intraplay with now-spective (in the present moment of emergent being), and retrospective (backward looking) manners of sensemaking. The agential aspects of antenarrative are in its intraplay with materiality.

This introduction begins with some practical applications, then posits a triadic model of three genres of storytelling that are in intraplay with one another and material conditions, and then develops current approaches to antenarrative and how they participate in shaping the future of organizations.

Practical—Antenarrative ways of storytelling that shape the future of organizations are highly practical. I teach undergraduate and master's students in my small-business consulting class and PhD students in our seminar on complexity systems to do several collective storytelling interventions to change the cycle, and change the rhizome-assemblage of Las Cruces & Mesilla Valley Arts Scene. 'Ante' your 'bet on the future!' 'Chaos' does not mean disorder (that's just noise or cacophony). Chaos is not just entanglement to the neglect of order. Chaos is movement whose order is hidden, subterranean, preconscious. Its antenarrative chaos of subterranean (rhizome) order and complexity dynamics of storytelling (defined as interplay of antenarrative, living story, and linear narrative) that are the subject of the handbook we coauthors are putting forward.

Triadic Model of Storytelling—Storytelling is the domain of discourse we focus upon. Storytelling has three genres that are in intraplay: narrative, living story, and antenarrative (See Figure I.1). Let's define each, how they intraplay, and scholarly work that has been done to sort that out.

Narrative is the dominant force in the storytelling domain, and for millennia has focused on the past, on form, and structure, but not looked much at all at the future or at agency (Barney et. al, 2010; Boje, 2010). Narrative has turned living story spaces into rather rigid places, and just ignored transformative antenarrative processes altogether.

Narrative for millennia has required story to be " . . . a whole . . . a whole is that which has beginning, middle, and end" (Aristotle, 350 BCE:

Figure I.1   Storytelling triad model.

1450b: 25, p. 233). This I call the BME narrative. Similarly, Weick's (1995) approach to narrative is whole, BME plot, and retrospective. Part of the problem is that narrative is treated as a thing (a particle, some stackable texts) or just dead text, whereas much of storytelling is more of a wave. Czarniawska (2004), for example, defines a 'petrified narrative' as the basis of a strong corporate culture, where the retrospected past has sedimented and can guide the future. A related problem in retrospective sensemaking narrative that Currie (1998) identifies is they petrify (or stabilize) so quickly there is a lack of noticing of the dynamics of living story networking.

Whereas Czarniawska (2004) acknowledges Boje's (1991) fragmentation and terse narrative processes of change, where storytelling is preferred sensemaking currency of organizations, Gabriel (2000) objects to saying a story is terse, or implied, instead of being worked out in its emotive appeal. A key constraint of narrative is monologism: Bakhtin (1973, p. 12), for example, says, "Narrative genres are always enclosed in a solid and unshakable monological framework." Derrida (1979, p. 94) also sees narrative as hegemonic. There is something else going on in the storytelling domain beside the work on narrative, its retrospection and petrification, such as living stories, ones we are embedded in, are more in the now. And is on the move.

Living Story—Living story is all about movement, the tour, a founding of story spaces, a networking in the unfolding present, where each story is dialogically relational to another one, and must be told to tell of another social relationship, another context. Living stories are often without beginning, and are never-ending (unlike narrative). There is for Bakhtin a "Dialogical manner of story" (1981, p. 60). Derrida (1979, pp. 99–100), for example, treats story more in terms of their reflexivity web of story to other stories. And for de Certeau (1984) stories are spatializing, tours, all about movement, and founding spaces. Living stories are morphed by narrative into something highly abstract and linear as narratives go. Narratives erase the living story "little wow" moments. It's a rather deadening, fossilizing, petrifying, and reifying process that narrative undertakes. Finally, we turn to a phenomenon that is also like living story on the move but is much more a 'bet' on the future, something that morphs and does not settle down just yet into narrative order.

Antenarrative—Antenarratives are self-organizing frontiers, fragments that seem to cling to other fragments, and form interesting complexity patterns of assemblage relationships to context and one another (Boje, 2001a, 2001b, 2001c, 2002, 2003, 2005, 2007a, 2007b, 2007c, 2008, forthcoming). The work has been extended in collaboration (Boje & Rosile, 2002, 2003; Boje, Rosile, Durant, & Luhman, 2004; Boje, Rosile & Gardner, 2007) and inspired additional independent work in the field of antenarrative (Barge 2004; Collins & Rainwater, 2005; Eriksen, 2006; Ericksen et al., 2005; Vickers, 2005; Yolles, 2007). Antenarratives are a bridging of past narratives stuck in place with emergent living stories. The opposition of places and spaces comes from Michel de Certeau (1984). Antenarratives are on the move, founding spaces, whereas narratives have settled into places. On the bridge story, spaces become narrated into just places, and narrative places can be displaced into living story spaces. This exchange is what shapes the future of organizations.

Next I introduce the reader to collective dynamics of storytelling complexity and chaos. Antenarrative is the bridging between narrative places and living story spaces.

The Intraplay of the Three Genres in Storytelling Domains—Narratives are in place, and living stories are forever founding spaces of movement, trajectory, and itinerary.

> Collective Storytelling Dynamics is defined as the intraplay of linear narrative, living story networking in the now, and antenarrative bets on the future.

This figure continues to combine my work on antenarratives (Boje, 2001a) with de Certeau (1984) place and space opposition, and the White and Epston (1990) *Narrative Therapy* work (restorying). Narrating reduces living story spaces to abstraction. Restorying recovers the 'little wow moments' (as I call them) from narrative oblivion, restoring living story into an antenarrative of the future, a new frontier, shaping the future of organizations. Table I.1 gives a summary of key points.

The narrative is before antenarrative and tends to erase the details of living story, leaving all the 'little story moments' that spacialize on the editing floor. Narratives "traverse and organize places; they select and link them

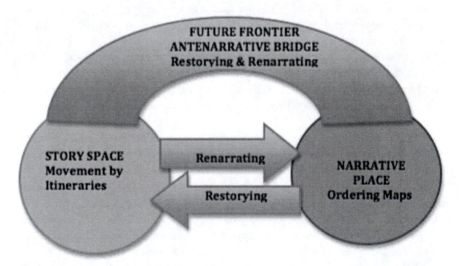

Figure I.2   Antenarrative as bridge between living story space and narrative place maps.

Table I.1   Contrasts of Triadic Storytelling Genres

NARRATIVE	LIVING STORY	ANTENARRATIVE
1. Abstract	1. Dispersed	1. Transformers
2. Monological	2. Polylogical	2. Polylogical
3. Whole	3. Web of Relationships	3. Packs
4. BME	4. Multiplotted	4. Multiplotted
5. Linear	5. Nonlinear	5. Transitioning
6. Retrospective	6. Now & Here	6. Unfolding
7. Centripetal (centering)	7. Centrifugal (differing)	7. Heteroglossic
8. In Place—fossilized	8. Founding Space by movement	8. Unsettling

together; they make sentences and itineraries out of them. They are spatial trajectories (de Certeau, 1984, p. 115). "Every story is a travel story—a spatial practice" (p. 115). Narrative reduces living story movement spaces to a place of stability and order and univocality.

SHAPING THE FUTURE: AGENCY AND STORYTELLING

Agential Storytelling Theory

I have been sorting out an agential approach to storytelling. I began following Karen Barad's (2007, p. 181) work on agential realism while in Denmark, when Anete M. Camille-Strand introduced me to it. She presented that work at Standing Conference for Management and Organization Inquiry in April 2010 (Camille-Strand, 2010, p. 1), in an action research project to effect "material storytelling."

Barad's (2007) *agential realism theory* ties discourse to materializing agency in a quantum physics theory of realism that is not positivistic. For Barad (2007, p. 139) "the notion of *intra-action* (in contrast to the usual 'interaction,' which resumes the prior existence of independent entities or realta) represents a profound conceptual shift." Barad assumes (2007, pp. 181–182) discourse and materiality are intraplaying, and not separated, as in classical approaches to mechanistic physics. Barad (2007, p. 181) views "space, time, and matter" as "mutually constituted through the dynamics of iterative intra-activity" rather than as an *interaction*. Ironically, it is in the 'native' American storytelling writing that postcolonial theory, post-classical narrative, and management/organization studies have ignored that one finds an important *intra-activity* of storytelling and materiality that is considered agential.

I began submitting journal articles on what I called 'Agential Storytelling Theory' (hereafter AST) in the past couple of years (Barney, Boje, Kach, Maynard-Patrick, McCulloh, Tobey, & Tourani, 2010; Boje, 2010).

"Storytelling is a way of participation in and is interdependent with material conditions of a living life-world" (Boje, 2010, p. 7).

In the first effort to tie storytelling to postcolonial theory (Boje, 2010, pp. 1–2), I asserted that representational narrative discourse ignores "*material-agentive-storytelling* practices" that are so salient to '*native*' American '*indians*' (Allen, 1992; Cajete, 2000; Owens, 2001; Vizenor, 1994, 1996, 1998, 1999—to name but a few).[1]

Allen's (1992) material-agential-storytelling perspective is rooted in "the oral tradition [that] has prevented the complete destruction of the web [of identity that long held tribal people secure], the ultimate disruption of tribal ways" (p. 45, bracketed additions, mine). Allen is convinced the tribal person "knows that living things are subject to processes of growth and change as a necessary component of their aliveness" and "is not symbolic in the usual sense" because it also has a "material dimension" (p. 62). Tribal peoples' storytelling is to "embody, articulate, and share reality" and to "actualize" and shape its direction with "the forces that surround and govern human life and the related lives of all things" (p. 56).

For Cajete (2000), storytelling is materialist, and the old charge of animism is for the posthumanist Cajete, an attention to interdependence of humans with the cycle regeneration and transformation of life on Earth. (Cajete, 2000. p. 95). Euro-American narrative, by contrast, is a second-order representational experience of being in interdependent relationship with the world. Narrative is a representational blueprint or map, "detached" and "estranged" (p. 24).

In the postcolonial storytelling paper (Boje, 2010), I relied on Owens's (2001, pp. 172–173) observation that seminal postcolonial theorists marginalized native American literature: "Edward Said [1993] . . . this celebrated father of postcolonial theory dismisses Native American writing in a single scathingly imperial phrase as 'that sad panorama produced by genocide and cultural amnesia which is beginning to be know as 'native American literature'; Homi Bhabha is totally silent about indigenous Native American writing; and the lone exception is Trinh Minh-ha's . . . inclusion of Leslie Marmon Silko's storytelling, and giving passing note to Native American writers Momaday, Joy Harjo, Vizenor, and Linda Hogan."

Vizenor (1994, 1996, 1998, 1999) applies poststructuralism, critical theory, and dialogical theory to accentuate a version of living stories that is a resistance to dominant colonizer narrative (Boje, 2010). Stories connote a special sense of materiality, what Vizenor (1998, p. 15) calls *transmotion,* defined as "that sense of native motion and an active presence, [that] is *sui generis* sovereignty" and "a reciprocal use of nature, not a monotheistic, territorial sovereignty." Storied transmotion is a material "presence in stories, an actual presence in the memories of others, and an obviative presence as semantic evidence" and in a Bakhtinian sense "a dialogical circle" (p. 169) and "in a 'dialogical context,' the conversions of [ethical] answerability" (p. 27, bracketed addition, mine; see Boje, 2010). Stories are a transmotion, and a virtual sense of presence in animated and embodied native memories that, like Cajete, includes, in a posthumanist philosophy, animal memories.

Agential Storytelling Theory (AST) "posits 'agential' as an 'intra-play' of discourse (including storytelling & sensemaking) entangled with materiality" (Barad, 2007, p. 181) accomplished, in part, by 'textual mediations' (Smith, 1990, p. 209).

Some storytelling patterns are full of noise and cacophony. *Others patterns emerge from time to time. One can learn to read the antenarrative linearity and cycles, but the spirals and rhizome-assemblages are a bit more difficult to discern.* Next, I explore these types of antenarrative shapes. Currently, there are four types of antenarrative: linear, cycles, spirals, and rhizomes. These are in dynamic interplay.

TYPES OF ANTENARRATIVES

Linear Antenarrative: Linear antenarrative is beginning middle end (BME) plot structure. It reduces life to the three-act play (first threshold, crisis, and climax) of the linear hero's journey. This BME narrative line is retrospective flatland storytelling (storytelling life reduced to a line). The prospective antenarrative, by contrast, is forward looking, an attempt at futuristic scenario making. The linear antenarrative challenge is to navigate future waters, to get from point A to B, in situations where there is not complete situational knowledge of outcomes.

A simple example is goal setting in planning the future. The goal setting antenarrative assumes a linear sequence with initiatory event A as the starting point, then in sequence, to B, C, and so on. The linear antenarrative assumes there will be no surprises, no departures from the beginning, middle, end scenarios. It also assumes that there are no shadow events, such as X, Y or Z that will disrupt the course of the planning antenarrative. If we project past onto the future (working backwards from imagined goal-finish to the starting point A), we have future-perfect antenarrative in short- and long-term memory: imagining future as completed and reverse engineering steps (backwards from I-finish) to get there (to A our starting point) brings us back to prospective narrative.

This kind of linear thinking in antenarrative (and retro-narrative) is highly instrumental. It is a utilitarian ethics. It assumes, in linear antenarrative terms, we can know the end (goal, outcome, result) and lay out linear steps to get there. It assumes the predictability of ends, cause-effect chains, and root cause location of beginnings. Western managerialist thinking is linear and hierarchical.

In cognitive science, prospective memory is a linear scenario (antenarrative) for the future by remembering to take an intended action (delayed retrieval) on cue. Work by Melissa Guynn (2003) uses laboratory studies of simulations to research prospective memory processes: "Individuals remember to execute event-based intended actions by deploying . . . attentional resources to monitor . . . target events."

The problem, goals (futuristics) are disrupted (short-circuited) by storytelling cycles and rhizomes. Next we look at two more kinds of prospective sensemaking, but these are nonlinear: cycles and rhizomes.

Karl Weick's (1995) work on narrative stresses retrospective sensemaking is a backward-looking framework of narrative. The work of Dennis Gioia and colleagues treat prospective sensemaking as a future-oriented process that envisions the future as having already occurred (as in future-perfect tense). An alternative to future-perfect sensemaking is to image the future as emerging and evolving in less linear ways. Boje (2007), for example, looks at prospective processes that are cyclical or networked (such as in rhizomatic processes). Rhizomes (Deleuze & Guattari, 1987) are assemblages that do not follow linear paths. In either approach to prospective sensemaking, strategizing the future often results in reinterpretations of the past and accenting what gets focused upon in the present. Both prospective approaches treat the historical past as malleable, as narratives reinterpret to align with future prospects and what is noted about the present. We take prospective a new direction, in cycles and rhizomes.

Cyclic Antenarrative: Thinking in terms of cycles (such as seasons, life, or event cycles), instead of lines of events, has been part of indigenous thinking (Cajete, 2000; Fixico, 2003) before colonization by structural-functionalist-linear modeling (Sandoval, 2000; Smith, 1999) that reduces complexity to a flatland (1 or 2 dimensions on a time-line chronology).

Socioeconomics behaves in cycles, not lines. In the preceding image, late contraction alternates with early contraction, bonds and stocks move up and down, and market cycles shift. If you try to bet on the future, using linear modeling, you will lose your investment. Cycles have been part of indigenous premodern thinking. Cycle thinking was picked up in modernity (in Enlightenment project), again by reclaiming some classical Greek ideas.

Plato's Cycles includes Fire, Air, Earth, and Water (see also Native and Indigenous views); Ether, Gas, Liquid, Solid; Dry, Warm, Moist, Cold, Passive to Active and back. One cycle is phase space transitions such as thermodynamics of heating ice, to get water, and then steam. Another example is phase cycles discussed since Plato's *Republic*: a pattern of governance would cycle between timocracy (aristocracy), formation of oligarchy, the emergence of democracy, and the eventual collapse into tyranny and beginning the cycle anew. There are other types of cycles. Nietzsche (1956) theorized that constellation of forces happens from time to time to create an "Eternal Return" pattern. Nietzsche was critical of Plato for making his cycle of governance only flow one way. More complex and dynamic phase transition is nonchaotic strange attractors in torus bifurcation (Zhang, Kong, Yu, & Chu, 2008). When an attractor introduces instability (disorder), then predictions of transitions between phase states become uncertain as multiattractors, noise, and chaotic itinerancy occur (Sauer, 2003).

McCloskey (1990) makes a very important and relevant point: storytelling with cyclic (stage-by-stage metaphors/models such as life cycle) are too abstract to be reliable in tell us about the future.

> If the stories of past business cycles could predict the future there would be no surprises, and by that fact no business cycles.
> (McCloskey, 1990, p. 96)

This because the cycles people story predict quite badly. We saw this with Enron, as people held onto their stock even as the bankruptcy became inevitable. "But if business cycles are unpredictable to the actors they are unpredictable to the drama critics, too" (p. 96). In short, "the extrapolated story contradicts the model" (p. 96). What I get from this is that if we flesh out a web of living stories, it can contradict the simplistic life cycle (or other cyclic metaphor of stage sequences). As we do so more contradictions arise. To me, antenarratives are bundles, weakly linked assemblages, not yet petrified into a tight narrative frame, complete with its stage metaphor.

> The story of business cycles can organize the past, but it contradicts itself when offered as a prediction of the future. (p. 95)

What McCloskey does with this is look at counterfactual scenarios: "What If" history characters had made this or that critical turn (inflection points, in Yue Cai's 2007 dissertation), and then we have some other future? For example, in the horseshoe nail, the antenarrative point is the nonlinearity of this counterfactual scenario, where for the want of this nail, or the blacksmiths that made them, there is a change of history. Such horseshoe nails are way below the comprehension (sensemaking) of aggregate, abstraction, level of the cycle narrative (Example: acorn—> sprout—> sapling—> tree—> shaped by environment forces; or life cycle: entrepreneur, takeoff, maturation, decline).

> For want of a nail, the show was lost; for want of a show, the horse was lost; . . . for want of a battle, the kingdom was lost and all for the want of a horseshoe nail.
> (McCloskey, 1990, p. 87)

Second (related) main point: McCloskey comes out against the BME narrative, for its linearity. McCloskey tells us one of the pitfalls of economists' storytelling includes the telling of beginning, middle, and end as "in stable models the small beginnings stay small for a long time" (McCloskey, 1990, p. 21). "In stable models the small beginnings stay small for a long time" (McCloskey, 1990, p. 21), and are not picked up by the grander narratives. Why? The small beginnings can become a butterfly effect, changing a cycle of repetition into a spiral of increasing difference. Complexity theorists/scientists/practitioners look at the storytelling in the unforeseen consequences. Narrative privileges particular plots for special attention, but does not explain the dynamics that matter to complexity. Complexity folks use a storytelling inquiry that does not stop at the surface. Complexity folks are immersed in storytelling, but it is a storytelling with its own traditions and ways of knowing.

To me the storytelling, as you know by now, is triadic; linear narrative meets living story web (collective level), and antenarratives shape the future. To me the storytelling triad in consulting is too narrative addicted, and the complexity science is better served with more balance in what I call the 'storytelling triad.' Yes, we want to retrospect the narrative, and see the abstract, and make it communicated in an elevator pitch. But we also want to look at emergent patterns, and in situ, and lived experience, and ways of shaping futures in dialogic nonlinear ways. Narrative works best at understanding something in retrospect, something that already happened. A living story web can become dialogic, can be pluralistic, can be co-generative in a self-organizing way. Some narratives, living stories, and antenarratives don't help. "We swim all day in wrong stories told by liars, incompetents, and the self-deluded" (McCloskey, 1990, p. 3).

We can make the antenarrative bet that if two or more stages are about the same as in the past, the cycle will unfold, in the future, such that the next stage is predictable. However, there are times when cycles go out of control, and, instead of a cycle, we are really in a spiral.

Spiral Antenarratives—One problem is that most of the cyclic stage-by-stage models of organizations are rather linear (bent-line) affairs. Giles Deleuze (1994, p. 21) says, "spirals whose principle is a variable curve and the trajectory of which has dissymmetrical aspects as though it had a right and a left." Only in the abstract, do revolving antenarrative cycles play out in perfect curves posited in representational abstractions. It is the differences that intraplay with the repetitions that are important to understand.

Gary Saul Morson (1994) theorizes shapes of time, in acts of backshadowing, sideshadowing, and foreshadowing. Backshadowing is a retrospective sensemaking, sideshadowing is now-spective (allowing for multiple shadows in the present), and foreshadowing is the stuff of antenarratives.

In foreshadowing, there are opportunity casts, as any one trajectory is only one shadow of a field of possibilities.

How do antenarrative spirals behave? Morson (1994, pp. 63–66) describes the vortex spiral, where there is more freedom of movements and choice away from the center. I wrote about nonlinear storytelling in relation to complexity in a theory chapter with Ken Baskin (Boje and Baskin, forthcoming). Here I want to note that at the center of the vortex there are few antenarrative options, few moves, and it's futile to struggle. It is best to wait till the spiral opens up, more choices are apparent, and one can break free. Determinist linear-narrative is a different shaping of time, positing a linear (or cyclic) recurrence of past into future. For Morson, fate is a narrative line from the future into the present determining all the moves. Linearity is all those myths of inevitability, where the past is traces as inevitable (Morson, 1994, p. 66). Vizenor (1994, p. 146), while not writing of spirals, does suggest that there is no continuity between representational narratives and the referred-to world. Structuralist narrative work has biased our observation to look at repetition, but not at the differences. In our analysis of 100 years of Sears Roebuck annual reports, we found important relationships between the storytelling and material conditions (Barney et al., 2010). We looked at each year of Sears' storytelling as a spiral of sideshadowing ways, out of which one or several were incorporated into the reporting. Others not chosen were not nonexistent; they were merely silent and would emerge in other years when the context and situation shifted.

How do you change a spiral? In the spiral-to-the-bottom foretold in the antisweatshop movement, the apologists for sweatshops foretell an antenarrative of spiral-to-the-top, a path for Third World workers to overcome poverty and oppression (Boje, 2007c). These two spirals influence and change each other. Each movement is making countermoves to the other's spiral. One might hope that a spiral could be transformed into a predictable, recurring cycle, but I suspect this rarely occurs. More likely a spiral becomes part of a more rhizomatic assemblage.

Rhizome Antenarrative: Rhizome antenarratives are nonlinear itinerant processes that do not behave as stable lines or cycles (Deleuze & Guattari, 1987). A rhizome is more than a spiral, a different field of action and agency. "A rhizome ceaselessly establishes connections between semiotic chains, organizations of power, and circumstances relative to the arts, sciences, and social struggles" (Deleuze & Guattari, 1987, p. 8). Rhizomes occur in nature and in the social environment; for example, a rhizome in your yard would be crabgrass, irises, or in the desert trumpet vines. A rhizome sends out shoots aboveground; for example, strawberries send out runners and form another strawberry plant (tuber) and those form other rhizomes, and so on. Potatoes send roots underground forming more potatoes. Social rhizomes look at covert underground and aboveground dynamic movements, the formation of covert cells.

In my work on globalization antenarratives (Boje 2007c), I developed an analysis of globalization as interplay of rhizome antenarratives, and two linear antenarratives (road to the top and road to the bottom). Bougen and Young (2000) looked at the rhizomatic processes of bank fraud and auditors' attempts to detect bank fraud. Auditors using linear analyses could not detect an already escaping present. Policy prescriptions could not corral the continuous movement of fraud into the future. There was a bank fraud panic in the 1890s and a stock-market rhizome in the 1920s, the Enron rhizome of 1990s, and our most recent as-we-speak crisis—mortgage-banking crisis. Boje and colleagues' work traces patterns of rhizomatic antenarrative clustering in the Enron crisis (Boje & Rosile, 2002, 2003; Boje, Rosile, Durant, & Luhman, 2004).

In each of these examples a rhizome formed with a set of covert transactions whose detection even by experts came too late to prevent crisis and tragedy. A proper study of rhizomatic collective dynamics would assess how people keep investing in patterns and ignoring the signals that a tuber's roots not only can be seen belowground, but they are ignoring the aboveground symptoms. Rhizomes are bonded by information you don't have.

The Socioeconomic Approach to Management (SEAM) small-business consulting training in rhizomatic patterns of the arts scene serves to identify what we call balance points in early detection to disrupt or destroy ongoing rhizomatic crises.[2] Rhizomes in the arts scene are nonlinear. Why? Because as a linear antenarrative prospectively tries to make the future a line path to a goal, there is a tuber breaking forth from the ground. An organization comes into the scene to organize it into lines. The arts scene resists by forming a counterorganization (tuber), as a nonline, a nonlinear flight. Rhizome is not a cycle. The cycles are recurring. The rhizome just keeps extending in all directions, until an obstacle, and then goes up, down, around, or cracks through.

The tubers that form can shoot up from the (cover) subterranean or descend from the visible vines crawling along the ground. The key facet of rhizomes is movement. They don't stand still; they are not lines.

Therefore, developing antenarrative skills allows for a greater possibility of intervention to disrupt a rhizomatic spread. To disrupt a rhizome or break out of a recurring cycle of doom, it is necessary to understand something I call 'Collective Storytelling Dynamics.'

COLLECTIVE STORYTELLING DYNAMICS (CSD)

Collective Storytelling Dynamics (CDS) is the interplay of antenarratives, linear narratives, and living story networking. CSD applies this complexity to three interdependent storytelling genres: narrative retrospective sensemaking, living story networks unfolding in the present, and antenarrative prospective sensemaking into the future. CSD is all about patterns of complexity of storytelling sensemaking (Boje, 2008, introduction).

Peter Hunter says, "People are very complex, when several people interact the situation is even more complex. When we try to control people we will always fail because we have no way of controlling their complexity."[3] When linear antenarratives (goal setting, plans, etc.) are attempted as managerial control in transorganizational complexity, the result is one fiasco after another. The reason is that complexity is full of rhizomes and cycles, not just lines to achieve utilitarian ends, goals, plans, aspirations, or instrumental intentions.

Morin's (2008) complexity theory has three principles of collective behavior: collective dialogic (order and disorder); recursion of social products and their effect happening simultaneously in ways that break out of linear cause-effect thinking patterns (Abbott, 1998); and holographic complexity that theorizes multiactor interplay of dimensional facets.

The beauty of a hologram is that you get to see 360 degrees around sphere. Holographic images (Boje, 2008) have a sphere of multiple facets in more than three dimensions. Each facet contains info about all the relations to the other facets and dimensions. Boje's (2008, chap. 2) holographic theory of storytelling complexity is that indigenous cultures had more 'holographic awareness' of complexity processes (Cajete, 2000; Fixico, 2003) before the flatlanders of modernity reduced storytelling to linear models in Western narrative of one and two dimensions (Abbott, 1988). To understand the rise of linear modeling in modernity, we have to look at the history of Western narrative.

Narrative Retrospective Sensemaking (past): Western narrative thinking tends to be linear retrospection (Abbott, 1988; Cajete, 2000; Fixico, 2003). Linear antenarratives are forward-looking (prospective), whereas narratives are more often backward-looking (retrospective) sensemaking. The backward and forward sensemaking approaches interplay with now-sensemaking resulting in CSD.

Modernity picked up Aristotle's (350 BCE) classical Greek model of linear narrative and made it the mainstay of storytelling (reducing all storytelling to linear relationships). Since Aristotle, narratives are defined as having a plot line—a beginning, a middle, and an end (BME). In linear BME, anything out of the line gets erased out of awareness. Bakhtin (1973, p. 12), for example, says, "Narrative genres are always enclosed in a solid and unshakable monological framework." Derrida (1979, p. 94) also sees narrative as hegemonic. Weick's (1995) approach to narrative is whole, linear (BME) plot, in retrospective sensemaking.

As stated earlier, narrative retrospection is by definition backward looking. A narrative that is (retrospectively) stabilized as recurring pattern recognition involves the potential problems of reductive and confirmatory bias. In order to make the plotline linear, people compulsively insert or exclude events and characters to abstract (misplaced) coherence.

'Petrified narrative' for Czarniawska (2004) is the backbone of strong organization cultures, but this approach ignores retrospective elimination of key characteristics important to recognizing distinct complexity of emergent situation (Dooley & Van de Ven, 1999; Nicolis & Prigogine, 1989) such as emotional contagion (Barsade, 2002; Lishner, Cooter, & Sald, 2008). This presents the danger for threat analysis in highly charged emotional contagion situations of an inadequate assessment of the present, or an analysis primarily influenced by negative emotional conditions that limit the ability of individuals to have a broad view of the current situation.

Nonlinear storytelling patterns get marginalized as reconstructed past takes precedence over thorough analysis of the reproductive processes that are emerging. First, Gherandi and Poggio (2007, pp. 39–40) propose narrative in male-dominated environments display gender differences. Male stories are developing marked-out linear paths that are set by choice, rather than chance.

A second problem in retrospective sensemaking narrative that Currie (1998, p. 98) identifies is they petrify (or stabilize) so quickly there is a lack of noticing of the dynamics of living story networking. There is filtering of the present through past lens at a very high rate of speed in order to reproduce a familiar pattern, and then project it onto the future. Narrative consigns the present to the past so quickly it subverts recognition of more authentic scenarios of the future.

Living Story Network (present): A second facet of (holographic) storytelling (CSD) is what we can call living story networking (Boje, 2001a, 2007a, 2008). A person's living story denotes or implies (between-the-lines) relationships to other stories ("I cannot tell you this story, without unfolding another story, and anther relationship to other stories").In Being present in the moment of Being, people share the living stories that are unfolding now and here, in their lives. Each living storytelling is a social act of relationship to others' living story networks currently unfolding. Living stories unfold in the Present (nowspective), without traceable beginnings or knowable end. One's living stories constitute a web of relationships in what Bakhtin (1993) looks at as a dialogical process in the present, in once-occureent event-ness of-Being.

Living story networks are by definition, nonlinear (Boje, 2001a, 2007a, 2008, chap. 11). People and scenes are networked (webbed) together in three or more holographic dimensions. "There is no [narrative or linear antenarrative] timeline, the story does not progress, there is no central character who goes out to experience adventures, there is no future and no past, there is only the now."[4]

The relationship to neuroscience is that living stories constitute episodic memory. Traditional approach to living story networks is a static and linear structural-functional and pragmatic view of relationships as instrumental ethics.

A dynamic holographic approach to living story networks looks at emergence and unfolding changes in relationships in the now (now-spective, as opposed to retrospective or prospective). This can expand the horizon of instrumental or practical ethics into what Bakhtin (1990, 1993) calls 'answerability' ethics. Answerability ethics is now-spective. It's our answerability in-the-moment-of-Being, in the now and here, in the midst of unfolding living story networks, in our relationships to others, to their living stories, which have just become complicit with our own living story. We either turn away, play the bystander, become apathetic to others' harm, or we make a choice, now and here, to be answerable to our complicity, to our role in living story networks.

CONCLUDING SUMMARY

In Collective Storytelling Dynamics (CSD) there is an important interplay among retrospective-linear-narrative, living-story-now-section-networking, and antenarrative-bets-on-the-future that has intra-activity with materiality. The collective dynamics of Agential Storytelling Theory (AST) are at the very heart of social storytelling complexity sensemaking. Trying to fit all storytelling dynamics into a flat line, viewed backwards, has been the obsessive task of Western narrative. Trying to discern one's answerability in living story networking happening in the now and here is one way to break out of narrative prison. Another way is to engage in antenarrative prospective sensemaking. The four kinds of antenarrative prospection are linear, cyclical, spiral, and rhizomatic. The linear/cyclic antenarrative seek to replicate past patterns into the future, whereas the spiral/assemblages connect the Nowness unfolding in once-occurrent-ness to the field of future possibilities. We are only beginning to explore what happens when cycles become spirals and more rhizomatic antenarrative amplification intraplay with materiality. Clearly it's time to develop an agential approach to storytelling, one situated in social interactions, where storytelling has material force.

NOTES

1. Throughout, lowercase 'indians' and 'native' are used, following Vizenor (1998), to denote a resistance to the colonizer and their Euramerican hyper-real simulations, because the Americas is not Columbus's India and 'native' is still being colonized.
2. See http://talkingstick.info for work done since 2007 on arts scene rhizomes.
3. "Complexity at Work," online article—http://www.top-consultant.com/UK/Editorial/Article_display.asp?ID=1584.
4. Source of quote on nonlinear storytelling (bracketed additions, mine)—http://www.widen.org.uk/responsiveenvironments/projectmanagement/sboard.htm.

REFERENCES

Abbott, A. (1988). Transcending general linear reality. *Sociological Theory*, 6(Fall), 169–186.

Allen, P. G. (1992). *The sacred hoop: Recovering the feminine in American Indian traditions.* Boston: Beacon.

Aristotle. (1954). *Aristotle: Rhetoric and poetics.* Intro by Friedrich Solmsen; rhetoric translated by W. Rhys Roberts; poetics translated by Ingram Bywater. New York: The Modern Library (Random House). (Poetics was written 350 BCE)

Bakhtin, M. (1973). Problems of Doestoevsky's Poetics (R. W. Rostel, Trans.). Ann Arbor, MI: Ardis.

———. 1981. The Dialogic Imagination: Four Essays. Austin: University of Texas Press.

———. (1990). *Art and answerability.* Edited by Michael Holquist & Vadim Liapunov. Translation and Notes by Vadim Liapunov; supplement translated by Kenneth Brostrom. Austin: University of Texas Press. From Bakhtin's first published article and his early 1920s notebooks.

———. (1993). *Toward a philosophy of the act* (translation and notes by Vadim Liapunov; Michael Holquist & Vadim Liapunov, Eds.). Austin: University of Texas Press.

Barad, K.(2007). *Meeting the universe halfway: Quantum physics and the entanglement of matter and meaning.* Durham/London: Duke University Press.

Barge, J. K. (2004). Antenarrative and managerial practice. *Communication Studies 55*(1), 106–127.

Barney, C. E., Boje, D. M., Kach, A. P., Maynard-Patrick, S., McCulloh, G, Tobey, D., et al. (2010). Agential Storytelling Theory: Materiality sensemaking within organizing enactments across a century of Sears Roebuck annual reports. Under review. Working paper available from dboje@nmsu.edu

Barsade, S. G. (2002). The ripple effect: Emotional contagion and its influence on group behavior. *Administrative Science Quarterly, 47*(4), 644–675.

Boje, D. M. (1991). Organizations as storytelling networks: A study of story performance in an office-supply firm Administrative Science Quarterly, 36, 106–126.

———. (2001a). *Narrative methods for organizational and communication research.* London: Sage.

———. (2001b). *Flight of antenarrative in Phenomenal Complexity Theory, Tamara, storytelling organization theory.* September 20, paper to honor Professor Hugo Letiche and his work on Phenomenal Complexity Theory, for the September 24 and 25 Conference on Complexity and Consciousness at Huize Molenaar (Korte Nieuwstraat 6) in the old center of Utrecht, Netherlands. Retrieved June 1, 2010, from http://business.nmsu.edu/~dboje/papers/ante/flight_of_antenarrative.htm

———. (2001c). *Antenarrating, Tamara, and Nike storytelling.* Paper prepared for presentation at "Storytelling Conference" at the School of Management, Imperial College, 53 Prince's Gate, Exhibition Road, London, July 9, 2001. Retrieved June 1, 2010, from *http://business.nmsu.edu/~dboje/papers/ethnostorytelling. htm*

———. (2002). *Critical dramaturgical analysis of Enron antenarratives and metatheatre.* Plenary presentation to 5th International Conference on Organizational Discourse: From Micro-Utterances to Macro-Inferences, Wednesday 24–Friday 26 July (London).

———. (2005). Empire reading of Manet's execution of Maximilian: Critical visual aesthetics and antenarrative spectrality. *Tamara Journal, 4*(4), 118–134. Retrieved June 1, 2010, from http://peaceaware.com/388/articles/20052.pdf

———. (2007a). *Handbook of narrative inquiry: Mapping a new methodology.* Jean Clandinin, Ed., pp. 330–354) London: Sage.

———. (2007b). The antenarrative cultural turn in narrative studies. In Mark Zachry & Charlotte Thralls (Eds.), *Communicative practices in workplaces* and the professions: Cultural perspectives on the regulation of discourse and organizations.* NY: Baywood Pub Co.

——. (2007c). Globalization antenarratives. In Albert Mills, Jeannie C. Helms-Mills, & Carolyn Forshaw (Eds.), *Organizational behavior in a global context* (pp. 505–549). Toronto: Garamond Press.

——. (2008). *Storytelling organizations,* London: Sage.

——. (2010). *Towards a postcolonial storytelling theory that interrogates tribal peoples' Material-Agential-Storytelling ignored in management and organization studies.* Under review, and working paper available from dboje@nmsu.edu

——. (forthcoming). Antenarrative in management research. *The Sage dictionary of qualitative management research.* London (2,500 words). Accepted 2006. Draft available at http://business.nmsu.edu/~dboje/690/papers/Antenarrative%20in%20Management%20research%20May%2014%2005.pdf

Boje, D. M., & Baskin, K. (forthcoming). *Dancing to the music of story.* Charlotte, NC: Information Age Press. See Chapter 1 on complexity.

Boje, D. M., & Grace Ann Rosile. (2002). Enron whodunit? *Ephemera, 2*(4), 315–327.

——. (2003). Life imitates art: Enron's epic and tragic narration. *Management Communication Quarterly, 17*(1), 85–125.

Boje, D. M., Rosile, G. A., Durant, R.A., & Luhman, J. T. (2004). Enron spectacles: A critical dramaturgical analysis. Special issue on theatre and organizations edited by Georg Schreyögg and Heather Höpfl. *Organization Studies, 25*(5), 751–774.

Boje, D. M., Rosile, G. A., & Gardner, C. L. (2007). Antenarratives, narratives and anaemic stories. In *Storytelling in management* (pp. 30–45). Nasreen Taher & Swapna Gopalan (Eds.). Dehradun, India: The Icfai University Press. (Note: was based upon paper presented in Showcase Symposium, Academy of Management, August 9, 2004, in New Orleans.) See conference version http://peaceaware.com/McD/papers/2004%20boje%20rosile%20Gardner%20Academy%20presentation%20Antenarratives%20Narratives%20and%20Anaemic%20ones.pdf

Bougen, P. D.; & Young, J. J. 2000. Organizaing and regulationing as rhizomatic lines: Bank fraud and auditing. *Organizaion.* Vol 9 (1): 459–475.

Cai, Yue. 2006. Story strategy dialogisms at Motorola Corporation. Unpublished dissertation, Management Department, New Mexico State University.

Cajete, G. (2000). *Native science: Natural laws of interdependence.* Santa Fe, NM: Clear Light Publishers.

Camille-Strand, A. M. (2010). *Material storytelling as identity re-work.* Paper presented to the April 2010 meeting of Standing Conference for Management and Organizational Inquiry (sc'MOI).

Collins, D., & Rainwater, K. (2005). Managing change at Sears: A sideways look at a tale of corporate transformation. *Journal of Organizational Change Management, 18*(1), 16–30.

Currie, M. (1998). *Postmodern narrative theory.* New York: St. Martin's Press.

Czarniawska, B. (2004). *Narratives in social science research.* London: Sage.

Dalcher, D., & Drevin, L. (2003). Learning from information systems failures by using narrative and antenarrative methods. *Proceedings of SAICSIT,* 137–142.

de Certeau, M. (1984). *Practices in everyday life.* Steven F. Rendall, Trans. Berkeley/London: University of California Press.

Deleuze, G. (1994). *Difference and repetition.* Translated by Paul Patton from French, 1968 text, *Difference et Repetition* (Presses Universitaires de France). New York: Columbia University Press.

Deleuze, G., & Guattari, F. (1987). *A thousand plateaus: Capitalism and schizophrenia* (B. Massumi, Trans.). Minneapolis: University of Minneapolis Press.

Derrida, J. (1979). Living on: Borderlines. In H. Bloom (Ed.), *Deconstruction and criticism* (pp.75–176). London: Continuum Publications.

Dooley, K. J., & Van de Ven, A. H. (1999). Explaining complex organizational dynamics. *Organization Science,10*(3), 294–321.

Eriksen, M. (2006). Antenarratives about leadership and gender in the U.S. Coast Guard. *Tamara Journal for Critical Organization Inquiry, 5*(4), 162–173.

Eriksen, M., Van Echo, K., Harmel, A., Kane, J., Curran, K., Gustafson, G., et al. (2005). Conceptualizing and engaging in organizational change as an embodied experience within a practical reflexivity community of practice: Gender performance at the U.S. Coast Guard Academy. *Tamara Journal for Critical Organization Inquiry, 4*(1), 75–80.

Fixico, D. L. (2003). The American Indian mind in a linear world. New York/London: Routledge.

Gabriel, Yiannis. (2000) Storytelling in organizations, New York: Oxford University Press.

Gherardi, S., & Poggio, B. (2007). *Gendertelling in organizations: Narratives from male-dominated environments*. Copenhagen: Copenhagen Business School Press.

Guynn, M. J. (2003). A two process model of strategic monitoring in event-based prospective memory: Activation/retrieval mode and checking. *International Journal of Psychology, 38*(4), 245–256.

Lishner, D. A., Cooter, A. B., & Zald, D. H. (2008). Rapid emotional contagion and expressive congruence under strong test conditions. *Journal of Nonverbal Behavior, 32*, 225–239.

McCloskey, D. (1990). *On narrative: If you're so smart: The narrative of economic expertise*. Chicago, University of Chicago Press.

Morin, E. (2008). *On complexity* (Robin Postel, Trans.). Cresskill, NJ Hampton Press.

Morson, G. S. (1994). *Narrative and freedom: The shadows of time*. New Haven/London: Yale University Press.

Nicolis, G. & Prigogine, I. 1989. Exploring Complexity. NY: W.H. Freeman & Company.

Nietzsche, F. (1956). *The birth of tragedy* (1872) and *The Genealogy of Morals* (1887) (F. Golffing, Trans.). New York: Anchor Books.

Owens, L. (2001). As if an Indian were really an Indian: Unamericans, Euramericans and postcolonial theory. *Paradoxa, 15*, 170–183.

Sandoval, C. (2000). *Methodology of the oppressed: Theory out of bounds*. Minneapolis/London: University of Minnesota Press.

Sauer, T. (2003). Chaotic itinerancy based on attractors of one-dimensional maps. *Chaos, 13*(3), 947–952.

Smith, D. 1990. The Conceptual Practices of Power: A Feminist Sociology of Knowledge. Boston: Northeaster University Press.

Smith, L. T. (1999/2008). *Decolonizing methodologies: Research and indigenous peoples*. Duneden, NZ: University of Otago Press.

Vickers, M. H. (2005). Illness, work and organisation: Postmodern perspectives, antenarratives and chaos narratives for the reinstatement of voice. *Tamara: Journal of Critical Postmodern Organisation Science, 3*(2), 1–15.

Vizenor, G. (1994). The ruins of representations: Shadow survivance and the literature of dominance. In Alfred Arteaga (Ed.), *Another tongue: Nation and ethnicity in the linguistic borderlands* (pp. 139–167). Durham, NC: Duke University Press.

———. (1996). The origins of essentialism and pluralism in descriptive tribal names. In Winfried Siemerling & Katrin Schwenk (Eds.), *Pluralism and the* limits of authenticity in North American literatures (pp. 19–39). Iowa City: University of Iowa Press.

———. (1998). *Fugitive poses: Native American Indian scenes of absence and presence*. Lincoln: University of Nebraska Press.

———. (1999). *Manifest manners: Narratives on postindian survivance*. Lincoln: University of Nebraska Press. Hanover, NH: Wesleyan University Press.

Weick, K. E. (1995) *Sensemaking*. London: Sage.

White, M., & Epston, D. (1990). Narrative Means to Therapeutic Ends. New York: Norton.

Yolles, M. (2007). The dynamics of narrative and antenarrative and their relation to story. *Journal of Organizational Change Management, 20*(1), 74–94.

Zhang, Y., Kong, G., Yu, J., & Chu, Y. (2008). A special type of attractor and transitions in a delayed system. *Physics Letters A, 372*(38), 5979–5983.

Part I

Individual, Gender, and Group Antenarratives

Introduction to Part I
Individual, Gender, and Group Antenarratives

In writing these section introductions, I intend to play with the chapter authors and their material, to have a dialogue, something dialogical, that will help bring about this new field of antenarrative inquiry.

I was fortunate to invent the theory of "storytelling organization" which I defined as a "collective storytelling system in which the performance of stories is a key part of members' sensemaking and a means to allow them to supplement individual memories with institutional memory" (Boje, 1991: 106). There was not yet a term to talk about the packs of future shaping accounts that were part of the sensemaking currency of storytelling organizations. In the 1995 article on Disney as Tamara-land, I started to look more closely at the complexity of storytelling organizations, at the variety of simultaneous storytelling in the Now, and how one kept pace with all the telling happening in different rooms (spaces) at the same time. I knew that there was something missing, some process shaping the future of organizations.

In 2001 I invented the term *antenarrative* by weaving the concept through every chapter after the book without them had been accepted, and after the final copy proofs:

> "This fragmented, non linear, incoherent, collective, unplotted and improper storytelling is what I mean by the term antenarrative" (Boje, 2001: 1).

I did this at the final rewrite, because the initial publishing contract forbade any new ideas, but I decided to break the rules and move in a new direction. After working with antenarrative for a few years, I defined antenarrative as follows: "Antenarratives are prospective (forward-looking) bets (antes) that an ante-story (before-story) can transform organization relationships" (Boje, 2008, p. 13). I began to look at storytelling as a holographic triadic of retrospective narrative, living story webs of now-relationships, and various sorts of antenarratives of prospective sensemaking. I believe the current book goes beyond by getting at the holographic aspects of storytelling.

As the chapter authors began working this past decade with antenarrative theory and research, their studies in this new book, point out how antenarratives are agential, giving rise to future events and situations that would not take place by retelling a retrospective narrative. It is the traversing that is not just some sort of social construction, but an ontological act of enactment. The materiality of storytelling, in all its corporeality, in its intra-play with material Being, with ecology, with bodies, and with quantum physics waves, is a new vista of theory and research in storytelling.

My understanding of antenarrative is being informed by collaboration with the authors of this book. As I understand them, antenarratives are travelers, in packs, moving in and among deep material contexts, morphing situations as they traverse. Antenarrative packs are not just meaning-making, but assemblages that are world-making. For me, antenarrative is much more a verb, not a noun, not ever *singular*, and always *iterative*. When antenarrating stops moving, stops being a morphing hoard of travelers re-combining, and finally stops iteratively changing context to affect future potentiality, then antenarrating-processes becomes just narrative-reduction, stuck and fossilized into some past-ness of individual or collective memory. Many organizations are stuck in the past, unable to invent futures that depart from replication.

Narrative tries to couple with antenarrating, to make linear or cyclic replications, but that is just past-representation volition to control the shape of the future, and keep it as it was. Linear and cyclic antenarrating turns out to be narrative just being future-controlling.

Several main contributions are made by this book. Perhaps the major one: Sensemaking is not only backward looking, retrospective narrative, but also prospective antenarrative. Second, the enactment process is iterative, which means the narrative stuck-in-the-past cannot successfully map the unfolding process in the Now-ness of Being, in the event-ness of enactment. Third, a veritable wave function that is holographic storytelling is occurring as sensemaking enactment folds past, present, and future into one another, in iterative acts of sensemaking. Finally, this book explore the ways the past narrative is ill-equipped to account for the unfolding enactments as people and material actants unfold an entire field of potentialities. So many futures are co-generated that are nonlinear, not controlled by precedent cycles, that the concepts of spiral, and all those Deleuzian rhizome-assemblages, mean whole new ways of sensemaking are being invented that our chapter authors set out to explore in their disciplines as wide-ranging as corporate strategy, math education, information technology, banking, and social movements.

The chapters in the first section, address how antenarratives move, how they unfold, refold, sort, sift, change, transform, and shape the future field of potentiality by working iteratively, connecting, making differences in reality, between individual and group roles, as well as between group and larger collective situations. Antenarratives are present in philosophy, education, strategy, marketing, accounting, theology, law, and literature. What is new about antenarrative is it gives some alternative to linear thinking and the same approaches in business to instrumental ethics and managerialist control.

Frits Schipper and **Barbara Fryzel's** Chapter 1 explores responsible use and power of antenarratives. Antenarrative is a kind of resistance force to managerial control that makes narrative representation a tool. This chapter starts by describing 1) various areas in which the notion of 'power' is being used, and 2) different modes of using it. These philosophers say that the important contribution that antenarrative makes is the focus on variety and having some ethically answerable complicity with a connection to the rationalizing forces of narrative. The chapter authors pay particular attention to the relationship of power and rationality. The practical contribution is contextualizing the intra-play of antenarrative and antenarrating in some constitutive situation change that presupposes power, but what kind? Power requires answerability for its use. Schipper and Fryzel raise the issue that antenarrative power is both in epistemology (knowing) and ontology (Being). Empirically, antenarrative is constitutive of Being-ness, acting in concert with other antenarratives, in a moving assemblage. Antenarrating has power to bring about something in a process, *power over* is the reality-effect brought about by antenarrating, and *power with* is about the means by which effects of Being are realized in specific situations by antenarrating. The final part of the chapter focuses on power and (ante)narrative, discussing semantic power, closure, and responsible use and abuse of power, referring to the example of Flextronics and use of narratives in air traffic safety. For Schipper and Fryzel the coupling of narrative to linear-cyclic antenarrating is rather instrumental-control, all about, mean-end chains. Spiral antenarratives, and what I am calling rhizomatic-assemblages, do not have such grand aspirations to control the outcome, just co-generating. The authors seem here and there to agree with William James that *life is before narrative*, before its does all that abstracting, reduction, and marginalizing of little 'wow' moments of individual and group experience. For Schipper and Fryzel, it's the expulsion of experience by narrative that is where antenarrative comes into play. What do they add and contribute to antenarratology? As they see it, antenarrative and narrative are in a twofold connectivity (1. as proto-narrative anticipation of potential story or antenarrative to be, and 2. as narratives coming before antenarratives). Both ways of connection come together in their composite term, 'ante(-)narrative.'

Jawad Syed and I develop in Chapter 2 a 'negotiated diversity management' antenarrative approach that changes the cycle of ways the multiplicity of living stories are typically being excluded by official retrospective-narratives they call, 'retro-narratives.' Retro-narrative constructs the identity of oftentimes culturally diverse employees. Like, Schipper and Fryzel's chapter, this chapter is about power. Syed and I critique of the diversity management narratives that promise economic gains and use technocratic rationality, but subvert the importance of unequal power relations. We suggest a triadic theory of storytelling, where such managerialist (often linear) narratives are one aspect, and opposed by two other kinds of storytelling: the living story of people in unequal power relations, and antenarratives (defined as ante, a bet, and before narrative fossilization sets in). We are interested in how non-linear (spiral and rhizomatic) antenarratives interplay with stabilized, often linear (sometimes recurring-cyclic) narratives and more fragmented living stories of people situated in unequal power relationships in organizations. We suggest that diversity management makes rather managerialist bets about the future situation of diversity in organizations. What is necessary is to cultivate antenarratives that present a critical appraisal of the future, and a counterforce to narratives whose (retrospective) sensemaking is stuck on the past.

Diane Walker's Chapter 3 contributes a *Tesseract Antenarrative Model* to enable schools and other organizations to move from linear narratives to multidimensional antenarratives for holistic critical antenarrative literacy. She is concerned about the ethics of No Child Left Behind, and wants to teach math literacy in a new way, using Tesseract Antenarratives. She happily engages in resistance using her critical pedagogy. Her model is based on mapping individual personal stories onto factor lattices to represent a multidimensional storytelling hologram. She uses mathematical drawings, photos, and sculptures to represent relationships between the factors of whole numbers. By mapping stories onto the factors, she conceptualizes a shape-shifting four-dimensional tesseract that illustrates the stories within stories and around and between stories. Walker wants to help teachers and students use her holographic storytelling to make connections between math, literacy, and other content areas. This can provide an antenarrative way of producing personally satisfying and meaningful works of literature and art. In sum, Walker's Tesseract Antenarrative Model introduces holographic complexity into storytelling in teaching and learning.

Grace Ann Rosile's Chapter 4 is an antenarrative and ethics analysis of catching her students cheating. This chapter builds an antenarrative analysis of causes of cheating by identifying the type of antenarrative represented by each unfolding perspective: linear, cyclical, spiral, and rhizomatic. Her contribution is to theorize a link between antenarrative-potentially used to explain the causes of cheating and the narrative theme emerging and cohering from four sorts of antenarrating, and finally identifying the ethical perspective she finds most compatible with the results of this antenarrative becoming narrative process. Linear antenarrative reflects an applied, rule-based (cause-effect or crime-punishment) ethics. Cyclic antenarrative, in the cheating, brings out pleas for Aristotelian virtue ethics. Spiral antenarrating is about a sort of instrumentality (greatest good for the most folks). And Rhizomatic (assemblage) brings forth more of a Bakhtinian answerability ethics, an emotion-volition to intervene in the social, recognize one's complicity in the assemblage of cheaters and non-cheaters, and to change the situation producing the cheating.

Kevin Grant's Chapter 5 takes us into spirituality practices of leaders. It is about the antenarrative analysis of the 'metanoia' experience. A metanoia experience is a spontaneous, unpredicted transpersonal encounter that really gets your attention. Grant analyzes my own close encounter with transpersonal, a contemporary miracle, and a munchable sign that it was time to devote myself to storytelling. Some leaders do not change behavior as a result. For other leaders, it can mean that what they do next is life-changing, deeply transforming the poetics of everyday life, including changing how they think and feel, and maybe turning-about, acting in organizations a whole lot differently. Metanoia, therefore, is the unpredictable outcome of the living story relational encounter with the transpersonal. What makes it an antenarrative, not the linear or cyclic sort, but one that spirals or results in a re-assemblage, whose outcome is unpredicted? In Gnostic Christianity, metanoia means awakening of shared intuition and direct knowing of the highest ultimate reality, that is, God, and for others, it's a close encounter with some higher power. The relationship of metanoia to antenarratives is all about the 'bet' on the future, as the metanoia process unfolds, and leaders Grant studied have to make a choice to change or not change not just their thoughts, feelings, and behavior, but their Being-ness in each moment of once-occurrent Being. In other words, the metanoia can be not just epistemological change of knowing, or the change of doing that comes from knowing-differently, but a much deeper more profound ontological change of Being-ness in the life-world.

Majella O'Leary and **Kim Economides'** Chapter 6 helps us understand legal antenarratives of twenty lawyers they studied, and like Rosile's chapter, explores their embedded ethical reasoning in the entire storytelling process. They remind us that lawyers, since the ancient Greeks, are accomplished storytellers, combining rhetoric, conversation and dialectic questioning to negotiate the fate of clients. In their study, O'Leary and Economides came across lawyers accounts of their practices that seemed fragmented, inconclusive, full of hesitancy, apprehension, and even superficiality, with no coherent resolution of underlying tensions of the business lawyer's conduct, as one might suspect from the poetics of Aristotelian narrative. Such narratives are said to detail action-plots, mood, scene-sequence, and character. The hesitant lawyer-informants seemed good candidates of Yiannis Gabriel's business-folks whose lack of poetics is a narrative deskilling in modern organizations. It was at this point that the chapter authors turned to antenarrative theory and methods to explore the practices of lawyers. As they put it, 'The lawyers' narratives essentially are antenarrative: they are future-orientated and, on occasion, they display real bravery in facing up to a difficult and uncertain future.' The lawyers antenarrating lacks the sort of closure one expects of narrative-retrospection, and moves in an opposite direction, raising serious concerns about the uncertainty of lawyer's future survival, and what kinds of ethics are possible in that tenuous future, with expected increased ethical self-regulation intra-twined with more and more commercialization of practices, while trying to resist the profit (instrumental) motives.

In sum, all-in-all, the chapters in section one are about resistance, ethics, and antenarratives that do not fit the mold of pre-narratives, proto-narratives, or retrospective sensemaking narratives. The chapters are about the uncertainties of practices in storytelling that do not meet the Aristotelian Poetics of linear or cyclic narratives. The chapters depict an antenarrative process, one unfolding a moral struggle, perhaps a metanoia of inspiration or at the very least an encounter with a future not easily predicted from replicating the past.

1 Antenarrational Presuppositions

A Philosophical Reflection on Responsible Use of Power and (Ante)narrative

Frits Schipper and Barbara Fryzel

1 INTRODUCTION

Narratives are present in many kinds of human activity. They are being used and studied in different fields such as philosophy, theology, law, and literature. There is a growing interest in narratives in connection with management and organization too. In case of the latter, they sometimes come into focus as alternative ways of looking at reality, alternative, that is, for what is sometimes called 'logico-scientific thinking,' which easily can be connected to instrumental rationality and control. On the other hand, however, narratives are sometimes considered as presenting new tools of management. In marketing, for instance, it is said that narratives (about companies, products, brands) create new ways of 'connecting' with customers.

It seems that narratives as such are not beyond the kind of rational control just mentioned. Hence, taking narratives on their face value, seeing them as a kind of original 'reality,' might stimulate an uncritical attitude towards them. In order to cope with this, David Bojé has introduced the concept of 'antenarrative.' He argues that an eye for what lies 'before' the narrative is needed. The notion of antenarrative is trying to accomplish this, bringing into focus "[the] counter-acting forces of the ante-narrative variety" (Boje, 2005; Boje et al., 2004); they are "incoherent and unplotted tellings" (Boje, 2001, p. 8).

The quotation just given presents antenarrative variety as a kind of resisting force. Moreover, looking at antenarratives is seen as a way of "theorizing the power to narrate differently" (Boje et al., 2004; see Boje, 2008, p. 1, narrative as "centring force of control and order"). Both, seeking an alternative kind of thinking mentioned ealier and looking for new marketing tools, also refer to the power of narratives (resp. Tsoukas & Hatch, 2002, p. 1004; Learned, 2007, p. 1). However, the authors mentioned do not reflect on the notion of power itself (see also Ricoeur, 1998, p. 278; Williams, 2007, p. 313). So it seems that narratives and antenarratives both involve 'power' and that thinking of them *pre*supposes the notion of power; power as 'antenarrational.' In this contribution we will reflect on the notion of power, giving a philosophical explication, and elaborate its relationship with rationality and antenarratives. A relevant general issue is the justifiability and (ab-)use of (narrational) power.

We will start by describing i) various areas in which the notion of 'power' is being used, and ii) different modes of using it. After this the notion of power will be clarified, also paying attention to the relationship of power and rationality. The final part focuses on power and (ante)narrative, discussing semantic power, closure, and responsible use and abuse of power, referring to the example of Flextronics and use of narratives in air traffic safety.

2 VARIOUS AREAS AND USES

The concept of power is used in different contexts and for various reasons. We now start by saying a few things about the first.

2.1 Contexts

In physics and the technical sciences, the term 'power' has a specific, uncontested, often quantified meaning. Besides, it functions in the social sciences, humanities, theology, to name a few. In philosophy worth mentioning are ethics, social-political thought, philosophy of law, philosophical anthropology, and metaphysics. Generally speaking, we can say that the concept of power is being used descriptively in explanations of reality (natural, social sciences, daily life), and in evaluations, normative analyses, gauging the meaning of realities (philosophy, daily life too).

'Power' in connection with the social world is often being used together with other terms such as 'authority,' sovereignty,' 'influence,' 'force,' 'vigour,' 'might,' to mention some of the most obvious. In the social sciences many current issues are imbued with references to 'power,' such as 'gender,' 'labour relations,' symbolic power (Bourdieu). Also more specific subject matters, studied in management and organization MO, like 'workplace *resistance,*' 'organizational hierarchy,' 'empowerment'—Boje (2001) talks about the 'empowering' and 'disempowering' analysis of narratives—and 'company loyalty' involved studies and explanations in terms of 'power.' Exercise of power can also manifest itself in bending the laws, defining legal duties, and so on. People able to do this are part of the "power elite" (Mills, 1956). In a broader sense also, corporations might be part of it, their power referring, for instance, to lobbying (Fryzel, 2005).

In ancient thought (the concept of) 'power' is used in connection with politics, political philosophy, and theology. Shortly after the Renaissance, power became related to knowledge (Bacon). Another issue is power and causal relationships, used to realize future goods (Hobbes). Centuries later, Nietzsche considered power as the all-pervasive essence of reality (including life). Legitimating (use of) power has been a subject matter of philosophy from its early beginnings. A move to the opposite has been made by Nietzsche in connection with the view just mentioned: power merely *is* and active just because it is power; so, there is no need for any kind of justification.

Many of us would consider this just-mentioned last step to be unsatisfactory. Twentieth-century philosophical thought about power (e.g., Arendt, Derrida, Guardini, Habermas, and Russell) is in line with this feeling: in human affairs power requires responsibility and purpose, which lies beyond. It is noteworthy that in this setting 'power' becomes more or less value-neutral. Neutrality is also involved in Foucault's idea of power as an unpersonal disciplining force, which can raise resistance. The same can be noted regarding sociology and organization theory; see, for instance, Max Weber's definition of power as the chance to realize one's will over and against those of others and Wright Mills's view that real power is a means residing within major institutions. Also Weick's view of power and sense-making can be mentioned here (Weick, 2005).

2.2 Uses

Three main ways of using the concept of power can be distinguished

- in explanations
- in philosophical characterizations
- in normative evaluations

Explanatory Role

We may think of the natural sciences as well as the social ones. In connection with the latter, power comes into focus concerning individuals, groups and other social entities like organizations and states, asking why they behave in a particular way. This question can be answered differently using various explanatory strategies. Some of them refer to the notion of 'power': i) the behavior in question is either a matter of being induced by the 'power' of another entity, party, institution or whatever, or ii) it is explained, saying that the actor has been using its own 'power' in order to achieve some end (later we will relate this to means-end rationality). In both cases, intentionality plays a role, in the former perhaps to a lesser degree. These ends can be of many kinds, some of them even being the maintenance or enhancement of one's 'power.'

Philosophical Characterizations

When Bacon identified knowledge and power or when Foucault remarked that knowledge (claims) always depend on a "régime of truth" (Foucault, 1980, p. 131), power is playing a role in matters of epistemology. A more sociological statement is made when it is said that, actually, "power defines what counts as knowledge" (Flyvbjerg, 1991, p. 27). Ontological issues can involve references to power too. For example, when a cause is seen to have the 'power' to produce its effect. An example would be the mechanistic view of reality as, basically, constituted by causal relations, the causes having effective 'power.' Also the Nietzschean identification of life and power ('will to power'), or even wider of power and reality, can be mentioned here. Of course, how such matters are considered more in detail depends on metaphysical views involved. More specific examples are the power of money (Simmel, 1989), organization, that is, the view that power is "constitutive" of organization (Clegg, 1990, p. 84), and language as power. In the same vein, is it sometimes said that power is the "pillar of the social fabric of governing structures and regimes" (Clegg c.s. 2006, p. 343). Saying this is indeed beyond any kind of empirical characterization. One could also ask the question whether narratives have such a kind of constitutive power.

Normative Function

This concerns various things such as i) attributing responsibilities and authorities, widening them or setting limits to them, ii) attributing liabilities, all variations on the theme of 'noblesse oblige,' and iii) judging and evaluating existing situations in terms of 'power relations' and of human capacities from a normative point of view. Liability especially comes into focus when some damaging events have happened which a particular actor, considering its responsibilities and 'power,' could and should have prevented. In law and applied ethics this use of 'power' is not uncommon. In actual situations, however, it might turn out that the more power an actor has, the more he can avoid being held liable. About 50 years ago, Wright Mills saw the power elite not as people who are fulfilling important duties but as those who "determine their duties as well as the duties of those beneath them" (Mills, 1956, p. 286). From a particular normative societal point of view this might be questioned: the more 'power' a person, company, or whatever has, the heavier the responsibilities may be. Not living up to this responsibility can arouse resistance, inside as well as outside organizations.

Looking at the just-given outline, it is clear that skipping the notion of 'power' from our vocabulary would severely limit our potential of explaining, understanding, and evaluating the world we live in. It is time now to get a clearer grasp of the concept of power.

3   PHILOSOPHICAL COMMENTS ON THE CONCEPT OF POWER

In this section we will start by giving an explication of denotation of power, including three modes of power that need to be distinguished. We will proceed by giving attention to factual and normative conditions related to the exercise of power. Because narrative is sometimes linked to instrumental rationality and control, sometimes seen as beyond (see introduction), a more detailed analysis of the relationship of rationality and power is relevant. Hence, we conclude this part considering the relationship of power and rationality.

3.1 Definition of Power

During history, authors have made different qualifications and distinctions related to various contexts in which (the concept of) 'power' is applied. For example, Aristotle, in his *Metaphysics* (1972), defines power (potency) as a "source of movement or change which is in another thing than the thing moved or in the same thing qua other." This definition is applicable to human and natural affairs. The same kind of generality one can find in Leibniz when he considers power as the possibility to change. Apart from these, one can find definitions especially related to human beings and social reality: power is "the production of intended effects" (Russell, 1967, p. 25); "with power, one party can get the other to do what the latter normally would not do" (Kramer, 1998, p. 264; see also Dahl, 1957); "power corresponds to the human ability not just to act, but to act in concert" (Arendt, 1970, p. 44). Arendt reserves power exclusively to human beings, a view which also has other defenders, for example, Guardini (1965, pp. 12, 13). For the question whether the concept of power should or should not be confined to human beings, see Morriss (2002). We will now give the following definition of power:

> *In its most general sense, "power" means the relatively durable capacity an entity has of bringing about an effect in an orderly way, or, in the midst of changing realities, to continue an existing situation in that way.*

This definition especially emphasizes the 'formative' character of power, not limiting it to human beings.[1] Considered such, different kinds of entities, natural ones (a river), technical artifacts (cars, engines, computers), animals (elephants, beavers), people, social entities (company, government, rules), conceptual entities (hypothesis, theories), and so on can be considered to have power as long as they have the capacity as described earlier (whether it is active or not). The definition does not refer to what power base is being involved. This base can be of many kinds, such as physical properties, formal authority, charisma, and so on, depending on the kind of entity. The usual content of power is the ability of making other people do things which they would otherwise not do (Dahl, 1957). This is nothing but a sociological specification of its general meaning, resulting in the so-called 'relational concept' of power. However, from a general philosophical point of view this concept is too limited. The definition given earlier makes power distinct from 'influence.' Whereas the former is to be considered as a relatively durable disposition of an entity to effectuate something in an orderly way, the latter accentuates the actual changes made and is more contingent. Power is relatively inescapable, whereas influence is not. So, people can be influential without having real power.

As already indicated, 'power' can get a specific meaning when linked to particular contexts, which also specifies the power base. Concerning human beings, the 'orderly way' can, for instance, be specified by referring to *intentions*. With natural entities (e.g., water having the power to extinguish fire), only physical laws and conditions come into play. If technical artifacts are being involved, the situation becomes more complicated. Moreover, in social reality the capacity and the effects concern people or other social actors, and the link between both involve so-called 'power relations,' some of which are imbued with formal authority (e.g., a police officer). In the financial world, actual power sometimes depends on the amount of money involved, sometimes on formal authority. Especially the present financial and economic crisis motivates to demand a strengthening of the formal authority of controlling bodies. Some authors link 'power' exclusively to intentions. When the concept of power is taken in the general sense presented earlier, this is not necessary; only in particular contexts comes this special link to the fore, as might be the case when we speak of 'corporate power.' In section 4 power will be related to narrative.

3.2   Power To, Over, and With

Concerning the concept of power, some important distinctions need to be made, that is, between *power to*, *power over*, and *power with*. With the expression 'power *to*,' emphasis is laid upon the capacity of bringing about something, just as it is formulated in the definition. 'Power *over*' focuses on the reality in or at which the effect is brought about. Finally, 'power *with*' underlines, if there are any, the entities, means, with whom the effect is being realized.[2]

A particular person may be supposed to have the power *to* lift objects up to a certain weight. Its actualization means that power *over* the object is exercised, doing so, for example, *with* muscle power. However, if a pulley and rope are being used, the '*with*' involves these artifacts in particular, at the same time the potential amount of mass increases. The power *over* is now exercised straightly on the rope and indirectly on the objects lifted. When cooperating with someone else on an equal basis, the power *with* involves two people without one having power *over* the other. Sometimes, vocal expressions are being used in order to create a shared rhythm in pulling the rope. When not peers, some kind of power *over* may effectuate the coordinated action. Bourdieu (1994, p. 107) gives attention to power *with* words. In commenting on Austin's speech-act theory, he is saying that power does not reside in the very words but is "delegated power of the spokesperson."

Power *to* can't be without power *over* and power *with* being involved. In thinking about social reality, 'power *over*' is often emphasized: the power of one individual *over* another, the power of an institution *over* people, and so on. However, understanding actual situations requires the other notions of power as well. For instance, the government has power *to* impose levies. As such it depends on the force of law, tax rules, and a whole system of organizations: that is, power *with*. The result is power *over* what people do with their money. If done properly, everything in this case has a legal foundation.[3] The latter brings in the issue of conditions on which power depends.

3.3   Conditions

In actual situations, exercising power refers to particular conditions. These can be of two kinds, that is, factual and normative ones. The first category refers to the necessary empirical conditions, the second to matters of legitimacy.

3.3.1   Factual

For having power *with* a pulley, it needs to be attached to a fixed point above the lifted object and the rope must be strong enough, not too elastic, and so on. Otherwise there will be no lifting power. Hence, there are unavoidable 'conditions de pouvoir.' Realizing them can involve power too, here again particular favorable conditions will have to exist, and so forth. Also, in social reality the conditions are crucial. Having power *with* depends on specific requirements, differing according to the situation at issue. However, we cannot say that power is necessary and sufficient in order to create the conditions. Consider, for instance, power *with* peers. Whether it concerns friends, colleagues, companies, or whatever, the willingness to cooperate is crucial and 'forcing' it is likely to be unproductive. Having power *with* organizations depends on the proper functioning of them. However, organizations are more than simple instruments. They constitute a complicated reality of their own: organizational rules, overall culture, subcultures, formal and informal organization, power relations, people, integrity (risks), knowledge, and so on. Having power *with*, therefore, very much depends on all being in concert, a situation of which it is hardly imaginable that it can be effectuated by power alone.

3.3.2   Normative

Normative conditions refer to matters of legitimacy. Questions like 'power for what reason?' and 'when is the exercise of power justifiable and when not?' are relevant here. Especially concerning society, they have been part of philosophy since long ago. Saying that a situation shows 'abuse of power' or the existence of an 'unacceptable power balance,' or just the opposite, always depends on answering the question 'power for what reason?' The latter refers to normative views concerning society and human life, or to specific values related to different kinds of practice (government, business, health care, education, etc.).[4]

3.4   Power and Rationality

During the Enlightenment period it was believed that reason and rationality alone would do away with sheer power, with unjustified authority, and so on, a line of thought which still finds its advocates. A bit naïve, perhaps, but its philosophical stand that power needs something beyond is not unsound. However, one can also find the view that rationality itself is a "form of power" (Flyvbjerg, 1991, p. 132) or that power can reign over rationality.

In order to become a bit more clear about the issue of power and rationality, we start by giving a brief explication of what rationality is about. Next, the focus is on rationality as power. The section will conclude by paying attention to power over rationality.

3.4.1   Rationality

Generally speaking, rationality is intelligently and wisely accounting for thinking and acting, finding good warrants for both (Schipper, 2009). It can be involved in decision making, knowledge claims, formulating intentions and plans, and so on. Acting according to plans or being active in the midst of evolving situations—to which the acting itself also contributes—requires rationality too.

Sometimes, rules and procedures, algorithms, are involved. On other occasions reference is made to general criteria (maxims), making judgments. It may be that the issue is finding effective, efficient means for attaining particular ends. The main question can also be what goals are to be achieved and on what basis they have to be formulated and selected. Especially this may refer to values (truth, justice, health, for example). Feeling and emotion can be among the reasons for doing something too.

However, intelligence and wisdom require that procedures, rules, emotions are never followed blindly, that criteria by which judgments are being made match situations at issue and that the values are understandable. They also demand us to be conscious of the fact that seeking effectiveness and efficiency may lead to preoccupations; tunnel vision might result, and meanings given to particular values may be too narrow or not contextualized enough (Schipper, 1998). Of course, concentration on rules, finding effective/efficient means, or using general criteria is often needed. If so, then what is in use are, respectively, algorithmic, instrumental, means-end, and judgmental rationality. However, they are only possible aspects of rationality in a wider sense. Considering them as paradigmatic might just result in unintelligent and unwise thinking and acting. To prevent all this, critical reflection is basic (Schipper, 2001, 2003, 2009).

3.4.2   Rationality as power

Earlier, rationality is related to thinking and acting.[5] Thinking remains within the conceptual realm, whereas acting involves an interference with the (e.g., physical, material) world. When considering rationality as power, it makes, therefore, sense to distinguish between thinking and acting related to, respectively, conceptual/semantic power and productive power.

Conceptual Power

As said, 'power' means the relatively durable capacity an entity has of bringing about an effect in an orderly way, or, in the midst of changing realities, to continue an existing situation in that way. Algorithms, for example, involve control of decision processes (power *to*), while determining outcomes (power *over*). The outcomes are, for instance, statements, formula, schemes, and so on, concerning a particular subject matter. As long as the rules and procedures do their job, this power (to and over) functions rather autonomously. Eventually there is some actor having power *with*. Look further at judgments based on general criteria, maxims in terms of which decisions are being made, for instance, concerning plans, deciding about effective means, and so on, using relevant information. Although autonomy of the process compared to the actors is lacking, the outcomes still come about in an orderly way, or a reconstruction can be made in that sense. Here too here there is a power to decide, defining the outcome (power over). Strictly speaking, the outcomes all remain within the conceptual level (statements, plans, formulated decisions, particular judgments etc.). We will, therefore, speak of *conceptual power*. When looking at resulting meanings, we can also say that *semantic* power is involved. For the sake of clarity, it is important to realize, however, that 'meaning' is used here in a broader sense than just linguistic meaning. For instance, concerning plans this meaning also involves differences they would make in reality, whether this is to be values positive, and so on.[6]

Productive Power

Means-end, instrumental, rationality concerns finding effective and efficient[7] means and using them to realize particular ends, that is, the acting side of rationality. We speak of 'means-end' rationality when the conceptual side is underlined; 'instrumental' rationality emphasizes actually achieving the ends. The latter is related to *productive power*, the means *with* which the power is exercised. Realizing the factual conditions (see section 3.2.1) is often also a matter of productive power.

In the case of reflection, it does generally not make sense to seek control over the outcome. Openness, crucial for reflective rationality, is beyond this. However, this is not saying that reflection, for instance, on the content given to 'efficiency,' does not demand much mental strengths, or that, as far as the meaning of judgments is involved, semantic power is completely absent.

3.4.3   Power over Rationality

Flyvbjerg (1991, 2001) argues that things often happen the way they do because power reigns over rationality, defining what is considered to be real, what actually counts as knowledge in the situation, and so on. We try to understand this by keeping various aspects of rationality in mind.

When algorithms in use are selected and implemented by the exercise of power *over* the people, there is power *over* this side of rationality. The same may happen to criteria. Also the definition/selection of ends can be a matter of power *over*, rather subtle or bluntly explicit. The following statement is a case of the latter: "This is what you have to strive for; otherwise you will be fired." However, it is hardly imaginable that choosing effective means can be a matter of power *over* people's minds; doing so will very likely be unproductive or create huge problems. Moreover, the reflective aspect is really at odds with power over, that is, over rationality. If so, then it would not be real reflection anymore.

Hence, we can conclude that power *over* rationality can only be active in a limited way. Studying what is actually being the case, which is what Flyvbjerg does, is asking a 'questio facti.' The 'questio juris' concerning power and rationality is much different, however. It introduces the philosophical issue of proper and responsible use of power, pointing to using it with intelligence and wisdom.

4   POWER AND NARRATIVE

When relating power and narrative, we need to have an idea about the latter. Narratives are many; fictitious, real life, backward looking, future oriented, complicated, or simple, and so on, some of them having all these characteristics. Key aspects are that they concern particular entities, actors, concrete actions, events, teleological traits, expectations, and intentions, placed into a more or less meaningful whole. So, narratives have an internal "nonrandom connection" (Toolan, 2001, p. 6). Some authors underline the plot-like character of this whole (e.g., Ricoeur). However, when narrative is future oriented, for instance, concerning intended actions, emplotment is likely to be less important. In this case, for example, reference to values may co-constitute the meaningful whole. Finding an adequate general (linguistic or philosophical) definition is, therefore, not easy and definitions are hardly without any critique.[8] Compared to logico-scientific thinking, narrative is more life near, because it refers to individual actors and situations. Whether this life is real, fictitious, past, present, or future does not make a difference for the narrative qua narrative.[9] However, a certain narrative has its own possible abstractions; for instance, certain matters may be excluded, particular voices not taken into account. It is here that the notion of antenarrative comes in (Boje, 2001, p. 17), pointing to antenarrative variety (see introduction). As we see it, ante and narrative have a twofold connection, i) as the anticipation of a (potential) story, and ii) as narratives coming before another narrative; both are taken together in the expression 'ante(-)narrative'.

In what comes next, concentration will be laid on two relevant issues. The first is the role of semantic power, with closure and the possibilities of relating as relevant subject matter. In connection with this, attention will also be given to ante and narrative. The second, final, important issue will be responsible use of power in connection with narrative, referring to the example of Flextronics and use of narratives in air traffic safety.

4.1 Ante, Narrative, and Semantic Power

In section 3.4.2 it was argued that it makes sense to distinguish conceptual and productive power, with semantic power as a submode of the first. Semantic power is nothing less than the power to create or define meaning, taken in a wide sense (see footnote 6). The 'meaning' connected to narrative is potentially also rather broad and does match the one just referred to. We will first look at power and narrative closure.

4.1.1 Semantic Power and Closure

Semantic power is the capacity to create or constitute a particular *meaning* in an orderly way. Narratives, as orderly wholes of symbols, just have this capacity and can, therefore, be seen as having semantic power. In terms of distinctions made in section 3.2, it concerns a power *to* create meaning, *with* the symbolic means in use (e.g., linguistic ones). Saying this is laying a different emphasis compared to Bourdieu's notion of symbolic power, which focuses more on the use of symbols to exercise power *over* people (see section 3.2). Power can also be part of a story itself, for instance, the "mystical powers" of Sherlock Holmes (Toolan, 2001, p. 88), but that is not what we have in mind. Semantic power also has to meet factual and normative conditions, starting with regard to the symbolic means that are being used, for instance, language. As far as wider meaning is involved, the normative can also relate to issues beyond this, for instance, concerning the legitimacy of meaning. All this is preserved when semantic power—also connected to narratives—is part of real-life situations. In this case the normative conditions especially point to the proper use and abuse of semantic power. We will come back to this issue in the next section.

Closure

A certain narrative creates a particular meaning. The well-known example of the simple narrative, 'The queen died and then the king died of sorrow,' already shows this.[10] Although different matters are being present, such as the sense of their relationship and emotional causality, there is one meaning. So, a *closure* of meaning is involved. Time references can also add to this. For instance, expressions like 'once upon a time' and 'after this the world never was the same any more' already create certain time horizons, that is, closure of past and future respectively. Nonfictional stories, such as official company narratives about founders, are no exception. They also have semantic power and closure. Now it is important to see what both can do to ante(-)narratives.

Ante(-)narrative

As said earlier, talking about ante(-)narratives involves double possible emphasis: pointing to what is before a particular narrative, and to a kind of proto-narrative. However, what is ante(-)narrative and narrative is circumstantial. If, for example, a judge in court gives a narrative account of what has happened in a particular case, the declarations made by the witnesses are indeed ante-. When the attention lies on the story told by a particular witness, what first was ante- now comes into focus and the ante(-)narrative shifts too, for instance, to things not told by the witness. *Compared* to the (hopefully) balanced narrative of the judge, what a witness tells is likely to be less inclusive and perhaps less coherent. Apart from this, however, the story of a witness can be coherent enough to constitute substantial meaning, probably having its own ante(-)narratives.

Now, it is important to realize that shifting focus also means that semantic power and closure shifts too. Seeing something as ante(-) decreases semantic power. Moreover, semantic power can organize, that is, shape and select, also what is 'ante' in its own terms. If so, then this force is exercised *over* another symbolic entity. When, for example, the official company story about the founder is already present and later on its narrational 'roots' are explored, this can become manifest. Now a critical reader might say that what comes into focus in such a case is only *seemingly* 'ante'; actually it is just a *post*-narrational image of the past. Such a reaction is indeed quite understandable and it illustrates that the ante(-) is considered only in connection to something else; speaking of the 'real' *ante* seems to be impossible. Moreover, if the ante is seen as ante(-)narrative, in the sense referred to earlier, the point of reference of this concept still is coherent, plotted, narrative. This also decreases semantic power. Only by bracketing this point of reference is it possible to see them as narratives in their own right; only then is there a chance that their semantic power becomes manifest.

4.1.2 Connecting Narratives

The previous section suggests that there are several ways in which ante and narrative are, or become, related. The first remains within the range of power *over* symbolic entities. The abovementioned company story and its roots would be an example; the connections made sustain narrative closure. The second way takes a move beyond. The link made between ante and narrative is based upon taking the first as narratives in their own right, being reflectively conscious of their potential semantic power.

An interesting example of the latter was front-page news in the Dutch media. It concerns Flextronics, an electronics manufacturing services (EMS) provider focused on delivering complete design, engineering, and manufacturing services to automotive, computing, consumer digital, industrial, infrastructure, medical, and mobile organizations, headquartered in Singapore. They also have a plant in the Netherlands (Venray). As far as social responsibility is concerned, Flextronics is saying that it:

> "continuously strives to improve its environmental performance and supports its customers through services, products, and new technologies that minimize environmental impact. Flextronics adheres to the highest ethical standards of practice with our customers, suppliers, partners, employees, communities and investors, and to providing a safe and quality work environment for our employees."[11]

This is part of the narrative told by the company about itself. Flextronics came into the news because the union filed a lawsuit against it at the court in 's Hertogenbosch. The reason for the union to take action is that employees became sick after having been exposed to several toxic substances, i) some applied in cleaning sea containers used for shipping products from the countries were they are fabricated, and ii) others evaporating from packaging and products, without warning or giving them appropriate protection; the management of Flextronics denies the latter. On the of July 29, 2009, several employees (of Polish origin) were interviewed on TV, telling their stories about becoming sick after unloading containers and what happened next. The key meaning of what they said is just the opposite of " . . . a safe and quality work environment . . . " (see preceding quotation). Because the management had enforced a speaking ban on employees, they had their faces and voices made unrecognizable.[12] The legal procedures just started. Hence, it is not possible to assess the outcome already. It is clear, however, that semantic power and closure are important for understanding the situation.

The official company story tolerates only particular antenarratives matching the official narrative's meaning. That's why management, sticking to this meaning, came with its ban. That's also why workers appeared on TV, telling their own substantial narratives.

What is just said is linking symbolic entities beyond narrative closure. By bringing the issue to court, the union helped create a new situation in which, eventually, the judge will have to come up with his own narrative. If things are going as to be expected in court, the official company narrative and those of employees will be presented, with their respective meanings. During the judicial process, they are also functioning as 'antenarratives,' as 'bets,' and in the end as antenarratives to the narrative of the judge, a narrative on which his/her verdict (if any, of course) is based. As far as semantic power and closure are concerned, there is a kind of 'movement' too. In the first phase, semantic power and closure of the involved narratives are manifest; next they are being transcended, and finally become bracketed because the power and closure of the judge's narrative are taking control. It is worth noticing that the latter narrative is (should be) based on values which are constitutive for judicial practice. If one of the parties does not want to accept this, the case might be taken to a higher court. If so, the situation then is changing again and the judge's narrative is becoming ante(-)narrative itself. The whole process, however, requires that the potential semantic power stays related to (reflective) rationality in the field of law.

The previous example is from a judicial context. However, the same situation could also be approached from other perspectives, such as business ethics. If so, then linking the narratives is done within another field. Yet, the indicated scheme of movement and the role of semantic power and rationality remain the same, although the values involved may be different.

4.2   Responsible Use of Power

The question of whether power is exercised responsibly or not is a philosophical one; another way of putting it is asking about normative conditions and good reasons for the use of power. We will now address some aspects of it, especially in connection with narratives.

In the introduction, it was mentioned that narratives are sometimes used for the sake of power. This comes close to Bourdieu's notion of symbolic power, in which power *over* people is exercised with symbols, in our case *with* narratives. Power *with* narratives depends on the semantic power discussed previously. Factual and normative conditions apply here too. The first refers to the technicalities of exercising power. The normative ones to the question whether the power at issue is exercised properly and for good reasons, hence, in a responsible way. This applies to power *over* people's behavior, *with* narratives, as well as to semantic power, which is power *over* meaning. Both concern a power *to* control. So, relevant for this paper are the following questions:

- *When is power* to *control to be considered as part of responsibility?*
- *When is power* over *people's behavior and* over *meaning suitable?*
- *When is power* with *narratives recommendable?*

Posing the first two questions is not addressing an empirical subject matter; they are philosophical ones indeed. The last question also allows an empirical interpretation in the context of answers to the other two.

It should be clear that answers will depend on the kind of practice and on actual situations. Take, for example, the second question. When creativity is involved (in R&D, in the arts, etc.), power over people's behavior and over meaning cannot be a general option (Schipper, 2001).[13] However, if it is the case that knowledge claims are scrutinized (e.g., in connection with the development of drugs), then power over meaning is necessary; we must be sure that concepts in use are unambiguous. Yet, it is also clear that power over meaning is not sheer power; it is based on previous relevant knowledge. At the same time, seeking power over behavior in this setting is not wisdom. If the intention is to find novel ideas and insights, power over meaning very likely will be counterproductive. However, when it comes to the production of drugs, it might be just the opposite; power over behavior, for instance, by implementing strict rules coming into focus.

The things said thus far already point to the direction in which answering the first question should go:

If creativity is essential, power to control is no option; when potential hazard is high, power to control is part of responsibility.[14]

Air traffic would also be a good example. Because of potential safety risks, for instance, semantic power over meanings used in communication is part of responsibility. Now look at power with narratives. If it turns out that a particular narrative, for instance, about the Tenerife air disaster of March 27, 1977, contributes to raising safety consciousness (an empirical matter), then using it as a means of power to is a viable option. Hence, power with this narrative is recommendable.[15]

Control over meaning may also involve control over narratives. Control over narratives implies power over their—then bracketed—semantic power. In connection with the previous example, this means it will be checked carefully that the intended safety message is present, and with good reason; in the end the semantic power of the narrative can be manifest again. On the other hand, if the intention is to gain new insights about safety, then power over crew members' narratives is not very wise because they are a potential source; seeing them as antenarratives is a start, to be followed by considering them as narratives having their own semantic power. In section 4.1.2 we argued that what counts as ante(-)narrative is circumstantial, making it also possible that an antenarrative is actually a 'post-' one, opening the door for irresponsible power over meaning. The case of Flextronics can be interpreted in this way. Seemingly, the management wants to have power over the stories of the employees, making allowed tellings into postnarratives. In terms of knowledge responsibility, it would have shown more wisdom if management would have been willing to learn from employees. If so, no good reasons for the indicated power intention would exist. A much better option could also start with seeing the tellings as antenarratives, subsequently focusing on them as substantial meanings, and then linking them among each other and contributing to the narrative the company 'wants' to tell. All this goes beyond closure, just the opposite of what happened.

5   CONCLUDING REMARKS

During the last two decades there has been a growing interest in narratives, for instance, in philosophy, organization studies and (socio-)linguistics. Being active with philosophy in connection with management and organization, we think that getting more insight into the relation of narratives, rationality, and power is important. Narratives can be involved in various modes of rationality, and power is an important element of—thinking about and acting with—narratives. That is why we first of all embarked on a philosophical tour in order to find an explication of the concept of power, relating it to rationality subsequently, and, finally, sought its connection with ante(-)narratives. The latter is important because it addresses narrative variety.

Our effort is not only motivated by a theoretical interest but has practical ends in view as well. The connection between both is made by the questions discussed in section 4.2 about responsible use of power. The answers differentiate according to situation, the kind of practice or field, and values involved. As far as ante(-)narratives, dealing with their variety and linking them—also beyond closure—are concerned, the answers also have to share this nuanced approach. Saying this is also contextualizing the distinction of antenarrative and narrative. Eventually, what to do depends on intelligence and wisdom, that is, situational rationality.

NOTES

1. Later on, in section 3.4.2., we will make a distinction between *semantic* and *productive* power. The former stresses its formative character in connection with statements, plans, etc., i.e., meaning taken in a wide sense, the latter in relation to (material) reality.
2. As far as we know, it was Mary Parker Follett (1941, p. 101) who introduced the notion of 'power with.' She especially had power with other people, in terms of cooperation, in mind. Arendt's (1970, p. 44) view of power as the ability to act in concert seems to be in line with this idea.
3. Laying these foundations is in many countries dependent on a proper functioning of Montaigne's three different powers and particular checks and balances.

4. Resistance can be interpreted as an effort to change the factual and normative conditions of a particular exercise of power.
5. We will not discuss the question whether and in what sense thinking is a kind of acting.
6. In terms of the well-known distinction between syntax, semantics, and pragmatics, semantics is especially connected with truth conditions. Our use of 'semantics' also includes aspects of pragmatics (what difference would it made in reality) and normative meanings. It can also refer to the notion of 'sense,' in German "Sinn," e.g., the sense of work. Hence we use the term more widely than is done traditionally.
7. Some authors see an intimate connection between power and efficiency. For example, Clegg cs. (2006, p. 7) makes the following statement: "to oppose efficiency to power as totally distinct and separate terms is to miss, entirely, that it was a concern with efficiency that gave birth to power in management and organizations. . . ." What they have in mind here is, according to their judgment, the wrong dichotomy of the sociology of organizations as concerned with power, and management theory as exclusively linked to efficiency. Whatever this may be, it is worth noticing that Clegg cs. considers efficiency-oriented management as a "political economy of the body" and as a "technology of power" (op. cit., p. 26) making a connection with ideas of Foucault.
8. Sometimes a difference is made between narrative and story, in which case story is supposed to be authentic/spontaneous, proactive, narrative as more or less constructed and backward looking (see, e.g., Boje 2008, p. 4). Boje (2001, p. 118) sees narrative as the emplotment of story. Sometimes story is considered to be the meaningful whole itself, narrative the particular symbolic means used. A sharp distinction is not easy to find, and in the present argument we will use both expressions, perhaps a bit naively, as denoting more or less the same.
9. In Philosophy there is also the discussion whether life *is* narrative or *before* narrative (Williams, 2007). We will not go into this discussion either.
10. This story has the "single temporal juncture," sometimes considered as minimal demand for being a narrative (Toolan, 2001, p. 148).
11. http://www.flextronics.com/about/pages/socialresponsibility.aspx; July 30, 2009.
12. http://www.novatv.nl/page/detail/uitzendingen/7139/Giftige+gassen+in+con tainers+leiden+tot+aanklacht; July 30, 2009.
13. This can be linked to Boje's notion of "emergent stories" (Boje, 2008, p. 54).
14. However, this should be taken with wisdom. The statement is a general one, not directly applicable to all situations, especially those in which creativity is needed while at the same time risk is very likely.
15. See http://aviation-safety.net/database/record.php?id=19770327–1.

REFERENCES

Arendt, H. (1970). *On violence.* New York: Harcourt.
Aristotle. (1972). *Metaphysica: The works of Aristotle translated into English.* Sir D. Ross, Ed. Oxford: Clarendon Press.
Boje, D. (2001). *Narrative methods for organizational and communication research.* London: Sage.
Boje, D. et al. (2004). *Antenarratives, narratives and anaemic stories.* Paper presented at the New Orleans Meeting of the Academy of Management. http://peaceaware.com/McD/papers

———. (2005). *Antenarrative*. Las Cruces: New Mexico State University Press.

———. (2008). *Storytelling organizations*. London: Sage.

Bourdieu, P. (1994). *Language and symbolic power*. Cambridge: Polity Press.

Clegg, S., cs. (1990). *Modern organizations*. London: Sage.

———. (2006). *Power and organizations*. London: Sage.

Dahl, R. (1957). The concept of power. *Behavioral Science, 2*(3), 201–215.

Flyvbjerk, B. (1991). *Rationality & power: Democracy in practice*. Chicago: University of Chicago Press.

———. (2001). *Making social science matter*. Cambridge: University of Cambridge Press.

Follett, M. P. (1941). *Dynamic administration*. London: Pitman & Sons.

Foucault, M. (1980). *Power/knowledge: Selected interviews and other writings, 1972–1977*. Colin Gordon, Ed. Brighton, UK: The Harvester Press.

Fryzel, B. (2005). Governance of corporate power networks. *Finance and Bien Commun. The Enterprise. Matter and Form(s), 23*(Winter).

Guardini, R. (1965). *Die Macht*. Würzburg, Germany: Werkbund Verlag.

Kramer, R. (Ed.). (1998). *Power and influence in organizations*. London: Sage.

Learned, A. (2007). *Marketing through stories: The selling power of narrative*. Retrieved June 1, 2010, from http://www.marketingprofs.com/marketing/online-seminars/108

Mills, C. W. (1956). *The power elite*. New York: Oxford University Press.

Morriss, P. (2002). *Power: A philosophical analysis*. Manchester, UK: Manchester University Press.

Ricoeur, P. (1998). *Hermeneutics and the human sciences*. Cambridge: Cambridge University Press.

Schipper, F. (1998). *Rethinking efficiency*. Electronic publication. Proceedings World Congress of Philosophy Boston 1998. Retrieved June 1, 2010, from http://www.bu.edu/WCP/MainOApp.htm

———. (2001). Creativity and rationality: A philosophical contribution. *Philosophy of Management, 1*(2), 3–15.

———. (2003). Philosophising outdoors. *Practical Philosophy*, Autumn 2003, 68–67.

———. (2009). Excess of rationality: About rationality, emotion and creativity. *Tamara Journal, 7*(4), 160–175.

Simmel, G. (1989). *Philosophie des Geldes*. Frankfurt am Main, Germany: Suhrkamp.

Russell, B. (1967). *Power*. London: Unwin Books.

Toolan, M. (2001). *Narrative: A critical linguistic introduction*. London: Routledge.

Tsoukas, H., & Hatch, M. J. (2002). Complex thinking, complex practice: The case for a narrative approach to organizational complexity. *Human Relations, 54*(8), 979–1013.

Weick, K. (2005). Organizing and the process of sensemaking. *Organization Science, 16*(4), 409–421.

Williams, B. (2007). Life as narrative. *European Journal of Philosophy, 17*(2), 305–314.

Wrong, D. (2004). *Power: Its forms, bases and uses*. New Brunswick, NJ: Transaction Publishers.

2 Antenarratives of Negotiated Diversity Management

Jawad Syed and David M. Boje

INTRODUCTION

Given the extraordinary socioeconomic, demographic, and technological changes taking place in the world today, business organizations and academic institutions are increasingly engaging in more innovative ways of managing. Adler (2006) and Allison (1988) suggest that simple linear solutions conventionally advocated in the economics literatures are no longer valid for today's complex business environment. This chapter identifies storytelling as one such nonlinear process that may be deployed for effective management of workforce diversity.

Adler positioned her argument and emphasized the need for 'hope' in the complex context of the political conflict in the Middle East. Allison positioned his arguments against linearity amidst management strategy models. We argue that storytelling offers one possible pathway towards hope. Although we share Fisk's (2006) concern when he laments different, politically separated narratives, and also critical race scholars' concerns when they question the very foundations of the liberal order such as equality theory and legal reasoning (Delgado & Stefancic, 2001), we believe there is hope, and that 'it is human to have hope' (Elie Wiesel, cited in Rourke, 2002). Indeed, if human action always achieved its intended results, there would be no space for stories (Gabriel, 2000).

Cultural diversity is a global phenomenon. The world's nearly 200 countries consist of about 5,000 ethnic groups, with about two-thirds having at least one substantial minority, an ethnic or religious group that constitutes at least 10% of the population. There are 110 countries with ethnic populations constituting more than 25% of the population, and another 42 countries with ethnic minorities in the range of 10 to 25% of population (UNDP, 2004). This means that each country would need to develop its unique response to diversity management within public policy and business organizations.

In this chapter, we develop a 'negotiated diversity management' approach from an antenarrative approach that changes the cycle of ways the multiplicity of living stories are typically being excluded by official retro-narratives constructing the identity of oftentimes culturally diverse employees. We argue that orthodox approaches to diversity management are influenced by hegemonic mainstream perspectives on diversity and how it ought to be managed. Storytelling gives voice to marginalized individuals and groups whose perspectives are otherwise suppressed in the 'mainstream' organizational structures and routines. Because of its imaginative and subversive nature, storytelling has the potential to offer holistic and critical, yet invisible, discourses on diversity management. We argue that one possible approach to deciding among mainstream and marginalized stories is through dialogic negotiation, which will provide for the creation of what is termed 'negotiated diversity management.'

We critique diversity narratives that promise economic gains and use technocratic rationality, but subvert the importance of unequal power relations. We suggest a triadic theory of storytelling, where such managerialist (often linear) narratives are one aspect, and opposed by two other kinds of storytelling: the living story of people in unequal power relations, and antenarratives (bets about the future; an ante is a bet and a before-narrative). We are interested in how nonlinear (cyclic and rhizomatic) antenarratives interplay with stabilized, often linear narratives and more fragmented living stories of people situated in unequal power relationships in organizations. We suggest that diversity management makes rather managerialist bets about the future situation of diversity in organizations; what is necessary is to cultivate antenarratives that present a critical appraisal of the future, and a counterforce to narratives whose (retrospective) sensemaking is stuck on the past.

DIVERSITY AND POWER

Diversity is typically defined as the degree of heterogeneity among team members on specified demographic dimensions (Ely & Roberts, in press). Culturally diverse groups 'collectively share certain norms, values or traditions that are different from those of other groups' (Cox, 1993, pp. 5–6). Such groups are usually associated with power differentials in organizations (Ragins, 1997; Ridgeway & Berger, 1986). The idea of a multicultural organization implies that the usual privileged positions must be dismantled, and that power mechanics are transformed (Cavanagh, 1997; Marsden, 1997). However, to what extent diversity management can enable such transformation remains in question (Kamp & Hagedorn-Rasmussen, 2004; Syed & Kramar, 2009).

Whereas issues of power differential and effective management of multicultural communities have become increasingly important in the last few decades, it is a fact that despite the diverse composition of the population and workforce in most countries, diversity management remains largely marginal in political institutions as well as in business organizations (LGI, 2007). Whereas there has been some progress towards equality and diversity in the last few decades, critical race scholars have demonstrated that national laws and labor policies continue to be predominantly shaped by the powerful members of the society (such as white males in the U.S. context), whereas the perspectives of the marginalized groups (such as ethnic minorities and women) remain generally ignored (e.g., Calmore, 1992; Solorzano & Yosso, 2001; Syed, 2007).

Gabriel and Willman (2005) argue that, over time, scholars have realized that relations of power are built into the very language that levels all humans to the undifferentiated condition of the mainstream or natural. Not unlike Adler (2006), Gabriel and Willman refer to a political example, this time the anti-balkanization, to illustrate that dialogue, not integration, is more likely to reduce hostilities and enhance understanding. They term integration at the cost of identity and individuality as a misleading notion, such as in the context of the current debate surrounding the future of the European Union.

Similar attempts towards integration with the 'mainstream' are evident in other national contexts, such as Australia. Syed and Kramar (2010) report the 'multicultural rollback' within the mainstream Australian media and politics. Through a much-publicized emphasis on Australian values, ethnic minorities are being urged to abandon their cultural practices in order to integrate and assimilate into the mainstream Australian society. In an effort to shift the emphasis away from fostering diversity and towards increasing integration among migrants, the government is canvassing substitute words and notions to explain how ethnic communities ought to integrate into Australian society (Hart, 2006, p. 3). Recently in 2007, the Australian government scrapped the word 'multicultural' from the name of the Department of Immigration and Multicultural Affairs as part of a major revamp of Australia's ethnic policy.

From an employment perspective, such moves towards integration or assimilation may be seen as opposite to the spirit of diversity and multiculturalism. Indeed, they are inconsistent with the 'dialogue among civilizations' and similar international projects such as the United Nations Global Compact, which urges businesses to support a sustainable and inclusive global economy (Cooperrider, 2004).

Supporting the need for a more inclusive stance towards management, this chapter argues for developing and engaging with multiparty stories in the workplace in order to arrive at a meaningful notion of diversity management. To achieve that goal, the chapter uses storytelling to develop an inclusive framework that provides for the creation of what is termed 'negotiated diversity management.'

RETHINKING DIVERSITY ANTENARRATIVES

Orthodox (or 'mainstream') diversity antenarratives, we argue, end up offering little more than classical 'cross-cultural training' as their bets on the future. These are coupled with narratives of history that point to economic or technocratic outcomes of diversity and erase the unequal power aspects. Contrast linear petrified (official) narratives with participants' own living stories in their world of lived experience in the organization; there are apt to be major disparities between the training narratives of diversity management success (or failure) and the people's own living stories. For example, Kalev, Dobbin, & Kelly (2006), based on an extensive review of various diversity management approaches, point out how most of the time there is either mixed result or it makes the situation worse (e.g., in terms of minority promotions).

It is, however, a fact that organizationally, polyphony is always present, even though it may be silenced by a hegemonic discourse of linear petrified narrative. Studies suggest that the polyphony of perspectives can trigger creativity and innovation, and that a polyphonic organization has the flexibility to cope with a fast-changing environment (Hazen, 1993; Kornberger, Clegg, & Carter, 2006). We argue that a polyphonic approach to diversity may be helpful to develop an awareness of privilege (or lack of it), enabling a pluralistic and realistic framing of diversity management in the workplace.

Further, diversity management has a social significance that reaches far beyond the workplace, occasionally reinforcing or challenging conservatism in the society. For example, the Productive Diversity policy in Australia is predominantly focused on the economic benefits of diversity management, and is, in this pursuit, largely dependent on quantitative research. Such policies tend to ignore the complex cultural-environmental challenges faced by culturally diverse employees, and lack the richness offered by qualitative narratives (Ho, 2006; Syed, 2007). Viewing dialogic story in relation to more stable narrative orders may provide a critique of this practice, and help in understanding the limitations of orthodox practices of diversity management.

Feminist Critique

A feminist critique of the state of workplace diversity offers some insight into the fundamental issues that need be addressed if diversity management is to succeed (Calas, 1992; Thurlow, Mills, & Mills, 2006), such as the potential of backlash towards marginalized groups, and a fuzziness surrounding the concept of diversity management (Jones & Stablein, 2006; Syed, 2007). In a study of women managers' stories of gender, Olsson (2000) used storytelling to examine the role of organizational myths and stories in the definition of leadership as heroic masculinism. The study classified attitudes towards women managers in three interrelated categories: invisibility, sexuality, and stereotypes. The stories suggest that women's career journeys are not only shaped by their competencies or abilities but also by stereotyped attitudes encountered along the way (p. 302). The study reveals how women's stories may 'break the silence' and expand official organizational myths about women's experiences in the workplace.

Race Critique

Critical race scholars have unraveled the primacy of the 'mainstream' perspectives in the institutions and practices of diversity management. They challenge the usual claims that governments, organizations, and other institutions make vis-à-vis objectivity, meritocracy, race neutrality, and gender equity. Their studies suggest that such traditional claims act as a camouflage for the self-interest, power, and privilege of the dominant group(s) in society (Calmore, 1992; Cox & Nkomo, 1990; Solorzano, 1997; Solorzano & Yosso, 2001). In the U.S. context, Ely, Thomas, and Padavic (in press) note that white persons as a group have higher status and hold more formal organizational and political power than do racial or ethnic minorities. Research on how cultural diversity can impact group interactions shows that inequality at the societal level creates asymmetries in minority groups' experiences at the interpersonal level (e.g., Tropp & Pettigrew, 2005). Most notably, ethnic minorities often suffer from 'power deficits' that 'may deter them from expressing their unique ideas' under conditions that would not deter whites (Swann, Polzer, Seyle, & Ko, 2004, p. 22).

Global Context

National and global contexts will provide different starting points for understanding what counts as diverse, and the extent of equality legislation in a country is also important to keep in mind. Recent work from sociology and cultural studies on intersectional analyses (Kersten, 2000; Prasad & Mills, 1997) attempts to think of gender, race, class, and other identity markers 'together' when describing and theorizing the subject position and life experiences of organizational members. We suggest that moving out of a diversity management discourse and into one where there are living unfolding stories of these identity markers (Somers, 1994) will prove to be a way to make relationships and provide important contextual insights for antenarrating different cycles and rhizomatics.

We see 'managing for diversity' as being a proactive, ongoing strategy that creates a culture within which people appreciate and can capitalize on individual differences—regardless of changing legal, demographic, and economic conditions. For example, Chavez and Weisinger (2008) explore an approach to diversity that goes beyond managerialist models. They look at the 'well-being of the worker' and the kinds of 'distinctive skills and experiences' that are in the worker's experience. Instead of managing diversity to get technocratic or economic results, the idea is 'managing for diversity' as a proactive change in organizational culture and strategy. There is a change proposed to the conventional narrative of diversity management, as well as what we are calling an antenarrative of how well-being becomes a bet on the future of the human condition. Their philosophy, however, needs to be extended beyond the classroom to an organization intervention.

The foregoing demonstrated the need for holistic and subversive stories instead of the mainstream or institutional narratives of diversity management. In the next section, we will discuss the implications of dialogic interplay of antenarrative, narrative, and story for diversity management.

THEORY OF STORYTELLING TRIADIC

Storytelling is increasingly used in employment contexts to make sense of the past and the present, to evaluate organizational resources, and to build future plans and strategies. In particular in Weickian sensemaking there is a recent shift to balance retrospection with prospection (Weick, Nord, & Walter, 2005; also see Boje, 2007; Ricoeur, 1992).

Özbilgin and Tatli (2006) suggest that individuals use stories in order to stake their claim in limited organizational resources, to legitimize their past actions as well as prospective future plans. The same is true in the broad field of diversity management, in which policymakers, employers, employees, and other stakeholders draw on competing stories in order to justify, promote, and implement their strategies. In story ethics, there is recognition that a life plan to realize Aristotelean 'Good Life' depends on the compelling nature of story, what Bakhtin (1990, 1991) calls answerability, what Ricoeur (1992) and others call responsibility, and what Levinas calls summoning responsibility (Hand, 1989). Story ethics is more about the social fabric of story in action than just text, which is more the subject of narrative (its structure, readability, followability, interplay of reader and author, etc.).

The underlying premise of narrative inquiry in organizations is the belief that individuals make sense of their world most effectively by telling stories (Clandinin & Connelly, 1994; Wiltshire, 1995). Within the culture of a social collective like an organization, narratives can take the form of a living story (Boje, 2005). Here, stories are fragmented; their shreds are collected together with those from other stories, in a disparate, random, and spontaneous fashion over time, by diverse individuals in the collective. However, from an interpretive research perspective, the historical truth of a story is not the primary issue (Riessman, 1993, p. 64). Instead, the intended meanings of the stories constructed by diverse storytellers are more important (Bailey & Tilley, 2002).

We consider in this chapter a triadic of very different storytelling practices. We argue that narrative tends to exclude, to be more abstract about time and place, to erase the specifics. This is valuable for generalization, but can become a sort of monologic. Living story is more tactical (in de Certeau's [1984] sense, the practice of everyday life), and is more grounded in relationships, in times and spaces that are contemporary. Antenarrative practices are all about movement and transition. Antenarrative provides a sort of bridge across narratives implanted in place that are stabilized (petrified, in Czarniawska's concept). There are two forces of movement, one where narratives that are dominant get restoried, so that erased (neglected or marginalized) aspects of the past become the basis for a new living storability. The other force is renarrating, where as narrative tends to do, the array of living stories are integrated, homogenized, and somewhat totalized into an overriding logic. Such logics are strategic, in that they focus attention, but overused—become stereotypic, leaving out the nuances, and the importance of the play of differences.

Antenarratives create a fictional frontier, a bridge between narrative place and living story spaces, and a surprising transformation. It is the antenarrator that makes a frontier, a bridge for narrative places ('where Billy the Kid was tried, or Pat Garrett was shot, or Albert Fountain and his son disappeared') and once again makes them into practiced story spaces. And the antenarrator can give narrative license to make story space into a practiced place. Antenarrative does this by opening a bridge, a frontier to transform one into the other, story into narrative, or narrative into story, and allow their return. Figure 2.1 gives an overview, a map of the Antenarrative Bridge between narrative past and living story relationships emerging at present.

Living story concerns spaces that embody movement, gesticulating, walking, talking, and finding pleasure that for de Certeau (1984, p. 13) "indefinitely organizes a *here* in relation to an *abroad*, a 'familiarity' in relation to a foreignness." Narrative is more about ordering practices that stall movement, set boundaries. Living stories are disordering practices, giving by itinerary a new insight, by tour, a moving force, one that displaces, undoes, and is more carnivalesque. Narrative, by contrast, is more

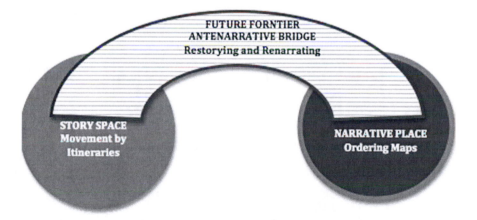

Figure 2.1 The antenarrative bridge between story and narrative.

the spectacle. Story space itineraries that become places, put in the narrative flag, play the program tape at a particular site, for the tourists.

A storytelling tour is made up of movements, transgressions across a territory, one that redefines the creative economy, the ways arts and cultures are knowable by consumers, advocates, and producers. In storytelling, the antenarratives (some of them) bring forth reemergence, crossing bridges beyond the frontiers on the tour, by giving story spaces that are disordering relationship, and by giving some narrative-ordering objectivity. The joint result of the storytelling tours is to displace and respace the creative economy.

Changes comes from the reemergences of frontiers in the alien place of an organization, city, or community and by recrossing the frontier bridge where the antenarrative travelers find ways to link the story spaces of itinerary with the narrative topological maps (where narrative flags are staked in place). Antenarrative creates frontier from the double game of narrative and living story, where each can by metamorphosis become its opposite, then return.

Figure 2.2 (rooted in Smith, 1990, p. 152) describes two antenarrative circuits of storytelling. Each arrow in this figure is a set of unique antenarrative practices. Smith does not use the term "living story," preferring to call it "primary narrative" and "ideological narrative." We, however, deploy the notions of living story and dominant narrative in this description and incorporate the antenarrative practices of transformation of one into the other. Living story, we argue, is situated in the materiality of making sense of actual lived socioeconomic experience.

The two antenarrative circuits of transformative practices are quite different. Here, "E" antenarrative is a generative (in social cogenerative) sensemaking, where the teller is filling in with their sense of context and direct experience of extended context. "I know just how she felt" because "something just like that happened to me" (Smith, 1990, p. 162). In this

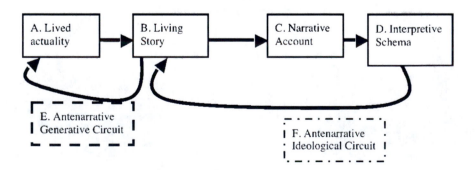

Figure 2.2   Two antenarrative circuits of storytelling.

"E" circuit the teller is filling out the living story expression by providing the transitions from extended context.

In the "F" antenarrative circuit, it is a socioeconomic division of labor, and the narrative account "C" is constructed by the interrogation of interpretative schema "D," which erases, sorts, edits, and renarrates living story "B" but has no connection to direct lived actuality "A." In the "F" antenarrative circuit, the supplements are contextual extensions the teller inserts, to make sense as they tell. It is especially obvious when it is the very first time of the telling and all the temporal sequence is uncertain, not yet sorted. We recognize this in ourselves, when the living story has an embodiment, and it is not just words, but the body is vibrating the telling. There can be a rupture between the two antenarrative circuits in the situation of diversity, where living stories are filtered and transformed to conform to interpretive schema. There may be differences of interpretations and only what is relevant and within boundaries survives the interpretative practices. The interpretive schema sets out what particulars it is interested in, and the rest of the living story is not noticeable or permissible.

Another theoretical possibility is to explicitly model the circuit from a small group perspective, and, in a second step, to enlarge it to an interaction model, for example, 'two antenarrative circuits in opposition' with reference to two interacting parties (power holders and disadvantaged groups). This small group model may be considered on both sides, that is, power holders and non-power holders communicating among themselves and with the other group.

In studying Smith's (1990) standpoint theory, we identify two very different standpoints relevant to diversity. One way to look at it is that the circuits can be in hegemonic relationship, where the "F" circuit, as it embeds in to social division of labor of authors, readers (including media reporters), becomes an ideological socialization that bleeds across into the "E" circuit, making even direct experience mediated by ideology. Smith is taking a highly situated approach to story and narrative, not a literary form or poetics approach. In the "F" circuit there are practices of interrogation and cross-examination (reminiscent of Derrida's concern about narrative); the practices assemble narrative that strips down living story of any contextual extension and most of its remains are monologically ordered (which is relatable to Bakhtin's concerns about narrative always being monologic). In terms of diversity, there is a lot of erasure, and a substitution of dominant ideological narrative for one's living story of actual experience.

For example, Boje's recent fieldwork on art and artists in New Mexico suggests that the state with its arms into the local has just such an antenarrative "E" circuit, and it sets up a juncture, a gap with the lived experiences of (mostly) women artists in the southern part of the state, and more of a male population of artists in the northern part of the state (where the state capital is located). The southern arts scene appears to be in the shadow of Santa Fe's arts scene. And there is not only gender but also racial differences. What is evident from this case study is that there are two antenarrative circuits in opposition; and change may be created at the juncture of the two antenarratives. Whereas perspectives on the way the state does its reporting can be thought to be about an "F" antenarrative circuit, individual artists' (subversive) stories may be categorized as an "E" circuit.

The foregoing suggests that diversity and power intermingle in complexity patterns that cannot be changed by linear approaches. Rather, cycles of inequity must be put center stage and more emergent designs of diversity imagined that allow for cogenerative antenarrating of future possibilities that go beyond standard recipes. In short, our main contribution is a critical theory (one rooted in Deleuze & Guattari's [1987]) that we believe can be useful in rethinking diversity and power.

NEGOTIATED DIVERSITY MANAGEMENT

Applying these debates to the context of diversity management in organizations, it can be argued that it is not just narratives which are important, but also the contexts which help establish which narratives are privileged and why (and vice versa). Boje's (2001) antenarrative approach may be useful to unravel the privileged and neglected narratives. Boje defines antenarrative as 'the fragmented, non-linear, incoherent, collective, unplotted, and pre-narrative speculation, a bet' (p. 1). The approach may help challenge the conventional diversity management discourse based on hegemonic mainstream stories. It may enable researchers to abandon the usual single-voiced and single-authored narratives and in the process adopt an antenarrative stance (Clark, 2002).

Boje (2001) describes a number of methods to draw out a multivoiced story within its context. The following is a summary of Boje's antenarrative methods also highlighting its relevance to diversity management.

The first method is deconstruction analysis, which exposes the taken-for-granted viewpoint of a story to its marginal or excluded opposite. The story is then reversed by putting the marginal at the center. This leads to a new perspective in which a story is resituated beyond excluded voices and singular viewpoint.

The second method is grand narrative analysis. Grand narrative analysis helps tease out the 'local' stories that are embedded in and possibly resisting the grand narratives ('regimes of truth'). This requires a comparison of the differences between the macrostory and microstory. The process may enable many local stories to emerge from the shadows.

Related to the previous approach is microstory analysis. Microstories focus on groups who are more usually excluded from historical narrative (e.g., ethnic minorities and women). Microstory analysis helps trace acts of resistance by the 'little people' to the 'elitist' grand narratives that control their lives. Consequently, the dominant narratives can be re-narrated in a more multi-voiced text' (p. 61). The interplay between the multiple narratives generates new meaning and understanding of a previously taken-for-granted phenomenon.

Intertextuality refers to a complex web of 'inter-relationships ensnaring each story's history and situational context with other stories' (p. 91). A story is always embedded in a broader chain of signifying systems that both constitutes, and is constituted by, the story. The methodological task is to disentangle a story's intertextual network of attributed and unattributed links to other stories (p. 92). By exposing the chain of sign systems that give a story authority, it becomes a denuded and plural entity in which different interpretations are possible.

Story network analysis permits the diagrammatic representation of links among people, groups, organizations, story themes, and other actors. It seeks continually to display the flow line by mapping how the different elements of a story, such as context, teller, and audience, interlink over time. It can provide critical information on the ever-shifting relationships between the elements that comprise the storytelling event.

Causality analysis unravels the too tidy narrative accounts because of their ability to 'sweep aside the random occurrence, coincidence, the misattributions' (p. 102). Instead of focusing on the reality of the causal attributions, an antenarrative approach is concerned with examining how particular views of causality emerge and become widely accepted.

Plot analysis offers a conceptual structure that permits the analysis of stories through an interplay between pre-understanding, emplotment, and embedded contextuality. A plot is not a clearly articulated causal chain that links events and episodes together but tends to be a loose collection of elements. These are a precursor to our ability to follow the plot of a story and make sense of it by 'grasping together' the events, characters, and actions as it is related *in situ* (embedded contextuality).

Finally, theme analysis is about what gets left out of theme taxonomies as well as the interrelationships between the cells within classifications. The focus is, therefore, on the polysemous (multiple meanings and interpretations) by encouraging a dialogue between researchers as they co-construct themes from the data.

Boje's (2001) antenarrative approach has a number of implications for the diversity management paradigm in organizations. In addition to highlighting the importance of comparing diverse stories, the approach may help examine how antenarratives transform in intertextual ways with various narratives about diversity and discrimination in the workplace.

Diverse stories embedded in and reflecting the organizations' culture may mitigate against the maladies that organizations frequently impart to their members (Gabriel, 2000). The relevance of multivoice stories stems from the fact that they echo the voice, thinking, and perception of diverse individuals and groups in the organizations.

For example, Davies (1996) offers an evolutionary approach to monitoring and evaluation of an industrial development project, termed the most significant change. Developed in the context of a microcredit development project in Bangladesh, the approach incorporates the collection and systematic interpretation of stories. The approach was subsequently applied in an industrial development project in Australia (Dart, 2000).

There are three main parts to Davies's approach: establish domains of change; set in place a process to collect and review stories of change; and conduct a secondary analysis of the stories. In the first stage of the process, the evaluation audience identifies the 'domains' of change that they think need to be monitored at the project level; for example, changes in practice. This process is a discrete activity and need only occur once. Various research techniques may be deployed in this process such as the Delphi technique. Unlike performance indicators popular in business organizations, such nominated 'domains' of change are not precisely defined but are left deliberately fuzzy. Instead, it is left to individuals to interpret what they feel is a change belonging to any one of these categories.

The next stage involves the collection and review of stories of significant change (according to the defined 'domains' of change that had been nominated using the Delphi process). The stories are collected by those most directly involved in the project delivery. Diverse individuals at various levels of the project hierarchy then review a series of stories, selecting those they think represent most significant accounts of change. The stories are selected through an iterative voting process, to generate as much consensus as possible. The process requires the participants to document and present their rationale for selecting those stories. This information is then shared with the storytellers and the project leaders. This feedback and monitoring system may be seen as a slow but extensive dialogue up and down the project hierarchy.

Annually, the selected stories are circulated amongst the project leaders, along with the criteria used by the review fora. Finally, at a roundtable meeting, policymakers are asked to review and select the stories representing the most significant accounts of change. In addition to the production of such a document comprising stories and reviewers' interpretations, the whole process is monitored and additional analysis is carried out.

Davies's approach seems to be consistent with Czarniawska's (1999, p. 22) narrative approach in field research, which involves: watching how the stories are being made; collecting the stories; interpreting, analyzing, and deconstructing the stories; putting together your own story and comparing with other stories. Indeed, different methods of doing narrative research are not mutually exclusive; they may add up and overlap, as the whole process of organizing can be seen as storytelling (Czarniawska, 1997).

Drawing on research on storytelling by Boje (2001), Davies (1996), Czarniawska (1999) and Gabriel (2000), a dialogic model can be identified reflecting a participatory approach towards understanding and framing diversity management in the workplace (Figure 2.3). The model is based on the premise that diversity management needs to be a multiparty process involving reciprocity, dialogic negotiation, and democratic contestation among various groups.

Figure 2.3 represents a conceptual model of negotiated diversity management. The first stage involves the collection of antenarrative, narratives, and living stories from diverse individuals and groups within the organization representing mainstream and marginalized narratives. Such stories may represent individuals' workplace experiences, for example, implications of their cultural identity in recruitment and selection or performance management. The participants from each cultural group may be encouraged to

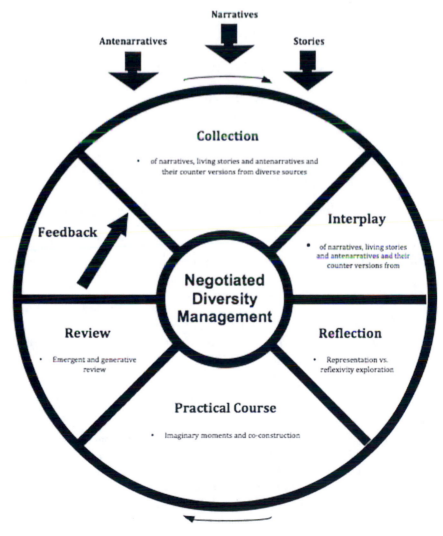

Figure 2.3   A dialogic storytelling approach to negotiated diversity management.

share their particular perspectives and beliefs about the most salient issues surrounding their jobs and the workplace in general. They may identify such issues based on real-life incidents in the workplace, preferably those issues that offer scope for strong collective emotional engagement. Microstory analysis, deconstruction, and intertextuality methods can be used to identify any discrepancies and acts of resistance by the 'little people' to the 'elitist' grand narratives that control their work lives.

In the second stage, participants review the interplay of antenarratives, narratives, and stories. In Oswick et al.'s (2000) terms, this stage is about reconstituting reality by writing a plurivocal script. For example, participants may endeavor to arrive at a coherent narrative of critical incidents, such as ethnic or racial bias in recruitment or training. They can also produce divergent counterstories, opening up to the possibility of alternative readings of the events. Antenarratives trace the pre-stories and the possibilities to transform the relation of narrative to counterstory. The aim is to move from a fixed position of 'monological reality' to a more transitory position of 'dialogical fiction' of diversity management.

The third stage involves the discussion of representation of identity and reflexivity. In this stage, representatives from diverse groups engage in collective reflexivity process, situating the variety of narratives and stories offered by culturally diverse employees. In terms of prospective sensemaking, the focus is upon stories peeking out of the margins. We argue that instead of a managerialist consensus, the process should focus on developing generative imagination based on dialogic negotiation and inclusive environment. This can be achieved through reflexivity on more complex understanding of diversity, representing a significantly rehumanized view of 'the other' (Gergen, McNamee, & Barrett, 2001).

The next stage involves identifying practical courses of action in light of dialogic negotiation. Needed in the process are imaginary moments in which participants co-develop a new framing of diversity management. These imaginary moments not only sow the seeds for co-construction but also shift the position of the participants from combative to cooperative. One possible way is through locating *superordinate goals* (Gergen et al., 2001). For example, feminist radicals and conservative traditionalists may join in a mission against sexual harassment. The challenge is not so much to consider the future in terms of fixed starting points but through dialogic negotiation to co-construct a viable future.

The final stage involves review, which reflects the fact that negotiated diversity management is a dynamic, ongoing process, based on generative interaction of diverse groups and individuals. The feedback arrow from the review to the storytellers represents the cyclical and reflective nature of negotiated diversity management.

The contribution of our proposed dialogic process is that it considers the interplay of administered narrative with more diverse stories in designing and implementing more generative and inclusive policymaking activities of diversity management. Such policies, we hope, will address the issues of participatory decision making and multiculturalism. Although conflict resolution may not be achieved in many situations, negotiated diversity management may nevertheless help in developing an increased understanding, appreciation, and reflection, which in turn is likely to lead to changes in individual and organizational behavior.

In Figure 2.3, the dialogue in the dialogic negotiation aspect of the storytelling approach may happen in the section on 'interplay' as well as in 'reflection' and 'review.' 'Reflection' may take place within diverse (conflicting) groups; 'practical course' consists of imaginary moments (any member can participate in these moments) and co-construction (between diverse groups). 'Review' may be taken by each separate group as well as through a collective dialogue. 'Feedback' may be given not only from one group to the other but also from diverse groups to the organization.

On a conceptual level, narrative and antenarrative may be treated as part of the deviation-countering and deviation-amplifying forces of organizational transformation (Boje, Rosile, & Gardner, 2004). The implication for management theory is that when there are narrative forces for standardization, there are also counteracting forces of the antenarrative variety. These counteracting forces have been traditionally missing in the official narratives of diversity management.

In the absence of an enabling diversity culture within and outside the organization, there is no guarantee that the proposed dialogic negotiation process will lead to an outcome which is satisfactory for power holders and non-power holders. A piecemeal or disjointed approach to negotiated diversity may result in an unchanged system (power holders push through more of the same), or a failed system (power holders try to push through more of the same, but trigger a revolution). In such a scenario of disjointed implementation and negative backlash, the circle may break down at some point or may enhance the power of a single group. The circle may also break down if non-power holders would not unveil their stories, because if these stories would be understood and rightly interpreted by the power holders, the knowledge could be used to destroy the little power left to the non-power holders.

It is therefore important that a dialogic negotiation approach is understood and implemented in a holistic manner in organizations and is also supported through an enabling environment. From a public policy perspective, a dialogic negotiation approach will involve the consideration of diverse stories in designing and implementing regulatory, procedural, and substantive policymaking activities of diversity management. Such policies will address the issues of participatory decision making, empowerment, and multiculturalism. Various perspectives will need to be taken into account to introduce a diversity focus into managerial practice as well as into conflict resolution.

A participatory political system may be seen as an ideal enabling environment for negotiated diversity management. Such a system guarantees members of ethnic groups their legitimate rights and needs. In its broad sense, civil society would include political parties, professional bodies, trade unions, and other nongovernmental organizations on the community and national levels. Such associational network is the nerve of a participatory political system (Ibrahim, 2000). Indeed, a meaningful diversity management is hard to achieve in the absence of a power-sharing mechanism at the sociopolitical level, that is, one which provides adequate mechanisms to ensure the participation of all major groups in decision making. This will result in improved awareness as well as harmony about the goals, functions, and impacts of different organizational processes (LGI, 2007).

CONCLUSION

This chapter highlighted the role of storytelling as a collaborative experience in designing and realizing diversity management in organizations. It identified storytelling as a valuable research approach to collect and make sense of various stories related to diversity and equal opportunity in the workplace. It argued that the future of diversity management could be secured by adopting a participatory culture.

The proposed negotiated diversity management offers a new participatory approach towards managing a culturally diverse workforce. The approach is based on the premise that storytelling can be effectively harnessed for participatory evaluation only when the collection of stories is coupled with a process of systematic and collective interpretation. Indeed, such interpretations themselves may tell another story, and the process of collective interpretation may have several beneficial outcomes for evaluation utilization.

The chapter has argued that storytelling is particularly helpful in highlighting voices of ethnic minorities and other marginalized individuals and groups. Indeed, it is not just ethnic minority persons who would gain from having a voice on issues related to diversity and difference, for example, Dingle's (2005) study of preservice white teachers, which gave voice to the teachers' beliefs about race, culture, and their potential ability to teach students who may not look like themselves.

Researchers may wish to consider the economic and sociopolitical contexts in which diversity management takes place. An important component of the antenarrative is the evolution of industrial relations and its implications for diversity management. Palmer's (2003) study demonstrates that the methods to promote diversity in the workplace have not been conventional industrial relations methods. Conventional industrial actions, such as strikes, are far less likely to be mobilized to attack forms of discrimination that divide, rather than unite, the industrial workforce. Instead, the main changes that have come have been through the national politics. Thus, diversity management remains in large shaped and constrained by legislation rather than industrial negotiation. Political campaigns and strategies, in turn, require sufficient numbers of people who self-identify with and are prepared to lobby for a particular identity group, and are concentrated in ways that can put pressure on a political constituency.

Given the evolution of antidiscrimination legislation in various national contexts (e.g., Palmer, 2003; Solorzano, 1997), it can be argued that the balance of advantage to the discriminated groups, such as ethnic minorities and women, is more likely to depend on the balance of power in national politics. For instance, referring to the relative lack of power associated with the aboriginal population in Australia than their counterparts in the U.S., Canada, and New Zealand, Palmer discussed the extraordinary difficulty of developing political support in Australia. Whereas such lack of support may be attributed to a long history of aboriginal peoples' disenfranchisement and scattered communities, it may also be attributed to a shortcoming of a majoritarian democracy in which the powerful mainstream enjoys unchecked authority, at times overruling the interests of marginalized minorities.

Perhaps one possible way forward is to negotiate and implement diversity management at multiple levels, that is, macronational, meso-institutional, and microindividual, instead of the conventional single-level conceptualization of diversity management (Syed & Özbilgin, 2009; Syed & Kramar, 2009). On a political level, the approach may be treated as consistent with the notion of a consociational system, which encourages cross-cultural dialogue and guarantees the participation of all cultural units in important political decisions in a society (Chryssochou, 1994; Lijphart, 1997).

REFERENCES

Adler, N. (2006). The arts and leadership: Now that we can do anything, what will we do? *Academy of Management Learning and Education, 5*(4), 486–499.

Allison, M. T. (1988). Breaking boundaries and barriers: Future directions in cross-cultural research. *Leisure Sciences,10,* 247–259.

Bailey, P. H., & Tilley, S. (2002). Storytelling and the interpretation of meaning in qualitative research. *Journal of Advanced Nursing, 38*(6), 574–583.

Bakhtin, M. M. (1990). *Art and answerability.* In M. Holquist & V. Liapunov (Eds.). Austin: University of Texas Press.

———. (1991). *Toward a philosophy of the act.* Translation and notes by Vadim Liapunov, in M. Holquist & V. Liapunov (Eds.). Austin: University of Texas Press.

Boje, D. M. (2001). *Narrative methods for organizational and communication research.* London: Sage.

———. (2005). From Wilda to Disney: Living stories in family and organization research. In J. Clandinin (Ed.), *Handbook of narrative inquiry.* London: Sage.

———. (2007). *Storytelling organization.* London: Sage.

Boje, D. M., Rosile, G. A., & Gardner, C. L. (2004). *Antenarratives, narratives and anaemic stories.* Paper presented at the Annual Meeting of Academy of Management. All Academy Symposium "Actionable Knowledge as the Power to Narrate," New Orleans, August 9.

Calas, M. (1992). An/other silent voice? Representing "Hispanic woman" in organizational texts. In A. J. Mills & P. Tancred (Eds.), *Gendering organizational in organizational texts* (pp. 339–383). Newbury Park, CA: Sage.

Calmore, J. (1992). Critical race theory, Archie Shepp and fire music: Securing an authentic intellectual life in a multicultural world. Southern California Law Review, 65, 2129–2231.

Cavanagh, J. M. (1997). (In)corporating the other? Managing the politics of workplace difference. In P. Prasad, A. J. Mills, M. Elmes, & A. Prasad (Eds.), *Managing the organizational melting pot: Dilemmas of workplace diversity* (pp. 31–53). Thousand Oaks, CA: Sage.

Chavez, C. I., & Weisinger, J. Y. (2008). Beyond diversity training: A social infusion for cultural inclusion. *Human Resource Management, 47*(2), 331–350.

Chryssochou, D. (1994). Democracy and symbiosis in the European Union: Towards a confederal consociation? *West European Politics, 17*(4), 1–14.

Clandinin, D. J., & Connelly, F. M. (1994). Personal experience methods. In N. K. Denzin & Y. S. Lincoln (Eds.), *Handbook of qualitative research* (pp. 413–427). London: Sage.

Clark, T. (2002). Book review. *Human Relations, 55*, 717–745.

Cooperrider, D. (2004, October). *The global compact leaders summit: Final report* (pp. 1–42). New York: United National Global Compact.

Cox, T. (1993). *Cultural diversity in organizations*. San Francisco: Barrett-Koehler Publishers.

Cox, T., & Nkomo, S. (1990). Factors affecting the upward mobility of black managers in private sector organizations. *Review of Black Political Economy, 18*(3), 39–48.

Czarniawska, B. (1997). *Narrating the organization: Dramas of institutional identity*. Chicago: University of Chicago Press.

Czarniawska, B. (1999). *Writing management: Organization theory as a literary genre*. Oxford: Oxford University Press.

Dart, J. (2000). Stories for change: A systematic approach to participatory monitoring. *Proceedings of the Fifth World Congress on Action Learning, Action Research and Process Management* (ALARPM). University of Ballarat, Australia.

Davies, R. (1996). *An evolutionary approach to facilitating organisational learning: An experiment by the Christian Commission for Development in Bangladesh*. Centre for Development Studies, Swansea, UK.

de Certeau, M. (1984). *The practice of everyday life* (S. F. Rendell, Trans.). Berkeley/London: University of Californian Press.

Deleuze, G., & Guattari, F. (1987). *A thousand plateaus: Capitalism and schizophrenia* (B. Massumi, Trans.). Minneapolis: University of Minnesota Press.

Delgado, R., & Stefancic, J. (2001). Critical race theory: An introduction. New York: New York University Press.

Dingle, J. (2005). *Let the dialogue begin: University and the White preservice teacher*. Doctoral dissertation submitted to the graduate faculty of North Carolina State University, Raleigh.

Ely, R. J., & Roberts, L. M. (in press). Shifting frames in team-diversity research: From difference to relationships. In A. P. Brief (Ed.), *Diversity at work*. Cambridge: Cambridge University Press.

Ely, R. J., Thomas, D. A., & Padavic, I. (in press). Team racial learning environment and the link between racial diversity and performance. *Administrative Science Quarterly*.

Fisk, R. (2006), "Different narratives in the Middle East", *The Independent*. 16 December. Available at: http://www.independent.co.uk/opinion/commentators/fisk/robert-fisk-different-narratives-in-the-middle-east-428657.html, Accessed 12 October 2010.

Gabriel, Y. (2000). *Storytelling in organizations: Facts, fictions and fantasies.* Oxford: Oxford University Press.

Gabriel, Y., & Willman, P. (2005). For dialogue rather than integration. *Human Relations, 58,* 423–427.

Gergen, K., McNamee, S., & Barrett, F. (2001). Toward a vocabulary of transformative dialogue. *International Journal for Public Administration, 24,* 697–707.

Hand, S. (Ed.). (1989). *The Levinas reader.* Oxford: Blackwell.

Hart, C. (2006). Multiculturalism is a dirty word. *The Weekend Australian,* p. 3, 4 November 2006.

Hazen, M. (1993). Towards polyphonic organization. *Journal of Organizational Change Management* 6(5), 15–26.

Ho, C. (2006). Migration as feminisation? Chinese women's experiences of work and family in Australia. *Journal of Ethnic and Migration Studies, 23*(3), 497–514.

Ibrahim, S. E. (2000). Management and mismanagement of diversity: The case of ethnic conflict and state-building in the Arab world. *Management of Social Transformations,* UNESCO MOST Discussion Paper Series, No. 10.

Jones, D., & Stablein, R. (2006). Diversity as resistance and recuperation: Critical theory, post-structuralist perspectives and workplace diversity. In A. M. Konrad, P. Prasad, & J. K. Pringle (Eds.), *Handbook of workplace diversity* (pp. 145–166). London: Sage.

Kalev, A., Dobbin, F., & Kelly, E. (2006). Best practices or best guesses: Assessing the effectiveness of corporate affirmative action and diversity policies. *American Sociological Review, 71,* 589–617.

Kamp, A., & Hagedorn-Rasmussen, P. (2004). Diversity management in a Danish context: Towards a multicultural or segregated working life? *Economic and Industrial Democracy, 25,* 525–553.

Kersten, A. (2000). Diversity management: Dialogue, dialectics and diversion. *Journal of Organizational Change Management, 13*(3), 235–248.

Kornberger, M., Clegg, S., & Carter, C. (2006). Rethinking the polyphonic organization: Managing as discursive practice. *Scandinavian Journal of Management, 22*(1), 3–30.

LGI. (2007). Local government and public service reform initiative. MMCP Activities: Training in Diversity Management, February 15.

Lijphart, A. (1997). The puzzle of Indian democracy: A consociational interpretation. *American Political Science Review, 90*(2), 258–268.

Marsden, R. (1997). Class discipline: IR/HR and the normalization of the workforce. In P. Prasad, A. J. Mills, M. Elmes, & A. Prasad (Eds.), *Managing the organizational melting pot: Dilemmas of workplace diversity* (pp. 107–128). Thousand Oaks, CA: Sage.

Olsson, S. (2000). Acknowledging the female archetype: Women managers' narratives of gender. *Women in Management Review, 15*(5/6), 296–306.

Oswick, C., Anthony, P., Grant, D., Keenoy, T. and Mangham, I. 2000. A dialogic analysis of organisational learning. *Journal of Management Studies, 37*(6): 887–901.

Özbilgin, M., & Tatli, A. (2006). *Storytelling and diversity management.* Paper presented at the 9th Storytelling Seminar, Norwich Business School at UEA, June 29–30.

Palmer, G. (2003). Diversity management, past, present and future. *Asia Pacific Journal of Human Resources, 41*(1), 13–24.

Prasad, P., & Mills, A. (1997). From showcase to shadow: Understanding the dilemmas of managing workplace diversity. In P. Prasad, A. Mills, M. Elmes, & A. Prasad (Eds.), *Managing the organizational melting pot: Dilemmas of workplace diversity* (pp. 3–30). Thousand Oaks, CA: Sage.

Ragins, B. R. (1997). Diversified mentoring relationships in organizations: A power perspective. *Academy of Management Review, 22,* 482–521.

Ricoeur, P. (1992). *Oneself as another* (Kathleen Blamey, Trans.). Chicago: University of Chicago Press.

Ridgeway, C. L., & Berger, J. (1986). Expectations, legitimation, and dominance behavior in task groups. *American Sociological Review, 51*(5), 603–617.

Riessman, C. K. (1993). Narrative analysis. *Qualitative Research Methods Series,* No. 30. Newbury Park, CA: Sage.

Rourke, M. (2002, April 29). His faith in peace endures. *The Los Angeles Times,* p. E1.

Smith, D. (1990). *The conceptual practices of power: A feminist sociology of knowledge.* Boston: Northeastern University Press.

Solorzano, D. (1997). Images and words that wound: Critical race theory, racial stereotyping and teacher education. *Teacher Education Quarterly, 24,* 5–19.

Solorzano, D., & Yosso, T. (2001). Critical race and Latcrit theory and method: Counter-storytelling Chicana and Chicano graduate school experiences. *International Journal of Qualitative Studies in Education, 14*(4), 471–495.

Somers, M. R. 1994. The narrative constitution of identity: a relational and network approach. *Theory and Society,* 23: 605–649.

Swann, W. B., Jr., Polzer, J. T., Seyle, D. C., & Ko, S. J. (2004). Finding value in diversity: Verification of personal and social self-views. *Academy of Management Review, 29,* 9–27.

Syed, J. (2007). "The other woman" and the question of equal opportunity in Australian organisations. *International Journal of Human Resource Management, 18*(11), 1954–1978.

Syed, J., & Kramar, R. (2009). Socially responsible diversity management. *Journal of Management and Organization, 15*(5), 639–651.

———. (2010). What is the Australian model of managing cultural diversity? *Personnel Review, 39*(1), 96–115.

Syed, J. and Özbilgin, M. (2009), "A relational framework for international transfer of diversity management practices", *International Journal of Human Resource Management,* Vol. 20 No. 12, pp. 2435–2453.

Thurlow, A., Mills, A., & Mills, J. (2006). Feminist qualitative research and workplace diversity. In A. Konrad, P. Prasad, & J. Pringle (Eds.), *The handbook of workplace diversity* (pp. 217–236). London: Sage.

Tropp, L. R., & Pettigrew, T. F. (2005). Relationships between intergroup contact and prejudice among minority and majority status groups. *Psychological Science, 16*(12), 951–957.

UNDP. (2004). *Human development report 2004: Cultural liberty in today's diverse world.* New York: UNDP Press.

Weick, K.E., Nord, W. R. (2005), Review of "Managing the future: Foresight in the knowledge economy", Academy of Management Review, Vol. 30 No. 4, pp. 871–873.

Wiltshire, J. (1995). Telling a story, writing a narrative: Terminology in health care. *Nursing Inquiry, 2,* 75–82.

3 The Tesseract Antenarrative Model
Mapping Storytelling to Multidimensional Factor Lattices in Mathematics

Diane Walker

The creation of a poem, or mathematical creation, involves so much sense of arrival, so much selection, so much of the desire that makes choice—even though one or more of these may operate in the unconscious or partly conscious work-periods before the actual work is achieved—that the questions raised are very pertinent . . . The poet chooses and selects and has that sense of arrival as the poem ends; [s]he is expressing what it feels like to arrive at [her]his meanings. If [s]he has expressed that well, [her]his reader will arrive at [her]his meanings. The degree of appropriateness of expression depends on the preparing. By preparing I mean allowing the reader to feel the interdependences, the relations, within the poem. (Rukeyser, 1949)

INTRODUCTION

I am proposing a *Tesseract Antenarrative Model* to enable schools and other organizations to move from linear narratives to multidimensional antenarratives for holistic critical antenarrative literacy. This model is based on mapping personal stories onto factor lattices to represent multidimensional storytelling that makes connections across time. Factor lattices are mathematical drawings and sculptures that represent factors of whole numbers. We can make more sense of our lives through storytelling by using a model of a shape-shifting four-dimensional tesseract to illustrate the stories within stories and around and between stories, much like a web, but with more depth and complexity. As the Tesseract Antenarrative Model continues to emerge, it can aid teachers and students in using storytelling to make connections between math, literacy, and other content areas, and it will provide a mechanism for producing personally satisfying and meaningful works of literature and art.

WHAT IS A LINEAR NARRATIVE?

This curriculum-connecting activity is offered as an antidote to the spirit-breaking *No Child Left Behind* Act (2002), which shatters students, teachers, and knowledge into isolated and quantifiable bits and pieces because of its limiting emphasis on standardization. According to Freire (2000), the teacher-student relationship is fundamentally narrative in character, and the narrating subject and her listening objects become "lifeless and petrified" (p. 71). The result is that education suffers from what Freire called "narration sickness" (p. 71). In order to elaborate on how the Tesseract Antenarrative Model supports a healthier and more connected curriculum in teaching and learning, while providing a creative outlet for self-expression, I will describe how it relates to the work being done in storytelling organizations (Boje, 2008).

Since the time of Aristotle's *Poetics* (350 BCE/1954), a linear narrative has had a beginning, middle, and end. This is referred to as a BME by Boje (2008, p. 9). A linear narrative, a BME, is a "whole telling" and it is "usually a backward-looking (retrospective) gaze from the present back through the past" (p. 7). Essentially, it is a whole and it is the plot. Characters, dialogues, and themes are sorted into one plot that "changes little over time" (p. 7). There are some definite challenges to this linear-thinking narrative in schools. These challenges include the fact that linear thinking is a like a cage, or a box, that is limiting, rather than expansive. Linear thinking is one-way; it looks backwards into the past. Linear thinking is not creative; it is looking at what has already happened. Also, linear thinking structures experiences into a static cognitive map; there is not much in the way of transformation happening. Lastly, linear thinking is monological; the conversation is with yourself, rather than with others (dialogical). Storytelling introduces the dialogical conversation.

WHAT DO WE MEAN BY STORYTELLING AND ANTENARRATIVE?

Boje (1991) defined story as "an oral or written performance involving two or more people interpreting past or anticipated experience" (p. 111). He later modified it to include "an architectural expression interpreting or expressing experience." By story, Boje (2008) means a 'highly dialogized story' (Bakhtin, 1981, p. 25), that is, a "polyphonic (many-voiced) story," but also "dialogized with multi-stylistic expression, diverse chronotopicities, and the architectonics of interanimating societal discourses" (pp. 262–263). The primary elements of storytelling as set forth by Boje (2008) include narrative linearity w/BME, which looks mostly behind us into the past (*retrospective*), the living story unfolding, or that which is happening now (*in the now*), (which I term the *now-spective*), and antenarrative, bets on the future (*prospective*), which is what we believe the story could be in the time to come, nor should we forget the *transcendental* and the *reflexive* (p. 5, italics in original). Hence, Boje's "living story" unfolding "is in between dead and alive, between forgotten fragments and revitalizing those into one's own life" (p. 239). Living story is "collective ongoing, simultaneous, fragmented, and distributive storying and restorying by all the storytellers reshaping, rehistoricizing, and contemporalizing" (p. 239). One is seldom in living story alone. "The living story fabric is a complex collective-weave of many storytellers and listeners who together are co-constructing" in order to transform antenarrative (pp. 239–240). This transformative narrative implies that we are always in relationship to each other. According to Costa and Garmston (2002), we can never not be connected.

Antenarrative was invented and defined by Boje (2001) as "fragmented non-linear, incoherent, collective, unplotted and improper storytelling." Antenarrative has a double meaning: ante means a "bet" and ante means "before," so that an antenarrative is a "bet" on the future "before" it is lived in story (p. 1), for example, before it is stabilized into BME narrative. He further adds, "Story is an account of incidents or events, but narrative comes after and adds 'plot' and 'coherence' to the story line." In this antenarrative concept, Boje asserts that "telling can be about the future" (p. 7), and thus antenarrative is a bet on the future in a process he names *prospective* sensemaking (pp. 1–2, italics in original). Stories are antenarrative when they are told "without the proper plot sequence and mediated coherence preferred in narrative theory" (p. 3).

Under Boje's (2007) descriptions, there are four types of antenarratives:

1. Simple: a linear bet on the future (e.g., a plan or goal), replaying past onto the future.
2. Cycle: a web that connects past onto future as recurring fixed stages in sequence.
3. Spiral: connecting living story present-ness to the future possibilities.
4. Rhizome: a set of relationships aboveground (conscious) and below-ground (out of awareness.) (See Deleuze & Guattari, 1987.) that connects present unfoldment to the future potentialities.

I am proposing a fifth type of antenarrative, represented by the multidimensional Tesseract Antenarrative Model, which is based on mapping stories onto mathematical models called factor lattices. This model was first presented to the New Mexico Council of Teachers of English on October 24, 2008.

THE TESSERACT ANTENARRATIVE MODEL

This Tesseract Antenarrative Model introduces space–time as the fourth dimension of antenarrative to represent a model of past, present, and future narratives all coexisting at once in space–time. This fifth antenarrative is proposed to represent antenarrative amongst stories that show how every story is in relationship to other stories. The Tesseract Antenarrative Model is named for the particular term for the special representation of divisors for the whole number 210. A full discussion of the factor lattice for 210 will follow shortly.

Critical Antenarratology

The Tesseract Antenarrative Model relies on Boje's work on antenarrative (2001) and storytelling organizations (2008) to extend his concept of *critical antenarratology* (2008, p. 241, italics in original) to people in teaching and learning institutions. Boje (2008) defines critical antenarratology as "a method to trace and pre-deconstruct an ongoing interweaving living story narrating and antenarrating that is always composing and self-deconstructing" (p. 241). It is a powerful method of making meaning out of the experiences in the storytelling organizations we call schools because it calls for reflection and action, much like the conscientization of Friere (2000). Storytelling is emotive-ethical sensemaking (Boje, 2008, p. 262), and has become increasingly invalidated or ignored in schools (Rendon, 2009).

Critical antenarrative is rooted in the critical theory of the past and informs critical pedagogy (Apple, 2000, 2004; Apple & Buras, 2006; Freire, 2000; hooks, 1994; Kincheloe, 2005; Macedo, 1994; McLaren, 1998; Shor & Pari, 1999; Wink, 1999). A common criticism is made by scholars that standardization and assessment have become more important than the people that are being measured (Meier, 2002; Meier & Wood, 2004; Kohn, 1999, 2000; Kozol, 1991; Sleeter, 2005). The Tesseract Antenarrative Model provides methods for teachers and learners to reclaim their right to tell stories and make meaning from them (Rendon, 2009; Spring, 2000, 2007; Witherrel & Noddings, 1991).

Critical Pedagogy

When personal stories are given their rightful place as the center of learning, learning can transcend the limited standardization of knowledge that people in schools are being measured by (hooks, 1994; Kohn, 2004; Sleeter, 2005). For this storytelling, holistic critical literacy is defined as an extension of the contributions of the many critical pedagogues over time into a view that encompasses learning in its multidimensional totality, or wholeness (Arendt, 1958; Holt, 1964, 1967, 1969; Miller, 1996, 2000a, 2000b; Miller & Nakagawa, 2002; Nakagawa, 2000; Palmer, 1997, 2004). This notion includes a practical and relevant application of the principles of conscientization (Freire, 2000), caring and happiness (Noddings, 1984, 2003, 2005) and the significance of education to life (Krishnamurti, 1953, Noddings, 2006). This notion encompasses holistic learning in its widest sense by asking people to reflect on their lives by telling stories. These stories will inevitably cross several disciplines, including literacy, mathematics, science, history, and art.

These are the major questions to be explored in this article: How do "storytelling" and "antenarrative" apply to a mathematical model? How can we make a visible model of the primary events or points in time that constitute some of the relationships of our stories before, in, around, below, above, and across time? How can students, teachers, and others transform their literacies by participating in their own telling, writing, reading, performing, and creating of their own stories? These questions will be explored by showing how mathematical models can be used to model antenarrative.

HISTORY AND CONTEXT OF THE
TESSERACT ANTENARRATIVE MODEL

The seeds of the Tesseract Antenarrative Model were sown during my eighth-grade year in a little village in northeastern New Mexico (population ~ 200). On a cold December day, my favorite math teacher, Sam Walker (no relation), handed me a mathematics journal. He said, "There is an article in here you might enjoy. Why don't you read it and see what you think?" The title of the article was "Factor Lattices," and it had been written for teachers by a math educator (Kenney, 1970). I found the article absolutely fascinating. Seeing my interest, he encouraged me to do a project for the local science fair. Subsequently, I spent many happy hours working on a math/science fair project over several months. I made drawings and models of all of the factor lattices of numbers from one to one thousand, and titled my project "*Finding Patterns in Factor Lattices.*"

I remember being totally engaged and thrilled with the mystery, challenge, and marvelous order that I found in doing the work. I felt enormous satisfaction when I figured out a new pattern for myself. I became so engrossed in the project that time seemed to stand still (Csikszentmihalyi, 1990). During one crystal-clear especially frigidly cold work session, at about midnight, I heard a rapping upon the window to the village school science classroom. Startled, I looked to the window, and saw my mother beckoning me to go home. I distinctly remember feeling quite resentful that there were not more hours in the day for me to do my work. I regretted having to go home to sleep. That was one of the many times that I recall becoming single-mindedly in pursuit of a topic that fascinated me (See Abbot, 1884, and Feynman, 1999). In addition to several other awards, that project went on to win the top prize in the New Mexico State Science, Math and Engineering Fair, and influenced my lifelong devotion to math and science learning.

Over the years, with similar enthusiasm, I have shown friends and teachers how to draw and model factor lattices to find the largest common denominator (LCD) and the lowest common multiple (LCM) of a number. I am now revisiting factor lattices almost 40 years later because of new interests in poetry, storytelling, and art, due in great part to my participation in the Borderlands Writing Project at NMSU, led by Dr. Kyle Shanton. I have found enormous pleasure and joy in discovering writing as a powerful outlet for thoughts, feelings, and ideas about life and have developed a keener respect for writing from our experiences. The engaging and challenging writing project, together with the fortuitous meeting with the inventor of antenarrative, led me to reflect on my early education years. My love affair with the village school and the village people gave birth to my sustained passion for teaching and learning.

The roots of the Tesseract Antenarrative Model were nourished during my dissertation studies after I met the world's foremost scholar on storytelling in organizations (Boje, 2008), and the inventor of antenarrative (Boje, 2001), at New Mexico State University. I was struggling with how to get my ideas about education into a form that would most accurately represent the topic of my dissertation study, which was about what made people happy in schools (see Noddings, 2003). I wanted a model that would more closely match the notion that, as learners, we are much more than standardization, assessments, and politics lead us to believe (Holt, 1989; Macedo, 1994). I was grappling with the obvious limitations of supposedly "objective" quantitative research and the subjectivity of qualitative research, whereupon the researcher's limited representation of the participant's experience is not the whole truth. According to Riessman (1993), "Our narratives about others' narratives are our worldly creations." She continues, "All we have is talk and texts that represent reality partially, selectively, and imperfectly" (p. 15).

In my experiences as a teacher and learner I have noted that there is much sadness and sorrow, frustration and anger in teaching and learning organizations. As a critical pedagogue, a person who critiques pedagogy, I want to express a holistic view of teaching and learning that is holographic (Talbot, 1991) and transcendent. My simple definition of a critical pedagogue would be "a person who critiques teaching and learning, does not like what she sees, and tries to figure out ways to see and do things differently." As an educational practitioner, I have a deep concern about my observations of unhappiness in teaching and learning, and yet I am conflicted because I continue to enjoy myself tremendously in teaching and in learning. I have begun asking how we can promote and sustain enthusiasm for a more connected education that brings us collectively more happiness (see Noddings, 2003; Spring, 2007). I believe the Tesseract Antenarrative Model leads us towards more happiness in education.

WHAT ARE FACTOR LATTICES?

Factor lattices are abstract mathematical representations that can be drawn or modeled. They utilize a conceptual understanding of points and line segments to represent the mathematical relationships between the factors (divisors) that divide a number. These factors determine the geometric structure of each factor lattice. Certain common representations show specific relationships between all of the whole numbers that divide any whole number. As a number increases, it follows that there are more factors, so that the representation and the relationships between numbers becomes increasingly complex. Based on the geometry of factor lattice design, some points will represent prime numbers. A prime number is a natural number that is divisible by only two natural numbers: itself and the number 1. A single point would represent a single factor, say, the number 1, and only the number 1. Two points would represent two factors, say, 1 and 2, connected by a line segment. Three points would represent three factors, say, 1, 2, and 3, which would be connected to each other by line segments, and include other relationships. Four points would represent four factors, say, 1, 2, 3, and 5, connected by line segments, and other relationships. Finally, five points would represent five factors, say, 1, 2, 3, 5, and 7, connected by line segments, and more relationships.

In these mathematical representations of relationships, assumptions are made that all points are the same size, all line segments are of same length, and all angles are right angles. The result is that a geometrical representation can be imagined for every whole number, where each point, or vertex (location where more than one line segments meet), is represented by a factor of the number. Numbers are connected to each other in particular relationships. For example:

- $1 = 1$ (a point, Zeroth Dimension Factor Lattice, 0-D)
- $1 \times 2 = 2$ (a line segment; linear, First Dimension Factor Lattice, 1-D)
- $1 \times 2 \times 3 = 6$ (four line segments forming a square, Second Dimension Factor Lattice, 2-D)
- $1 \times 2 \times 3 \times 5 = 30$ (six squares forming a cube, Third Dimension Factor Lattice, 3-D)
- $1 \times 2 \times 3 \times 5 \times 7 = 210$ (a cube within a cube, a hypercube, also known as a tesseract, Fourth Dimension Factor Lattice, 4-D)

Constructing the Factor Lattices

Imagine a point in space. It is a 0-hypercube (Figure 3.1). A point is imagined to be zero dimensional (O-D) because it has no width, length, or height, and is infinitely small. Every point is identical to every other point and has the same exact measurement, because it has no dimension. The point below is a two-dimensional attempt to draw a nondimensional point representing the zeroth dimension. The point represents the number 1.

In mapping to storytelling, it is a point of nothingness: It is an infinitely small point with no dimensions, a place where storytelling has no point. It is not yet a story; it is a possibility for a story. If we take the zero-dimensional point and extend it outward in any direction, we form what is termed mathematically a 1-hypercube. If we place another point at the end of the line, we then create a line segment (Figure 3.2).

Figure 3.1   Factor lattice for the number 1, 0-D, A point.

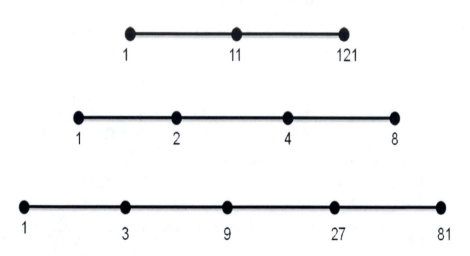

Figure 3.2   Factor lattice for the number 2, 1-D: A line segment.

Figure 3.3   Factor lattices for the numbers 8, 81, and 121, 1-D: Line segments.

All line segments are one-dimensional (1-D) because they differ in size by only one measurement, length. (They all have the same width and height, which is infinitely small.) If we were to expand the line infinitely, it would cover one-dimensional space. The factor lattices for all prime numbers are line segments—either singular, or multiple for numbers that are powers of primes (e.g., 11 to the 2nd power, 2 to the 3rd power, 3 to the 4th power (Figure 3.3).

In mapping to storytelling, it is a simple BME linear antenarrative: At one point is the beginning, where I began first grade. The line segment is the middle, and is the time between the beginning and the end. At the other point is the end, where I finished first grade (Figure 3.4).

I began first grade.   I finished first grade.

Figure 3.4   Mapping storytelling to the factor lattice for the number 2.

Now, if we take the first dimensional line segment and extend it in any direction that is exactly perpendicular to the first direction, we create a square, which is termed a 2-hypercube (Figure 3.5). All squares are two-dimensional (2-D) because they differ with each other in size by two measurements—width and length. (They all have the same height, which is infinitely small.) All of the edges are the same length, which is infinitely small, and all of the angles are right angles. If you expanded the square infinitely, it would cover two-dimensional space. Examples of two-dimensional cyclical antenarrative in governing are a timocracy, an oligarchy, a democracy, and tyrants. Examples from cycles in nature would include the birth, growth, and death of plants and other living things.

In mapping storytelling to the factor lattice (Figure 3.6), I begin the second grade. I learned science at home and I read science books at school. I finished the second grade.

If we take the noninfinite square and extend it in a third direction, perpendicular to both of the first two directions, we create a cube, a 3-hypercube (Figure 3.7). All cubes are three- dimensional (3-D) because they differ with each other in size by all of the three measurements that we know of—height, width, and length. Similarly to the square, all of the

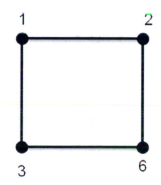

Figure 3.5   Factor lattice for the number 6, 2-D: A square.

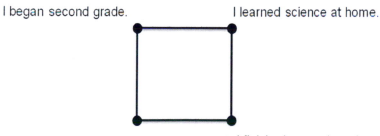

Figure 3.6   Mapping storytelling to the factor lattice for the number 6.

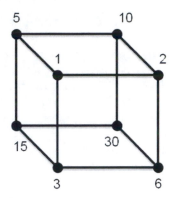

Figure 3.7   Factor lattice for the number 30, 3-D: A cube.

edges within a single cube are the same length, and all of the angles are right angles. If you expanded the cube infinitely in all directions, it would cover three-dimensional space. We add the third dimension with the third prime factor, 5. We remind ourselves, however, that the drawing we see is a two-dimensional representation of a three-dimensional model.

In mapping to storytelling, the story increases in complexity (Figure 3.8): I began each school year. During each school year, I learned science at home and I read science books at school. I did this for 12 years.

The third dimension is approximated by the term 'rhizome' used by Deleuze and Guattari (1987) to describe theory and research that allows for multiple, nonhierarchical entry and exit points in data representation and interpretation (p. 6). Rhizome is a botanical term for a tuberous plant that includes irises, potatoes, ginger, and spreading plants such as crab and Bermuda grass, other grasses, and trumpet vines. Deleuze and Guattari (1987) summarize their concept of a rhizome with these notions: "The rhizome connects any point to any other point." Further, "It is composed not of units but

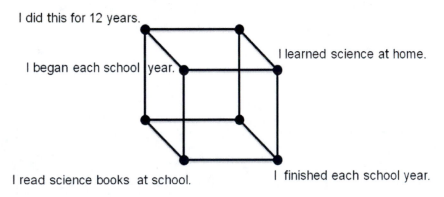

Figure 3.8   Mapping storytelling to the factor lattice for the number 30.

of dimensions, or rather, directions of motions." The rhizome "constitutes linear multiplicities with *n* dimensions having neither subject nor object, which can be laid out on a plane of consistency, and from which the One is always subtracted (*n*-1)." Lines make up the rhizome. "We call a 'plateau' any multiplicity connected to other multiplicities by superficial underground stems in such a way as to form or extend a rhizome" (pp. 21–22). Additionally, Deleuze and Guattari (1987) state, "A rhizome has no beginning or end; it is always in the middle, between things, interbeing, *intermezzo*" (p. 25, italics in original). The Tesseract Antenarrative Model extends their definitions into the fourth dimension: (*n*-1) becomes (5–1), or 4, and allows for an inclusion of multiple un-linear beginnings, middles, and ends. They further premise that "knowledge is negotiated, and the learning experience is a social as well as a personal knowledge creation process with mutable goals and constantly negotiated premises." In teaching and learning, rhizomes can be a means of framing knowledge creation and validation.

To demonstrate how the Tesseract Antenarrative Model provides a method to map the holographic complexity of stories onto a mathematical model, we can take the noninfinite cube of the third dimension and extend it in yet another direction perpendicular to the first three. How can we do this? It is impossible to do within the restrictions of the third dimension. However, it is possible to imagine abstractly within the fourth dimension (4-D), known as time–space. The shape that results from this extension of a cube into tetraspace is called a tesseract, or 4-hypercube (Figure 3.9). All

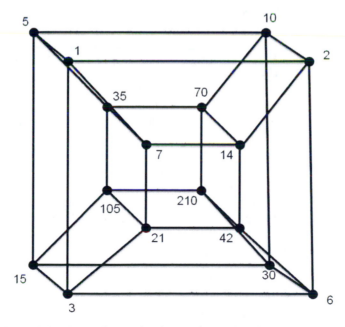

Figure 3.9 Factor lattice for the number 210, 4-D: A tesseract.

tesseracts differ from other tesseracts in size by four measurements (equal to each other within a single tesseract)—width, length, height—and trength (a term specific to the tesseract) in which a cube within a cube is imagined.

THE TESSERACT ANTENARRATIVE MODEL: MAPPING STORIES ONTO FACTOR LATTICES

Tesseract is the term used for the geometric construction of the factor lattice for the number 210. It provides for a two-dimensional drawing or a three-dimensional model of a four-dimensional (4-D) relationship. If you expanded the tesseract infinitely, it would cover four-dimensional space. Similarly to the square and cube, all of the edges within a single tesseract are the same length, and all of the angles are right angles. Each of the 16 vertices of the tesseract represents a different factor for the number 210. Each number has a relationship to 210 and to every other number.

In order to give an example of mapping stories onto factors, I have chosen to use a poem. Stories, or antenarratives, can be mapped onto the tesseract by substituting one stanza from my poem for each of the 16 factors, allowing each of the 16 stanzas to be mapped to a different vertex. The result is that the tesseract antenarrative becomes more complex because of the stated and unstated relationships amongst the stanzas. The antenarrative reflects time all at the same moment as the antenarrative moves between retrospective, now-spective, and prospective. An example is provided in the poem on the opposite page.

The Tesseract Antenarrative Model allows for the transformation of stories into tesseract antenarrative by replacing points and relationships of numbers to each other, with stories and relationships of stories to each other across space–time. The tesseract lends itself to more fully describing the relationships between stories as they become increasingly complicated, providing holographic complexity (Talbot, 1991). A longer version of the poem could have been written as an autobiographical essay. Even so, it would not visually describe the whole of my life story. My antenarrative is present in the around and in-between spaces of the model; only the poetic short version of my antenarrative is made visible. Any antenarrative that is written or spoken is always an approximation. It can never be the whole story. In the Tesseract Antenarrative Model, it is possible to start the poem at any stanza, and still retrieve the essential narrative, because each stanza is in relationship to the whole story. By doing this, the antenarrative can shift from one point to another.

Tesseractive Webs

The assumption that all measurements in a tesseract are identical implies an impossible yet continuous movement—a shape-shifting in, out, around

I Am Poem

I am from the brilliant stars.
And the dust of the earth.

I am from the birds and the bees.
From a gringo cowboy sperm cell and a broomcorn Hispanic egg.

I am from the cold mountains and the hot valleys.
I am from a village near a volcano and three crosses near a river.

I am from chopping wood and carrying water.
From fresh milk and vegetables and commodities and food stamps.

I am from barbed wire and windmills.
And butchered sheep and chickens.

I am from sweet peas stolen from the garden.
And hot tortillas with melted butter and Karo syrup.

I am from *La Gente y Los Remedios*.
I am from my people and the remedies.

And from *La Gente Loca y La Gente Buena*.
Y los santos tambien.

And from the Crazy People and the Good People.
And the saints too.

I am from my Grama and Grampo.
And from my tias and tios and primas.

From my aunts and uncles.
And my cousins, too.

I am from lazy summer days.
And hard work.

I am from struggle.
And from survival.

I am from my friends and from my daughter.
And still I am from indigenous and from education.

I am from biology, chemistry and physics.
I am from everyone from life itself.

I am from love.
And will be until space-time ends.

Figure 3.10 I am From. Poem by Diane Delida Walker, 2007.

and between—which allows it to shape-shift in every dimension. I name this shape-shifting *tesseractivity*—that which models the tesseract antenarrative—storytelling in the fourth dimension. Further, if we imagine that the lines are curved in space–time (Einstein, 1915/1961), then the tesseractivity becomes more transformative. In this curved antenarrative tesseract model (Figure 3.11), storytelling continuously undergoes transformative shape-shifting. If we imagine each tesseract to represent one story, then a *Tesseractive Personal Web* of different stories could represent one person. If we imagine one tesseract to represent one person, then many people interacting with each other will form a *Tesseractive Community Web* of storytellers. Finally, if we imagine each person with a tesseractive web of stories, then we can imagine a multidimensional tesseractive web of many stories of many people tesseracting across the earth, which I name a *Tesseractivity Holistic Web*. We are all in relationship to each other, with some stories (or some people) having a greater influence than others on the storytellers and storylisteners.

Some results of this antenarrative tesseractivity are the simultaneous interplay of tesseracts, with multiple storytellers and storylisteners in a

Figure 3.11 Model of curved tesseract. Photograph by Diane Delida Walker, 2010.

curved tesseractive web. In this model, we get perspective in how stories relate to each other and are influenced by the other surrounding tesseractive webs. We get dialogic, in that people are talking and listening to each other, and we get reflexivity, in that every participant is continuously self-reflecting. Lastly, using Boje's (2008) notions of antenarrative, we can imagine that time is prospective, now-spective (unfolding), and retrospective all at the same moment, as also posited by de Broglie (1970):

> In space–time, everything which for each of us constitutes the past, the present, and the future is given in block, and the entire collection of events, successive for us, which form the existence of a material particle is represented by a line, the world-line of the particle. (p. 114)

Further, de Broglie states that although space–time appears to be successive aspects of "slices" of the material world, in reality, space–time exists prior to our knowledge of the events that will constitute it (p. 114). The Tesseract Antenarrative Model does not presume to tell the whole story, nor to assume that stories are easily told in 16 points. It is a model to illustrate how stories from one person or a group of people relate to each other. The deceptive "rigidity" with regard to the length of line segments and size of points in the factor lattice mathematical model does not need to translate into a rigidity of antenarrative. By Boje's (2008) definition, antenarrative is morphing, or shape-shifting, and the stories of teachers and learners can do the same. By using this model, teachers can encourage students to tell more stories about their lives, and subsequently use those stories to plan their lives. The details and lengths of antenarrative can be determined by the participants.

What about More Dimensions?

At this time, the number of dimensions most often discussed by quantum physicists is 13 (Greene, 2003). A fifth-dimensional factor lattice remains a puzzle to be solved, or at least enjoyed (see Abbott, 1884). It would be too complicated to draw or model the fifth dimension without talking in detail about quantum physics, the holographic universe (Talbot, 1991), and parallel universes (Greene, 2003). It would be helpful to know much more than we "know" about the universe.

HOW ARE FACTOR LATTICES DRAWN AND MODELED?

Drawings for factor lattices can be made using a pencil or pen to draw the points, or vertices, connected by the line segments up to and including the fourth-dimension factor lattices. The factor lattice model for a point can be any spherical object, including the nonsustainable craft Styrofoam balls, rubber balls, or roundish objects from nature, such as a cranberries and other berries. Factor lattices for prime numbers and for multiples of prime numbers can be modeled by using a round object, or modeling clay which has been rolled into balls, to represent the points, or vertices. Tinker Toy sticks, pick-up-sticks, wooden skewers, and toothpicks can represent the line segments that insert into the point models. These objects of similar lengths, widths, and diameters can be used to make models of all the two-, three-, and four-dimensional factor lattices.

The tesseract model requires a bit more work. It can be modeled by making the larger cube out of dense Styrofoam balls and skewers. The smaller cube that fits within the tesseract can be made using smaller dense Styrofoam balls, modeling clay or cranberries, and toothpicks for the line segments. The smaller cube can fit within the larger cube by cutting skewers to the right size so that the smaller cube is suspended within the larger cube, while remembering that the cubes are abstractly the same size. This exercise requires the use of spatial intelligence to construct the tesseract in the mind. The points are by definition the same size and the line segments are the same length, resulting in the unavoidable observation that any physical

Figure 3.12 Stories mapped onto tesseract vertices. Photograph by Diane Delida Walker, 2010.

model is an imperfect representation of the tesseract. Depending on their length, words, phrases, stanzas, or stories can be mapped onto the tesseract model by cutting them out of paper and using a straight pin to pin them to each vertex. The shape-shifting tesseract can be modeled by capturing the reflection of the tesseract model in a curved mirror (See Figure 3.11). In the next picture, Figure 3.12, the tesseract is seen with the stanzas from the *I Am From* poem mapped onto the vertices of the Tesseract Antenarrative Model. The antenarrative must include some bets on the future in order to tell a more complete story.

TEACHING AND LEARNING POSSIBILITIES FOR THE TESSERACT ANTENARRATIVE MODEL

The Tesseract Antenarrative Model introduces holographic complexity into stories told and shared in teaching and learning. Stories that are mapped onto the vertices are antenarrative when they are told, "without the proper plot sequence and mediated coherence preferred in narrative theory" (Boje, 2001, p. 3). This tesseract model provides multiple entry points for a story, and allows for 16 different entry points (Deleuze & Guattari, 1987). Various combinations are possible for teaching and learning situations. For example, one student could provide all 16 entry points, or two students could provide eight entry points, or 16 students could provide one story for one point. The tesseract antenarrative model provides a method for making the abstract idea of storytelling and relationships between stories more appealing to teachers and learners, and engages more of the multiple intelligences (Gardner, 1983).

Possible results of mapping stories onto vertices of a tesseract are a transformation from linear thinking (monological) to quantum (polylogical) thinking in multidimensions, and a transformation from monovoice synthesis (one voice) to polyvoice (many voices) synthesis (Boje, 2008). Additionally, tesseract antenarrative travels from linear chromotopic to polychromotopic (retrospective/now-spective/prospective interplay [Boje, 2008]). Knowledge is transformed—from the "banking" method of education (Freire, 2000, p. 72), where knowledge is deposited into students and withdrawals are made at will—to reflective conscientization (Friere, 2000, p. 75), where there is shared understanding through creation, mutability, and negotiation (Deleuze & Guittari, 1987). Finally, storytelling and storylistening are transformed from static student-as-listener models to dynamic models of student and teacher as coparticipants.

The Tesseract Antenarrative Model extends the possibilities of Boje's (2008) concept of critical antenarratology (p. 241) to people in the organizations we call schools. Making meaning for ourselves out of the stories we have lived, are living, and are "betting" on should not be reserved for philosophers or the fringes of educational practice (See Krishnamurti, 1953).

In fact, Boje (2008) states that the stories of the little people are often marginalized and cut off (p. 242). Czarniawska (2004) notes, "Other people or institutions concoct narratives for others without including them in a conversation; *this is what power is about*" (p. 5, italics in original). I am telling this tesseract antenarrative about myself as I try to make meaning of my own life, and find personal power as my own storyteller. This is one example of my attempt to see my life as a whole: where I came from, where I am, and where I am going. I am making a "bet" that teachers and learners will find happiness and pleasure in utilizing the Antenarrative Tesseract Model in the "future."

Each and every time that I visit the tiny village where I grew up, and when I am able to see the amazing tesseract of our Milky Way, I am awed by the fact that physically we are essentially visible collections of atoms in relationship to other atoms. However, atoms are not all we are: We are story tellers and story listeners. Like Rukeyser (1949), I wonder that the "universe is made up of stories not atoms" and that we are able to ponder our place in the universe here on this small mostly blue point in time/space: "What lies behind us and what lies before us are small matters compared to what lies within us" (attributed to Ralph Waldo Emerson or Henry David Thoreau).

REFERENCES

Abbot, E. (1884). Flatland. Retrieved September 09, 2009. http://www.ibiblio.org/eldritch/eaa/F02.HTM
Apple, M. (2000). *Official knowledge* (2nd ed.). New York: Routledge.
———. (2004). *Ideology and curriculum* (3rd ed.). New York: Routledge.
Apple, M., & Buras, K. (2006). *The subaltern speak*. New York: Routledge.
Arendt, H. (1958). *The human condition*. Chicago: University of Chicago Press.
Aristotle. (350BCE/1954). *Aristotle: Rhetoric and poetics* (W. Roberts and I. Bywater, Trans). New York: Random House.
Bakhtin, M. (1981). *The dialogic imagination: Four essays by M.M. Bakhtin*. (Ed. by Holquist). Austin: University of Texas Press.
Boje, D. (1991). The storytelling organization: A study of storytelling performance in an office supply firm. *Administrative Science Quarterly, 36*, 106–126.
———. (2001). *Narrative methods in organization and communication research*. London: Sage.
———. (2007). *Chapter 17: Globalization antenarratives. Organizational behavior in a global context* (A. Mills, J. Helms-Mills, & C. Forshaw, Eds.). Toronto: Garamond Press. Retrieved September 06, 2009. http://peaceaware.com/vita/paper_pdfs/Boje%20(2008)%20Globalization%20Antenarratives.pdf
———. (2008). *Storytelling organizations*. London: Sage.
Costa, A., & Garmston, R. (2002). *Cognitive coaching: A foundation for Renaissance schools* (2nd ed.). Norwood, MA: Christopher-Gordon.
Csikszentmihalyi, M. (1990). *Flow: The psychology of optimal experience*. New York: Harper & Row.
Czarniawska, B. (2004). *Narratives in social science research*. London: Sage.
de Broglie, L. (1970). In *Albert Einstein: Philosopher-scientist* (P. A. Schilpp, Ed.). La Salle, IL: Open Court.

Deleuze, G., & Guattari, F. (1987). *A thousand plateaus: Capitalism and schizo-phrenia.* Minneapolis: University of Minnesota Press.

Einstein, A. (1915/1961). *Relativity: The special and general theory.* New York: Random House.

Feynman, R. (1999). *The pleasure of finding things out: The best short works of Richard P. Feynman.* Cambridge: Perseus.

Freire, P. (2000). *Pedagogy of the oppressed.* (30th anniversary edition). New York: Continuum.

Gardner, H. (1983). *Multiple intelligences: The theory in practice.* New York: HarperCollins

Greene, B. (2003). *The elegant universe: Superstrings, hidden dimensions, and the quest for the ultimate theory.* New York: Vintage.

Holt, J. (1964). *How children fail.* New York: Pitman Publishing Company.

———. (1967). *How children learn* (5th ed.). New York: Pitman Publishing Company.

———. (1969). *The underachieving school.* New York: Pitman Publishing Company.

———. (1989). *Learning all the time.* Reading, MA: Addison Wesley.

hooks, b. (1994). *Teaching to transgress: Education as the practice of freedom.* New York: Routledge.

Kenny, M. (1970). Factor lattices. *Mathematics Teacher, 63*(8), 647–651.

Kincheloe, J. (2005). *Critical pedagogy.* New York: Peter Lang Publishing.

Kohn, A. (1999). *The schools our children deserve: Moving beyond traditional classrooms and "tougher standards."* New York: Houghton Mifflin.

———. (2000). *The case against standardized testing: Raising the scores, ruining the schools.* Portsmouth, NH: Heinemann.

———. (2004). Test today, privatize tomorrow: Using accountability to "reform" public schools to death. *Phi Delta Kappan, 85*(6), 569–577.

Kozol, J. (1991). *Savage inequalities: Children in America's schools.* New York: Crown Publishers.

Krishnamurti, J. (1953). *Education and the significance of life.* New York: HarperCollins.

Macedo, D. (1994). *Literacies of power: What Americans are not allowed to know.* Boulder, CO: Westview Press.

McLaren, P. (1998). *Life in schools: An introduction to critical pedagogy in the foundations of education* (3rd ed.). New York: Addison Wesley Longman.

Meier, D. (2002). *In schools we trust: Creating communities of learning in an era of testing and standardization.* Boston: Beacon Press.

Meier, D., & Wood, G. (2004). *Many children left behind: How the No Child Left Behind Act is damaging our children and our schools.* Boston: Beacon Press.

Miller, A. (1996). *The drama of the gifted child* (Rev. ed.). New York: Basic Books.

Miller, R. (2000a). *Caring Education & Meaningful Democracy* (Reimagining Politics and Society Conference, New York).

———. (2000b). *Caring for new life: Essays on holistic education.* Brandon, VT: Foundation for Educational Renewal.

Miller, R., & Nakagawa, Y. (2002). *Nurturing our wholeness: Perspectives on spirituality in education.* Brandon, VT: Foundation for Educational Renewal.

Nakagawa, Y. (2000). *Education for awakening: An Eastern approach to holistic education.* Branden, VT: Foundation for Educational Renewal.

Noddings, N. (1984). *Caring: A feminine approach to ethics & moral education.* Berkeley: University of California Press.

————. (2003). *Happiness and education.* Cambridge: Cambridge University Press.

————. (2005). *Educating citizens for global awareness.* New York: Teachers College Press.

————. (2006). *Critical lessons: What our schools should teach.* Cambridge: Cambridge University Press.

Palmer, P. (1997). *The courage to teach: Exploring the inner landscape of a teacher's life.* San Francisco: Jossey-Bass.

————. (2004). *A hidden wholeness: The journey toward an undivided life.* San Francisco: Jossey-Bass.

Rendon, L. (2009). *Sentipensante (sensing/thinking) pedagogy.* Sterling, VA: Stylus.

Riessman, C. (1993). *Narrative analysis: Qualitative research methods.* Volume 30. Newbury Park, CA: Sage Publications.

Rukeyser, M. (1949). *The life of poetry.* New York: A.A. Wynn/Current Books.

Shor, I., & Pari, C. (1999). *Critical literacy in action: Writing words, changing worlds.* Portsmouth, NH: Heinemann.

Sleeter, C. (2005). *Un-standardizing curriculum: Multicultural teaching in the standards-based classroom.* New York: Teacher's College Press.

Spring, J. (2000). *The universal right to education: Justification, definition, and guidelines.* Mahwah, NJ: Lawrence Erlbaum Associates.

————. (2007). *A new paradigm for global school systems: Education for a long and happy life.* Mahwah, NJ: Lawrence Erlbaum Associates.

Talbot, M. (1991). *The holographic universe.* New York: HarperCollins.

U.S. Government. (2002). Elementary and Secondary Education Act. No Child Left Behind. Public Law 107–110. Retrieved September 08, 2009, from http://www.ed.gov/policy/elsec/leg/esea02/index.html

Wink, J. (1999). *Critical pedagogy: Notes from the real world.* New York: Addison Wesley Longman.

Witherrell, C., & Noddings, N. (1991). *Stories lives tell: Narrative and dialogue in education.* New York: Teachers College Press.

4 The Antenarrative of Ethics and the Ethics of Antenarratives

Grace Ann Rosile

INTRODUCTION

I sat there unable to believe the words coming out of my mouth. Surely these were lines from some low-rated cops-and-robbers TV-movie, having no place in higher education. Yet here I was, telling this young man that if he gave me the names of the other students involved in this cheating episode, his penalties would be lighter. How did I get here?

When I discovered evidence of a systematic plan for widespread cheating in my senior-level business strategy class, I found myself headed for a story I did not like. It seemed I would be the villain, failing a whole group of senior students, many of whom had been planning to graduate that term.

If I was not the villain, then those students I caught cheating must be the villains, daring to flout the rules designed supposedly for their own benefit. Identifying and punishing the "bad guy(s)" seemed the obvious moral choice. But which of the students were bad guys? Or was I a bad guy? How could I change this story so neither I, nor my students, were the bad guys?

I wanted to do the right thing, once I figured out what that was. And I wondered if the right thing would allow me to sleep at night and want to get up and teach the next day. Thus began my search for a way to change this emerging story from a disaster to a "teachable moment" (Rosile, 2007).

I sensed that I was at a portentous point. The cheating episode could be the sad ending of my teaching tale ("Teacher Retires After Embarrassing Cheating Scandal") hardened into "the" story as a retrospective narrative of what happened. Or I could intervene now, in the moment of the living story, where antenarrative possibilities abounded. In restorying what had already happened (Rosile, 1998; Rosile & Dennehy, 1998), I could choose the antenarrative threads I preferred and weave a different future ("Cheating Episode Enhances Ethics in the Classroom").

Antenarrative (Boje, 2001) refers to the fragments of life before we have had a chance to form ideas about what "really" happened. Antenarrative influences our subsequent narratives, which we create with retrospective sensemaking (Weick, 1995). Antenarrative warrants attention because it is forward-looking, it contains the seeds of the future, and it shapes the future behavior. I will suggest a link between the type of antenarrative potentially used to explain the causes of cheating and the narrative theme emerging from this antenarrative, the response to the theme, and finally the ethical perspective most compatible with the results of this process.

In sum, antenarrative prospective sensemaking is followed by narrative retrospective sensemaking, which then triggers behavioral responses. These responses fall under the domains of different ethical perspectives. The result is that ultimately, our choice of antenarrative influences our ethical perspective and the focus of our corresponding ethical actions.

ANTENARRATIVE: FOUR TYPOLOGIES

Previous work (Rosile, 2004a, 2004b, 2006) employed antenarrative analysis to identify four perspectives on the root causes of academic dishonesty (cheating). This chapter builds on that antenarrative analysis of causes by identifying the type of antenarrative represented by each perspective: linear, cyclical, spiral, and rhizomatic (Boje, 2001). The antenarratives I encountered while floundering my way through this cheating experience demonstrate all of Boje's (2001) four antenarrative types. The type of antenarrative employed is significant because it contains the roots of subsequent narratives.

I begin with an explanation of each of these four types (linear, cyclical, spiral, and rhizomatic), including examples of that type of antenarrative from the cheating case already introduced. Then I offer a typology of antenarrative causes of cheating, summarized in Table 4.1. Table 4.2 groups retrospective narratives of cheating using the same dimensions as Table 4.1. Next, Table 4.3 suggests a link between certain prospective antenarratives of cheating and particular retrospective narratives of cheating. Finally, Table 4.3 also shows that these pairs of antenarratives and narratives each correspond to a particular ethical perspective.

Linear Antenarratives

When I interviewed the students accused of cheating, many of their antenarratives were linear with a sin-repent plot. A few students immediately confessed and said it was a stupid thing to do, they should never have done it, they were under pressure, and this seemed a way out. A few denied everything until confronted with powerful evidence. Only one persisted in denials; other charged students told me this holdout stood in the hall outside my office trying to persuade them to all stick together in denying everything. I had to appreciate the solidarity argument, but their cause was not so noble.

After admitting guilt, the students' antenarratives tended to be linear cause-and-effect plots: others cheat so it is OK for me to cheat too; my cheating does not affect anyone else; my special circumstances force me to cheat; the tests are too difficult, so the only way to pass is to cheat; the others who do well must be cheating too.

CYCLICAL ANTENARRATIVES

The institution's antenarrative from administrators was cyclical, with evidence of cheating triggering a round of investigation, charges, findings, punishment, and potential removal of the punishment (for example, no further offenses within a specified period allowed the removal of the transcript notation about academic dishonesty). These cycles of crime and punishment may adapt to changing circumstances with different sorts of rules. In the cheating case discussed here, the cheaters used new technology: text messaging via cell phones. This form of cheating was not possible a scarce year earlier. Once discovered, it triggered a whole set of new rules banning cell phones and electronic devices during exams.

In the debate about the culpability (if any) of business schools in regard to the recent burgeoning of corporate scandals, Anderson (2003) and Stablein (2003) suggest that what and how we teach may send an unintended message about moral choices in the business world. Stablein (2003), a professor of business himself, asks us to critically question the fairness of our classroom practices: do we model respect or oppression in the classroom? Perhaps we have adopted oppressive pedagogies (Freire, 1970, 1995) which contribute to perpetuation of oppression in the work world. This argument constitutes a cyclical cause–effect antenarrative.

Another aspect of cyclical antenarrative emerges from the results of negative publicity. The cheaters hurt the reputation of the whole class, the university, and beyond. Such notoriety in turn comes back to harm the reputation of all students from that university (or country, as in the case of China, where it is commonly believed that cheating is widespread).

While conducting my research and workshops on cheating, I discovered that many department heads, administrators, and universities try to cover up cheating to protect the image of the institution. This has the unfortunate unintended effect of allowing cheating to go unpunished, thus encouraging more cheating. Paradoxically, institutions which are proactive may appear to have more cheating simply because more of it is detected and prosecuted. These are cyclical patterns of antenarrative.

Spiral Antenarratives

The cyclical antenarrative can spiral out of control. If students cheat now, what will they do in the so-called "real world"? Perpetuate Enron-type behaviors? If as many as 86% of all students have been reported as cheating for over 20 years in self-report-data-based research (McCabe & Trevino,

1995), then where are those students today? Could some of them be cheating faculty members? Proliferation of high-level research scandals suggest the answer is yes, and further, that such cheating begins as early as middle school science fairs (Shore, 2005).

Cheating is not confined to the academic arena, as documented in Calahan's *The Cheating Culture* (2004). Athletics, journalism, engineering, medicine, and of course the perennial favorite, politics, are among the domains that have demonstrated public-confidence-shaking levels of unethical behaviors (Calahan, 2004).

Spiral antenarratives are not necessarily negative. "Appreciative" pedagogy (Yballe & O'Connor, 2000) seeks to establish positive spirals. Shifting the focus away from what is wrong, and appreciating our strengths and potential for good, can initiate spirals of positive, future-oriented dynamics in the classroom and the workplace.

Spiraling antenarratives seem to have a self-reinforcing dynamic that escalates the effects with each cycle. Thus, knowledge of cheating incidents seems to reinforce the antenarrative that everyone is doing it so I might as well cheat too. The more unethical behavior is punished and publicized, the more jaded public attitudes seem to become. One wonders if the *Wall Street Journal*'s regular column entitled "Executives on Trial" has had any impact on the decrease of numbers of students enrolling in a business major. It is possible that such paradoxical reactions are merely part of another cycle, a cycle of extremes before cultural norms can shift.

Rhizomatic Antenarratives

My own antenarratives of this cheating episode were searches for meaning, which Boje (2001) and Gioia and Mehra (1996) call "prospective sensemaking." My initial antenarratives were linear cause-and-effect variations on a theme: How could they do this to me? How can I teach after this? How can I face students and tell them they have failed for cheating? Notice the focus on Oh, poor me; this is all about me.

Eventually I moved to cyclic antenarratives: What caused this? Why did this happen to me? How can I prevent this from happening again? Then I began to think ahead. What will I say to the class about completing their group projects with so many teammates missing? How will this affect the mood in the classroom? I had visions of a funereal atmosphere and recalled research on survivorship issues in downsized companies—and shuddered to think that could become my classroom, a group of morose, depressed survivors.

Then my antenarrative became rhizomatic. Like the root systems of plants that send out runners, or a map of a road system, rhizomatic patterns are networks of nodes and interconnections. The rhizomatic antenarrative has multiple connections with other antenarratives.

After the shock and self-blame and embarrassment of this cheating incident began to wear off, I realized the 20% who cheated are not the whole story. If 20% cheated, surely another 20% knew about it and did nothing. In addition, this particular variety of cheating (via text messaging) required an out-of-class confederate to text in the illicit information, extending the network of people involved to beyond the classroom.

I began to focus on rhizomatic antenarratives. Both the active collusion and passive complicity of participants comprise a network of rhizomatic antenarratives which, over time, can contribute to a "cheating culture." Due to this culture aspect, the claim that my cheating does not affect anyone else is spurious for many reasons, including the result that one person's cheating feeds the "everyone-does-it" antenarrative.

Similarly, the linear "victimless crime" antenarrative argues that cheaters only hurt themselves. However, a rhizomatic antenarrative links cheating to the quality of feedback available to the instructor regarding the class. If it appears to me as instructor that a sufficient number of students are doing reasonably well on exams, I assume they are learning the material. I do not get the required feedback to know if the material is too difficult, if my teaching methods were not as effective as they appeared, or if students are lacking some prerequisite knowledge to integrate this new material. Thus the cheating antenarrative is rhizomatically connected to the instructor's consideration of teaching and testing methods.

The more attention I paid to rhizomatic antenarratives of connectedness, the more I saw the hidden, indirect, yet far-reaching effects of cheating. I realized three things: (1) There are no innocent bystanders; (2) Cheating is just as much about the noncheaters as it is about the cheaters; and (3) We are all cheaters.

ANTENARRATIVE TYPOLOGY OF CAUSES OF CHEATING

And Now, Back to Our Story: Antenarrative of an Ethical Dilemma

When I first heard about the cheating, the antenarrative (storyline in development) seemed to be "Ungrateful Students Cheat in Caring Professor's Class." Didn't they realize how hard I worked to make my class interesting, even enjoyable, educational, and passable? Many of the students in this senior capstone class had been in previous classes of mine. I liked to think they signed up for my section out of interest and appreciation, not because I might be seen as "easy" and someone with whom they could get away with little work and/or much cheating.

Here was the system I had evolved into: After a quiz or exam was started, I posted the correct answers on the wall just outside the classroom. I also issued each student a color-coded small square of paper on which to record answers. On their way out, students could check their small slip of paper with the answers on the wall and figure out their grade on the spot.

Table 4.1   Antenarrative Typology of Causes of Cheating

	Insider/Emic Antenarratives of "Us"	Outsider/Etic Antenerratives of "Them"

Micro
Internal
Attributions/
Speculations
	I. Cause-Effect Linear
	   Antenarratives
	
	"A few bad apples"
	
	Personal morality of students
	Student demographics
	Grade inflation
	   Pressure/expectations
		II. Rhizomatic Interconnected
		    Antenarratives
		
		"Beating the system"
		
		Teachers helping students to
		   cheat
		teacher failure (tenure system)
		Commodification of education

Macro
Internal
Attributions/
Speculations
	III. Cause-Effect Cyclical
	     Antenarratives
	
	McDonaldization of
	   Education"
	
	Multiple-choice testing
	Administrative role of faculty
	Grade inflation/expectations
	New technology
	"Enronitis" (hubris)
		IV. Spiraling-Out-of-Control
		    Cyclical Antenarratives
		
		"Systematic Abuse of Power"
		
		Educational capitalism
		Abuse of teachers' powers
		Standardized testing/
		   performativity
		Irrelevant curriculum

Adapted from Rosile, G. A. (2004a). "McCheating: Narrative Analysis of Root Causes," in C. Gardner & A. Alkhafaji (Eds.), *Business Research Yearbook* (vol. 11).

Several students who had been in my basic organization behavior class were now in this senior-level class. They knew my system. Apparently their enrollment in a second class with me coincided with the advent of text messaging via cell phone. They saw an opportunity. Whereas only two or three had accomplices outside the room, a few others benefitted by getting the little square slip of paper passed unobtrusively to them as the text-message-informed students left the room.

At first, I blamed myself. This contributed to my initial reluctance to prosecute those who cheated. Yet as I spent a weekend considering all sides of this situation, I finally concluded that the issue was much larger than a few cheaters. Even though more than 20% were suspected of cheating, the majority had not cheated. How could I best serve them? Not by ignoring those I was fairly certain had cheated.

I did not want to accuse someone falsely; such an accusation alone could be damaging, even if dropped later. At the same time, if guilty parties escaped unpunished, then the harsh penalty of failure in the class would seem to fall especially hard on those unlucky enough to be caught. This led me to conclude that if I were to prosecute and fail some, I wanted to be as

Table 4.2   Retrospective Narratives of Cheating, Responses, and Ethical Perspectives

	Insider/Emic Narratives	Outsider/Etic Narratives
Micro Internal Narratives, Response, Ethical Perspective, and Strategies	I. Crime and Punishment Theme Question Micro Practices Applied/Rule-Based Ethics Applied ethics exercises Negotiated syllabi/students' rights Ethics statements/pledges Procedural justice	II. Collusion and Complicity Theme Question Conflicts of Interest, Pragmatism Answerability Ethics Support/reward skilled teaching "De-schooling society" Technology serves teaching, not reverse Pay for skills, not just for degree
Macro External Narratives, Response, Ethical Perspective, and Strategies	III. Classroom-Culture Theme Clarify Values and Cultural Norms Virtue Ethics Class as learning organization Taboo topics out of the closet Philosophy/ethics in curriculum Custom massification Distributive justice	IV. Complete-Corruption Theme Employ Critical and Liberatory Pedagogy Instrumentalism and Pragmatism: Greatest Good for Whom? Decommodification of education Resefine education, learning Link classroom with societal outcomes Social justice

sure as possible that I had identified all guilty parties, avoiding as much as possible the system of making an example of a few unlucky ones.

This reasoning led me to look more favorably upon the suggestion of the "sting," of planting a series of false answers to see which students had that same pattern of 18 out of 24 false answers. It would be highly unlikely, even virtually impossible, that anyone would have the complete pattern of 18 wrong answers by chance.

THE ETHICS OF ANTENARRATIVE

I set up the "sting" with 18/24 incorrect answers posted during the next exam. Seven students' papers showed all 18 incorrect answers. Two more students were subsequently identified by more than one student as also having cheated. They confessed when confronted.

After failing and removing from class seven (of a final total of nine) students whom I determined to be cheating, I gave a 20-minute speech to the class about what had happened, why I did what I did, and what I thought needed to be done to prevent cheating in the future. I also talked about my personal views of ethics and education, and my feelings about what had happened. Then I asked the students to write what they thought of the situation.

I collected anonymous written comments (antenarratives) from 26 students. I identified 49 topics or issues in those 26 submissions. Those 49 topics were grouped into 11 themes. Previous work (Rosile, 2004b) provides a full transcript of those comments, as well as a detailed analysis of the themes.

To begin my antenarrative analysis, I created an antenarrative typology which is an elaboration and extension of earlier work (Rosile, 2004). I chose two dimensions for this typology. The first dimension reflects whether the speaker is talking about themselves as an individual or member of a group versus talking about the "other." This dimension I call Us and Them.

The Us/Them dimension is supported by Attribution Theory, which has demonstrated significant biases in the way we attribute causes of behaviors, depending on whether we are discussing ourselves or some "other" person(s). We tend to attribute another's failure to their poor internal qualities like weak character or lack of skills. Our own failures we tend attribute to external factors such as the difficulty of the undertaking, or luck (Nelson & Quick, 2008, p. 85).

The second dimension is micro (individual level) versus macro (group or organizational-level) behaviors. These two dimensions, Us/Them and Micro/Macro, yield four quadrants. The domain of each quadrant includes its antenarrative type, its narrative theme, a typical response to that theme, and an ethical perspective compatible with that quadrant's characteristics. The quadrants are displayed in Table 4.3. I will explain each of these quadrants next.

Q I Linear Antenarratives and Applied/Rule-Based Ethics

Quadrant I is the Me/Us perspective. It is "emic" because it comes from the people or culture under consideration, rather than being imposed from outside that culture. The focus is on specific micro behaviors which come from my/our internal personal qualities of moral character, skills, and abilities. This quadrant yields the Linear Antenarrative of cause-effect. The pattern here is to protect self-image by separating the good self from the (rare) bad others. I call this "A few bad apples," and it leads to a "Crime-and-Punishment" theme. This theme triggers the response of questioning specific behaviors (micro practices) by those bad apples.

This micro, internally focused approach is the domain of applied or practical ethics. Kant's (1900) "categorical imperatives" are an example of rule-based applied ethics. The imperatives are universal rules or principles to guide individual behavior in all situations. The Ten Commandments would be an example of Kantian categorical imperatives. This perspective addresses the specific microlevel behaviors of Quadrant I (individual actions), judging some behaviors to be good and others bad.

Q III Cyclical Antenarratives and Virtue Ethics

Quadrant III is also the Me/Us perspective. It is emic in that judgments emerge from within our group rather than being imposed from the outside. Quadrant III shifts to the macrolevel of systemic behavior, and this system level is viewed as constituting external forces impinging on the group, for example, "McDonaldization" (Ritzer, 2000). The antenarratives here are cause-effect cyclical, with the theme of "Classroom Culture." This theme triggers the response of reexamining our values and social norms which give rise to the culture.

Quadrant III's macro, externally focused approach is compatible with the domain of virtue ethics. Aristotle (Crisp, 2000) used the concept of virtue to identify moral behaviors as the actions of a virtuous person, or "what the mature person with a 'good' moral character would deem appropriate" (Ferrell, Fraedrich, & Farrell, 2010, p. 157). Behaviors directed towards the highest good, towards happiness, are virtuous. Virtue ethics is sometimes called "character-based" ethics because it is based on the development of personal characteristics which predispose a person to behave in accordance with those virtues. Quadrant III's systemic-level and cultural focus makes it compatible with virtue ethics because the definition of virtue is embedded in the values of a given society.

Q II Rhizomatic Antenarratives and Answerability Ethics

Quadrant II is about Them. It is etic because the views and judgments are imposed from outside the group or culture. The focus is on specific micro behaviors which come from the internal personal qualities of members of the Them group. The antenarratives here are rhizomatic. We see those others as people trying to beat the system, and engaging in collusion and complicity for personal gain. Conflicts of interest, organizational politics, and collusion behaviors, such as teachers helping students to cheat so that both look better to evaluators, are some of the issues falling in this quadrant.

This micro focus looks at individual corruption, collusion, and complicity as a result of external forces. Answerability ethics addresses such situations because it calls for individuals to be answerable (take action) to influence systemic-level wrongs (Belova, 2008; Boje, 2008).

Q IV Spiral Antenarratives and Instrumental/Pragmatist Ethics

Quadrant IV, like Quadrant II, is also about Them, but the focus is on macro (group-level) external forces. The antenarratives here are spiraling out of control. The self-reinforcing systemic pressures act on groups in ever-escalating waves of abuse of power leading to corruption, which leads to further abuse of power and so on. This macro focus looks at systemic-level corruption as a result of powerful external forces. Critical theory and liberatory pedagogy question these systemic-level forces.

Whereas some would say the instrumentalism and pragmatism of ethics in the business world are the cause of the deplorable condition of "business ethics," it is the critique of instrumentalism and pragmatism that is relevant in Quadrant IV. Such critique of the deepest assumptions of instrumentalism and pragmatism holds the best hope for unraveling and shifting this spiral antenarrative. Based on the idea that what is good is that which is practical and workable, instrumentalism and pragmatism are often viewed as similar. Proponents include John Dewey and Charles Sanders Peirce.

Antenarratives, corresponding narratives, and compatible ethical perspectives are displayed in Table 4.3.

ANTENARRATIVE ETHICS INTERVENTION

According to Kohlberg (1969), the higher levels of cognitive moral development encompass a larger sense of community. Cognitive moral development (Nelson & Quick, 2008) suggests that concern only for oneself is a very immature level of moral reasoning. The higher levels of moral consciousness consider not just the self but the family, community, nation, and all humankind. So too antenarratives may be placed in a hierarchy of complexity, with the rhizomatic level incorporating all simpler types (linear, cyclical, and spiral). This suggests that rhizomatic antenarratives are inherently more conducive to higher levels of moral judgment, because they tend to incorporate a broader perspective.

I employed a speech to the whole class, to attempt to shift the direction and weight of the antenarratives I uncovered in my personal interviews with students and in my research on classroom cheating. I wanted students to see a bigger picture. I hoped they would see beyond linear cause-effect antenarratives, beyond cycles and spirals, to appreciate the complex interconnectedness of the rhizomatic antenarratives. I hoped the perspective of rhizomatic antenarratives would bring them to a greater appreciation of answerability ethics. I wanted to be answerable myself, and to inspire them to be more answerable regarding classroom integrity.

Based on the anonymous written comments of 26 students yielding 49 differently themed comments, I found that 20/49 comments reflected the rhizomatic antenarrative and answerability ethics (Quadrant III). When analyzed by person, 13/26 individuals made statements that indicated a rhizomatic antenarrative. Of those 13, 10 specifically mentioned answerability and their enhanced desire to be proactive in future cheating situations. Following are two such examples (Rosile, 2004b):

Table 4.3 Linking Antenarratives, Narrative Themes, Responses, and Ethical Perspectives*

	Insider/Emic Antenarratives of "Us"	Outsider/Etic Antenarratives of "Them"
Micro Internal Attributions	I. <u>Cause-Effect Linear Antenarratives</u> "A few bad apples" Leads to: <u>Crime-and-Punishment Theme</u> Response: **Question Micro Practices** Ethical Perspective: **Applied/Rule-Based Ethics** STUDENT COMMENTS (12/49 = 25%) #1 This stinks . . . I feel naive and cheated . . . I felt unfairly treated . . . this will catch up to them . . . they will pay (someday) . . . (they) should be thrown out of the University . . . great injustice to the rest of the class. #9 (the university should) ensure students are neither tempted nor able (to cheat). . . .	II. <u>Rhizomatic Network of Antenarratives</u> "Beating the system" Leads to: <u>Collusion-and-Complicity Theme</u> Response: **Question Conflicts of Interest, Pragmatism** Ethical Perspective: **Answerability Ethics** STUDENT COMMENTS (20/49 = 41%) #3 I didn't even hear comments about cheating . . . wish I was more observant . . . I too am the oblivious student. #5 Thank you . . . My hat's off to you . . . Thanks for standing up for us . . . I support you . . . Thank you for sharing those experiences. #6 You have changed the way I think. . . .
Macro External Attributions	III. <u>Cause-Effect Cyclical Antenarratives</u> "McDonaldization of Education" Leads to: <u>Classroom Culture Theme</u> Response: **Clarify Values and Cultural Norms** Ethical Perspective: **Virtue Ethics** STUDENT COMMENTS (9/49 = 18%)#2 I feel ashamed . . . I apologize for my peers . . . feeling disappointed . . . I was upset . . . I feel bad for them but they should be made an example of.#10 (one who cheated) I feel terrible . . . I realize how wrong this was . . .	IV. <u>Spiraling-Out-Of-Control Cyclical Antenarratives</u> "Systemic Abuse of Power" Leads to: <u>Complete Corruption Theme</u> Response: **Employ Critical and Liberatory Pedagogy** Ethical Perspective: **Instrumentalism and Pragmatism: Greatest Good for Whom?** STUDENT COMMENTS (7/49 = 14%)#4 There have always been cheaters and there always will . . . it is everywhere . . . from 3rd grade spelling test up to the CEO of Enron . . . corporations rob people for profit . . . cheating is a viable option.#11 Cheating is wrong . . . it hurts the whole, even those that never cheat.

I have been in other classes where students have cheated and I always looked the other way. I figured that as long as I'm not cheating it's not my problem. But after hearing you speak and going through this experience in this class, I feel like I should have said something in the past. The idea that it wasn't affecting me was wrong because it does. I struggled in this class on my tests and when others got better grades it affected me, and others around me. I see it not only affects me but also the integrity of my college. Thank you so much for sharing your heart with us in class. You have changed the way I think about my responsibility as a person. I won't look the other way either, and I hope others won't also.

When I began to hear "rumors" about how people passed exam #4, I was *very* upset because my initial thought was that nothing would be done. I study very hard and felt unfairly treated because I assumed people would get away with wrong-doing. Today, my entire opinion of this college, you as a professor, and this class has improved immensely because you took a stand on something that needed immediate attention. All I can say at this point is "My hat's off to you!"

I was overwhelmed at the effectiveness of my intervention. As the icing on the cake, 6/49 comments were thanking me for my efforts!

CONCLUSION

In conclusion, each of the four types of antenarratives (Boje, 2001) presented here encourages a particular compatible ethical perspective. In the cheating case example, rhizomatic antenarratives encouraged adoption of answerability ethics (Bakhtin, 1970, 1993). My intervention of a heartfelt speech to foster rhizomatic antenarratives appears to have had two results. First, students saw things differently when they were able to see connections of the rhizomatic antenarratives. They saw deeper, hidden, and far-reaching effects of an act of classroom cheating. Second, students expressed a greater willingness to be more proactive in noticing and doing something about classroom cheating. This is the essence of answerability, arrived at through the ethics of the antenarrative.

REFERENCES

Anderson, J. A. (2003). Ethics in business and teaching. *Management Communication Quarterly, 17*(1), 155–164.

Bakhtin, M. (1990). *Art and answerability* (M. Holquist & V. Liapunov, Eds., & V. Liapunov, Trans.). Austin: University of Texas Press.

————. (1993). *Toward a Philosophy of the Act* (Michael Holquist and Vadim Liapunov, eds; translation and notes by Vadim Liapunov). Austin, TX: University of Texas Press. (From Bakhtin's early 1920s notebooks; 1993 is first English printing).

Belova, O. (2008). No alibi in ethics: Bakhtin's philosophy of the act and the question of answerability in business. In D. Boje (Ed.), *Critical theory ethics for business and public administration*. Charlotte, NC: Information Age Publishing, Inc.

Boje, D. M. (2001). *Narrative methods for organizational and communication research*. London: Sage.

————. (2008). *Storytelling organizations*. London: Sage.

Calahan, David (2004). *The Cheating Culture: Why More Americans are Doing Wrong to Get Ahead*. Orlando, FL: Harcourt, Inc.

Crisp, R. (Trans). (2000). *Aristotle: Nichomachean Ethics*. Cambridge: Cambridge University Press.

Ferrell, O. C., Fraedrich, J., & Ferrell, L. (2010). *Business Ethics* (7th ed.). Mason, OH: Southwestern, Cengage Learning.

Freire, Paulo. (1970). *Pedagogy of the oppressed* (Myra Bergman Ramos, Trans.). New York: Seabury.

Freire, Paulo. (1995). *Pedagogy of hope*. New York: Continuum.

Gioia, D. A., & Mehra, A. (1996). Book review of Weick, K. E., *Sensemaking in Organizations* (1995). *Academy of Management Review, 21*(4), 1226–1240,

Kant, I. (1781/1900). *Critique of pure reason*. New York: The Colonial Press.

Kohlberg, L. (1969). Stage and sequence: The cognitive developmental approach to socialization. In D. A. Goslin (Ed.), *Handbook of socialization theory and research* (pp. 347–480). Chicago: Rand McNally.

McCabe, D. L., & Trevino, L. K. (1995). Cheating among business students: A challenge for business leaders and educators. *Journal of Management Education, 19*(2), 205–218.

Nelson, D. L., & Quick, J. C. (2008). *Understanding organizational behavior* (3rd ed.). Mason: OH. Thompson/Southwestern.

Ritzer, G. (2000). *McDonaldization of society: New century edition*. Thousand Oaks, CA: Pine Forge Press/Sage Publications.

Rosile, G. A. (1998). Restorying for strategic organizational planning and development: The case of the scifi organization. In J. Biberman & A. Alkhafaji (Eds.), *Business Research Yearbook, 5*, 689–694.

————. (2004a). McCheating: Narrative analysis of root causes. In C. Gardner & A. Alkhafaji (Eds.), *Business Research Yearbook* (vol. 11).

————. (2004b). Ante-narrative analysis of students' reactions to cheating in class. *Crossing frontiers in quantitative and qualitative research methods* (vol. 2). Proceedings of the First International Co-Sponsored Conference Research Methods Division Academy of Management, held March 18–20, 2004, in Lyon, France, pp. 1141–1152.

————. (2006). Retrospective and antecedent narratives of cheating. *Annual Review of Management and Organization Inquiry*.

————. (2007). Cheating: Making it a teachable moment. *Journal of Management Education, 31*(5), 582–613.

Rosile, G. A., & Dennehy, R. F. (1998). Restorying for personal and organizational change. In N. M. Bodensteiner (Ed.), *Southwest Academy of Management Proceedings*, March 5–7, 275–276.

Shore, Bruce M. (2005). "Cheating Among Faculty" unpublished paper presented at the October 2005 Annual Conference of the Center for Academic Integrity, Virginia Tech University, Blacksburg, VA.

Stablein, R. (2003). Teaching business ethics or teaching business ethically? *Management Communication Quarterly, 17*(1), 151–154.

Weick, K. E. (1995). *Sensemaking in organizations*. CA: Thousand Oaks. Sage.

Yballe, L., & O'Connor, D. (2000). Appreciative pedagogy: Constructing positive models for learning. *Journal of Management Education, 24*(4), 474–483.

5 The Creative Spirit of the Leader's Soul

Using Antenarratives to Explain Metanoia Experiences

Kevin Grant

INTRODUCTION

This chapter begins with the theme "the human soul is not meant to be understood." However, the leader's soul evolves through the poetics of everyday life. Using this as a theme, a metanoia experience is introduced to explain an individual's transpersonal encounter. After the encounter, the person decides to change the way they feel and think. As the leader experiences an unpredictable event, a story begins to evolve where we begin to see significant behavioral changes in the person's life. Thus, the story is considered to be an antenarrative because of the unpredictable outcome from the occurrence and the leader's need to move away from the path they once predicted. This chapter will explain the experience of having a metanoia and why leaders go through this encounter. Using antenarrative theory, developed by Boje (2001), this encounter reveals a morphing process where a story begins to develop as the individual moves through this unexpected and spontaneous event.

Most people would agree that good leaders are good storytellers (Boje, 1991). Stories help inspire action because they transport the listener to an experience of events by conveying emotion and creating a picture of what happened, and why it happened. Stories help change our minds and in doing so change our behaviors. Storytelling is an important skill for leaders because it takes us away from the ordinary experience and seizes our attention. In fact, stories can help us set aside the practical experiences of life so in the end the soul can be served. This is what this chapter is about; it's about the stories of two leaders who experienced a transpersonal experience and adapted new behaviors which brought about new meaning and purpose in their lives.

Leaders recognize transpersonal (spiritual) leadership is the development of one's self, who goes beyond their own ego and serves others while influencing the organization to create a genuine outcome of care. Reading about these experiences we begin to understand the leader's creative spirit through antenarratives as the leader's soul began to take shape. Grounded theory explaining antenarrative by Boje (2008) brings about new meaning to storytelling.

Most stories have a beginning, middle, and end (BME), meaning they are retrospective or looking back; however, living stories go on forever. In a living story there is no beginning and the ending is not in sight. Living stories of leaders who experience a personal transformation are best understood using the theoretical concept of antenarrative introduced by Boje (2008). When using the theory of antenarrative to explain a personal transformation, it is best described as a "pre-narrative" or a "bet" (ante) that you can tell the antenarrative will become a living story that is world-changing and transforming. Antenarrative is some kind of morphing connective of narrative and living story; therefore, it is prospective sensemaking (looking-forward) to transform the future with storytelling (p. 1). Antenarratives are the pre-story that reveal the leader's soul while providing insight into their own creativity after they have found meaning and purpose in their life. Stories shared by leaders who experienced a transcendent experience ended with the individual expressing a higher calling in life.

When leaders talk about their higher calling they are expressing a greater sense of transcendence, or having a feeling of being called through one's work or vocation. Those who practice spiritual leadership, because of their higher calling, influence their followers and have a high regard for one's self and developing good quality relationships with others. This in turn helps create a greater sense of meaning and purpose with the capacity to effectively manage one's surrounding world, the ability to follow inner convictions, and a sense of continuing growth and self-realization.

The purpose of this chapter is show how antenarratives can be used to explain a metanoia experience or a deep personal transformation. The experience coming from having a metanoia is termed in the Greek as a shift of mind or moving from the old way of thinking to a new way of thinking. A metanoia experience is when a leader makes a "shift" (change) of "mind" (thoughts and feelings) and as a result is transformed to a follower-centered leader. In other words, the leader has a change in the way they think and feel, or take on a new behavior.

METANOIA

The word 'metanoia' literally means transcendence of the mind. In the Gnostic action of Christianity, it took on the meaning of an awakening of shared intuition and direct knowing of the highest ultimate reality, that is, God. Upon asking individuals concerning a personal metanoia experience, the individual will respond by speaking of something bigger than him- or herself where they felt a sense of being connected (Korac-Kakabadse, Kouzmin, & Kakabadse, 2002). People attempt to recapture these feelings of being a part of something bigger than him- or herself because of having a metanoia experience that they will continue to search for this experience again for the rest of their life.

Sanford (1970) speaks of metanoia as being a "turning about" rather than being sorry for something we have done. The turning about is the "reversal of one's self and of one's life" (p. 111). Sanford (1970) contends that "metanoia includes turning away from our identification with our outer masks, and confronting what lies behind that mask: what looks like an inner adversary or enemy" (p. 111).

Applying the metanoia experience to the theory of antenarrative means the experience is a "bet" on the future. A leader who has a metanoia, which is spontaneous and unexpected, is considered a bet on the future; as the metanoia process takes place, the leader does not know what the final transformational outcome will be because the leader is forced to make a decision to change or not to change their behavior. However, the outcome from the experience is known after, not before. Thus, after the leader is transformed, a living story is shared with others that is difficult to explain. Boje (2000a) views this experience by leaders as a discovery to becoming a "spiritual leader" which requires moving beyond one's self.

The design of this chapter is to introduce metanoia using storytelling from an antenarrative perspective. However, the limitation is, when these stories are read later on in the chapter, we will know the beginning, middle, and end (BME) of the story. Therefore, my attempt is to explain how one moves through the metanoia and why this experience is an antenarrative and eventually evolves into a living story when told to others. To fully understand stories from individuals who described this experience, specific terminology is required.

TERMS DEFINED

Mind

Ryle (1949) provides a descriptive meaning of "mind" which does not stand for another organ. It signifies my abilities and proneness to do certain sorts of things and not some piece of personal apparatus without which I could not or would not do them (p. 168). Therefore, the mind functions to give us a way of discussing the person's capacities, abilities, and activities (Sayward, 1983).

Spirituality

Mitroff and Denton (1999) defined "spirituality" as one being connected to one's self, others, and the entire universe. The idea of being connected to one's self, others, and the entire universe is called "interconnectedness" (Mitroff & Denton, 1999). When a person senses interconnectedness at work, the person brings more of themselves to work where they feel they can deploy their full creativity, emotions, and intellect at work (Mitroff

& Denton, 1999, p. 83). This definition of interconnectedness agrees with Howard's (2002) thinking whereby humans are inextricably made up of mind, body, emotions, and spirit. In conclusion, we are all looking for meaning in life (Howard, 2002) and spirituality is about interconnectedness within the world, along with our desire to tap into our deeper resources (Mitroff & Denton, 1999).

Spiritual Leadership

Fry (2003) defines spiritual leadership as the "values, attitudes, and behaviors necessary to intrinsically motivate one's self and others so that they have a sense of spiritual survival through calling and membership" (pp. 694–695). In this chapter, spiritual leadership is treated more as an observable phenomenon occurring when a person in a leadership position embodies spiritual values, such as integrity, humility, compassion, agapao, and altruism, thereby creating the self as an example of someone who can be trusted, relied upon, and admired. Spiritual leadership is demonstrated through behavior, whether in the individual's ethics, compassion, or respectful treatment of others (Reave, 2005). Spiritual individuals are more likely to demonstrate spiritual leadership, but a person does not have to be spiritual or religious to provide spiritual leadership (Reave, 2005).

Spiritual Values

"A value is an enduring belief that a specific mode of conduct or end-state of existence is personally or socially preferable to an opposite mode of conduct or end-state of existence" (Rokeach, 1973, p. 5). "Therefore, values are multifaceted standards that guide our conduct in a variety of ways" (p. 13). The growing literature about spirituality in the workplace produces an emerging consensus on which spiritual values are primary or core. The emerging consensus is summarized in the following list (Kriger & Seng, 2005, pp. 302–311):

a) Forgiveness
b) Kindness
c) Integrity
d) Compassion/empathy
e) Honesty/truthfulness
f) Patience
g) Courage/inner strength
h) Trust
i) Humility
j) Loving kindness
k) Peacefulness

l) Thankfulness
m) Service to others
n) Guidance
o) Joy
p) Equanimity
q) Stillness/inner peace

Spirit

"Spirit refers to the vital energizing force or principle in the person, the core of self" (Fairholm, 1996, p. 11). Spirit in the Bible is translated from the Greek word 'pneuma' (Shawchuck & Heuser, 1996). There are two meanings of pneuma: life's breath or the breath of life, and wind or the force of wind that blows (p. 121).

Soul of the Leader

The title of this chapter is called the creative spirit and soul of the leader. The title came after much researching and writing on spiritual leadership over a six-year period. In my research I found leaders do change the way they think and feel, whereas those who observe the leader's new behavior will ask the question "What happened?" The leader answers by stating they had an experience which is difficult to explain. The reason is because in most cases the leader will describe the experience as an emotionally charged experience. From this specific experience the person changed from who they were to who they are.

The key word in the title is 'soul,' which links to the type of story that is shared in this chapter. Spiritual writers use "soul" to speak not about something a person has but about who a person most deeply is. According to Benefiel (2005), her understanding of soul is a deep essence of a person who may find expression through religious faith or it may find expression in other ways (p. 21). A simpler understanding is the emotional and relational depth of the leader and their yearings to develop and evolve into what the leader wants to become.

The *Catholic Encyclopedia* (2009) defines soul as the ultimate internal principle by which we think, feel, and will, and by which our bodies are animated. The term 'mind' usually denotes this principle as the subject of our conscious states, whereas "soul" denotes the source of our vegetative activities as well (Maher & Bolland, 1912, p. 1).

Living from soul is living from the core of our true nature, where divine energy infuses our being with loving wisdom. Then the divine image in which Scripture says we are made is freed to shine through our being and doing. When we are empowered to live from soul in our daily activities, we become a blessing to life (Edwards, 1997).

The Creative Leader

The other key word in the title is as important as soul and that is "creative." An understanding of a creative leader is one who is fully engaged and using all their creative gifts to make the organization better. Creative leaders understand that leadership is a shared responsibility and fosters an environment that is committed, loyal, and productive. Using their creativity the leader reaches their higher calling which came through a personal emotionally charged experience which is called metanoia.

Understanding of these terms provides insight about an encounter described by individuals who experience deep change and personal transformation called the "dark night of the soul," which is similar to having a metanoia.

DARK NIGHT OF THE SOUL

When an individual begins their metanoia journey usually they are in the middle of a difficult experience such as a divorce, a loss of a loved one, a depression, a business failure, or a nagging emotion which will not go away. For some, these problems or situations are to be solved, whereas in most cases these problems become a source of great despair. Moore (2004) describes these difficult times as not a "surface challenge but a development that takes you away from the joy of your ordinary life" (p. XIV).

Many leaders who reach a point in their life where they are faced with a challenge try to solve the problem so they can be happy. However, happiness is a sensation that evaporates quickly, and the problem never gets solved. Hoping the problem will fade away, people spend most of their time avoiding life's problems and channel them towards ambitions, addictions, and preoccupations. Examples of this are observed in leaders who become workaholics, ignore their families, engage in medications to numb the pain, and begin to isolate themselves from others.

Moore (2004) contends a dark night is a person's way of returning to the living. However, when one has the feeling of going beyond self and discovering something more powerful than what he is humanly capable of doing, it is called a "state of liminality."

USING ANTENARRATIVE IN STORYTELLING

What follows are two stories by leaders who experienced transpersonal transformation or metanoias. The tendency is to read the stories with a beginning, middle, and end because the story is being retold and the authors are being retrospective. However, these stories can also be read using the antenarrative theory. Each author is describing their metanoia not knowing what the ending will be.

Narrative may be seen as a deterministically constituted structured expression of a thematic story about an event or set of connected events. If antenarrative is pre-narrative, then it may develop into narrative through the use of patterning processes given that a set of events can be conceptualized and related (Yolles, 2007, p. 76). It is also maintained in phenomenology that access to reality is mediated through consciousness and its attendant capacity for understanding. For many, understanding comes from knowledge, and knowledge is acquired from the experience of phenomenal reality (p. 82).

Metanoia Stories

The first story is retold by David M. Boje, who developed the theory of antenarrative. The backdrop in David's story is his personal search for meaning and purpose in his life, after a personal trauma he experienced in the Vietnam War. The story begins after David came home from the war and he begins to search his soul to determine his future or higher calling. Following is David's transcribed story which he describes as his metanoia experience.

"THE POTATO CHIP STORY" (BY PERMISSION, MAY 15, 2009)

A Storytelling about Transcendental Situations

1. **Narration:** David is usually too busy to notice things, like the rhythm of time. But, he realized this rhythm after facing lots of rejection at UCLA. It was 1982, and he just decided to slow down, do nothing, read his bible, and figure out a path for his life. It can all be about taking time to do some reflexivity, to tune into something transcendental, where something quite spiritual may happen.
2. **David:** (Trying to decide between doing story or more quantitative kinds of research) "OK God, what do you say? I could do either. Be quantitative or do the qualitative story research . . ."
3. **God:** (no answer).
4. **David:** (Opens NIV Pictorial Bible,1978; picks a page at random, opens to pp. 10–11, begins to read: He decides to substitute the word 'story' for passage.)

SCENE 2: The Miracle
5. **David:** "OK God, it seems to me, if this is a sign, that story research is the way to go.
   Yet, I am kind of a skeptic. I therefore humbly request a sign. Not a lightning bolt, but a definite sign."
6. **God:** (no answer)

7. David: (takes a break, goes from 5th floor to 1st, to the Potlatch (coffee & snack room). David puts in 35 cents, and clicks A12, for some Potato Chips. The chips and candy hang in the machine on metal spirals. The spiral turns and a bag of chips drops into the slot. But, the spiral keeps turning (11 more times).

8. David: (speaking aloud to himself) "It can't be. There are 12 bags of chips in the bin."

SCENE 3: In Elevator

9. David: (hands bag to student) "I prayed to God for an answer to a question. I put in my money and got 12 bags of chips. Here have one!"

10. Student: "You think it's a miracle?"

11. David: "Don't know. Does God work through machines."

12. Student: "My guess is God can do anything in anyway."

13. David: (going to each secretary on 5th floor) "Can you believe it? I put a question to God, asked for a sign. I put in 35 cents and got 12 bags of potato chips."

14. Secretary 1: "12 is a biblical number."

15. David: "There are 12 apostles."

16. Secretary 2: "The 12 tribes of Israel."

17. David: "I think there are 12 angels."

18. Secretary 1: "12 gates."

SCENE 4: Dénouement

19. David: "Thanks God. I'll take the chips as a sign that story is the path I will take from here on out." (to himself, 'Guess a machine miracle is the kind that takes some faith to believe in.'). The next day. David is in the Potlatch (1st floor coffee & snack lounge).

20. David: (to man serving the machine): "May I ask you a question?" Serviceman: "Sure, what is it?"

21. David: "Is there anything wrong with this machine?"

22. Serviceman: "Not that I know of. Why do you ask?"

23. David: "I was in here yesterday, and I put in 35 cents, and 12 bags came out. The thing just kept spitting them out."

24. Serviceman: "No cannot be. You see you put in the coins, and it will only allow this here thing to turn just once. Its part of the safeguard of the mechanism . . ."

25. David: "So you are sure, that the machine cannot just keep turning out chips?"

26. Serviceman: "No way."

SCENE 5: Changed Behavior

27. Spiritual Leadership—Where does inspiration come from? Slowing down, meditation and prayer, worked for me. Spiritual leaders tune

in, and respond. And every once in a great while, miracles do happen. I've had several. Orienting your leadership on a spiritual place, is another way to go.

It should be noted that this transcript is taken directly from David's personal life experience, and a descriptive transpersonal experience which he termed his metanoia.

The second story comes for the biblical text in Psalms 25. The story is King David's (KD) personal metanoia from a paraphrase by Pul, a Franscian Sister (1983). David's personal reflection explains his metanoia and how his behavior was transformed.

THE JOURNEY THAT IS METANOIA

A Paraphrase of Psalm 25

1. One more time I stretch my heart to receive your word.

2. Difficult as it is for me to trust you, I want to abandon
3. My old enemy, fear.
4. You ask me again that I take up the journey
5. That is metanoia.
6. That I prepare myself for new moments of fidelity.

7. I mean today these words so oft-prayed:
8. Make known to me my path—
9. Show me the way you would have me follow—
10. Guide me as I discern the signs and the signals
11. Of your beckoning—
12. I have been waiting upon your word.

13. I know that grace is never lacking
14. And that strength and courage will be bestowed
15. I know that my weakness is not the obstacle,
16. Nor my slowness to convert.
17. You remind gently, ever and again, of own restless search.

18. In so many little ways you point the one way.
19. At my first response you plant peace in my heart.
20. I know that change is inevitable.
21. I know that I cannot retreat from poverty and the demands
22. Of our human community.
23. Your words will haunt me until I surrender.

24. When fear prompts me to distraction and excuse,

25. You place in my path a need I cannot refuse.
26. I experience so much fullness and I taste the promise
27. Of your support.
28. For surely when I dare to go where I fear to go,
29. I become aware of the security of your friendship.
30. And my eyes are on your face in the faces of those I meet,
31. And my feet are freed for walking.
32. Keep looking at me, and look after me,
33. For I feel so very alone and unsure
34. I drain my energies wrestling with the unknown
35. And my destination remains but a shadow (pp. 333–334).

LINKING METANOIA TO ANTENARRATIVE

Both authors' experiences are portrayed as a metanoia experience. Any individual who is experiencing a metanoia will state this is a before story or an antenarrative because of the unpredictability of the current encounter. After having the metanoia the person becomes reflective or is looking back and thus the story becomes living. By retelling these two living stories, similar themes begin to evolve explaining why a metanoia is an antenarrative. It should be noted that when a person is moving through a metanoia the eventual story is evolving, which is why it's an antenarrative. Because it is experiential, it is only through the experience that the final living story is revealed.

What follows is a table that explains why a metanoia experience is considered an antenarrative. Using Boje's explanation of antenarrative, the following table was designed to compare and contrast antenarrative to metanoia. So far the chapter has established that an antenarrative is a pre-story or looking ahead. In other words, the living story is evolving; therefore it does not have a true BME yet. In the same context a metanoia is a pre-story where the leader is looking forward, while their behavior is morphing. The final outcome of the story may take time, but as the actual metanoia takes place the leader is beginning to move through personal transformation.

Using the table's themes, several explanations are made as to why metanoias are considered antenarratives. From these explanations a narrative analysis of the two stories can be developed to better understand the metanoia experience.

Unpredictable

The unpredictability of a metanoia means it's unplanned, spontaneous, unexpected, or unprompted. In the first story, Boje receives 12 bags of chips unexpectedly and links the event to a sign from God. Because the event is spontaneous, Boje is not sure why this is happening and the story is fragmented; therefore, it's considered a pre-story. There is no cohesive accomplishment of a narrative where we see a BME to the story. We are

Table 5.1   Comparison of Metanoia to Antenarrative

Theme	Metanoia	Antenarrative
Unpredictable	Unexplained, unplanned, and spontaneous	Fragmented, non-linear, incoherent, and unplotted
Not a Story Yet	The story is beginning to evolve, morphing	Pre-narrative specula-tion or being before
Undetermined Out-comes	Not sure what will happen	Asks the question "What next?"
Forward Looking	Anticipate the outcome and even have expectations of personal transformation	A collective memory
Becoming a Living Story	After the metanoia occurs it becomes retrospective—metanoias occur again or loop back	Eventually the antena-rrative becomes a living story with a BME

left guessing what will happen to Boje and we try to piece the pre-story together to generate some type of meaning.

In the second story King David (KD) is in the process of repeating another journey called metanoia. The author can only describe what happened in the past, but now he is not sure what the new metanoia experience will reveal. KD mentions in his personal journal that "new moments of fidelity" will occur but he is not sure what the outcome will be. The key point in using the term 'unpredictability' is that both the antenarrative and metanoia are answering the question "What is going on here?"

Not a Story Yet

Throughout both stories there are comments by both authors indicating their experiences are evolving and it is "not a story yet." Both authors are moving through their metanoia experience hoping to find out the true meaning of their experience. With metanoias the person is morphing and experiencing a personal transformation with an unpredictable outcome. In the same context, antenarrative is a pre-story or a before story and, as Boje stated in his definition of antenarrative, the story is also morphing.

Undetermined Outcomes

With both the antenarrative and metanoia there is no predetermined outcome. Not having the ability to predict the outcome, both authors are telling their story with a bet on a future outcome that is life changing. As the antenarrative begins to evolve from the metanoia experience, the person becomes emotionally charged because the leader is working through a radical change in the way they feel and think. As the person describes their emotions we are not quite sure how the person's behavior will be transformed. In Boje's story he discovered a new construct called spiritual leadership. From his experience he adapts a more meditative state or prayerful approach to his leadership.

In KD's case he begins to describe his transformation as having a greater security in God and building new relationships with others. Although David has a transformational outcome, uncertainty was always on his mind.

Forward Looking

Having the ability to predict the future always brings about a sense of comfort and assurance. With any outcome, necessary adjustments are made to reduce stress. The metanoia experience involves unpredictability about the future as one awaits future outcomes. Once the outcome is known, the person takes on a new outlook of how to lead. The same is true with antenarratives; the story is evolving and the future is being formed as the person creates their story. Once the story is complete, the person uses personal reflection (looking backwards) to better understand the situation and study lessons learned. From these lessons the person can look forward with new behavior and perspective.

Becomes a Living Story

Once the antenarrative is complete, it now has a BME and is retold as a living story for others to learn from. Maybe the story will lie dormant for a period a time, but retold to bring about new meaning for others. As others analyze these living stories again, new perspectives bring about new meaning and purpose in those reading the story.

IMPLICATIONS FOR LEADERS

This section points out significant implications leaders gain from using antenarratives to better understand individuals as they move through change in the workplace. The only constant variable in the workplace is change, where individuals begin to feel a sense of loss, anger, frustration, and grief. Many are looking for answers to their pain and frequently look to leadership to carry their burdens and come up with new solutions. This period of confusion or uncertainty leads to leadership sensemaking.

Sensemaking

There are many definitions of sensemaking; for me it is the transformation of raw experience into intelligible worldviews. It's a bit like what mapmakers do when they try to make sense of an unfamiliar place by capturing it on paper. But the crucial point in cartography is that there is no one best map of a particular terrain. Similarly, sensemaking lends itself to multiple, conflicting interpretations, all of which are plausible.

Sensemaking involves turning circumstances into a situation that can be comprehended in words and moves towards a springboard of action. Using sensemaking means looking backwards to rationalize what people are doing or answering the question "What does this event mean?" People are essentially saying, This event makes no sense and want to know what the story is. Answering the question "What's the story?" emerges from retrospect, connections with past experience, and dialogue among people. Answers to the question "Now what?" emerge from presumptions about the future, articulation concurrent with action, and projects that become increasingly clear as they unfold. When people then ask "Now what should I do?" this added question has the force of bringing meaning into existence, meaning that they hope is stable enough for them to act into the future, continue to act, and to have the sense that they remain in touch with the continuing flow of experience.

Changed Behavior

As leaders, the tendency is to fix the situation as well as the individual. However, the individual is going through an emotionally charged experience with uncertain outcomes. Emotions and behavior are raw and as leaders we should be aware of their pain. Managerial books have failed when people are searching for meaning and a reason to hope for the future. What these books have failed in doing, leaders can do in times of confusion and collective pain (Dutton, Frost, Worline, Lilius, & Kanov, 2002). During times of confusion and pain, leaders demonstrate acts of compassion which influence a response by others to be compassionate in the organization.

'Compassion' means to be together with someone's pain. The prefix 'com' means together with and the word 'passion' has the same root as the word 'pain' (Heifetz & Linsky, 2002). According to Boyatzis, Smith, and Blaize (2006), compassion is defined as having three components: (1) empathy or understanding the feelings of others, (2) caring for the other person, and (3) willingness to act in response to the person's feelings. Compassionate leadership is characterized by long enduring leadership which makes a positive difference (Briner & Pritchard, 1997). A compassionate leader is one who seeks the greatest good for the individual, the group, and the mission (Briner & Pritchard, 1997). The compassionate leader feels the pain of individuals and seeks to help them reach their goals, aspirations, and dreams (Briner & Pritchard, 1997; Boyatzis, Smith, & Blaize, 2006).

Leaders can come alongside those who are feeling the pain of change and listen to their antenarrative stories. After listening to the emotions of the individual, the leader can identify behavior traits and determine the willingness of the person to move through change. The antenarrative discussion helps the leader to begin predicting the outcome from the stories, although the story is still morphing. This brings the leader closer to the workplace rather than making reactionary decisions after the story is complete.

By listening and interpreting antenarratives of individuals, the leader's intentions are to serve others, which creates meaning and purpose in the inner self. This then creates an organizational culture where caring for others and self initiates a sense of membership and value.

CONCLUSION

To summarize, this chapter highlights several distinguishing features of metanoia and antenarratives. Both come from a genesis of disruptive ambiguity or a sense of uncertainty. Not knowing what the future story will become, the individual is asking "Now what?" As the story evolves through personal transformation, the individual begins to experience a change in the way they feel and think.

Unfortunately we hear about the story after it happens and ask the question "What's the story?" Being retrospective, the person retells their story. However, the new story will become an antenarrative when the individual asks the question again "Now what?" and begins to bet on the future. The metanoia experience loops back where we see individuals have multiple metanoias and experience multiple transpersonal shifts of mind. This type of antenarrative is best described as a cycle antenarrative rather than linear.

Leaders need to recognize that individuals are moving through their emotions and feelings trying to discover meaning and purpose in their lives. Knowing this, leaders must listen to the stories of others and begin to anticipate what the ending behavior of the individual will be.

REFERENCES

Benefiel, M. (2005). The second half of the journey: Spiritual leadership for organizational transformation. *The Leadership Quarterly, 16*(5), 723–747.

Biberman, J., & Whitty, M. (2005) (Eds.). *The spirit and work reader* (introduction). Retrieved August 8, 2008, from http://business.nmsu.edu/~dboje/Conferences/IntrotoSpritualCapitalism.html

Boje, D. M. (1991). Organizations as storytelling networks: A study of story performance in an office-supply firm. *Administrative Science Quarterly, 36,* 106–126.

———. (1994). Organizational storytelling: The struggles of premodern, modern, & postmodern organizational learning discourses. *Management Learning Journal, 25*(3), 433–461.

———. (1995). Stories of the storytelling organization: A postmodern analysis of Disney as "Tamara-Land." *Academy of Management Journal, 38*(4), 997–1035.

———. (1999, June 29). *Storytelling leaders* (lecture notes). Retrieved December 15, 2007, from http://business.nmsu.edu/~dboje/leaders.html

———. (2000a). Approaches to the study of spiritual capitalism. pp. xxv–xxxii in Jerry Biberman & Michael D. Witty (EDS.) "Workplace and Spirit." Scranton Il. University of Scranton Press.

———. (2000b). *Theatrics of leadership: Leaders as storytellers and thespians.* Retrieved December 15, 2007, from http://business.nmsu.edu/~dboje/teaching/338/theatrics_of_leadership_links.htm

———. (2001). *Narrative methods for organizational and communication research.* London: Sage.

———. (2008). What is antenarrative? Draft available at: http://cbae.nmsu.edu/~dboje/papers/what_is_antenarrative.htm

Boyatzis, R. E., Smith, M. L., & Blaize, N. (2006). Developing sustainable leaders through coaching compassion. *Academy of Management Learning & Education, 5*(1), 9–24.

Briner, B., & Pritchard, R. (1997). Compassionate leadership. *Executive Excellence, 14*(19), 6.

Dutton, J. E., Frost, P. J, Worline, M. C., Lilius, J. M., & Kanov, J. M. (2002). Leading in times of trauma. *American Dietetic Association, 102*(7), 1014.

Edwards, T. (1997). Shalem news. *Shalem Institute for Spiritual Formation, 21*(1).

Fairholm, G. W. (1996). Spiritual leadership: Fulfilling whole-self needs at work. *Leadership & Organization Development Journal, Bradford, 17*(5), 11.

Fry, L. W. (2003). Toward a theory of spiritual leadership. *The Leadership Quarterly, 14*(6), 693–727.

Heifetz, R., & Linsky, M. (2002). *Leadership on the line.* Boston: Harvard Business School Press.

Howard, S. (2002). A spiritual perspective on learning in the workplace. *Journal of Managerial Psychology, 17*(3), 230–242.

Korac-Kakabadse, N., Kouzmin, A., and Kakabadse, A. (2002). Spirituality and leadership praxis. *Journal of Managerial Psychology,17*(3), 165–182.

Kriger, M. P., & Seng, Y. (2005). Leadership with inner meaning: A contingency theory of leadership based on the worldview of five religions. *The Leadership Quarterly, 16,* 771–806.

Maher, M., & Bolland, J. (1912). Soul. In *The Catholic Encyclopedia.* New York: Robert Appleton Company. Retrieved August 30, 2009, from New Advent: http://www.newadvent.org/cathen/14153a.htm

Mitroff, I. I., & Denton, E. A. (1999). A study of spirituality in the workplace. *Sloan Management Review, 40*(4), 83–92.

Moore, T. (2004). *Dark night of the soul.* New York: Gotham Books.

Puls, J. (1983). The journey that is metanoia: A paraphrase of Psalms 25. *International Review of Mission, 72*(287), 333–334.

Reave, L. (2005). Spiritual values and practices related to leadership effectiveness. *The Leadership Quarterly, 16*(5), 655–687.

Rokeach, M. (1973). *The nature of human values.* New York: Free Press.

Ryle, G. (1949). *The concept of mind.* Totowa, NJ: Barnes & Noble.

Sanford, J. A. (1970). The *kingdom within: The inner meaning of Jesus' sayings.* Philadelphia: J. B. Lippincott.

Sayward, C. (1983, December). Minds, substances, and capabilities. *Philosophy and Phenomenological Research, 44*(2), 213–225.

Shawchuck, N., & Heuser, R. (1996). *Managing the congregation.* Nashville, TN: Abingdon Press.

Yolles, M. (2007). The dynamics of narrative and antenarrative and their relation to story. *Journal of Organizational Change Management, 20*(1), 74–94.

6 Understanding Legal Antenarratives

Majella O'Leary and Kim Economides

INTRODUCTION

How should one understand and interpret the stories that lawyers tell? In this chapter we extrapolate methodological lessons arising out of our previous research investigating stories that reveal latent ethical dilemmas in legal organizations (Economides & O'Leary, 2007). Lawyers' narrative accounts may appear superficial, fragmented, or inconclusive because often there is no resolution of underlying tensions that underpin professional and business conduct. As social scientists interested in collecting and analyzing qualitative data, we have become increasingly drawn to narrative analysis. The explanatory power of stories and narrative knowledge in the wider study of contemporary organizations has been well documented, but these resources remain underutilized in studies of legal professionalism. Brown, Gabriel, and Gherardi (2009, p. 1) link narrative with organizational research, arguing that stories often contain moral judgments, are replete with deeper meaning, and frequently elicit strong emotional reactions. There is now a well-established tradition of research on narrative and storytelling in organizations (see, e.g., Boje, 1991, 1995, 2001, 2008; Currie & Brown, 2003; Czarniawska, 1997, 1998; Gabriel, 1991, 1995, 2000; Humphreys & Brown, 2002; Watson, 2000). Despite this progress, legal scholarship has concentrated narrative analysis on literary jurisprudence, with a few ethnographic studies using conversational analysis to explain relations between lawyers and their clients, both in court and in law offices. So far as we are aware, we are the first research team to apply narrative methods to legal and ethical decision making within the provincial law firm.

Having carried out extensive narrative research on the newspaper and financial sectors (see O'Leary & Chia, 2007; Knights & O'Leary, 2005; O'Leary, 2003) where research participants 'performed' by providing us with plentiful stories containing well-developed plots and characters, conjuring up rich organizational histories, we embarked on our narrative research in law firms in the belief that these were organizations containing significant repositories of stories. After all, lawyers are accomplished storytellers; and legal training, at least since ancient Greece and Rome, involved teaching advocacy (moral and legal) through an oral tradition placing heavy emphasis on rhetoric, dialectical reasoning, and the art of conversation (see, e.g., Berman, 1983). However, what we encountered was nervous apprehension as lawyers struggled to describe dilemmas arising out of their professional experience. Our seemingly hesitant informants perhaps did not appreciate the relevance of their personal stories or were concerned they might constitute a breach of confidence. We experienced strained encounters and listened to stories without detailed character, action, plot, mood, scenes—all the things we had come to expect and value. Lawyers' stories were at first glance somewhat superficial and failed to reveal any deep insights revealing the true nature of professional practice. At first we questioned our research methods: had we failed to develop rapport with our research participants? Or perhaps, rather than exposing limitations of our research technique, this lack of poetics may have revealed another quite different process: the narrative deskilling of modern organizations (Gabriel, 2000).

Eventually, we came to accept that not all of our research subjects were accomplished storytellers, and that parts of their professional lives needed to be shielded from interviewers. But most importantly, the stories we heard were terse, fragmented, and uncertain but mainly because the moral and professional issues typically facing lawyers invariably are very complex. Narrative coherence may be missing because often there is no resolution of the underlying and unstated ethical issues. The stories we heard often lacked detailed character, action, plot, mood, scenes, and so on—all the things normally associated with a coherent story—and many of our legal stories were in fact fragmented and inchoate, if not incoherent. Neither did the stories inform us of a rich history about the law firms; they certainly were not nostalgic. But this in itself is interesting and reveals something of the isolation of the individual lawyer as they grapple with ethical issues. The narratives were in fact often prospective and reflected underlying tensions the modern law firm struggles with as commercialization intensifies and commercial values conflict with professional ethics. The lawyers' narratives essentially are *antenarrative*: they are future-orientated and, on occasion, they display real bravery in facing up to a difficult and uncertain future.

Here we introduce our study of lawyers' antenarratives told by lawyers as they reflect on moral dilemmas arising in everyday work settings. Our broad aim was to examine the moral experience of lawyers in provincial practice. Our sample, based on 20 lawyers, was drawn from different firms across two cities, each with populations approximating 130,000. A series of in-depth interviews was carried out with lawyers representative of different echelons within their firms, ranging from new recruits to senior and retired partners, who also covered contentious and noncontentious legal work, and included specialists in criminal law, employment law, intellectual property, family law, personal injury, and commercial property. Each was asked to reflect on a situation where they faced an ethical dilemma whilst practicing law and to explain how they handled it. What lessons, if any, emerged—both for them and their firm—from the experience? More generally, we asked how particular law firms, or individual lawyers within them, learnt about ethical practice. We were far more interested in understanding processes for handling everyday ethical dilemmas and the induction of new recruits in professional conduct and culture than exposing the atypical, extraordinary practices of egregious lawyers that so often attract extensive media attention.

Our informants attempted to tell us stories as they reflected on the ethical dilemmas they experienced in their working lives. Through these stories we hoped to glimpse the embedded nature of ethical reasoning eclipsed by dominant positivist traditions in legal education and expose the emotional and ideological underpinnings that support practical legal reasoning, or 'thinking like a lawyer.' These stories hint at what may lie beyond the formal codes that purport to govern professional conduct and permit unique insight into how ordinary legal professionals in fact reconcile public and professional duties with private conscience. They reveal mostly the fears of lawyers about where the profession is heading.

Some lawyers struggled to think of ethical dilemmas, suggesting that they mechanically applied formal rules, whether substantive or procedural, and that therefore ethical dilemmas did not arise. As one participant observed: *Normally in law morality is drained out of the situation . . . ethics is not present in the practical training of lawyers . . .* They tentatively considered the issue of breaching client confidentiality as a 'safe' place to begin discussing ethics. This issue of client confidentiality was a common starting point for many of the lawyers and they deployed antenarrative as a kind of 'ground clearance' operation that prepared the way for deeper consideration of ethical conduct.

CONFIDENTIALITY

The implications of breaching client confidentiality typically sprung to mind when lawyers were asked to consider ethical dilemmas. The following narratives are antenarrative in the sense of 'preparing the ground' for a more serious discussion yet to come; they are experimental narratives in that they are used to explore the possibility of sharing more serious ethical dilemmas having established trust and rapport. This first antenarrative is set in a social rather than legal setting:

> *The nearest I ever came to breaking confidentiality was when I was involved in a case where one of the parties had a large art collection.*

> *I was out at a professional/social occasion. We were talking about art and a particular artist and I said, I have a case where my client has a large collection by this artist. One of the guests at the gathering said "Oh, that must be X". He had identified my client. It can happen easily in a small area.*

The characters here lack depth but the story could be seen as a useful 'throat-clearing' exercise allowing the lawyer to discuss the border separating his professional from his social life and how professionalism may be tested outside the physical boundary of either the law firm or court. This narrative is not elegant but is a useful 'icebreaker' that helps establish moral orientation and test the trust between the research subject and researcher. Confidentiality appears as an issue in which lawyers expected researchers to be interested once the concept of ethics is introduced. A very similar story shows how important it is to 'think before you speak,' especially in informal settings outside the office, in order to preserve client confidentiality:

> *I have divorced a significant number of clients in [the city] especially accountants and also barristers and solicitors. You can be constantly faced with ethical dilemmas when out socialising. At a drinks party at an accounting firm, one of the senior partners (a former client) introduced me to his colleague saying, "Oh, she did my divorce, she's excellent" and added to his colleague, "Oh you've done this before [got a divorce] but if you want to do it again, this is the woman you want to hire"! I was actually acting against this colleague in a very acrimonious divorce but of course I said nothing and just danced around the room to get away. Later he came up to thank me for maintaining confidentiality. For commercial lawyers that doesn't usually arise as a dilemma, they want to publicly announce whom they've worked for, but not so for family lawyers.*

The implications of breaching confidentiality here could appear relatively trivial but the story provides a safe testing ground to examine ethical dilemmas more thoroughly and to consider the wider context such as the increasing pressure on law firms to embrace commercial values. In the following account, disclosure is required by legislation, but although the lawyer begins with certitude on the need to report his client, this clarity soon gives way to uncertainty as other considerations are introduced:

> *If I know a client is involved in money laundering, even if it is just a suspicion, I have to report it even if it is a breach of client confidentiality. Do you betray a client if you have only a suspicion? And what if the client was regarded as invaluable to the business? Then you would be under serious pressure.*

This antenarrative prepares the ground for further discussion but also highlights the fact that ethical dilemmas for lawyers seem rooted in the future and relate to increased commercialization operating in an uncertain competitive environment that may well challenge, if not supersede, their professional code of ethics. The above account is certainly lacking in any closure and moves in the opposite direction to the narratives we are familiar with: it begins with some certainty about what constitutes professional ethics, raises serious concerns for future survival of the lawyer in both commercial and moral environments, and ends with the uncertainty of what will be possible/acceptable in the future. This uncertainty is also present in one of our few more 'poetic' stories with both plot and character and even linearity until the conclusion, where the narratives are incoherent and moral ambivalence remains:

> *We had an established client who came to us and reported that he had fallen down a lift. The lift gave way and he was badly injured and couldn't work. We were sent a video by the insurers showing our client up a ladder repairing his guttering . . . They had made him an offer and some of us thought he was malingering. However the lawyer running the case believed the client and instinctively felt that something wasn't quite right. In fact, what the insurance company had done was set up a camera outside our client's house and kept it there all day. He'd go up the ladder to fix the guttering but it would be too painful to stay up there for long so he'd come back down, so he was up and down all day; it took him ages to fix the guttering. But the insurers had edited the video in order to conceal his pain. If that lawyer hadn't believed the client, we'd have sold him short. After that he got a large sum of money. You should trust your judgement and trust your client. This to me focuses attention on what it is to be a good lawyer. . . . But lawyers won't always have the luxury of following their instincts like that and did the solicitors for the other side know that the video had been doctored?*

This story relates to a relatively ordinary case, although the lawyer involved cared enough to get the best deal possible for his client. What is interesting is that it is presented to us as a backlash against commercialization; lawyers are thinking about how they will promote ethical lawyering.

COMMERCIAL PRESSURES AND VALUES

One of the more dominant traits of legal practice in a competitive market is the imperative to be continually aware of commercial values. Trainees must therefore learn how to balance the need to be both profitable and professional. There are significant changes facing the business environment of law firms, and particularly following the Legal Services Act 2007, which opens up the legal services market to an unprecedented degree. This deregulation is not only confined to the UK legal profession. It appears to be global, in that professions almost everywhere are being forced to compete and to be accountable for their quality standards. Law is just one of many professions forced to accept a radical reshaping of its regulatory structure, and markets, at the start of the 21st century. In part this is due to external trends, for example, changing attitudes of competition authorities towards the profits professions have been able to accrue by virtue of their monopolistic power. This reflects a worldwide trend away from self-regulation towards external oversight over professional standards. Thus the introduction in the UK of the Legal Services Act 2007, which by 2011 will permit the establishment of Alternative Business Structures (ABS), structures that could well be owned by nonlawyers, fundamentally alters the legal landscape; and already Australia has allowed the formation of incorporated legal practices that are now listed on the stock exchange. There is therefore a huge potential for traditional ethical values to clash with newer intensified commercial ones. Similar pressures were noted 20 years ago when provincial lawyers pondered their futures post the Courts and Legal Services Act [CLSA] 1990, the legislation that began the process of breaking professional monopolies and signaling the loss of self-regulation for the legal profession, and opinion divided country lawyers into 'pessimists,' 'entrepreneurs,' 'specialists,' and 'fatalists,' with each group deploying different narratives predicting radically contrasting future outcomes (Economides, 1992, p. 118). Indeed, the pressure to put profit before clients is already with lawyers, as seen here in the following antenarratives that relate to a future already beginning to be played out:

> *I raised a concern with a senior lawyer that my client was pursuing an uneconomic case, and that we should really try to dissuade the client from being so gung-ho. My colleague advised me that if the client wanted to tear up £50 notes and flush them down the loo that was their prerogative. This is a great concern as competition intensifies and with the way things are going who knows if I will be forced to take clients who have no chance of winning their case.*

There is a fear that commercial pressure will place lawyers in a position where they are working against their personal code of ethics, and there is a sense that lawyers will need to protect themselves from such pressures and strive to maintain a sense of professional duty:

> *I have already experienced a compromising situation and we will all increasingly face these pressures. I was assigned to a case at completion where some well-known people were buying a parcel of land near . . . from another firm of solicitors . . . it was a tax scam . . . the boss asked me to shred the files . . . do you do what the boss wants not just think about what the client wants? . . . there is also the duty to the court*

... these are the dilemmas young lawyers will face ... they need to be aware of these pressures before they enter the profession ... they need to be aware of the drivers that can lead them astray.

The senior lawyer just mentioned believes that young lawyers are ill-prepared to cope with the moral dilemmas they will increasingly encounter in corporate law firms. He suggests a need for ethics training in order to give lawyers some basis for decision making when there is pressure from the firm.

There are courageous lawyers who claim that they would never be driven by commercial pressures and would always protect the vulnerable. We were told of lawyers who put themselves at personal risk of financial loss or even physical violence. What surprised us was the degree to which stories revealed both the vulnerability and modesty of lawyers themselves. This contrasted with the popular image of lawyers as being arrogant, opinionated, and always right. For example, lawyers on occasion believe strongly enough in a case that, although they know they may lose, they will still pursue it:

But there will always be cases where I am willing to act though I know I won't be paid, eg a custody case ... you look after the vulnerable. And in medical negligence cases ... I know of a solicitor who went the distance in the High Court and then to the House of Lords, then lost. But he was conscientious and believed in his client's case even though he knew that the client wouldn't have the means to pay him. He had 50 days in court in [another city] all on his own expenses. He makes a good role model.

Here the lawyer makes a promise with himself not to be swayed by a profit motive. In the aforementioned antenarrative, the lawyer refers to a role model; and indeed, the discussion of morality in the context of increasing commercialization shifts towards what it means and, more importantly, what it will mean to be a good lawyer.

THE GOOD LAWYER

The discussion swiftly moved to consider what it meant to be a good lawyer and whether this is likely to change as a result of increased commercialization. In this changing environment, what constitutes a good lawyer? Already, new recruits are told stories about 'going the extra mile' in the more commercial firms, stories which emphasize the profit motive which should underlie decisions.

There was a major client and a deal that had to be completed in a day. The deal involved development of land but there was one old guy who wouldn't move out. It has been his family home for generations. [Senior lawyer often held up as a role model] suggested personally visiting the old guy in his house. The old guy moaned about having to move this and that and said he'd need £200 (they thought it would cost thousands). This story is about being practical . . . some are good on the law but not very practical, they wouldn't think of turning up at the old guys home.

New recruits told us how expectations were set in terms of establishing a punishing work ethic that would be rewarded:

Peter, a commercial lawyer is held up to us as a good role model because of the sheer hard work he does, the hours he puts in. He has very demanding clients in commercial property. He brings a sleeping bag in and stays all night when necessary. This is what is expected of us in terms of values, dedication, clocking up hours . . .

Here again brave attempts are made to resist the profit motive, and to promote the notion that being a good lawyer involved striving for a good outcome for everyone. This seemed particularly important to some family lawyers who thought they had a greater moral responsibility to third parties as well as their immediate clients and that not everything can be subordinated to a dominant business culture:

As a family lawyer I won't just be governed by what is profitable for the firm. I must be able to take on board the impact of e.g. a divorce on others. A good family lawyer will always do this. You take the client down the road they are going to a conclusion and you explain the full consequences of what they are trying to do . . . The client I disliked most was the client who has most money. He was obnoxious and evil. He was most intelligent but had never been to school. He was a dealer, pure evil. He hated his wife and there was absolutely no reasoning with him at all. She had gone off with someone else and who could blame her. There was no reasoning with him. I kept thinking, you are quite evil. He was quite scary to act for because he was so intelligent. In the end, the only thing that I could do was to take him down the painful path where he would consider what would happen to his children if he proceeded in this way. I gave him a book about the effect of divorce on children and said before you go on, you must tell me that you have read this book. That produced a slight moderating influence on him. So I went the extra mile, I tried to change his behaviour although this was beyond the call of duty. I will always take clients on this journey to see the pain they will cause if they pursue their case regardless of how much money they have . . .

In the preceding account, the lawyer reflects on how she herself uses pro-spective storytelling as a means of achieving a fair outcome; she takes the client on a journey into the future in order to make clear the consequences of their legal action. The following lawyer is sensitive to the importance of ethics because, she argues, often formal legal rules run out. An ethical law-yer is one who protects his/her client, considers their well-being, but also is aware of wider duties to the court, to third parties, and possibly the public interest. This is far from the cynical commercial attitude:

> *As a young lawyer, I was in a mediation session. I saw the hairs on the back of the man's neck rise. My instinct told me something was wrong. The mediation finished and I spoke briefly to the client afterwards. But I left her and as she walked down through the car park he as-saulted her. I was a size 8 23 year old. None of the court security staff did anything but I ran down and got between them. Things flow out beyond the case. It is important not to leave a client behind. Today, I will always walk out with my client. Even in a controlled environment things can happen. It's about thinking down the line. Rules run out. Being a good lawyer means knowing what to do when the rules run out. This is what I will continue to teach to new recruits.*

The research we have presented depicts legal antenarratives of the moral struggle lawyers face as a result of the increased commercialization facing the legal sector. Lawyers begin with restraint and caution, some implying that the law is totalizing and there can be no ethical dilemmas for lawyers that the law won't provide an answer to. As they begin to reflect on the ethical dilemmas they confront, first through the exploration of the rela-tively benign antenarratives of confidentiality, they consider how the future might play out. Through antenarrative they recognize the importance of ethics and how, on occasion, the law is not enough. They begin to foresee a threatening future where morality and professional values will be displaced by commercial pressures as new legal structures emerge (some antenarra-tives depict this future as having already begun). The significant role of antenarrative, however, is to generate a courageous response and to demon-strate what it really means to be a good lawyer and how moral values can be preserved and passed on to new recruits. The antenarratives are at once a vow to be guided by professional values and a call to action.

REFLECTIONS AND CONCLUSIONS
ON LEGAL ANTENARRATIVES

The legal story space of law firms consists of few rich stories of organiza-tional history, with beginnings, middles, and endings. Even the one almost 'poetic' story we heard—that of the doctored video—although possessing a plot and some coherence, unravels before it ends with ambiguity over the future. Instead of poetic stories, we have terse stories—that of spending the night in the office—which embrace commercial values and antenarratives of possible futures.

The lawyers' narratives were certainly not nostalgic but neither were they postalgic (Ybeme 2004, p. 1), depicting an idealized future. Instead, these fragile prospectors related events of the past as a means of reflecting on the future and with some hope for changing that future (Boje. 2008, pp. 13–14). The antenarratives move in a linear fashion as past events are described but coherence is avoided at the last minute and they end in uncertainty. The antenarratives relate to a threatening future but are also a response to that future and an imagining of a better more ethical one. Through the antenarratives the lawyers talk themselves into action. Those who seemed isolated as they considered their moral dilemmas begin to consider the collective and call for formal ethics education, and indeed the antenarratives have been the seed for the development of ethics training for future solicitors (Economides & Rogers, 2009). The prospective futuring may be used too in order to educate the client to be responsible for the possible outcome of a legal action, and indeed our family lawyers already use this approach in divorce cases (see further Sarat & Felstiner, 1986). Perhaps lawyers' skills in storytelling are not so much about the generation of a coherent or poetic narrative as we first believed when embarking on this research, but instead involve creating an altruistic, even courageous, response to the future. The fragile legal antenarratives can perhaps be "the most powerful transformative sense-making of all" (Boje, 2008, p. 14).

REFERENCES

Berman, H. J. (1983). *Law and revolution. The formation of the Western legal tradition.* Boston: Harvard University Press.

Boje, D. M. (1991). The storytelling organization: A study of story performance in an office supply firm. *Administrative Science Quarterly, 36*, 106–126.

———. (1995). Stories of the storytelling organization: A postmodern analysis of Disney as "Tamara-Land." *Academy of Management Journal, 38*(4), 997–1035.

———. (2001). *Narrative methods for organizational and communication research.* London: Sage.

———. (2008). *Storytelling in organizations.* Los Angeles: Sage.

Brown, A. D., Gabriel, Y., & Gherardi, S. (2009). Storytelling and change: An unfolding story. *Organization, 16*(3), 323–333

Currie, G., & Brown, A. (2003). A narratological approach to understanding processes of organizing in a UK hospital. *Human Relations, 56*(5), 563–586.

Czarniawska, B. (1997). *Narrating the organization.* Chicago: University of Chicago Press.

———. (1998). *A narrative approach in organizational studies.* London: Sage.

Economides, K (1992). The country lawyer: Iconography, iconoclasm, and the restoration of the professional image. In P. A. Thomas (Ed.), *Tomorrow's lawyers* (pp. 115–123). Oxford: Blackwell.

Economides, K., & O'Leary, M. (2007). The moral of the story: Toward an understanding of ethics in organizations and legal practice. *Legal Ethics, 10*(1): 5–26.

Economides, K., & Rogers, J. (2009). *Preparatory ethics training for future solicitors.* (The Law Society, London, available at: http://www.lawsociety.org.uk/influencinglaw/policyinresponse/view=article.law?DOCUMENTID=419357)

Gabriel, Y. (1991). Turning facts into stories and stories into facts: A hermeneutic exploration of organizational folklore. *Human Relations, 44*(8), 857–875.

———. (1995). The unmanaged organization: Stories, fantasies and subjectivity. *Organization Studies, 16*, 477–502.

———. (2000). *Storytelling in organizations.* New York: Oxford University Press.

Humphreys, M., & Brown, A. D. (2002) 'Narratives of Organizational Identity and Identification: A Case Study of Hegemony and Resistance' *Organization Studies* May 2002 23: 421–447.

Knights, D., & O'Leary, M. (2005). Reflecting on corporate scandals: The failure of ethical leadership. *Business Ethics: A European Review, 14*(3), 186–199.

O'Leary, M. (2003). From paternalism to cynicism: Narratives of a newspaper company. *Human Relations, 56*(6), 685–704.

O'Leary, M., & Chia, R. (2007). Epistemes and structures of sensemaking in organizational life. *Journal of Management Inquiry, 16*(4), 392–407.

Sarat, A., & Felstiner, W. L. F. (1986). Law and strategy in the divorce lawyer's office. *Law & Society Review, 20*(1), 94–134.

Watson, T. J. (2000). Ethnographic fiction science: Making sense of managerial work and organizational research processes with Caroline and Tony. *Organization, 7*(3), 489–510.

Ybema, Sierk (2004) "Managerial postalgia: projecting a golden future", *Journal of Managerial Psychology, 19*(8), pp.825–841

Part II
Organization and Writing Antenarratives

Introduction to Part II
Organization and Writing Antenarratives

In **Jo Tyler's** Chapter 7, the organization she studies makes escalators. She points out that the dominant narratives that organizations like to tell about themselves routinely compete with living stories webs of relationships from the margins and shadows of an organization. In the case of a tragic workplace accident, an organization's grand narrative of safety is especially challenged. Tyler's analysis of antenarrative explores the intra-play between dominant historical narratives the company puts out, and the living, emergent, unfolding stories of the accidents and those intimately and tragically involved. As Tyler puts it, "These living stories may reveal actual practices in the organization that are challenging, sad, and that are out of alignment with the espoused organizational texts in the dominant narrative." In writing the storytelling, Tyler cautions us to watch how the authors of dominant narratives try to force fit a plot structure that cuts off the energetic vitality of the living (organic) stories, and pushes back an antenarrative that is more the spiral and rhizome-assemblage than any play it forward dominant narrative attempts to script a linear future. The antenarrating is a process with a trajectory. The organization participants fuel the antenarrating with desire for more, both for conforming linear futures and for those futures that spiral in non-linear more unpredictable timespace.

Lynette Drevin and **Darren Dalcher's** Chapter 8 looks at how actors antenarrate in the information systems world. They use a microstoria analysis to assess the little people's living stories that don't fit into or are just excluded from the dominant retro-narrative accounts of information system change in universities. These smaller voices often cannot be heard in the coherent dominant narrative's preference for bigger voices, higher up in the university totem pole. The web of living stories connections have 'too many versions' circulating, and the web keeps changing in relation to the plurality of contextual situations. Then there is the whole buy-in process where the antenarrating renegotiates the relation between past and future (in linear modes) or the antenarrating between present living story emergence that the futures with less linear foreshadows. The authors identify the contribution of the antenarrative approach as identifying and watching information system problem areas, such as small living stories of the Present, all swept away by the traditional narratology approaches. Narratives just over-generalize, tidy-up, and highlight, but miss the antenarrative stakeholder negotiated process of engagement and buy-in.

Yue Cai, myself, and **Clarinda Dir's** Chapter 9 focuses on strategy antenarrating in situations of complexity. They frame their contribution in pointing out that while there has been important work on antenarrative (such as by the authors of this book), in the field of strategy, which is all about shaping the future, the concept of antenarrative has not gained recognition in those coveted tier one journals of the Academy that determine ones tenure and promotion. Traditional approaches to strategy outside Barry and Elmes 1997 Academy of Management Review article, on storytelling and strategy, seem to stick to the traditional more linear antenarratives of the future, those linear planning models, with the coherent action plans, that pretend the future will be a progress narrative replay of the past. Traditional strategy approaches are backward looking, training students in case courses to plan for the future by analyzing retrospective narratives of the past. Antenarrative approaches to strategy can help organizations break free of being stuck in the past by trying to replicate it in some linear progress narrative. Antenarratives, such as spiral and assemblage, are more open-ended. The marginal living stories struggle to become those future dominant strategic narrative centers that can move a firm away from the blindness of a linear progress narrative, or some recurring cycle of organization and market stages (birth, growth, maturation, and decline). Strategy is obviously future oriented, but the problem with replicating dead narratives is a sort of Disney-effect occurs, with everyone asking, "What would Walt have done? Let's make that our strategic plan!" The danger is instead of looking at the Here and Now unfolding situation environment, the strategy makers cannot forget their dominant narrative way of antenarrating the same old future. The little exception living stories emergent Now, and one accumulating under the carpet (swept under the rug) need to antenarrate to deconstruct the dominant narrative strategy, especially when the situation has shifted radically. The chapter authors remind us that antenarratives persist in all shapes and varieties, and are dialogically negotiating the field of future potentialities. Just picking one dominant narrative is good for focus and branding, but leaves the antenarrative negotiation process in Morson's backshadows, sideshadows, and foreshadows. Yue Cai, in particular in this chapter, builds upon her dissertation study of how ten Mintzberg et al strategy schools. For example, the 'design strategy school' looks at how to create uniqueness, clarity and simplicity , iin narratives. Most strategy courses teach students under the label SWOT (strengths, weaknesses, opportunities, and threats). The positioning school focuses more on tactics of dealing with competitors, suppliers, etc. The leader in the entrepreneurial school is often characterized in a narrative as the heroic innovator, creating by acts of destruction of the old ruts to bring about some glorious new future.

Design and planning strategy schools are more mechanistic, more linear narrative, than the more organic-adaptive positioning and entrepreneurial schools. The chapter authors look at how to develop some alternative antenarrative strategy approaches, such as more cyclical and rhizomatic processes. The authors look at a proposition: antenarratives are most abundant prior to a strategic inflection, where different futures contend to be the next dominant strategy narrative. In the dialogical struggle, some living stories get silenced, others that emerge in a dynamic changing situation go unnoticed (the dominant narrative is too blinding to see them). Motorola Corporation is used as a context to explore the proposition.

Sergio Luis Seloti, Jr., and **Mário Aquino Alves'** Chapter 10 authors identify key sensemaking elements embedded in strategic alliance storytelling between competitors. They used the antenarrative method to study the multiple voices heard from newspapers and magazines, interviews, etc. as the fragments of storytelling of stakeholders assigning meaning to events. They noticed that interpretations of events by the competitors engaged in acts of cooperative alliance were so different as to constitute quite divergent sensemakings that led them to different alliance strategies and results. How is this possible? Seloti and Alves assert that the antenarrative process that makes alliances work out is quite tortuous and nonlinear path finding. Events vary in uncertainty and equivocality. The precedent events have an indeterminate wave (turbulent) effect and frequency into a particular field. The wave form carries into consequent events that can increase that uncertainty and equivocality as the antenarrating picks intra-plays with more contradictory interpretations, and as more information creates even more complexity to a situation. The events enactment process is therefore not only retrospective but prospective sensemaking, as the field of antenarrative futures widens and deepens with emergent strategies demanding quick decision responses, evoking more alternative scenarios for the strategic alliance that are unanticipated by retro-narrative sensemaking. And that explains why two alliance partners can do antenarrative enactment and sensemaking quite differently. In this theory move, the chapter authors make a significant contribution to Weickian sensemaking and enactment theories. It is the differences in the sensemaking practices of the alliance partners that allows them to process environment data differently. Further, the organization sensemaking processes are different from that of individuals because when people leave the organization, some sensemaking maps and norms remain. This means their ways of enactment are different. But how? While in the firm's employ, the individual(s) sensemaking preconception(s) is unique to each firm's environment situation. This uniqueness leads the sensemaking of the firm in different directions, and creates significant blind spots in antenarrating the future. In the blind spots significant environmental changes to a situation can go unnoticed in enactments by one or both of the alliance partners. In retrospective sensemaking the enactment process in prior work has only been viewed as a feedback cycle between environment and organizations, where retrospective information received and selected is retained in the enactment process. Seloti and Alves contribute the 'auto-realizable prophecies' type of antenarrative as synthetic to the (backward-looking) retrospective sensemaking. Hence Weickian sensemaking is related not just to the past, but also to antenarrative enactment processes, viewed as a wave function. The collaborative enactments among alliance partners as they antenarrate expand the field of possible futures, opening up more equivocality, co-generating options, making it less likely the alliance partners collude in a shared antenarrative enactment.

Teppo Sintonen and **Tommi Auvinen's** Chapter 11 uses sketches and drawings to visualize antenarrative sensemaking of the research process itself, as researchers make guesses about what happens in the flow of experience. Their major finding was that the research process was not contained in any sort of Beginning-Middle-End (BME) narrative. Attempts at linearity were dispelled by more spiral process drawings. Second, is the finding of a particular relationship between the physical act of drawing and the research process as an antenarrative unfolding and refolding occurring simultaneously in different places, as in the Tamara play. The drawings emerged and took physicality as the researchers made and read their interview transcripts. Drawings emerged at various times and places in the research process, not at any one time, or any concluding retro-glance backwards. In the antenarrating visualizations explore prospective sensemaking transformations as researchers picked up or drop out supplements, attachments, etc. in the unfolding enactment of each successive event context is negotiated but remains unfinalized. The chapter authors started drawing their intuition of material-things that existed elsewhere, and came into Being when they gave them figure, form, and thing-ness. The things existed elsewhere, but not in the Here and Now of their research. The thing-ness materiality emerged into physical existence in the linking of researcher drawings to antenarratives. A bet was made that the future-oriented prospective sensemaking drawings would enact futures be working out in drawings and sketches, clues to those futures. For example, the drawings pulled together embryonic ideas about the relationships between leaders and followers, as a story circulated around their organization. The drawings depict the empirical situation, the drawings becoming an actant (thing-actor) in the different times and places of the research process. In sum, Sintonen and Auvinen use antenarrative drawings to explore just how complex and nonlinear the research process can be. Theirs is a study of the dynamics of emplotment, as the heterogeneous relationship between concord and discord. The material texture of their drawings goes through acts of resemblance of composition, that allows multiple interpretations to co-exist. A concordant story can emerge as a consequence of drawing some emplotment, but does not conceive of the effects and influence each drawing has in the future by merely retrospective sensemaking (looking back on each drawing). This is because the living stories reduced to BME narrative sensemaking retrospections become the target for continuous sensemaking. The Tamara-aspect of the research process exemplifies that the Now-ness of the sensemaking (making sense Now). Researchers occupy particular physical spaces, but just as in the changing rooms of Tamara, they encounter a multitude of unexpected situations, and watch as their ideas veer off, flourish, change, or get written off. The drawings emerged in particular rooms, and material conditions. Yet, events occur simultaneous in other rooms, doing things the researchers are not aware of. They give the example of the Standing Conference for Management and Organization Inquiry (sc'MOI, see http://scmoi. org). The drawing s excited amazing interest in the conference participants. Chain reactions are set off in the various rooms, including sc'MOI, and the researchers heard new and unexpected stories from other in other rooms at the conference. The drawings, not the initial research topic, and the interest generated by the drawings, prompted the researchers into new directions. The main point of this chapter is that doing the antenarrative drawings generated unexpected experiences, led to further ideas in the future enactment of prospective sensemaking not controlled by BME retro-narrative, not pegged to some originary research question.

Anna Linda Musacchio Adorisio's Chapter 12 gives as true an account of the genealogy of antenarrative as I have ever read. Her focus is on the notion of antenarrative by highlighting the novelty of my articulation of the theory, and in the entering into the dynamic aspect of the relation between narrative and antenarrative. If we agree that narrative not only corresponds to a well-constructed account but rather to a crystallized version of it for an entire group or for an individual, we must recognize that forces towards narrative control are always at play in organizational contexts, at an individual as well as at a collective level, and can be detected at the utterance level. The stabilization of antenarratives into narratives can depend on the strength that ties an individual to a certain identity that 'drives' certain versions of the facts rather than others, on the desire that such individual has to conform to the accounts performed by others, or on the 'official' version that is shared among a certain group to which the individual seeks to belong. Not only is this process inevitable, but it is also very appealing to people when they start to narrate their lives in organizations. Adorisio witnessed this in her research with bankers of community banks in New Mexico. Her focus is on the social dimension of storytelling that is often neglected in narrative inquiry where there is a strong tendency in emphasizing the role of storytelling for its cognitive dimension. Yes, we do love narratives as they provide order and structure to our lives, but we love them also because they make us feel part of a group and secure our social identities with our interlocutors, at least in the worlds in which we tell and are listened. I was fortunate enough to accompany Adorisio on several of her banking interviews. We witnessed something quite amazing in how a franchise bank gobbled up community banks, then demanded that those who stayed employed cease remembering and cease storytelling their community bank, and instead adopt the fashioned narrative of the franchise bank.

7 Living Story and Antenarrative in Organizational Accidents

Jo A. Tyler

LIVING STORY AND ANTENARRATIVE IN ORGANIZATION ACCIDENTS

The dominant narratives that organizations like to tell about themselves routinely compete with stories from the margins and shadows of an organization. In the case of a tragic workplace accident, an organization's grand narrative of safety is especially challenged. In this chapter we slow down the events to examine the interplay between the historical narrative of safety and the living, emergent story of the accident and those involved. We can watch for attempts to preserve the dominant narrative, to force fit the emerging story into an orderly linearity that will fit neatly within its structure, and see the energetic vitality, the aliveness, of the organic story (Tyler, 2007), an antenarrative (Boje, 2001) that actively pushes back against narrative linearity with spiral and rhizomatic movement.

THE GRAND NARRATIVE

Elisha Graves Otis establishes his elevator factory. The next year, at the New York World's Fair, he proves his new product's safety mechanism: As he rides up and down upon the platform, (he) occasionally cuts the rope by which it is supported. . . . The New York Recorder's official artist, who had been idling all morning beneath the palms, set busily to work with his block and pencil, on a drawing which would be reproduced thousands of times and come to decorate Otis offices around the world, illustrating an event that has long since eclipsed the bigger show it was a part of. It wasn't Otis going up that dazzled the crowd—it was Otis not coming down with a crash after he slashed the hoisting rope with a saber. 'All safe, gentlemen,' he announced, as the brakes kicked in. 'All safe. . . .' For when Otis had severed the hoisting rope with his saber, the lift had fallen only a few inches, then stopped with a jolt. The mechanism was simple, it was automatic, and it promised to make the hoist safe for the first time in 2,000 years. By executing this stunt, before a gasping crowd, Otis had heralded the birth of the elevator industry (United Tecnologies History and United Technologies Highlights).

By way of introduction, we have this striking image, this artifact, a dazzling and classic narrative of an iconic hero-founder. So engraved or petrified is this narrative that there is the line drawing from the actual day of the event lodged on the company Web site and in the lobbies of its buildings around the world. It is a story embedded with messages to employees, customers, and other stakeholders about the company as an organization that is grounded in innovation, and imbued with a grand metavalue of safety. This narrative assures investors that it is safe to include Otis in their portfolios. Customers understand that they buy a history of safety when they purchase Otis products. Employees, hearing this story as part of their new-employee orientation, learn that they stand on the shoulders of a heritage that renders safe their participation in manufacture, installation, and service of Otis products. The focus on safety in training classrooms, on factory hallways and walls, reinforces this message: Otis means safety. These texts and associated images reinforce an implicit pact: Employees have a role in upholding this heritage, a shared responsibility with 'the company' for making sure that they, the firm, and its products are, indeed, 'all safe.'

This story matters to the organization and to the industry *writ large* because the vertical transportation business—the business of elevators and escalators—is indeed a dangerous one.[1] It *needs* stories of safety, and not just to create an image that will serve it well in the marketplace. In a constructivist sense, companies like Otis need to create a reality that will serve its people well against the backdrop of the workaday hazards of the field.

And still, despite its every effort to train, to persuade, to coerce its employees into a 'safe mode,' this narrative of Elisha Graves Otis at the New York World's Fair is not Otis's whole story. It is surrounded by competing stories that push at it, poking and prodding, endeavoring to change its shape, distend it, explode it. The job of the 'all-safe' narrative is to maintain its shape, to stay tidy and round in the face of these story pressures that jockey for visibility in their quest to escape from the eclipse of the narrative. The 146 industry-related deaths that the eLCOSH Web site reports occurred between 1992 and 2001 included 57 installers and repairmen.[2] So there are clearly other stories. They run the gamut of stories from 'close calls' to 'pure accidents' and a dozen shades in between. They are just as true as (some would say truer than) 'All safe, gentlemen. all safe,' but they are not 'produced' by the organization, narrated with affiliated images. They are not included on the company Web site, in the materials for the investors, or on the bulletin boards in the break-rooms, in recruiting materials for new employees. Rather, these are stories from the literal shadows of an elevator shaft, the top of a car, the back corner of a machine room, the pit of an escalator. They are stories that paint a sharp contrast to the message of safety as value, safety as priority, and they are not stories that enjoy regular telling at new-employee orientation. But they are told. Let me tell you one. It's one in which I had some direct involvement during my tenure in the industry.[3] Along the way, we can pause to gaze at the story through the lenses of antenarrative and living story.

THE ESCALATOR ACCIDENT

There is a procedure called "lock out/tag out." Mechanics are supposed to use it when they work on live equipment. It's more than just shutting the machine down. It's a process of isolating the machine from the power source, and then putting a bright tag on the power panel or switches so that they will not be restored to power until the services tasks are complete.

In the early 1990s, two mechanics on the job went to a department store to adjust a shaky escalator. They were behind schedule for the day, and agreed that one would get to work while the other went to fetch some hot drinks for both of them. The mechanic remaining on the site shut off the escalator and set up orange cones around the bottom of the escalator platform. Between the cones he strung bright tape declaring "danger" to passersby. Working from inside the taped zone, he began to take up the stair treads of the escalator, stopping for a while to chat with the manager of the store.

By way of background, in order to service an escalator you pull up the stair treads, separating them at the line of their interlocking metal "teeth." Lifting up the bottom landing reveals a small escalator pit. By situating himself in the pit, the mechanic can reach the escalator's principal mechanisms to service them. And, while standing in the pit, the mechanic's belly is just about in line with the jagged, alternating teeth of the exposed tread.

On this particular day in the department store, as the mechanic kneeled, bending over the equipment in the pit, a noise caught his attention. He rose up a bit so as to more easily identify the source of the sound when he caught sight of the moving stair tread. Alarmed, he began to straighten, just as the teeth of the tread edge bit into his belly, home to soft and vital organs.

His screams confused his buddy, who, sure that the mechanic would have finished the job in the time it had taken him to return with coffee and tea, had, in the absence of a tag, assumed that his associate had simply forgotten to restore power to the unit. In the long seconds that it took the returning mechanic to realize that the screams were in fact from the front of the escalator, the teeth had perforated the mechanic's skin, puncturing and crushing his tender innards. Horrified, his buddy pulled the switch down, turning the unit off. He ran to help pull the treads back and release his friend to the emergency medical technicians who swept him off, lights flashing, sirens wailing.

The story of the accident swept through the organization. How had it really happened? A terrible accident. Sloppy work. Poor partnership. Inadequate training. Bad scheduling. Too much pressure to meet the call-time statistics. The antenarrative was typical in its nonlinearity. It jumped from place to place quickly, reconfiguring itself with each telling, and often dropping some fragments in favor of retaining and emphasizing others. Different versions of the story appeared holographically at different levels and in different functions of the organization, the construction of each one linked to the place it was told, to the listeners who heard it, to the very quality of their listening. Supervisors, for example, infused their version with blame on management for putting too much emphasis on timing. Human resources versions added information about the condition of the victim. The administrators in the field offices told a version in which the central protagonist was not the accident victim but his buddy, who had flipped the switch turning on the machine—how he must feel, whether he had appeared back at work, and whether he would keep his job.

While the field workers waited to hear about the condition of their colleague, telling and retelling the story, senior management met on the seventh floor of the headquarters building and speculated about workmen's compensation claims. They discussed the possibility of the mechanic suing the firm, which was, after all, an American company. They crafted plans to address various scenarios—'endings' to the story that ranged from 'probable' to 'unlikely but possible.' It was indeed, they concurred, an unfortunate accident, but their real concerns were with harnessing or containing the antenarrative, imprisoning it, in Boje's (2006) terminology, in a tidier narrative which would erase the living story.

I first heard the story when I was called into that meeting on the seventh floor. It was not 'all safe.' No one invoked the great founder narrative. No one talked about history. They talked about the future. They worked prospectively. It was a nervously legalistic conversation intended to foster damage control and shift the ending of the story in a way that would best suit both the local management team and the big shots at corporate headquarters.

Meanwhile, on the floors below, out on the street, the story was streaming through the organization, listeners straining to discern new details in each version they heard, and incorporating them into the next version they themselves would tell. The story is moving rhizometrically through the organization.

Then there is a pause in this movement, as a new fact emerges and finds its place in the story.

The mechanic is going to survive. Everyone on the seventh floor agrees that this is good news. Fine news, indeed. It is true, he will never fully recover, but he is a "lucky" man. Despite his disabilities he will heal sufficiently to be functional. It is true, he will not be able to return to work in the field—but surely he will not want this anyway. Surely he will want to agree on some sort of settlement, and live a quiet life outside the industry. Just one level down, on the sixth floor, more specific contingency planning commences with lawyers murmuring over their computers and cold coffee in specialized tongues.

The lawyers on floor six are hungry for more of the story, for rhizomes that have not yet formed. They call me in for a conversation, hopeful that I can help them. They are filled with questions and instructions.

What will he be asking for? they want to know. How can we compensate him so that he will be less inclined to sue? How can we settle? Who has talked to him since he left the hospital? How is he adjusting? Whom has he been talking to? Who has the straight story? Who can give us the inside track? People must be talking out in the field. Go find out, they say to me, but be discreet, eh? Don't cause a stir. . . .

Those busily crafting narrative on the sixth and seventh floors agreed on at least one thing: that no matter what else transpired, they would arrive at one version of the narrative which they would all stand behind. In their vernacular, they would 'get their story straight' for the corporate folks, for any prosecuting attorney who might appear on the scene to represent the mechanic. They were looking for the story that they could build into or otherwise connect and leverage the petrified (borrowing from Czarniawska [2004]) historical narrative of safety. Their intent was to make this newly 'sanctioned' narrative so common that it would replace all other versions of the story, squeezing them out of the organization altogether. They invested a tremendous amount of energy in trying to anticipate the direction of the living story, and in planning contingencies that would shut down those rhizomes which least suited the organization, those which would present the greatest difficulty in manipulating into a 'proper' narrative version of events. But the story was too alive. They could not possibly anticipate every potential rhizomatic bulb and tentacle.

The mechanic is back on his feet, and wants to arrange to come to the office to visit with some of his colleagues. He calls me, the manager of training and development, to make an appointment. Surprised, I tell him I'll be happy to see him, and we fix the day and time. I inform the managers and lawyers on the sixth and seventh floors. "He sees you as safe," they suppose. "You need to talk him out of suing us. Make sure he understands that we want to work with him on this. Surely we can come to some agreement."

They have assigned me a role in the emerging story. I cannot anticipate what it will be. I am not interested in manipulating the narrative into a linear version that will suit the executives and the lawyers. I am only curious about the direction the story will take, out of so many possible directions.

> A few days later, the mechanic is sitting in my office drinking tea. After some pleasantries, he puts down his cup, and leans towards me a little. "Do you think they're going to fire me? I mean, I know it was my fault, sloppy work. I was in a hurry. It was a huge mistake and I've paid the price, right? And I know I can't ever work out in the field again, but I have an idea. I just don't want them to fire me. Do you think they're going to fire me?"

This twist in the story is completely unanticipated by those on the sixth and seventh floors, who only expect problems, who lack any trust that the injured mechanic might be a reasonable man, that he may have his own idea about the direction the story could take.

> "Oh, I don't think they'll fire you," I assure him. "What's your idea?"

Here I become a new character in (and new teller of) the story, and I have a chance to shape or direct its unfolding. There is a way in which I become responsible for certain decisions, choices about the plot of the story. I could tell the mechanic that management is vulnerable, for example, and that he has an opportunity to grab for a gold ring. I could advise him, nudge him in a direction away from the narrative that I know management is attempting to craft, the narrative as they hope it will take shape, but I do not. I have my own emerging and living antenarrative, as an expatriate, as a young female, as a defector from corporate headquarters. I make a choice to take action in the form of listening to the injured mechanic's version of the story, rather than attempting to shape the telling in a way that might make a difference for me. Because I do not even know what that shape might be, I become a naïve listener, and the quality of that listening allows for a fully unanticipated rhizome.

> "I want to come and work for you," the mechanic says, his eyes meeting mine squarely.
> "For me?"
> "I love this company," he explains in a rush. "I'm sorry about what happened, and I only want to come back to work here." He paused, and I waited. It felt like a long silence, and when I failed to break it, he continued.
> "My idea is that no one should ever be like me. No one should get hurt this way. And I can help. I know I can. I want to come and work in the training department. For you. I see what Peter does, and I can do it.

I can write training materials, and I could teach too, I think. But that's not the thing. The thing is, I want to tell my story."

"Your story?"

"Yeah, that's right. I want to go to every technical class, every safety class, and I want to tell people what happened to me, what I did. I want to show them my scars. I want them to see how I can't stand up straight. I want to tell them about how my life is different now, from the very moment I get up in the morning to pee. I can do that if I come to work for you. That's my idea."

This deviation from every single thing anticipated by management is so surprising that for a moment it literally takes my breath away. The story here leads me into a territory that is more foreign, more complex, more beautiful than all the unimaginative narrative possibilities envisioned by those on the sixth and seventh floors. I believe in that moment that it justifies my own failure to present the mechanic with their dreaded narrative option of the gold ring.

I tell the mechanic that I love his idea and I will see what I can do. I arrange a meeting on the seventh floor, and in it I tell management that I think there is a way to prevent the mechanic from suing. Even before they hear the idea, they are all for it. I lay it out for them. I explain that it will require additional budget for my area, an additional full-time head on my payroll. They are uncharacteristically generous. Instantly I have the head count, the travel budget. "Whatever you need," they tell me. "Just make it happen."

The mechanic comes to work for me. In each class, he lifts up his shirt to show his scars. In each class he tells his story, uncensored, in his own way, in his own words. In the evenings, participants talk about it in the pub. They retell it, living it in their mind's eye. At the end of the training they go home, and they tell their spouses, partners, children, and friends. Lock-out, tag-out errors drop precipitously. Word of the story reached European branches of the organization, and overseas managers invited the mechanic to visit them, to tell the story in their classes. Because it was difficult for the injured mechanic to fly, we requested funds to make a video, and he captured one version of the story on a tape for distribution to any trainer who wanted it. It even traveled to competing companies, because the mechanic successfully argued that safety transcends brand. The story stayed on the move.

And now I am telling it to you, here in this book. Maybe after reading it you will tell it to someone else. The 'all-safe' story is still trapped in an undead narrative, but that narrative is now less round, its once smooth surface now dappled by the story of the mechanic who was bit hard by the jagged teeth of an escalator.

IMPLICATIONS FOR PRACTICE IN ORGANIZATIONS

No story is inherently bad, or even good. Stories simply *are*. The more we try to manipulate them or silence them, the more likely they are to have effects on the protagonists, and on the organization, that feel negative, difficult, or scary. If practitioners, for example, those in human resources and organizational development, are trusted in the organization—an admittedly problematic notion that can often be overcome by the presence of a neutral third party such as a research partner—they may be in a position to elicit and hear stories that both support and run counter to the grand narratives of the organization. These living stories may reveal actual practices in the organization that are challenging, sad, and that are out of alignment with the espoused organizational texts in the dominant narrative. They are often drawn from the depths and the margins of the organization, places where real work is accomplished, but where there is little visibility to the leadership of the organization. When these stories do burst through the boundaries of the acceptable narratives to become visible to those 'in charge,' there is tremendous pressure on practitioners to harness them, to squelch them, or to sculpt them into a glossier, more acceptable version, one that is more in alignment with the already sanctioned organizational narratives. Examples of these stories are the middle manager who was in an executive meeting on Friday, but whose office was empty the following Monday; the 'high-potential' lesbian who was threatened by management and repeatedly denied promotions; the disabled applicant who was never interviewed because he was 'overqualified'; the reorganization effort that was explained as a way to increase productivity and resulted in laying off 21 workers just short of their full retirement and, lest we forget, the mechanic who was crushed, permanently disabled, by an escalator.

Listening seems critical to the process of unfolding antenarrative. The failure to recognize the voices from marginalized and liminal spaces of the organization results in practitioners whose truncated listening cannot properly interpolate discourse because the high and low frequencies, some portion of the "social voices of the era" (Bakhtin, 1981, p. 430), are excluded. Without the advantageous richness of the high strings and low basses that anchor the curve of the discourse, the practitioner is at risk for 'producing' single-faceted monophonic story/telling that fits neatly with the prevailing narrative and Bakhtin's concept of authoritative discourse. This whitewashed, sanctioned story/telling typically lacks the reflexive properties that make stories appealing to business listeners (Tyler, 2004). Valuable stories will be silenced, and listeners will range from discontent to angry.

This is problematic, because these listeners, protagonists in emergent, living antenarrative, have the power to act as a critical toggle switch in the success/failure of organizational development and change. All too often they are unable to find themselves in the linearly formulated narratives they hear from the primary spaces. They cannot situate themselves in narratives

(Bandura, 1986) that patently fail to reflect their work and the organizational context as they know it. Instead, they hear stories from a world of work—of social and physical processes—that fail to represent them in ways that matter. They hear an attempt to replace their stories with sanctioned story/telling of those in power that represents, instead, the espoused theories (Argyris & Schön, 1996; Brookfield, 1987) of the organization. As their voices are officially silenced, their stories ignored/denied, these listeners will tune out the organization's systematized telling. But there is no implication that these shadow stories will simply dissipate. They are not squeezed out by the official narratives in the primary spaces which align with, reinforce, and attempt to reproduce the espoused ontology of the organization.

Instead, their stories of the hegemony of the culture, the points of separation from the 'corporate' narratives will comprise in large measure their internally persuasive, ongoing, and often powerful contribution to the organizations' discourse (Bakhtin, in Holquist, 1981, p. 424). Deprived of primary spaces, sanctioned airtime in which they can make this contribution, they will fine-tune the channels of their social networks, using the stories as lubrication for clear transmission of their experience. Attempts to shut these stories down appear to make them stronger, not weaker. Practitioners end up trying to do damage control, create spin, consuming energy that would have been better suited to giving them voice sooner in forums where their meaning could be explored, their implications for the organization's story examined, where they could exhibit their power as a source of connection, or of novelty.

Lifting these kinds of stories up for public consumption may feel risky to practitioners, because they can expose the gap between the organization's espoused theory and its theory-in-use, but the greater risk may lie in not providing outlets in which they can be told, and heard. Employees will view tidy narratives as an attempt by management to gloss over real difficulties. Telling these stories can reorient the potency they have when they remain publicly undiscussable, but it takes some degree of courage and a willingness to live with and work through their unanticipated and unintentional consequences.

Practitioners who shy away from these stories imperil their own credibility. After all, a full range of stories are already being told in the organization, contributing to the discourse in a lively and powerful way. Raising the visibility of emerging antenarrative, following their nonlinear, spiraling, and rhizomatic flow, is an act of courage that will not go unnoticed by the members of the organization. Practitioners who ignore stories that are difficult—for whatever reason—run the risk of appearing naïve at best and manipulative at worst. Practitioners do not pursue these constructs because they themselves are cast in a system that they are at once asked to both stabilize and change, and the system itself has not been interpreted as capable of the elasticity and tensile strength that make this complex, multidimensional change possible. If stories are a way of releasing this energy out of context, it's no small wonder that tidy, positive narratives like 'All safe, gentlemen, all safe' stories that support the normal trajectory—up and to the right—are preferred to those living emergent stories of mechanics who, due to their injuries, will never again stand fully upright.

NOTES

1. Incidents involving elevators and escalators kill about 30 and seriously injure about 17,100 people each year in the United States, according to data provided by the U.S. Bureau of Labor Statistics and the Consumer Product Safety Commission. Injuries to people working on or near elevators—including those installing, repairing, and maintaining elevators, and working in or near elevator shafts—account for 14 to 15 (almost half) of the deaths. The two major causes of death are falls and being caught in/between moving parts of elevators/escalators." From the eLCOSH Electronic Library of Construction Occupational Safety and Health Web site, http://www.cdc.gov/elcosh/docs/d0300/d000397/d000397.html

2. "More than half of the deaths of those working in and around elevators—especially electrocutions and "caught in/between" and "struck by" deaths—were caused by failure to de-energize elevator electrical circuits or failure to ensure that elevator parts could not move while maintenance or repairs were under way. These causes resulted also in three of the five work-related escalator deaths." Ibid.

3. At the time of this story I was a training and development manager for a wholly owned overseas subsidiary of Otis. I tell this story through the lens of my own experience and recollection by way of providing a firsthand example from the industry.

REFERENCES

Argyris, C., & Schön, D. A. (1996). *Organizational learning II: Theory, method, and practice.* New York: Addison-Wesley Publishing Company.

Bakhtin, M. M. (1981). *The dialogic imagination: Four essays.* Holquist, M. (Ed.). Austin: University of Texas Press.

Bandura, A. (1986). *Social foundations of thought and action.* Englewood Cliffs, NJ: Prentice Hall.

Boje, D. M. (2001). *Narrative methods for organizational and communications research.* Thousand Oaks, CA: Sage.

———. (2006). Breaking out of narrative's prison: Improper story in storytelling organization. *Storytelling, Self, Society: An Interdisciplinary Journal of Storytelling Studies, 2*(2), 28–49.

Brookfield, S. (1987). *Developing critical thinkers.* San Francisco: Jossey-Bass.

Czarniawska, B. (2004). *Narratives in social science research.* London: Sage Publications.

eLCOSH Web site. Center to Protect Workers Rights. Retrieved February 2006 from http://www.cdc.gov/elcosh/docs/d0300/d000397/d000397.html

Holquist, M. (Ed.). (1981). *The dialogic imagination by M. M. Bakhtin.* Austin: Texas University Press.

Tyler, J. A. (2004). Strategic storytelling: The development of a guidebook for HRD practitioners using storytelling as a business strategy for learning and knowledge transfer. Doctoral dissertation, Columbia University, UMI Dissertation Abstracts.

———. (2007). Storyaliveness and powerful listening. *Electronic Journal of Radical Organizational Theory: Fifth International Conference on Critical Management Studies Proceedings.* Retrieved January 15, 2009, from http://www. mngt.waikato.ac.nz/ejrot/cmsconference/2007/proceedings.asp

United Technologies History. (n.d.). Retrieved February 12, 2006, from United Technologies website, http://www.utc.com/profile/facts/history.htm.

United Technologies Highlights. (n.d.). Retrieved February 12, 2006, from United Technologies website, http://www.utc.com/press/highlights/innovation.htm.

8 Antenarrative and Narrative

The Experiences of Actors Involved in the Development and Use of Information Systems

Lynette Drevin and Darren Dalcher

1 INTRODUCTION

Information systems (IS) are used so often and universally that we cannot even conceive a world without computerized systems. IS support important functions in most areas, including business, leisure, and science. Moreover, IS add to the competitiveness of companies, help with the continuous change that takes place, and underpin business activities. However, some of the systems designed to support these functions do not deliver their expected outcomes. Many references to failed or challenged systems are reported on in the media (see, for example, KPMG, 2005; Standish, 1999, 2001, 2004). A distinction is often made between failed systems that are canceled prior to installation and challenged systems that exceed their cost and schedule timelines and experience some trouble during development before eventually being put into operation.

The failure of IS should suggest the need for detailed investigation to seek out the real reasons for failure so that it may benefit future systems. A few approaches have been set forth by researchers to investigate failure situations (Flowers, 1996; Fortune & White, 2006; Lucas, 1975; Lyytinen & Hirschheim, 1987; Standish, 2001, 2004; Yardley, 2002). It is noteworthy that the same concerns have been expressed by researchers looking at failure phenomena for the last 35 years.

One of the approaches suggested for the understanding of IS failure situations is the interpretive approach, derived from the social sciences (Fortune & Peters, 2005). The foundation is that reality is socially constructed and reality could be understood through the interpretation of data. Dalcher (2004) suggests narrative methods where a failed or challenged IS situation can be seen as a special example of a case study, using the term 'case history.' The case history contains descriptions and observations of the actors and their perceptions and feelings, and thus will probably have a biased perspective. The failure situations, or negative experiences pertaining to a particular IS, can be described via the stories of the actors. Riessman (1993) states that the metaphor of 'story' implies that we create order and construct texts in our specific contexts. To narrate is to impose order on the flow of stakeholders' experience to make sense of events and past activities. There is, however, a problem with this view in the sense that we do not want to create order at this stage. The different actors involved may have many viewpoints on a particular situation, which they may share with the investigator. However, it might not be done in a very orderly way. We can therefore not refer to narrative order. This is where the terminology of antenarrative comes in. Boje (2001) liberates a story from having a beginning, a middle, an end, and a plot (Harmer & Pauleen, 2007). Antenarrative is seen as 'before story' or prenarrative. Most of the stories of the actors involved in an IS failure situation will be of such a nature, that is to say, incoherent, fragmented, and nonlinear. The goal of this chapter is to report on the application of antenarrative for the investigation of the experiences of actors involved in the development and use of an IS, thereby also generating new insights into narrative theory.

The layout of the rest of the chapter is as follows: The rationale of this work is given in section 2 along with the description of terminology used. In section 3, the background of the research project is described. Some methodological issues are reflected upon in section 4. The analysis and discussion of the results are presented in section 5 before finalizing the story, with some concluding remarks highlighting the value of the approach used and the wider contribution it offers.

2 RATIONALE AND TERMINOLOGY USED

The aim of this project is to use antenarrative approaches to make sense of the experiences of actors involved in the development and use of an IS. Usually many actors are involved when an IS is developed and additional ones join in when the system is put into use. Each actor has a role to fulfill; therefore, everyone will have their own story to tell about their expectations, experiences, and perceptions pertaining to the given system.

The Standish Group compiles biannual reports related to IT projects and their outcomes. The group labels the outcomes of IT development projects as successes, challenged projects, and failures (Standish, 1999, 2001, 2003, 2004).

- *Successful projects* are completed on time and within budget with all features and functionality as originally specified.
- *Challenged projects* are completed with budget or time limits exceeded and with fewer features and functions than originally specified.
- *Failed projects* are canceled before completion.

An example of a failure is the MasterNet trust accounting system of the Bank of America. The project suffered losses of $78 million and is known within the IT industry as a system that fell short of expectations (Glass, 1998). Challenged systems are finally used after many changes and improvements have taken place. It could be that some of the actors are satisfied with the system whereas others are not. It could be that certain aspects of the system are accepted by some actors and other aspects are not. The term 'failed situations' is used in this chapter to refer to situations where there is a deviation from the expectations of the actors.

Information System: An IS can be seen as a collection of people, data, processes, interfaces, and networks that are integrated for the purposes of supporting and improving the day-to-day functions and processes in a business, and provide problem-solving and decision-making information for management (Bentley & Whitten, 2007).

Narrative: Lieblich, Tuval-Mashiach, and Zilber (1998) state that humans are storytellers by nature and that, through stories, researchers can explore and understand the inner world of individuals. Clandinin and Connelly (2000) were influenced by John Dewey in their outlook of narrative where experience is the key. Narrative is a way of representing and understanding experiences. For this project, in the IS context, narrative inquiry is used to retrospectively untangle a web of actions and events as well as to gain insight into the experiences of actors.

Antenarrative: Boje (2001) introduced the term 'antenarrative methods' to take into account that stories appear to be told improperly; in a fragmented, multiplotted, and complex manner, for example, a story in an *ante* state of affairs before a constructed narrative is used to impose sense.

Actor: Any person who plays a role or participates during the development and/or use of an IS.

3   BACKGROUND AND DESCRIPTION OF THE CASE

An academic environment was chosen for this research project due to the accessibility of the information system and the actors. Initial discussions with the IT services director and further meetings on other formalities (such as taking into consideration the relevant ethical issues) resulted in the permission for progressing with the project. During initial meetings with IT personnel, the outlay and infrastructure of the different IS were discussed. It was then decided to study a certain complex IS having around 19 subsystems. These include systems dealing with student records, grade processing, student fees, accommodation, applications and admissions, and so on. This is contained in an environment called 'Student Administrative Systems.' We concentrated on three subsystems, namely grade processing, student fees, and student records. During these meetings, individuals (actors) were identified who could provide us with their experiences on the specific IS. Four distinct actor groups were identified and it was decided to involve actors from each of the groups.

A first meeting was held with one actor as part of a pilot study. The unstructured to semistructured interview lasted approximately 1 hour. Occasionally it was necessary to prompt for clarification as the actor was not a natural storyteller. (We experienced this to be the case with most of the involved actors.) The interview was transcribed and analyzed in a way such as described by Lieblich et al. (1998). The whole interview was investigated and then sections were interpreted in context with the rest of the narrative to get a feel for the data. Lieblich et al. propose a model to classify types of narrative analysis as follows:

- The *holistic approach* takes a story as a whole and sections are then interpreted in context with the other part of the narrative.
- With the *categorical approach* the original story is dissected as in traditional content analysis.
- The *content-based* approach refers to the content of an account to answer the questions why? what? who? from the teller's viewpoint.
- The *form-based* approach ignores the content of a story and looks at its structure, sequence of events, evoked feelings, and choice of words.

The preceding four approaches were evaluated for appropriateness in this study, and it was decided to use the first approach for initial analysis.

After the pilot study was interpreted and the results reflected upon, it was decided to use a few approaches for analyzing the data, as there is no single best way to conduct narrative analysis and interpretation (Cortazzi, 1993; Czarniawska, 1998; Mishler, 1995; Riessman, 1993). The three-dimensional narrative inquiry space of Clandinin and Connelly (2000) was chosen in order to get a comprehensive view of each actor's experiences with the IS under investigation. These include aspects such as time and continuity (past, present, future), situation (place), and interaction (personal and social). However, these aspects were only used for data gathering and not during analysis as the reporting phase did not make use of these dimensions as such. Another approach that was selected was the antenarrative notion (Boje, 2001), which will be described in this chapter. When the narrative approaches were investigated, antenarrative seemed to be an applicable way of studying the stories of the involved actors, as incoherency and multiplotted narratives were evident.

The meetings with the other identified actors were scheduled and interviews were held with 10 actors in total. Each interview lasted between 1 and 2 hours, during which the actor shared his/her experiences with the specific IS with the researcher. Recordings were made of each interview and the data were transcribed in text format.

The next section will look into the research methodology followed for this project.

4 METHODOLOGY AND ISSUES SURROUNDING RESEARCH PRACTICES

Two guidelines were taken into account during this project. Firstly, the view of Clandinin and Connelly (2000) that narrative inquiry studies the experiences of people was used in guiding the planning and conduct of the interviews with the relevant actors in order to encourage them to share their experiences related to the development and use of the IS. Secondly, the perspective introduced by Boje (2001) that antenarrative is the multivoiced, non-linear and unplotted storytelling was also utilized in uncovering and making sense of actors' experiences. This guideline was useful in our study because the 'stories' of the actors involved in the IS are accounts of events before plots or coherence are added to the storylines.

Clandinin and Connelly (2000) describe the research and practice of a few authors who included narrative in their work, thus adding new dimensions to narrative inquiries. The reported work stems from diverse disciplines such as psychotherapy, anthropology, organizational research, psychiatry, and teaching. The value of their work is in expanding the body of knowledge available for narrative work and in enabling us to borrow terms, theories, and metaphors from other disciplines. In doing so, practice and research are bridged. The current study borrowed from the narrative domain and imported new methods to the field of IS research. The experiences of actors involved with the IS were retold as their accounts and narrative methods could then be used as an adequate way of representing and understanding their experiences.

When the different narrative approaches were investigated for suitability, while acknowledging that there is no 'single recipe,' we found that the approaches that might be considered for the study of IS experiences had to take into account the fact that stories of actors involved in IS experiences are incoherent and unplotted. The selected approach had to look deeper, read between the lines, and look at the little stories, dualities, feelings, and bias. By using such approaches, the researcher is placed in a position to generate a more comprehensive description and explanation of events, especially in those situations that were not acceptable or agreeable to the actors involved in the IS.

Boje (2001) sets out eight antenarrative analysis options that can deal with fragmented and polyphonic storytelling. The alternative methods that Boje has assembled focus mainly on multistranded stories of experiences that lack collective consensus. The analytical process followed was the antenarrative as described by Rosile (2004) where a cycle through emic representation of the actors' experiences and the researcher's etic interpretation of their experiences of IS is taking place and is shaping the sensemaking of this phenomenon. The next section will apply the antenarrative approaches to an IS as experienced and reported by the involved actors.

5   PRESENTING THE FINDINGS THROUGH ANALYSIS AND INTERPRETATIONS OF THE ACTORS' EXPERIENCES

5.1   General

The antenarrative approaches selected for this study concentrated on the following themes:

- Deconstruction: Attention was given to aspects such as the following: looking for dualities, the other side of the story, what has not been said, and opposites and other voices.
- Story network analysis: Here the focus was on identifying the connections between stories.
- Microstoria analysis: This goes hand in hand with the previous two approaches, where not only the more 'official' standpoint is evaluated, but each actor's story is seen as important in order to get the complete picture of the phenomenon under investigation.

With these themes in mind, the recorded interviews were listened to and the transcribed interviews were read thoroughly to become more familiar with the stories. Fragments of the stories which were relevant and which focused on the topic of investigation were identified and analyzed. The preceding antenarrative themes as well as the context of the study were kept in mind while the analysis was done.

Four main groups of actors were identified, namely:

1. *SU*—super user, responsible for training, handling some changes, logging errors, evaluating change requests, passing on requests to IT, sometimes directly to the external software development company (*EC*).
2. *IT*—Employee from the University's IT division.
3. *U*—User of the system, e.g., secretaries, administrative people.
4. *EC*—Employee of the external company. The development and maintenance of the IS was done by an external company.

The first three groups are part of the university environment. The external company contracted out some development work to a company from abroad (*CA*) at a specific stage of the development of the project.

For this chapter, a single interview from each of the four categories was used for analysis.

The lines of communication and the ways in which the different actors interact are presented in Figure 8.1.

5.2 Analysis

Each interview was introduced by the researcher, stating the background and aim of the project. The actor was then asked to elaborate on his/her experiences with the IS under study. Specific areas were highlighted, such as:

- How do/does the specific subsystem(s) that they use fit into the broader system?
- What is their involvement with this system? How do they interact with others?

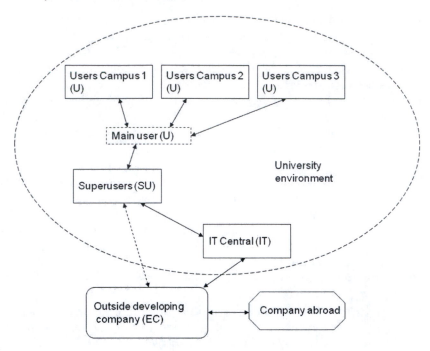

Figure 8.1 Communication and reporting lines.

- How were their experiences with, and perceptions of the system, through all the phases? How were their expectations, and the comparison with the reality they encountered?
- Specific successes and/or problem situations within the IS, and the improvements that can be made.

After reading intensively through the transcribed interviews, the following three broad topics emerged:

1. The views of the actors on success or failure within systems in general.
2. Views on problems experienced and dissatisfaction with the system.
3. The role of each actor, their feelings about the systems, and the interaction with other actors.

The following sections will give some of the views of each actor on the abovementioned broad topics.

5.2.1 Different Views on Success and Failure in Systems

When analyzing the data from each of the interviews it became clear that the focus of each actor on failure and success was on a different level.

For example, the *SU* put the blame for perceived failure almost fully on the users for wanting the functionalities very rapidly implemented. With this response, the posed question was not answered directly but there was implicit acknowledgment in the response that too little testing time may lead to failure:

> "Problems occurred as a result of the campuses being rushed to get new functionalities and in this way testing time was not sufficient."

The view from the *IT* actor on success was focused more towards the user:

> "One should adhere to the users' expectations and their workload must be reduced. The user should be empowered, service delivery must improve."

From the user side it was clear that they want a system that must be functional and correct:

> "The system should work smoothly. I don't want all sorts of errors."

The project manager from the outside company (EC) elaborated on her views on success and failure and thereby—between the lines—shows her many years' experience acknowledging that no IS can give 100% satisfaction to users:

> "Theoretically the system should be within budget, the users must be excessively happy, they must not complain about anything, but one never sees this. If a user gets 80%–90% of what he wanted, then you have succeeded."

EC viewed failure from the user's point of view and made the following statement:

> "The system is a failure if the user indicates that you have to stop the development because you are wasting their money."

5.2.2 Different Views on Problems Experienced within the System

The next broad theme that was identified by analyzing the account of each actor points towards the problematic areas experienced by the actors. During the interview the actors were asked to share their experiences with the IS in question, including any problems that were encountered.

The *SU* identified a few problem areas ranging from errors that occur in the system, lack of proper communication, and user and management demands that cannot always be met. This *SU* group has made a plan (appointed a main user) to handle the many queries from the users, thereby protecting the time they could spend on the important issues. It is interesting to note that this actor often used the diminutive form of nouns when referring to users and people—thereby implying superiority over users:

> "The system has many errors and the system does not have stability, and one thing leads to another. We are nowhere near the 100%. As users (diminutive form) realize there is more that systems can do, they ask for more functionalities."

> "The communication of errors poses a problematic situation. There are communication lines to *IT*, *EC* and different types of users. Users can be very bothersome and therefore we organized for a main user to stand between the *SU* group and the other users."

> "Sometimes management wants certain queries answered which are not possible to handle by the system."

The view of *IT* on experienced problems was much more focused on the level of technical issues. It was acknowledged that the system was too complex. There were references to human issues such as scope and feature creep, resistance to change, and training problems. Certain project management issues were also problematic:

> "This was a tall order for such a complex system. There were numerous interfaces; there were many errors when we went live."

> "We should not have tried to develop the complete system, rather used phasing in of parts."

> "It was problematic—the planning versus the reality at the end. You are not aware of what you don't know. There are a lot of uncertainties which make planning and estimating very difficult."

> "The user's expectations grow with time."

> "The users have resistance to change, and they panic if something is done differently."

> "With the new platform, the interfacing with a company from abroad was problematic in terms of communication, e.g. language and different time zones. This system is bilingual and that poses a challenge as well."

> "The data migration was problematic—it should have started earlier."

> "All the deadlines have not been met."

The user group experienced different types of frustration when using the system. These problems ranged from inadequate training to inflexibility, and from version problems to poor system performance. A few examples of statements reflecting the views of *U* are given:

> "The many versions of the system are very confusing. Errors are corrected but then in the newer version other errors emerge."

> "The system is very slow—especially during exam times when the grades have to be input into the system."

> "Sometimes some information is inaccurate."

> "The system is not flexible, and then some lecturers use their own spreadsheets to manage the grades which are then only submitted to the system as a final grade."

> "Training was not adequate."

EC also admitted to the complexity of the system and the need for flexibility resulting in frequent requests for changes. Improved communication and better planning were also mentioned. Scope and feature creep were experienced, as users needed new functions. Certain technical matters made things worse, such as slowness of data lines and new platforms that had to be used. There were also political and power struggle problems as well as language barriers when a company abroad (*CA*) got the contract for a specific phase of the system development. It seems that project management functions need to receive more attention:

> "Complexity of the system is high due to many functions and many subsystems."

> "New technology and software were used therefore the learning curve was high."

> "A lesson to learn was that planning must get serious attention. Work in phases."

> "It was not anticipated that data migration would be as difficult as it was in reality."

> "A lot of time was wasted waiting for the data lines (20%–30% of the time) due to working from two parts of the country."

> "Politically, you have to get users to believe in the product—to buy in."

"New problems and challenges arose with *CA*, such as:

- Approaches were different: e.g. reuse was high on the list of *EC* but not on the agenda of *CA*.
- Sometimes the *CA* asserted that something was not possible; then we had to search for the possibility and more often than not, it was possible.
- Language—English is a foreign language to the *CA* and they speak it with a heavy accent.
- Understanding of the academic environment needed to be communicated."

"We had problems with estimating time allocations and budgetary issues due to many uncertainties."

5.2.3   *Different Views on the Role of Each of Actor, Feelings About the System, and Interaction with the Other Role-Players*

The actors were asked to share their experiences of the IS being studied with the researcher. These included aspects such as their role, their feelings towards the system, and the interaction with other actors. It was evident after analyzing the interview data that the actor groups felt differently about some of these aspects. There were positive, proud feelings, some experienced frustration with the system, whereas others felt that many things were learned through this project (value added to the actor). There were also different perspectives on the interactions that had taken place between role-players:

SU has feelings of ownership and wants to protect the system as that of their group.

"I am very positive about the system."

"We work hard towards getting good results."

The role of *IT* is that of project manager and mediator. She likes to work under pressure and does not like the training aspect much. She also has a feeling of pride in the sense that the system gives more to users and students than similar systems:

"The system gives that something extra to students that other universities' systems do not have, e.g. own language as well as in English (other universities will only be in English)."

"In a sense the users are spoiled, and they don't realize what it takes to keep the system going."

U has the role of secretary and uses the system for grades, student records, and sometimes for financial transactions. The feeling of U towards the system was not positive—especially in the beginning. We can interpret this maybe as the resistance to change. The slow speed of the system at times also causes negative perceptions:

> "The frequent new versions are frustrating. The time it takes to enter the data and to generate reports is not acceptable."

The main role of EC is that of project manager at the external company that carries out the development and maintenance of the system. EC sees the learning curve as interesting. There is a feeling of compliance between the different parties involved. EC experienced much frustration with the testing. EC has a positive attitude and is not discouraged easily. As expected of an experienced project manager, EC often refers to project management aspects and throughout the interview she analyzes some of the problematic issues herself. She realizes that nothing regarding a project will be perfect:

> "The management of projects is sometimes underestimated."

> "There are always new things to learn in a project and this could be positive or negative."

> "Users can be very meticulous—especially when you don't involve them in all the system issues."

> "There are many challenges regarding the conditioning of the users— that is exhausting."

> "There will always be another 'rabbit out of the hat'—a surprise."

5.3 Discussion

The experiences of the actors were analyzed as antenarrative; no coherent flow or plot was evident. By using deconstruction analysis to look for dualities, or the other side of the story, or what has not been said, we may gain new insights into the phenomenon under investigation. Companies that develop and implement IS may learn from the views of actors involved in these systems. Although we have to be cautious in drawing general conclusions from this case, there is sufficient evidence to show that the different actor groups have different perceptions of the same IS in question ('very positive' vs. 'frustration'). They experience different feelings ('pride' vs. 'have to accept the system'). There are different views of the failure situations ('instability,' 'too many versions,' 'slow,' 'many uncertainties,' 'inadequate training'). Different stakeholder groups have different concerns, preferences, and values. These values and concerns play a part in shaping their views of systems. Their experiences will vary based on their viewpoint and perspective. Project management recognizes the need for stakeholder engagement and the case emphasizes the differences between distinctly different stakeholder groups and communities.

The story network analysis yields the connections between the accounts of the actors. We can see that the problems experienced by *IT* and *EC* (both in the roles of project managers) are on the level of project management issues (e.g., 'planning very difficult,' 'inadequate training,' 'deadlines not met,' 'complexity'). *IT*, *EC*, and *SU* were all very positive about the system ('give the user more than what is needed,' 'snug-fit system,' 'very positive'). Regarding their views on failure and/or success, *IT*, *U*, and *EC* were in agreement that the users must be satisfied ('adhere to users' expectations,' 'system should be available,' 'critical functions should work'). This is significant because it goes beyond the traditional criteria used in the project management domain, which often focuses on internal project management targets such as time, budget, and scope or functionality. User acceptance is crucial to the success of any system and different interest groups and stakeholders recognize the need for the system to satisfy their interests and needs.

Microstoria analysis has shown that all actors' stories have to be taken into account when investigating the phenomenon. Each actor has unique problems and 'lived' experiences from the specific IS. In this case it can be seen that the users may have 'smaller voices' that need to be heard ('it should be fast,' 'always available,' 'too many versions,' 'flexibility is a problem,' 'main user not always available'). This again emphasizes the need for different perspectives to be acknowledged and for the recognition that different stakeholders must be brought on board to ensure buy-in that will ultimately lead to the success of systems when new IS are introduced into organizations.

6   CONCLUSIONS

Success in developing IS systems requires recognition of the different interests involved (Dalcher, 2009). The IS system described in this case is very complex and contains many subsystems. By analyzing the experiences of the actors we see that the four groups have different perspectives and views which need to be taken into account.

After analyzing the actors' stories as antenarrative, the following examples of guidelines can be offered to be taken into account when future IS are developed:

- All different stakeholder groups need to be consulted.
- Attaining buy-in and establishing user trust in each group are essential.

- The number of change requests, and thereby the number of system versions, needs to be limited.
- Communication is crucial to success; developers should work towards improving communication lines between all actors.
- Planning should be improved and uncertainties have to be limited or clarified.
- Ambassadors and interfaces can support communication and ensure representativeness. Where large groups are involved there may be a need to increase the availability of the 'middle person' to handle the queries of the many users.
- Involvement and empowerment rely on the ability to interact with the system. Training should be planned and executed to ensure that the users will be empowered to participate and use the system.

The value of applying an antenarrative approach lies in better identifying the problem areas within this IS that normally cannot be obtained through traditional approaches such as postproject reviews and evaluations. When the small stories are looked into, the things that are perhaps unsaid emerge from studying the accounts given by the actors. Although we cannot generalize, some insights might be applicable to other systems as well. The findings highlighted earlier certainly support the ideas of engagement, buy-in, communication, and stakeholder engagement that emerge from adopting a more pluralistic view emphasizing the importance of different stakeholder groups in ensuring success. The lessons learned from the application of the methods described earlier can support the development of new information systems and can play a part in beginning to address the concerns relating to the high rate of failure in information systems. By making sense of mismatches and issues raised in past projects, especially those related to success, engagement, and satisfaction, we can learn the lessons from earlier events and thus begin the journey to improve development practice. On a higher level we can absorb the new insights gained from the case and use them to also extend narrative theory and practice, thus contributing back to the discipline from where we have borrowed.

REFERENCES

Bentley, L. D., & Whitten, J. L. (2007). *System analysis and design for the global enterprise.* Boston: McGraw-Hill.

Boje, D. M. (2001). *Narrative methods for organizational and communication research.* London: Sage.

Clandinin, D., & Connelly, F. (2000). *Narrative inquiry: Experience and story in qualitative research.* San Francisco: Jossey-Bass.

Cortazzi, M. (1993). *Narrative analysis.* London: The Falmer Press.

Czarniawska, B. (1998). *A narrative approach to organization studies.* Thousand Oaks, CA: Sage.

Dalcher, D. (2004). Stories and histories: Case study research (and beyond) in information systems failures. In M. E. Whitman (Ed.), *The handbook of information system research* (pp. 305–322). London: Idea Group Inc.

Dalcher, D. (2009). Software project success: Moving beyond failure. *UPGRADE, 10*(5), 42–50.

Flowers, S. (1996). *Software failure: Management failure*. Chichester, UK: Wiley.

Fortune, J., & Peters, G. (2005). *Information systems: Achieving success by avoiding failure*. Chichester, UK: Wiley.

Fortune, J., & White, D. (2006). Framing of project critical success factors by a systems model. *International Journal of Project Management, 24*, 53–65.

Glass, R. L. (1998). *Software runaways: Lessons learned from massive software project failures*. Upper Saddle River, NJ: Prentice Hall PTR.

Harmer, B., & Pauleen, D. (2007). *The work anytime anywhere mobility blues*. 4th QAULIT Conference, New Zealand.

KPMG. (2005). *Global IT Project management survey*. Retrieved October 31, 2007, from http://www.pmichapters-australia.org.au/canberra/documents/irm-prm-global-it-pm-survey2005.pdf

Lieblich, A., Tuval-Mashiach, R., & Zilber, T. (1998). *Narrative research*. Thousand Oaks, CA: Sage.

Lucas, H. C. (1975). *Why information systems fail*. New York: Colombia University Press.

Lyytinen, K., & Hirschheim, R. (1987). Information systems failures: A survey and classification of the empirical literature. In P. Zorkoczy (Ed.), *Oxford surveys in information technology 4* (pp. 257–309). New York. Oxford University Press.

Mishler, E. G. (1995). Models of narrative analysis: A typology. *Journal of Narrative and Life History, 5*(2), 87–123.

Riessman, C. K. (1993). *Narrative analysis*, Newbury Park, CA: Sage.

Rosile, G. A. (2004). *Antenarrative analysis of students' reactions to cheating in class: Crossing Frontiers in quantitative and qualitative research methods* (vol. 2). Proceedings of the first International Co-Sponsored Conference: Research Methods Division Academy of Management.

Standish Group. (1999). *A recipe for success*. Retrieved March 8, 2004, from http://www.standishgroup.com/sample_research/PDFpages/chaos1999.pdf

———. (2001). Extreme chaos. Retrieved March 8, 2004, from http://www.standishgroup.com/sample_research/PDFpages/extreme_chaos.pdf

———. (2003). Latest Standish Group chaos report shows project success rates have improved by 50%. Retrieved February 23, 2004, from http://www.standishgroup.com/pres/article.php?id=2

———. (2004). 2004 third quarter research report. Retrieved April 25, 2006, from http://www.standishgroup.com/sample_research/PDFpages/q3-spotlight.pdf

Yardley, D. (2002). *Successful IT project delivery: Learning the lessons of project failure*. London: Addison Wesley.

9   Strategy as Antenarrative Complexity

Yue Cai-Hillon, David M. Boje, and Clarinda Dir

INTRODUCTION

Antenarrative has became an important discussion topic in the research of organization theory and organizational change. However, the field strategy, the concept of antenarrative has not gained recognition as a way to investigate organization strategy changes.

The traditional approach to strategy is backward looking using standard case studies to teach strategists to plan for the future by reading the narratives of the past. By applying this approach, strategists were imprisoned in the dead narratives that denied the change of time.

Traditional strategy narratives are based on a set course from the past, and antenarrative approach to strategy is based on an open-ended course where each story does not have a set position in the future narrative. Antenarrative helps organizations break out of the narrative prison. This approach to strategy investigates the competing antenarratives of present time that struggle to create a story about the future. This approach is more suitable for the nature of strategy, which is future orientation.

In this chapter, we will evaluate the theory of storytelling organizations, its relation to system complexity, how strategy is reflected through storytelling complexity, and finally discuss antenarratives and narratives of strategy storytelling complexity.

STORYTELLING ORGANIZATIONS AND SYSTEM COMPLEXITY

Foucault (1977, p. 217) called stories "the vigilance of intersecting gazes" where a story is the irreducible substance of a story; whereas a narrative is the way these stories are related (Fiske, O'Sullivan, Hartley, & Saunders, 1983). Stories and narratives help us make sense of the storylines being told and the world we live in. Storytelling is constructed in the succession of the stories used as a tool or program for making sense of events (Gephart, 1991, p. 37). In an organization, people are in a constant state of narration and re-narration of the individual and collective's past, present, and future.

People use narratives to construct powerful stories. These stories are typically fictions in reflection of the individualized experiences (White, 1978). The organization is living in history while crafting history as competing antenarratives struggle to become the narrative center.

Czarniawska's (1997) theory of narrating organizations recognized narratives bridge social construction with a clear beginning, middle, and end. On the other hand, Boje (1991) took a mix of folklore and social construction view and considered that in storytelling organizations beginning, middle, and end are not so clear when aware of the presence of antenarratives.

Antenarratives refuse to attach to the beginning, middle, and end coherence of an organization narrative. They are the "in the middle" and "in-between" stories (Boje, 2001, p. 293) of a storytelling organization with collective, unplotted, and prenarrative speculations. The traditional narrative theory focuses on what has happened which is retrospective (backward-looking), whereas antenarratives are prospective (forward-looking). If we release story from narrative's prison and allow the antenarratives to emerge within organizations, then we have accomplished a true "Storytelling Organization" (Boje, 2006).

Strategy is future oriented. Yet, the traditional approach to strategy often is backward looking with a standard case-study approach that teaches strategists to plan for the future by reading and applying the narratives of the past. Antenarrative helps strategists to break out of this narrative retrospective prison by understanding the competing antenarratives of the present. Traditional narratives are set whereas antenarratives are open-ended and not set. Through this competition, marginal stories struggle to become the future narrative centers and create a story about the future. This analogy is much more suitable for the nature of strategy, being future oriented.

Antenarratives in a storytelling organization were dead narratives from the past but given a new meaning due to the changes in the contextual environment, forgotten narratives or hidden narratives controlled and marginalized by the narrative center, or embedded narratives within the dominant narrative and can only be discovered through deconstruction (Boje, 2001).

Given that antenarratives exist in all shapes and sizes, they are observed in every level of organization system complexity. According to Boulding (1956), there a nine levels of system complexity (Table 9.1); however, antenarratives find better comfort and freedom to emerge at higher levels of storytelling organization system complexities where the organization is more dynamic. At lower levels of complexities, antenarratives are tightly controlled by organization structure, history, and traditional and dominant narrative centers.

Organizations embrace multiple-strategy schools of thought. Each school corresponds to a level of storytelling organization complexity and environments for antenarratives to emerge. Strategy is a process of narrative and antenarrative.

Table 9.1   Boulding's Nine Levels of System Complexity

Nine Levels of "Storytelling Organization" Complexity

---

1. FRAMEWORK: unique property is mapping the types of narratives in use by "storytelling organization." Narrative maps, such as tragic, romantic, comedic, satiric, are dominant framework, but have forgotten "epic-story" interactivity with such narrative types.

---

2. MECHANISTIC: unique property is metrics to index time and travel motions of narratives throughout segments of the "storytelling organization." There are narratives about eras, summarizing everyday crisis points, but no biographical narration; time and space are mechanistic, imitative of machine metaphorization.

---

3. CONTROL: unique property is centralized first-order cybernetic control of narratives behavior with rule-based mechanisms of deviation-counteraction. Observed narrative -scripts are compared to idealized narrative by a core of specialists noting deviations from the rules. First cybernetics is a complication of machine metaphorization.

---

4. OPEN: unique property is second-order cybernetic deviation-amplification, which opposes the level 3 deviation-counteraction, to accomplish self-maintenance whereas a throughput of narratives of the environment are sorted, without much or any knowledge generation. Second cybernetics is further complication of machine metaphorization.

---

5. ORGANIC: unique property is division of labor among mutually interdependent parts, each with highly specialized narrators, not doing much more than filtering environments for positive or negative narratives. Organization metaphorization framework and machine cybernetics coexist with mimicry of tree or plant. Up to this level, narratives imprison story in sign re-presentations; mimicry of more polyphonic polylogic is emergent, not pronounced.

---

6. IMAGE: unique property is the beginning of self-awareness and the narrating teleologically. Storying image of organization is differentiated from throughput processing of environmental narrative. Small antenarratives (bet & before fragments that aspire to narrative coherence) can transform a petrified image story. Metaphorization is computer-screen image mimicry achieved through orchestrating stylistic dialogism strategically.

---

7. SYMBOL: unique is self-consciousness achieved through self-reflexive storytelling. Stories are self-reflexively co-produced and co-interpreted at symbolic level, not just mere signs or images. The chronotopicity of constructing the time/space conception of history is salient. Metaphorization is history mimicry through chronotopic dialogism.

---

8. NETWORK: unique property is self-reflexive awareness of organization situated in network of societal discourse that proscribes roles to organizations that organizations rescript. Architectonic interanimation of cognitive, ethical, and aesthetic discourses, of which story is domain, is manifest. Metaphorization is mimicry of computer network.

Continued

Table 9.1   Continued

---

9. TRANSCENDENTAL: unique is self-reflexive awareness of metaphysics of what is unknowable in opposition to what is knowable. Metaphorization is mimicry of spiritual enlightenment. However, the prior eight properties are still in interrelationship, including the Polypi dialogism of dialogisms of polyphonic, stylistic, chronotopic, and architectonic dialogism. Story has escaped narrative prison, but the narrative police are trying to arrest story, as always.

STRATEGY SCHOOLS OF THOUGHT

Mintzberg, Ahlstrand, and Lampel (1998) described strategy as an *elephant* composed by the 10 schools of thought and it is impossible to grasp the entire beast. Mintzberg and Lampel (1999) referred the 10 strategy schools as the 10 parts of strategy processes, strategy formation, and implementation processes. Each school of thought brings about a unique meaning to the strategic whole. Table 9.2 presents the sources of each school of thought, base discipline, the center voices, and its corresponding level of system complexity. It is important to remember that each higher level of system complexity embraces the lower levels of complexities prior to it.

The *design school* focuses on creating uniqueness, clarity, and simplicity through SWOT analysis (Andrews, 1951; Chandler, 1962) and planning.

Developed alongside the design school of thought, the *planning school* described the microlevel structures of the dominant voice, the decomposed strategies and programs (Ansoff, 1965), which discouraged the creativity behind the creation of uniqueness, clarity, and simplicity.

The *positioning school* focuses on tactics in reflection of the plan, intended to strategically comprehend and control the external world. This school of thought emphasizes the economic aspects of the organization in relation to its industry and environment (Porter, 1990; Sun Tzu, 500 BCE).

The natural instincts within an organization reflect the *entrepreneurial school* of thought. Similar to the planning and positioning schools, this vision, a niche, is used to comprehend and control the external world led by a dominant voice, the intuitive architect. A leader described in the entrepreneurial school is often considered a hero because they are innovators, where their behavior impacts the society. Yet, along with creation, there is destruction. The idea of " . . . only stepping out the old ruts, will bring new insights (Grove, 1996, p. 121)" aligns with Schumpeter's (1950) theory of entrepreneurial creative destroying nature.

The *cognitive school* focuses on the individual conceptions, where the strategies to make sense of the complexity and unpredictability of the external environment are constructed through individual creative interpretations, instead of rational maps of reality by the controller. Each individual is a fragment to an organization (March & Simon, 1958) collectively influencing an organic system (Kilduff, 1993).

As a learning organization, knowledge becomes the center and the core competency (Lindblom, 1959). The dominant voice under the *learning school* is no longer controlled by a person, which can be touched or felt. It is now an abstract sensemaking process that requires continuous consideration by the organization collective.

Power school emphasizes positions and tactics. At the micro level, the focus is on the natural interpretations by individuals of the political patterns, complexity, and unpredictability within the organization and the external world. At the macro level, the focus is on control, the control of the internal processes and external relations by the organization leaders. At a micro level, the central actors are the ones that hold power. It is about bargaining and negotiation among insiders of an organization. At a macro level, the central actor is the organization. It is about the leaders of the organization and their voices.

The *cultural school* is opposite to the power school, which focuses on the collective. This collective strategy tries to balance the dissonance between control and unpredictability of the external world. Strategy formulation is a social process that integrates the voices by the centers and marginal.

Environmental demands drive the strategies behind the *environmental school*. This school of thought focuses on the creation of a specific market position (niche) by responding to environmental conditions.

The *configuration school* integrates the previous schools with an emphasis on contextual importance. Under the configuration school, there is a place and time for every school of thought. This school reflects Boulding's (1956) types of predictable systems: framework, mechanistic, control, open, and simple organic.

The authorship of each school varies. Design, planning, positioning, 'macro' power, and entrepreneurial schools are led by one or multiple dominant voices. These voices are the controllers or centers of an organization. The cognitive, learning, cultural, 'micro' power, environmental, and configuration schools are lead by collective voices. These voices integrate the marginal into the centers that blurs the controls by the dominant voices.

As described earlier and shown in Table 9.2, design and planning schools are linear, structured, and predictable systems with a dominant narrative by the architects and planners. Positioning and entrepreneurial schools are open and organic systems with control exercised by the leaders using highly specialized narratives while interacting with environment. The cognitive and learning schools are image systems where learners, individuals, or organizations are self-aware and exercise creativity brought by the freedom of the minds. The power school is a network system where individuals or organizations are situated among societal discourses and dominance can be brought through self-reflexivity. The cultural and environmental schools are symbol systems where the individuals are self-conscious and only have meaning when being a part of the collective. Configuration school is a limited transcendental system. In a transcendental system, individuals and

Table 9.2   Mintzberg Ten Schools of Thought

Schools	Sources	Base Disciplines	Centers	System Complexity
Design	P. Selznick (1957), & Andrews (1951)	None (Architecture as metaphor)	Architects (Dominant and judgmental)	Framework Control Mechanistic
Planning	I. Ansoff (1965)	Some links to urban planning, system theory, & cybernetics	Planners (process oriented)	
Positioning	Schendel and Patten (1977), Michael Porter (1980 and 1985)	Economics (industrial organization) & military history	Analysts	Controlled Open Organic
Entrepreneurial	J. A. Schumpeter (1950), A. H. Cole (1959) & others in economics	None (although early writings come from economics)	Leaders (dominant yet intuitive)	
Cognitive	H. A. Simon (1947/1957), & J. March & Simon (1958)	Psychology (cognitive)	Minds (source of cognition no matter passive or creative)	Image
Learning	C. E. Lindbliom (1959), M. Cyert and J. G. March (1963), K. E. Weick (1969), J. B. Quinn (1980), & G. Hamel & C. K. Prahalad (1994)	None (perhaps some peripheral links to learning theory in psychology & education). Chaos theory in mathematics.	Learners (individuals or organizations)	

Continued

Table 9.2   Continued

Power	G. T. Alison (1971) (micro), J. Pfeffer & G. R. Salancik (1978), & W. G. Astley (1984) (macro)	Political science	Individuals (micro) or organizations (macro)	Network
Cultural	E. Rhenman & R. Normann late 1960s in Sweden	Anthropology	Collectivity	Symbol
Environmental	M. T. Hannan & J. Freeman (1977). Contingency theorists (e.g., D. S. Pugh et. al., late 1960s)	Biology	The environment	
Configuration	A. D. Chandler (1962), McGill University group, Mintzberg and Miller, etc., late 1970s; R. E. Miles & C. C. Snow (1978)	History	Periodic changes in leadership to reflect contextual demands	Transcendental

organizations are self-reflexive; the dominant narrative is no longer in control whereas the antenarratives breaks out of the narrative prison competing to become the new narrative.

Mintzberg and Lampel (1999) described these strategy schools of thought as being independent forms of strategy where organization can only experience one strategic form at one time. On the contrary, Adler believed that the schools are relational and applied concurrently in strategy formulation and implementation. The intention is to blend the approaches that can be best applied suitable to achieve organizational short- and long-term goals. No matter the blend, it must serve organizational transformation as well as perpetuation; satisfy the individual cognition and social interaction needs, and cooperative as well as conflictive relations; apply analysis and negotiation processes. All of this must be a response to the environment demand.

In this study of Motorola strategy change over the past 50 years, it is found that Motorola exploited multiple strategies simultaneously. Each strategy school represents an antenarrative with an emphasis on corporate, consumers, media, workers, activists, or researchers.

STRATEGY AS ANTENARRATIVE COMPLEXITY

Organizations live through life cycles coupled with numerous strategic inflections. These strategic inflections are often within competitions, technological changes, customer changes, supplier changes, complement product changes, regulation changes, and organizational changes. They often represent the antenarratives to a new strategy.

Strategic inflection points are defined as: "A time in the life of a business when its fundamentals are about to change" (Grove, 1996, p. 3). It occurs when the old strategy or narrative dissolves and gives ways to the new strategy narrative. The new strategy is intended to help the organization create opportunities and bring it to a new height, but it is just as probable to signal 'the beginning of the end' because it is often difficult to identify strategic inflections prior to its sprouting (Grove, 1996, p. 3). Therefore, responding to the winds of change in a timely fashion lessens a company's chances of becoming trapped in a declining state or letting attractive new growth opportunities slip away because of inaction.

Antenarratives are most abundant prior to a strategic inflection when stories compete to create a story about the future and become the dominant narrative. At a strategic inflection point, this struggle is silenced and one narrative emerges while others disappear back into the narrative prison. However, the narrative prison could never hold back the antenarrative as the environment changes. This is when old and new antenarratives once again compete to become the dominant narrative of the organization.

During the last 50 years of Motorola development, the company experienced multiple strategic inflections. By analyzing Motorola's annual report from 1966 to 2008 and Motorola's key activities between 1928 and 2008, three inflections were selected for this study to help understand how the discovery of the struggle among present antenarratives and storytelling complexity help organizations identify possible inflections and strategic change of the future. The inflections are 1967, 1987, and 2004.

Strategy schools and system complexities were identified through the investigation of Motorola's annual reports and corporate citizenship report (Table 9.1). According to Mintzberg (1999), it was assumed that an organization implements one strategy at a time during a given period. However, Motorola practiced multiple strategy schools of thought prior to, during, and even after a strategic inflection. This multiplicity reveals strategy complexity and the existence and struggle among strategy antenarratives.

Table 9.3   Motorola Strategy Inflection Complexity

	1966	1967	1968)
Common	Cultural School Organic	Cultural School Organic	Cultural School Organic
	Design School Symbol	Design School Symbol	Design School Symbol
Unique	Planning School Control	Planning School Control	Planning School Control
	Design School Controlled Open		
	Positioning School Open	Positioning School Open	Positioning School Open
	Environmental School Organic		
	Power School Network		
	1986	**1987**	**1988**
Unique	Entrepreneurial School Open	Entrepreneurial School Open	Entrepreneurial School Open
	Planning School Control		
		Design School Controlled Open	Design School Controlled Open
	Positioning School Open	Positioning School Open	Positioning School Open
	Environmental School Organic		
	Power School Network		
	2003	**2004**	**2005**
Common	Cultural School Organic	Cultural School Organic	Cultural School Organic
	Design School Symbol	Design School Symbol	Design School Symbol
Unique	Planning School Control		

Continued

Table 9.3   Continued

	Design School Controlled Open	Design School Controlled Open	Design School Controlled Open
Unique	Positioning School Open	Positioning School Open	Positioning School Open
	Environmental School Organic		Environmental School Organic
	Power School Network		Power School Network

It was found that the amount of presence of Motorola strategy storytelling antenarrative was determined by (1) number of strategy schools and (2) storytelling organization system complexity levels. Larger number of strategy schools was observed during the 21st-century strategy storytelling, which reflected a stronger presence of antenarratives. During the years prior to the strategic inflections, 1967, 1987, and 2004, the complexity levels were at higher levels compared to the year of strategic inflections, which also reflected a stronger presence of antenarratives.

The year 1967 was a megastrategic inflection due to the unpredicted event (false forecast in consumer products division resulted in tremendous loss) and planned event (mega expansion into many foreign countries resulted in large investment). The changes in strategy narration involve changes in theorized strategy complexity levels. The strategy narration for 1966, prior to the strategic inflection point, was dialogical with strategy antenarratives from both higher and lower complexity levels. In 1967 and 1968 strategy narration became rather linear and rested at a lower level of complexity. Perhaps the dialogical nature and the struggle among the strategy antenarratives in 1966 were an amplification of the megastrategic inflection point.

At a glance, the year 1987 did not distinctively represent itself as a strategic inflection point due to insignificant change in strategy narrations; yet, Motorola global expansion strategy was put forth during these years. This new dominant narrative is an extension to Motorola's 1967 meganarrative. During the years between 1966 and 1987, antenarratives emerged and died off as the new strategy was reinforced in 1987.

The year 2004 was an example of a gradual strategic inflection where strategy direction shift was linked with changes in leadership and leadership vision. This gradual narrative shift was the foundation for the new strategy narrative recognized in 2005. The strategy narration complexity was similar during the three years (2003, 2004, and 2005) when strategy antenarratives from both lower and higher levels of theorized complexities were observed.

Pondy and Mitroff (1974) pointed out that strategies are often formulated at an abstract higher level complexity whereas implementation has taken place at a more factual linear and structured lower level of complexity. Perhaps this is why formulation and implementation processes are disjointed. Nevertheless, higher level complexities give rise to antenarratives' freedom to express, be creative, compete, and the opportunity to become the new narrative; whereas lower level complexities only give room for production of structure, control, and clear authority.

CONCLUSION

Antenarrative is a new and complementary approach to the traditional strategy process. Beyond making sense of the narratives from the past, organizations ought to understand the competition among the stories of the present and how they struggle to become the future. Strategy antenarratives could be hidden and forgotten stories from within or outside of an organization, embedded stories that are discovered when looking in between the dominant narratives of the present, and dead stories from the past that are offered new opportunities due to changes in the environment.

By discovering storytelling organization complexities, we also discover the presence of strategy antenarratives and their place in the storyline. Higher levels of storytelling complexity give room for greater numbers of strategy antenarratives to present themselves in the competition for future narrative. As organizations live through their rollercoaster lifecycles, strategy antenarrative dialogism is most prominent before and after a strategic inflection point. Before the future is set in place, stories compete for their place in the storyline of control. As the dominant narrative is being set, the antenarratives restory and resituate themselves in search of the next opportunity. After a dominant narrative has been set and implemented, it becomes the past, which creates opportunities for new and existing strategy antenarratives to reemerge and struggle for their places in the future. The process is cyclical. As the organization grows, its dominant strategy narrative changes, a result of a continuous struggle among the persevering antenarratives.

REFERENCES

Allison, G. T. (1971). *Essence of decision: Explaining the Cuban missile crisis.* Boston: Little Brown.

Andrews, K. W. H. (1951). *Administrative action: The techniques of organization and management.* Englewood Cliffs, NJ: Prentice Hall.

Ansoff, H. I. (1965). *Corporate strategy.* New York: McGraw-Hill.

Astley, W. G. (1984). Toward an appreciation of collective strategy. *Academy of Management Review, 9,* 526–533.

Boje, D. M. (1991). The storytelling organization: A study of storytelling performance in an office supply firm. *Administrative Science Quarterly, 36,* 106–126.

———. (2001). *Narrative methods for organizational and communication research.* London: Sage.

———. (2006). Breaking out of narrative's prison: Improper story in storytelling organization. *Storytelling, Self, Society: An Interdisciplinary Journal of Storytelling Studies, 2*(2), 28–49.

Boulding, K. (1956). General systems theory: The skeleton of science. *Management Science, 2*(3), 197–208.

Chandler, A. D. (1962). *Strategy and structure: Chapters in the history of the industrial enterprise.* Cambridge, MA:. MIT Press.

Cole, A. H. (1959). *Business enterprise in its social setting.* Cambridge, MA: Harvard University Press.

Cyert, R. R., & March, J. G. (1963). *A behavioral theory of the firm.* Englewood Cliffs, NJ: Prentice Hall.

Czarniawska, B. (1997). *Narrating the organization: Dramas of institutional identity.* Chicago: University of Chicago Press.

Fiske, J., O'Sullivan, T., Hartley, J., & Saunders, D. (1983). *Key concepts in communication.* London: Methuen.

Foucault, M. (1977). *Discipline and punish: The birth of the prison.* New York: Vintage.

Gephart, R. P. (1991). Succession, sensemaking, and organizational change: A story of a deviant college president. *Journal of Organizational Change Management, 4,* 35–44.

Grove, A. S. (1996). *Only the paranoid survive.* New York: Doubleday.

Hamel, G., & Prahalad, C. K. (1994). *Competing for the future.* Boston: Harvard Business School Press.

Hannan, M. T., & Freeman, J. (1977). The population ecology of organizations. *American Journal of Sociology, 82,* 929–964.

Kilduff, M. (1993). Deconstructing organizations. *Academy of Management Review, 18,* 13–31.

Lindblom, C. (1959). The science of muddling through. *Public Administration Review, 19,* 79–88.

March, J. G., & Simon, H. A. (1958). *Organizations.* New York: Wiley.

Miles, R. E., & Snow, C. C. (1978). *Organizational strategy, structure, and process.* New York: McGraw-Hill.

Mintzberg, H., Ahlstrand, B., & Lampel, J. (1998). *Strategy safari: A guided tour through the worlds of strategic management.* New York: The Free Press.

Mintzberg, H., & Lampel, J. (1999). Reflecting on the strategy process. *Solan Management Review, 40(3):* 21–30.

Normann, R. (1977). *Management for growth.* New York: Wiley.

Pfeffer, J., & Salancik, G. R. (1978). *The external control of organizations: A resource dependence perspective.* New York: Harper & Row.

Pondy, L. R., & Mitroff, I. I. (1974). On the organization of inquiry: A comparison of some radically different approaches to policy analysis. *Public Administration Review, 34,* 471–479.

Porter, M. E. (1980). *Competitive strategy.* New York: Free Press.

Porter, M. E. (1985). *Competitive Advantage,* New York: Free Press.

Porter, M. E. (1990). "The Competitive Advantage of the Nations", New York: Free Press.

Pugh, D. S., Hickson, D. J., Hinings, C. R., & Turner, C. (1968). Dimensions of organizational structure. *Administrative Science Quarterly, 13,* 65–105.

Quinn, J. B. (1980). *Strategies for change: Logical incrementalism.* Homewood, IL: Irwin.

Schendel, D., & Patten, G. R. (1977). A simultaneous equation model of corporate strategy. *Management Science, 24*(15): 611–621.

Schumpeter, J. A. (1950). *Capitalism, socialism, and democracy.* New York: Harper & Row.

Selznick, P. (1957). *Leadership in administration: A sociological interpretation.* Evanston, IL: Row, Peterson.

Simon, H. A. (1947/1957). *Administrative behavior.* New York: Macmillan.

Sun Tzu. (500 BCE). *The Art of War.*

Weick, K. E. (1969/1979). *The social psychology of organizing.* Reading, MA: Addison-Wesley.

White, H. (1978). *Tropics of discourse: Essays in Cultural Criticism.* Baltimore: Johns Hopkins University Press.3+

10 Antenarratives, Strategic Alliances, and Sensemaking

Engagement and Divorce Without Marriage Between Two Brazilian Air Carrier Firms

Sergio Luis Seloti, Jr., and Mário Aquino Alves

INTRODUCTION

In some way, managers need to deal with this duality and go through an interesting challenge: how to make alliances work, even if the partner is also a competitor. The way they do that—and most of all, the way they make sense of that—is a tortuous and non-linear path made of stories and narratives, fragmented ideas, and discourses which drive us to an antenarrative way of constructing reality and sensemaking.

Strategizing processes may be impacted by internal and external issues. Governmental actions, competitors, new products, social changes, and a wide range of events impact on the process of strategizing, as well as the way managers see the environment and how they interpret what they see. If events change the way managers strategize and the process of strategizing also changes what they see, then we are talking about sensemaking about event-based strategies. In this chapter, we analyze the history of two Brazilian airline companies—TAM and VARIG—and how the events impacted the managers' decision making, driving them to establish a strategic alliance and how this alliance became the event that triggered other changes in firms' strategy leading to the alliances ending.

HORIZONTAL STRATEGIC ALLIANCE: SLEEPING WITH THE ENEMY

Strategic alliance is a commercial partnership which increases organization strategy efficiency, favoring mutual interchange of technologies, skills, and products (Yoshino & Rangan, 1996). They vary from a simple contract to the formation of joint ventures and must answer, simultaneously, to three characteristics:

- Legal independence: firms must keep control of themselves after alliance formation;

- Shared control and benefits: alliance performance shall be fruit of partners' action, and
- Continue mutual contribution in one or more areas to maintain alliance.

Cooperation is the social interdependence relationship where individuals with common goals work together and share information intending to achieve these goals (Deutsch, 2003). Cooperative strategies—such as strategic alliances formation—are used by firms to achieve their goals through cooperation instead of competition, focusing on benefits from collaboration, such as supply skills and resource needs in a different way from competitive strategies that seeks to gain advantage over other players (Child, Faulkner, & Tallman, 2005). Cooperative strategies are not necessarily alternatives to competitive strategies, but compose a different domain of possibilities that should be considered when planning the firm strategy.

Horizontal alliances are strategic alliances whose partners act in the same market as competitors. Also known as co-optation alliances, they have the potential to neutralize competition and bring complementary resources to the specific business involved in the alliance (Doz & Hamel, 2000; Nalebuff & Brandenburger, 1996). Even if it seems to be a paradox, horizontal alliances exist and are strategic choices in some cases, like establishing technology patterns, international goods trade or distribution, and strengthening small firms to compete with stronger ones (Das & Teng, 1998). In opposition of the hostile-forces idea (Porter, 1998), Powell (1990) notices the existence of an intricate collaboration network involving lots of firms, including ostensive competitors.

STRATEGIC ALLIANCE AS A SENSEMAKING PROCESS

"Organizations are open social systems who process environment data" (Daft & Weick, 1984, p. 285). There are significant differences between organization and individual interpretation processes. In organizational process, there are shared knowledge, mind maps, norms, values, and behaviors which remain in organizations, despite human resource changes. The way firms scan and interpret environment data is also different between them, in that the process is influenced by individual preconceptions which are rarely reproduced in another environment. These preconceptions tend to guide interpretation and action to confirm the preconception itself, reinforcing itself. Finding reasons for actions taken—and defending them—may lead the process in two different directions: while they produce meaning in the face of ambiguity, they also may create blind points to future analysis, always reinforcing the same concepts and ideas and, possibly, ignoring significant environment changes (Weick, 1988).

Figure 10.1   Relationship between scanning, interpretation, and learning. Source: Daft and Weick (1984).

Weick (1988) proposes the existence of a special kind of interaction between environment and organizations which creates sense in a feedback cycle. The process starts with the receiving and selection of information. Then this information shall be retained, in an enactment process. The enactment concept, according to the author, is a synthesis of some other concepts, such as auto-realizable prophecies, retrospective sensemaking, compromising, and social information processing. In a more recent work, Weick, Sutciffe, and Obstfeld (2005) say that sensemaking process involves the retrospective development of images which explains and justifies current actions. Retrospective sensemaking is the moment when someone "looks back at what said earlier from a later point in time when the talking has stopped" (Weick, 1995, p. 12). Hence, sensemaking process and especially retrospective sensemaking are related to past, not to future (Weick, 1995).

When talking about managers' perceptions and decisions, Vlaar, Bosch, and Volberda (2007) suggest that "managers must make choices" (p. 440) and these choices are not just choosing between two extremes, from competition to cooperation, but there are functions and dysfunction in each possibility. In this way, context, transactions characteristics, perceptions, and individual experience influence choices.

SENSEMAKING, NARRATIVES, AND EVENT-BASED STRATEGIES

From Weick's conceptual framework on sensemaking—mainly, retrospective sensemaking—derives that strategy must be viewed as narrative, that is, the use of language to construct meaning. *"A narrative approach assume that tellings of strategy fundamentally influence strategic choice and action, often in unconscious ways"* (Barry & Elmes, 1997, p. 432).

Thus, in order to understand a narrative approach to strategy, one must review the literature perspective on the subject.

NARRATIVES IN LITERARY STUDIES

Narrative is "a method to recuperate the past experience by the combination of a verbal sequence of causes to a sequence of events, which (one infers) really happened" (Labov, 1972, pp. 359–360). Narrative can also be defined as that discourse that refers to a past moment (or imagined as one) in relation to the moment of speaking (Dubois, Giacomo, & Guespin, 1998).

It is clear, then, how important the temporality factor is for character-izing narratives. Todorov (1990) understands narrative as the "chronologi-cal chaining and often causal discontinuous units" (Todorov, 1990, p. 62). That notion of discontinuity of narrative was first studied by the Russian formalists, particularly Vladimir Propp (1997). Based on the view of the short story as narrative, each one of the actions present in the enunciation, when examined under the perspective of its utility for the narrative, acts as functions. If we read all the functions, one after the other, we will see that a function occurs in relation to another by a logical and artistic necessity. We see that no function excludes another. They all belong to the same set and to several sets. (Propp, 1997; Todorov, 1990)

Drawing a parallel with the analysis presented by Vladimir Propp (1997) with regard to the historic roots of the fairy tale, one should bear in mind that narratives are not isolated from the universe of social institutions. On the contrary, they are born in this universe and—simultaneously—consti-tute it. Narratives, therefore, have the function of constituting imaginary and symbolic systems of a particular society (Berger & Luckmann, 1987). Every society creates a coordinated set of representations, through which it reproduces itself and which represents in particular the group to itself, distributes the identities and roles, expresses the collective necessities and the ends to be reached (Ansart, 1978).

In addition, narrative structures offer many opportunities for variations and combinations that raise the narrative to the status of strategy in the creation of meanings and in the structuring of discourses that constitute a symbolic universe. The schemes that result from the narrative strategy con-stitute an instance from which discourses are generated. Todorov (1990) simplified the idea of narrative theory whilst also allowing a more complex interpretation of texts with his theory of equilibrium and disequilibrium. The fictional environment begins with a state of equilibrium (everything is as it should be). It then suffers some disruption (disequilibrium), and, con-sequently, a new equilibrium is produced at the end of the narrative.

Events are the point of a narrative inflection, the point where the narra-tive suffers its transformation, where it creates new meanings, and gener-ates new narratives. An event is precisely situated in the effects of meaning. Event possesses an interesting political dimension that contributes to under-standing its role in language. It is via event that one can understand the change of meaning of a narrative. Narrative is also praxis; thus, an event entails a strategic potential for action.

Events as Triggers of Strategic Directions

After the paradigm shift towards interpretationism and postmodernism in the field of management studies in the 1980s, events have been considered as a unit of analysis to understand organization processes. As we showed earlier, Daft and Weick (1984) were among the first to highlight the utility of using the concept of event to analyze organization process, and Weick (1995) used the concept of event to give sense to sensemaking.

Events may be considered in different levels of analysis: from the ecological level to the individual level (Peterson, 1998). In terms of the connection of events and sensemaking, it is notable that we must consider, in terms of strategy definition, if one is to consider events are units of analysis, he/she must consider events at the organizational level of analysis because they will connect issues as strategic priorities and political goals to contingent contexts affected by uncertainty.

Whereas a stream of authors use field-configuring events such as meetings, congresses, and formal gatherings to analyze its influence over strategies (Lampel & Meyer, 2008; McInerney, 2008; Oliver & Montgomery, 2008), in this article we take a broader definition of events as triggers to strategic directions change, once they generate an inflexion on narratives that will define situations, reducing uncertainty or equivocality (Weick, 1979).

Events may vary according to their uncertainty and equivocality (Daft & Lengel, 1984). Uncertainty describes a well-precedent, discrete event that either has a somewhat indeterminate wave position (turbulent effect) or occurs as part of a wave form that appears with indeterminate frequency within a particular field. Retrospective sensemaking about the structure of antecedent and consequent events typical of narrative or establishing connections with a number of similar narratives structures in a field can reduce uncertainty. Equivocality is usually defined as an event with continuing ambiguity. Different and contradictory interpretations will not be resolved by adding information. On the contrary, further information may create more complexity to a situation. An equivocal event may be unprecedented and unique, or it may lack a determinate fit into a larger meaning framework of fields, perspectives, or potentials. Thus, recognizing that uncertainty and equivocality refer to similar but different contingencies implies admitting a broader domain of interpretation ambiguities to be analyzed.

Thus, events are the critical incidents that define—or redefine—scenarios and interpretations about these scenarios, more specifically, strategic alliance formation (Farjoun, 2002; Madhavan, Koka, & Prescott, 1998; Sawy & Pauchant, 1988).

Event-based strategies are related to emergent strategies and demand fast decisions. Eisenhardt (1989) demonstrated that fast decision processes usually use more information than the slower ones, demanding shrewd managers to do so. Because managers interpret the environment in different way,s their responses are also different and may lead to antagonistic decisions (Dutton & Duncan, 1987).

Methodology

In order to analyze the sensemaking strategizing processes, the present article uses multiple methodological strategies that have made it possible to search and interpret the data collected. The presented case has been developed by using different sources of data, as proposed by Eisenhardt (1989), such as company Web sites, newspapers (Earl, Martin, McCarthy, & Soule, 2004), magazine research, and in-depth interviews with managers involved in the studied strategic alliance. The airline interviews happened in 2003, while alliance was still 'alive,' and in 2008, after its ending. The newspaper, Web sites, and magazine research occurred during the first half of 2008 and covered from 2003 to 2008, the whole strategic alliance duration. These secondary sources were relevant to show the changing discourse, as well as making it possible to hear the multiple voices from narratives in the form of antenarrative fragments (Boje, 2001)

The case's choice took into account the relevance of the companies to the Brazilian air transport industry and, most of all, to its rarity. An alliance involving two or more big direct competitors is not an ordinary event. The alliance between TAM and VARIG—two of the three biggest airline companies in Brazil at the tim—is a precious case because it shows the early stages of an alliance between competitors, from the events that drove them to the alliance (the pre-alliance stage) to the end of this partnership, leading one of the companies to an almost collapse situation. Besides, this is a well-known event in recent Brazilian business history. These reasons justify the decision for the presented case (Eisenhardt, 1989).

We used the Critical Incident Method (Tjosvold & Weicker, 1993) to understand the strategic impacts of strategic alliance formation over enterprise choices, as used to understand entrepreneurs' network effects over competition and cooperation. A narrative and antenarrative analysis combination completes our methodological framework. Narrative analysis makes it possible to study fragments of texts, speeches, and interviews to compose the narrative. Most of these fragments are antenarrative elements, for they are pre-elements which will form the final narrative (Boje, 2001). Antenarrative provides flexible retrospectives about recent events that reveal unusual, unexpected patterns (Baskin, 2008).

Through a sensemaking perspective (Weick, 1998; Weick et al., 2005), we analyze the partners' choice, formation of alliance, reinterpretation and strategic change, and, finally, the end of this alliance in a narrative context. Antenarrative methods are used to scrutinize some narrative analysis (Yolles, 2007).

THE AIRLINE STRATEGIC ALLIANCE CASE

This was a case of a horizontal strategic alliance between two Brazilian airline companies in 2003, initially as a code-share agreement: each company would be responsible for selling 50% of the tickets of each flight, eliminating duplicated routes. Their first intention was to raise airship occupation and increase profitability (Binder, 2006). The agreement had been effective from March 10, 2003, to May 2, 2005.

The companies presented different profiles. The first one, TAM, is younger. Founded in 1963 as an air taxi company by some investors that were not keen to aviation, it was an employee named Rolim Amaro—the last pilot of the flight schedules, who became its major personality. In order to get his bosses' attention, Rolim—also known as 'Comandante Rolim'—began to please his passengers beyond the usual, so they would ask explicitly for him to take them on the next trips. This was an important fact, because it became the more valuable mark of TAM in the following years, which resulted in Rolim becoming a partner of the company. TAM was known as the best quality service company, getting some national and international quality prizes in 1993, 1994, 1995, and 1996 (Binder, 2006).

VARIG, the second one, was the leading airline company in Brazil for decades. It was founded in 1927, by Otto Meyer, a German entrepreneur living in Brazil. Five years later, VARIG earned its first governmental benefit: 15 years' tax exemption and a loan from the State. The Second World War, however, brought some restrictions to the German entrepreneur as Brazil joined the Allied forces, and, as a consequence, Otto Meyer resigned as company CEO in 1941. His successor, Ruben Berta, led the enterprise until 1966, when he died. Governmental benefits such as tax exemption and monopoly of important commercial routes—fruit of a very close relationship with governors—were present along its whole history (Binder, 2006).

The 1990s were turbulent years in Brazilian economics. In the early 1990s, free-market reforms evolved to deregulation and strong competition in almost all sectors in Brazil. The air transport industry suffered the effects of market deregulation and the volatile currency fluctuation: many airline were bankrupted. In 1998, despite their own losses, VARIG and TAM were considered the best positioned companies to answer to those changes (*Business*, 1998, p. 64).

Since economy stabilization, many Brazilian industry structures have transformed for several reasons. The airline industry was not different. Whereas stabilization brought new passengers to fly, currency devaluation raised fuel costs. The stabilization of the Brazilian economy in the middle of the 1990s, which opened new competition opportunities, brought new consumers and, most of all, new investments. Real, the new currency, was launched in June 1994 by Fernando Henrique Cardoso, head of the treasury department at that time. This new currency and economic plan raised people's purchasing power and allowed new passengers to fly for the first time. It was a great opportunity for airline firms in Brazilian industry, but also would bring more competitors in a short time. The economic crisis that affected the world economy in the late 1990s was also an important impact event. Currency devaluation at the beginning of 1999—pressed by the rising public deficit caused by the controlled exchange rate—raised costs, causing financial disequilibrium to all airline companies in Brazil. Fuel and maintenance costs are rated in dollars, so the operational costs rose. The recent increase in numbers of cunsumers was not sufficient to pay new costs and some traditional firms were bankrupted—such as VASP and Transbrasil. VARIG and TAM were in better situation, but still worrying: something must change.

The terrorist attack on the World Trade Center on September 11, 2001, in New York, and the entrance of a new competitor—GOL, a low-cost/low-fare company—were also relevant events. Generalized panic and new security expenses reduced airship occupation and—again—raised costs. Technology-intensive and simplified processes quickly lifted GOL to the third market position. Taking advantage of its low-cost strategy, GOL had a bigger profitability than its more important competitors—TAM and VARIG. When in a price war, these factors are surely decisive. GOL was rising too fast and stealing some passengers from TAM. In this time, VARIG was in very difficult financial position because of recent economics and global events. Although all those events are relevant, a powerful new competitor was certainly the most significant one, a key driver event.

As a response to this scenario, VARIG and TAM (the first and second biggest companies at the time) eventually decided to ally themselves through a code-sharing operation. Apparently, the agreement would lead to a future merger between the companies (Seloti, 2008). However, it did not happen. The joint operation started in March 2003. This code-sharing agreement consists in shared sales and flights. Both companies were responsible for selling 50% of airplane seats. They also shared the flying operation, through a scheduled planning of interpolated flights, removing duplicated flights. This strategy intended to cut operational costs and raise airship occupation rates. Therefore, both companies benefited. A former TAM executive mentioned that this agreement allowed VARIG to breathe and have some extra time to recover its finances.

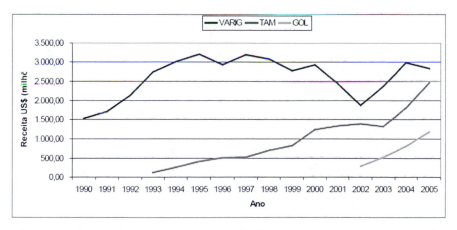

Figure 10.2 Total revenue evolution—1990 to 2005. Source: Resumo Anuário Exame Maiores e Melhores (1990–2005) apud Binder (2006), p. 195.

Whereas TAM tried to solve its financial troubles through operational efficiency—reducing costs and other administrative actions—VARIG, near bankruptcy, was loyal to its history and still pressed the government to help airline companies (Binder, 2009). Different mind-sets triggered different solution paths—and different storytelling. According to a former TAM executive, TAM had three reasons to join VARIG:

- **Governmental pressure.** The Brazilian presidency did not want a big airline company to break.
- **Slots in the major Brazilian airports.** VARIG had many slots and could share them with TAM. Because these slots are governmental concessions, they are quite valuable to the airline industry.
- **Hit the executive market.** VARIG was the preferred company for executive flights. TAM needed to break this preference, and sharing flights would be a good way to show itself to the executives.

However, VARIG executives truly believed the opposite. Their interpretation was that passengers were flying TAM aircraft, but preferred VARIG. With shared flights, "no one could notice in fact who the beauty was and who the beast was." Although this story does not makes sense in a first analysis, maybe the major VARIG reason to join the alliance was to have more time to get some governmental favors. But there is another possibility: VARIG really intended to merge with TAM in the near future. This would be a good solution for almost all, including the government. Political factors were placed to press for this solution, as said the former TAM executive: *"It would be bad news to government: 'Will VARIG bankrupt in my turn?'"* (Seloti, 2008, p. 101)

Seloti (2008) supposes TAM intended to merge initially, but its perception about this strategic alliance changed through time and it didn't want to join at the end. Whereas the intentions changed through time, the story didn't change. During the joint operation, TAM showed itself as a better services provider than VARIG. When the merger possibility began to disappear, TAM bought new airplanes and put them to fly the shared operation, as a signal of quality and modernity, as told by a former VARIG executive. These facts triggered the ruin of the alliance.

Near the end of the agreement, TAM and VARIG showed the market that their initial intentions had changed (Flores, 2004). VARIG's top executive in charge of managing the agreement was hired by TAM months after the end of it (Magnavitta, 2008). It is important to notice that, at the end, TAM was really stealing VARIG's passengers.

Discussion about the Case

Resources and skills complementarities are among the more relevant factors that influence the choice of a partner in a horizontal strategic alliance

(Child et al., 2005; Doz & Hamel, 2000; Nalebuff & Brandenburger, 1996). It is possible to find valuable resources and capabilities of each partner that really could complement the other. TAM and VARIG had something that was of interested the other. By VARIG's side, historical and political factors allowed having slots, international routes, a valuable brand, and, most of all, VARIG was preferred by executive travelers. This last resource, certainly, was the most coveted by TAM, but was also the result of the other factors. On the other hand, TAM had the technology to sell through the Internet, offering convenience and lower costs to consumers. It also had modern airships and the recognized superior service (represented by the red carpet at the airship door). There is evidence to support the idea that TAM took advantage of the proximity to 'learn' about VARIG, but VARIG did not do the same and saw its revenues fall after the code share ended.

The economic and political scenario and the strong market growth brought some possibilities, but it also brought the need for new managerial tools and cost controls. Binder (2006), however, remembers that cost controls in airline companies are not a simple task: exchange rates, fuel costs, occupation costs, and opportunity costs in case of low attendance. "A full airship isn't always a profitable flight" (p. 110).

CONCLUSION

The multiple voices heard (from interviews, newspapers, and magazines) as fragments of a narrative (Boje, 2001) helped us to listen to the entire history and understand the meaning, even better, the assigned meaning of what the events represented to each partner. This method is suitable to this project.

This chapter tried to identify sensemaking elements embedded in strategic alliance stories told by both sides. The interpretation given by each partner about the same event was so different that one of these sides could not be right. Or even both. Maybe these were just their stories, their interpretation about the same events, but divergent sensemakings led them to different ways, different alliance strategies, and also different results.

Maybe no one will never know the initial intention of TAM and VARIG, but what calls our attention is that perception and meaning—and then the narratives—change over time, impacted by new events, strategic changes, or just perception and signification changes.

As the stories change, everything changes.

REFERENCES

Alves, M. A., & Blikstein, Izidoro. (2006). *Análise de Narrativas*. In C. Kleinübig Godoi, R. Bandeira-De-Melo, & A. B. Silva (Eds.), *Pesquisa qualitativa em estudos organizacionais: Paradigmas, estratégias e métodos* (pp. 403–428). São Paulo: Editora Saraiva.

Ansart, P. (1978). *Ideologias, conflitos e poder* [Ideologies, conflicts, and power]. Rio de Janeiro: Jorge Zahar.

Barbosa, C. A. P. (2006). *Alianças estratégicas que usam a Web e seu impacto para a construção de vantagem competitiva em empresas de TI.* Dissertação de Mestrado em Administração de Empresas. São Paulo: Universidade Presbiteriana Mackenzie.

Barry, D., & Elmes, M. (1997). Strategy retold: Towards a narrative view of strategic discourse. *Academy of Management Review, V22*(2), 429–452.

Baskin, K. (2008). Storied spaces: The human equivalent of complex adaptive systems. *Emergence : Complexity and Organization, 10*(2), 1–13.

Benveniste, E. (1966). *Problemes de linguistique generale.* Paris: Gallimard.

Berger, P. L., & Luckmann, T. (1985). *A construção social da realidade* [The social construction of reality]. Petrópolis, Brazil: Vozes.

Binder, M. P. (2006). *Recursos e competências sob turbulência: Estudo longitudinal de três empresas aéreas brasileiras.* Dissertation. Administração de Empresas, EAESP/FGV.

Boje, D. M. (2001). *Narrative methods for organizational & communication research.* Sage.

Business: As free as a bird. (1998). *The Economist, 347*(8067), 64.

Child, J., Faulkner, D., & Tallman, S. B. (2005). *Cooperative strategy.* New York: Oxford University Press.

Daft, R. L., & Lengel, R. H. (1986). Organizational information requirements, media richness and structural design. *Management Science*, 554–571.

Daft, R. L., & Weick, K. (1984). Toward a model of organizations as interpretation systems. Academy of Management. *The Academy of Management Review* (pre-1986), 9. 284.

Das, T. K., & Teng, B.-S. (1998). Between trust and control: Developing confidence in partner cooperation in alliances. *The Academy of Management Review, 23*(3), 491–512.

Deutsch, M. (2003). Cooperation and conflict: A personal perspective on the history of the social psychological study of conflict resolution. In D. Tjosvold, M. West, & K. G. Smith (Eds.), *International handbook of organizational teamwork and cooperative working.* John Wiley & Sons.

Doz, Y. L., & Hamel, G. (2000). *A vantagem das alianças.* Rio de Janeiro: Qualitymark.

Dubois, J., Giacomo, M., & Guespin, L. (1995). Dicionário de lingüística [Dictionary of linguistics]. São Paulo: Cultrix.

Dutton, J. E., & Duncan, R. B. (1987). The creation of momentum for change through the process of strategic issue diagnosis. *Strategic Management Journal, 8*, 279–295.

Earl, J., Martin, A., McCarthy, J. D., & Soule, S. A. (2004). The use of newspaper data in the study of collective action. *Annual Review of Sociology.*

Eisenhardt, K. M. (1989). Building theories from case studies research. *Academy of Management Review 14*(4), 532–550.

Eisenhardt, K. M. (1989). Making fast strategic decisions in high-velocity environment. *Academy of Management Journal, 32*(3), 543.

Farjoun, M.. (2002). Towards an organic perspective on strategy. *Strategic Management Journal, 23*, 561–594.

Flanagan, J. C. (1954). The critical incident technique. *Psychological Bulletin, 54.*

Flores, J. (2004, March 23–29). Fight to survive. *Flight International.*

Gomes-Casseres, B. (2000). Strategy must lie at the heart of alliances. *Financial*

Lampel, J., & Meyer, A. D. (2008). Field-configuring events as structuring mechanisms: How conferences, ceremonies, and trade shows constitute new technologies, industries, and markets. *Journal of Management Studies, 45*(6), 1025–1035.

Madhavan, R., Koka, B. R., & Prescott, J. E. (1998). Networks in transition: How industry events (re)shape interfirm relationships. *Strategic Management Journal, 19*(5), 439–459.

Magnavitta, C.. (2008). *TAM anunciará saída de Wagner Ferreira nesta segunda. Jornal do Turismo*. Retrieved June 15, 2008, from http://www.jornaldeturismo. com.br/noticias/6-aviacao/16527-tam-anunciara-saida-dewagner-ferreira.html

McInerney, P.-B. (2008). Showdown at Kykuit: Field-configuring events as loci for conventionalizing accounts. *Journal of Management Studies, 45*(6), 1089–1116.

Nalebuff, B. J., & Brandenburger, A. M. (1996). *Co-opetição*. Rio de Janeiro: Rocco.

Oliver, A. L., & Montgomery, K. (2008). Using field-configuring events for sensemaking: A cognitive network approach. *Journal of Management Studies, 45*(6), 1147–1167.

Peterson, M. F. (1998). Embedded organizational events: The units of process in organization science. *Organization Science, 9*(1), 16–33.

———. (1998). Como as Forças Competitivas Moldam a Estratégia. In C. A. Montgomery & M. E. Porter (Eds.), *Estratégia: A Busca da Vantagem Competitiva* (pp. 11–28). Rio de Janeiro: Editora Campus.

Powell, W. W. (1990). Neither market nor hierarchy: Network forms of organization. *Research in Organizational Behavior, 12*, 295–336.

Propp, V. (1997). *As raízes históricas do conto maravilhoso* [The historical roots of the marvelous tale]. São Paulo: Martins Fontes.

Sawy, O. A. E., & Pauchant, Thierry C. (1988). Triggers, templates and twitches in the tracking of emerging strategic issues. *Strategic Management Journal, 9*(5), 455–473.

Seloti, S. L., Jr. (2008). *Sensemaking em alianças estratégicas: Busca, interpretação e ação*. Master of science in administration thesis. FGV, São Paulo.

Times, Mastering Management, October 16.

Tjosvold, D., & Weicker, D. (1993). Cooperative and competitive networking by entrepreneurs: A critical incident study. *Journal of Small Business Management*. 11–21.

Todorov, T. (1990). *Genres in discourse*. Cambridge: Cambridge University Press.

Weick, K. (1979). *The social psychology of organizing*. Addison-Wesley.

———. (1988). Enacted sensemaking in crisis situation. *Journal of Management Studies 25*(4), 305–317.

———. (1995). *Sensemaking in organizations*. Sage.

Weick, K. E., Sutcliffe, Kathleen M., & Obstfeld, David. (2005). Organizing and the process of sensemaking. *Organization Science, 16*(4), 409–421.

Vlaar, P. W. L., Van den Bosch, F. A. J., & Volberda, H. W. (2007). Towards dialectic perspective on formalization in interorganizational relationships: How alliance managers capitalize on the duality inherent in contracts, rules and procedures. *Organizational Studies, 28*, 437–466.

Yolles, M. (2007). The dynamics of narrative and antenarrative and their relation to story. *Journal of Organizational Change Management, 20*(1), 74–96.

Yoshino, M. Y., & Rangan, U. S.. (1996). *Alianças estratégicas*. São Paulo: Makron Books.

11 Visual/Picture as Antenarratives
Sketching the Research Process

Teppo Sintonen and Tommi Auvinen

"What is the use of a book," thought Alice, "without pictures or conversations?"

Lewis Carroll, *Alice's Adventures in Wonderland*

INTRODUCTION

Using pictures, sketches, and drawings to make sense of issues in research is not a new idea. For centuries explorers, missionaries, and adventurers have drawn pictures of what they saw, or imagined they saw (Mason, 1990). For anthropologists, drawings and pictures were almost the only way to represent other races before the era of photography (Collier & Collier, 1986; Comaroff & Comaroff, 1992; Mason, 1990). When photography became common, it presented new opportunities for visual representation. Photography allowed people not only to map and survey static places and objects, such as architectural constructs, fireplaces, tools, or clothes, but also to record social interaction, relations, and circumstances (Collier & Collier, 1986). Pictures have not only been figurative but also nonfigurative models as in Lévi-Strauss's (e.g., 1963, 1969) structural models describing social orders or ties of kinship.

Visualization has also been utilized in many fields of science and there are numerous different forms of visualization. For example, scientific visualization focuses on the use of computer graphics to create visual images. They are an aid to the understanding of complex, massive numerical representations of results or scientific concepts. In physics, medicine, and engineering, transparent substances like air or water may be colored in order to make observations. In our case, our fluid is the flux of stories in an organization (see Auvinen & Sintonen, 2009; Sintonen & Auvinen, 2009), and it has to be visualized to permit observation.

Visualization has much to do with antenarratives (Boje, 2001, 2008). An antenarrative pays attention to the speculative, the ambiguity of sensemaking, and guesses what is happing in the flow of experience. Antenarrating is what is before the story, the here and now, and is a bet on prospective transformation through supplements, dropping, and picking up meaning in each successive context, and remaining unfinalized.

Focusing on drawings and sketches used during a research process from the methodological point of view has been less common. This chapter considers drawings and sketches as a methodological means; not only in describing analysis or results, but also in a heuristic sense, to contrive new ideas. Our argument, which we elaborate here, is that Boje's antenarrative perspective can also be applied to the research process itself. We are taking into consideration the following aspects of antenarrative perspective: BME (beginning-middle-end) retrospective narrative, fragmented retrospective narrative, Tamara, and antenarrative. We focus on how these aspects intersect with the research process and the drawings and sketches created during the process. All of this is illustrated with the visualizations from our study.

We have drawn many sketches during our writing and analyzing processes and these sketches are a form of documentation of our work processes. In this chapter, we limit the examination to one, still ongoing, process. It focuses on leader's stories and it has resulted in two academic conference presentations (Auvinen & Sintonen, 2009; Sintonen & Auvinen, 2009).

In short, the following episodes took place during the research process: (1) after the preliminary reading of the data (leader's interviews), some intuitive models were drawn. (2) A seed of understanding or interpretation emerged about what the interview could be revealing. (3) We did some more sketches, without having a clear view of where they could lead. (4) After reading the subordinates' interviews, again some intuitive models were drawn. (5) The former visual sketches based on the leader's interview were developed further and reshaped. (6) We saw some of the drawings in different way. (7) We jumped back and forward between steps 1 and 6, until the deadline for the conference paper. (8) At last we edited a version of a paper that was presented at the conference with a visualization in the form of a cartoon. This is, of course, a simplification of the process. There was a lot of ambiguity and many unclear moments during it. It was not a linear process either; instead, it consisted of multidirectional moves often without exact planning.

VISUALIZATION OF THE RESEARCH PROCESS AS ANTENARRATIVE

David M. Boje's (2001) concept of antenarrative stems from the distinction between narrative and story. For Boje, narrative is a coherent account of an event or a sequence of events, which consist of plot, characters, and relatively linear temporal order. It appears in the form of BME. The function of the plot is to connect the events into one whole, which has a clear close. In contrast to narrative, a story is a bunch of incoherent fragments, which has no BME order. Whereas narratives usually appear in established contexts, stories have multiple manifestations in multiple instants. They appear simultaneously and overlap both temporally and spatially.

The prefix *ante* means that something exists before the proper and primary entity. Thus, antenarrative is something which exists before narrative. For Boje (2001), story is antenarrative in a sense that it precedes narrative. Narrative comes after story and makes it coherent by adding plot. *Ante* also has another meaning. It is a bet. This adds a speculative feature to antenarrative: it is a matter of guessing and traveling in ambiguity. The facet of story as antenarrative complicates the interpretation and understanding of stories. Whereas a narrative, as a coherent whole, is relatively easy to capture by retrospective sensemaking, a story evades all simple and unproblematic sensemaking (Boje, 2001; Weick, 2001).

In elaborating his concept of the organization of storytelling, Boje (2008) added more temporal dimensions to sensemaking. Sensemaking is not only backward looking, retrospective, but also takes place now, and can also be future oriented, prospective. He distinguishes eight ways of sensemaking according to these three temporal dimensions. We focus here on BME and terse fragments (which are in the sphere of retrospective sensemaking), Tamara (for the present or the now), and antenarrative as prospective sensemaking. They all have features that can help clarify the research process, and especially the visualizations created during the process.

By visualizing, we refer to the various ways to create or evoke pictures of many things and targets (cf. Hill & Levenhagen, 1995; Siirtola, 2007). Here we focus on the research process. Generally, visualization has something to do with imagination. According to Ricoeur (1994), imagination concerns both absence and nonexistence. Traditionally the term 'imagination' has been used in four ways. Firstly, to refer to the arbitrary evocation of things existing elsewhere, but which are absent here. Secondly, there are things, such as drawings and diagrams, which have a physical existence, but represent something else. Thus, they *take the place of* something. Thirdly, by use of imagination, we are able to bring to mind things that are not absent but are nonexistent. Fictional novels or dreams are examples of this kind imagination. Fourthly, there are things and representations which are absent and nonexistent for the outside observer but which tempt the subject attending in the instant to believe in the reality of the object.

Thus, when we are making drawings during the research process, we are also dealing with something which is absent or nonexistent. When we started drawing our first models, we had some intuition of things existing elsewhere, but they were still absent in the sense that we had not yet given them form or figure. The things existing elsewhere, but not yet here, are some intuitive ideas about the topic or targets of our research. When the sketches and drawings are made, their physical existence emerges. Imagination is a link between our drawings and antenarratives. As antenarrative is a bet and the subject of future-oriented prospective sensemaking, drawings are targeted at the future. Their meaning has not yet been clarified, and will perhaps never become clear, but they provide some clues to a future which can possibly be the subject of prospective sensemaking. In that way, drawings can be a means for the sensemaking and antenarrating end.

We present four examples of our drawings and sketches. All of them describe a situation in which a leader gets an idea for a speech in a meeting and he communicates it to his colleagues/followers. The reception is not that anticipated; the listeners become confused and even annoyed. The drawings are based on the impression which emerged while reading our interview data. The purpose of the drawings was to pull together and clarify the embryonic ideas that emerged concerning both the relation between a leader and his followers/colleagues, and also how a particular story he told to his followers circulates around the organization (see Auvinen & Sintonen, 2009; Sintonen & Auvinen, 2009). We should emphasize that the question of how well the drawings represent and describe the empirical situation, in this case the relation between a leader and his colleagues or subordinates, is not our focus. Instead, we accentuate the role the drawings played in the research process. All these drawings were born at different times and in different places. There are handwritten notes in Finnish on the drawings. They are translated into English following when necessary.

Drawing 1 (simple circles and an arrow) was made at the beginning of January 2009. It is the first sketch on the topic/theme and was drawn in the left margin of a printout of an interview transcript. The drawing was done in a researcher's office at the University of Jyväskylä, Finland. The notes in Finnish can be translated into English as follows: 'JK' initials of the leader interviewed (real name withheld); 'nykyinen kulttuuri' is 'present (organizational) culture'; 'pitäisi olla xxx visio' is 'should be the vision of the organization.'

Drawing 2 was made in the middle of January 2009 at the University library in Jyväskylä. It is drawn on the back of an interview printout, but not on the same sheet as drawing 1. Here too 'JK' refers to the initials of the leader interviewed.

Drawing 3 was drawn in the researcher's office in early February, 2009. It is drawn on the back of an interview printout, but not on the same sheet as drawings 1 and 2. The Finnish term 'Muurattu merkitys' can be translated into English as 'fixed meaning' (literally, walled-in meaning).

Drawing 4 was made at the beginning of March 2009, and also produced in the researcher's office. It is drawn on the back of a print of Walter R. Fisher's article published in *Argumentation* (1994).

Drawing 5 was made on April 3, 2009, in Orlando, Florida, USA. It is one of four overhead transparencies that were presented at the scMOI conference the next day. Furthermore, all transparencies were presented overlaid one on top of the other, together forming the complete picture. Due to space constraints we present only one of them here.

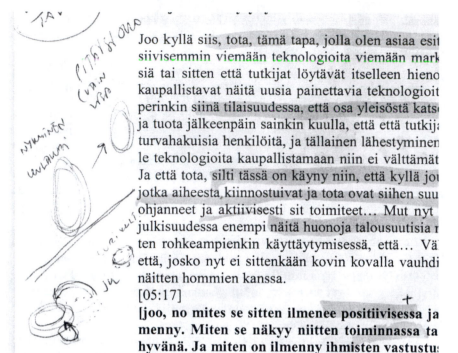

Joo kyllä siis, tota, tämä tapa, jolla olen asiaa esi‹
siivisemmin viemään teknologioita viemään mark
siä tai sitten että tutkijat löytävät itselleen hieno
kaupallistavat näitä uusia painettavia teknologioit
perinkin siinä tilaisuudessa, että osa yleisöstä kats‹
ja tuota jälkeenpäin sainkin kuulla, että että tutkij‹
turvahakuisia henkilöitä, ja tällainen lähestyminen
le teknologioita kaupallistamaan niin ei välttämät
Ja että tota, silti tässä on käyny niin, että kyllä jo
jotka aiheesta kiinnostuivat ja tota ovat siihen suu
ohjanneet ja aktiivisesti sit toimiteet… Mut nyt
julkisuudessa enempi näitä huonoja talousuutisia r
ten rohkeampienkin käyttäytymisessä, että… Vä
että, josko nyt ei sittenkään kovin kovalla vauhdi
näitten hommien kanssa.
[05:17]
[joo, no mites se sitten ilmenee positiivisessa ja
menny. Miten se näkyy niitten toiminnassa ta
hyvänä. Ja miten on ilmenny ihmisten vastustu‹

Figure 11.1   Drawing 1.

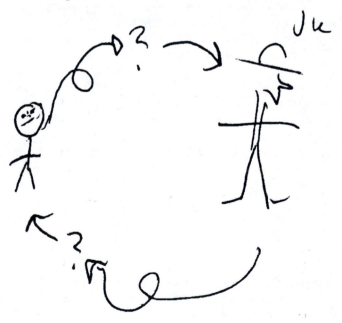

Figure 11.2   Drawing 2.

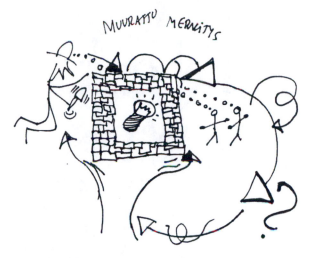

Figure 11.3   Drawing 3.

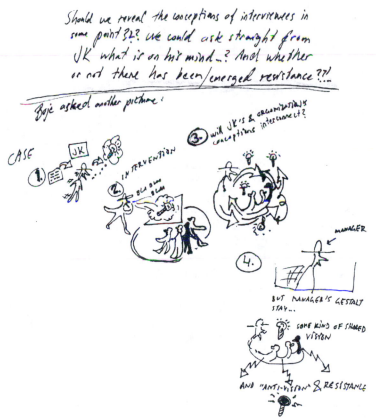

Figure 11.4   Drawing 4.

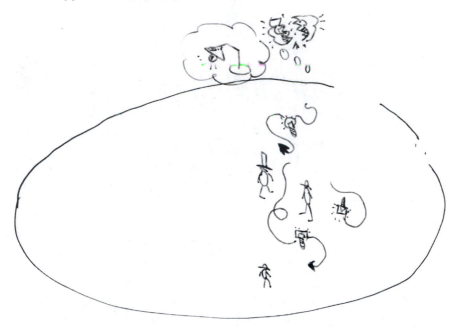

Figure 11.5   Drawing 5.

BME in the Research Process

Traditionally, and especially in quantitative research, research method text-books present the research process as a linear sequence of operations. The process has been illustrated in the form of a line or circle, which starts from planning and goes through steps like preliminary study, fieldwork, analysis of data, and preparing the final report. Thus, the research process has been described as having a linear BME structure. On the contrary, we argue here that the research process does not have such a clear BME structure, and we are trying to show how complex its actual structure can be.

There has been a debate on the existence of original or founding begin-ning narratives in organizations (Boje, 2008; Czarniawska, 1997, 2004). These kinds of narratives follow the BME structure and are usually immu-table, describing certain fundamental events of the foundation of organi-zations. Beginning narratives of organizations have their counterparts in research processes. Traditionally, ethnographies have started with an open-ing story, often a description of the researcher's operations and experiences during the fieldwork period (Aro, 1996; Clifford, 1986; Eräsaari, 1995; Marcus & Fisher, 1986). In opening stories, the research process has usu-ally been described in BME form and all the operations the researcher has undertaken as serving the process. Opening stories can be considered as small-scale grand narratives (see Lyotard, 1984) of the research.

Our research has no clear beginning, middle, or end and, furthermore, is not a founding narrative. It started with numerous little encounters, discussions, hints, and so on, which did not always lead in the same direction. Following Aristotle (1997), Ricoeur (1991a, 1991b, 1992) has argued that instead of speaking about a static structure (a plot), we should understand the dynamics of emplotment. It is a matter of the synthesis of heterogeneous elements, which might have nothing in common before the emplotment. In the emplotment, the synthesis of the heterogeneous, there is a tension between concord and discord. This tension is also apparent in our research process. During the process, we struggle to make sense of what we are doing, but never reach complete concordance.

Our drawings are examples of the tension between concordance and discordance. Although their shape, texture, and composition vary greatly, there are still some similarities connecting some of them. The resemblance between drawings 2 and 3 is easy to see, but on the other hand, drawing 4 stands out from the others, because there are no circles in it and it proceeds linearly. In addition, drawing 1 differs from the others by being very simple, and thus very difficult to make sense of. It is so general that it allows for multiple interpretations. Therefore, there is not such concordance between the drawings that they could form a linear BME narrative.

In the BME context, the sensemaking of the research process is retrospective (cf. Boje, 2008). The meaning of the process can be created after the episodes that took place in the process. This is also in accordance with Ricoeur's (1991a, 1991b) conception of emplotment. It is the process of emplotment which creates coherence between different elements of a story, and a concordant story may emerge as a result of emplotment. Thus, although we could not conceive and understand all of the meanings, effects, and/or influences our drawings would have in the future, it is possible for us to make sense of them afterwards, by looking back at what has happened. By emplotting different and discordant elements, we can make sense retrospectively. Viewers with at least some contextual information on the research topic will be able to discern the plot connection between the drawings retrospectively. The retrospective character of sensemaking in the BME context does not limit the quality of the possible interpretations or the number of possible interpreters. Different interpretations may exist depending on the sensemakers. This is because when the narrative has a coherent and fixed form (e.g., BME), it also has such an existence which allows it to become a target for continuous sensemaking.

Terse Fragments of a Research Process

Boje (2008) refers to two kinds of metaphors which illustrate two different ideas of narrative and/or story fragments. The first metaphor deals with narratives and the latter deals with stories. First, they can be understood as shards of pottery that archaeologists excavate. In this case, the shards will form a solid and complete pot. Similarly, the fragments of a story form a whole narrative, when assembled in the correct order. This conception can be interpreted in such a way that it refers to narratives that have a coherent structure and form. In this sense, it also implies that, in organizations, for example, there may exist coherent and solid narratives, although they might be broken into fragments. On the other hand, the pottery metaphor is problematic because it assumes that the pieces fit easily and exactly together and have a certain and fixed form. The second metaphor of fragmented stories is a mix of pieces of many puzzles. All the pieces have been cast into a pile and mixed together. It should be noted that the pieces are not from complete puzzles, but that the puzzles are missing pieces and parts and so are incomplete. We consider that this latter metaphor illustrates more accurately the manner in which organizational stories emerge, 'dance' and become interpreted and understood.

The drawings and sketches made during our research process are examples of the latter metaphor. They never formed any kind of a complete and coherent general view of the research. Instead, they changed many times: new layers were added and some were removed again; some parts were omitted or deleted. The drawings were not created in one session. Instead, they were products of an intricate and fluctuating combination of ideas which emerged at various times and places, often not even deliberately. They were drawn in places ranging from a researcher's office in Finland to a conference hotel in Orlando, Florida.

While doing the drawings there was a problem connected to terse fragments. Terse fragments (Boje, 2008) are thoroughly coded meanings which only an inner circle can understand. They consist of tiny hints, which may be verbal or nonverbal or even just a nod. Because the purpose of a drawing is to make sense, it matters what kind of figures are used in them. The problem lies in finding what kind of figures should be used in order to make the drawing understandable to the target audience. If they are too terse, only a minority of people will be able to make sense of the drawing. Of course, it is possible to manipulate the drawings to direct, or even misdirect, the reception of the drawings, but that was not our purpose.

In the drawings, there are figures representing human beings, referring to the leader and his colleagues/followers. We suppose that most of people in the field of organization studies can understand the conventional meanings of the figures. There are also circles endowed with arrows, straight or wavy, which are quite common in organizational charts. However, in this particular case it is not self-evident that the viewer interprets the circles as referring to the circulation of a story, especially in the case of drawing 1. Making sense of them requires at least some degree of knowledge in advance. For the inner circle, in this case the two researchers, the drawing process consists of a continuum of multiple hints we exchange. Sometimes we are able to make sense of things with the help of tiny nods in the immediate situation; sometimes the sense of the other's expressions eludes us.

Tamara in the Research Process

By Tamara, Boje (1995, 2001, 2008) refers to storying which takes place simultaneously in various spaces. He prefers the term 'storying' to 'story-telling,' because it includes more than only telling orally. Storying encom-passes not only spoken stories but also many visual methods, such as photographs, cartoons, and gestures to recount a story. This distinction also suits us, because we are dealing with visual issues. Tamara is a play in which the audience participates in the creation of stories. The audience wanders through different rooms in which they meet the actors. The actors reveal the stories of their characters to random members of the audience, while the audience reciprocates by trying to make sense of the play. Thus, Tamara exemplifies making sense now.

In some ways our research process reminds us of a Tamara kind of situ-ation. In general, while doing research many things occur both within a particular research project and outside of it. Researchers pursue the under-standing of multiple issues in places they physically occupy. Just as the audience changes rooms in Tamara, researchers encounter a multitude of unexpected situations, in which their ideas may flourish, be written off, or change their direction. For example, our drawings emerged in different places and conditions.

Events also occur outside of the research area, incidents of which the researchers are unaware in their now. In our case, one very influential chain of events took place before we got to know of it when the scMOI confer-ence was organized in 2008. The organizers did things of which we were not aware in the beginning, but which later led to our participation in the conference and the presentation of our drawings there. Thus, when we par-ticipated in the conference, we changed rooms as in Tamara, and heard new and unexpected stories from the other participants.

The Tamara style of research process raises an interesting problem for the control and organization of research processes. How tight and all embrac-ing a control can a researcher create for the process? Is it a matter of an unpredictable world, which produces unexpected situations and events? Or is it a matter of making sense, or giving an explanation, of loose and sloppily planned and realized processes? We argue that there is a tension between the two extremes. Researchers cannot fully control what is happening during the research process, because there are things that are beyond their control. Like the events which occurred in places where we were not present. On the other hand, this kind of contingency and randomness creates a need to explain the character of the process in a sensible manner.

Antenarratives in the Research Process

David M. Boje (2008, p. 13) defines antenarrative as follows: "Antenarratives are prospective (forward-looking) bets (antes) that an ante-story (before-story) can transform organization relationships." Antenarratives are also able to give rise to future events and incidents that would not take place otherwise. Here we look at two features of how antenarratives are involved in our research process. First, the presentation of drawings on certain occasions has led us to unexpected experiences. This concerns our drawings in general more than one of them in particular. Second, a specific drawing can have preliminary codes of meaning that may lead to further ideas in the future. Thus, they have a heuristic function for prospective sensemaking.

When we started to make drawings and sketches, we had no idea where they might lead us. We had just delimited the topic and collected enough data to start the analysis. Our purpose was to write an academic article and try to publish it in a (then undetermined) journal. Then we made a connection to David M. Boje, who invited us to present a paper at the scMOI conference in Philadelphia in 2008. At that moment, we did not have the slightest idea of the interest that our drawings would excite at the conference. We were surprised at the reception of the conference participants, and especially at the attention our drawings gained there. Thus, it was the drawings, not the conference paper itself, which opened up and led us to the point we are now in this research project. The drawings realized the prospective character of antenarratives by giving rise to these particular future events, which did not exist at the moment of drawing.

How can our drawings themselves be bets on the future? Although their appearance was not clear or definite at the moment of drawing, would they still constitute future-oriented embryonic concepts? The way we interpreted our drawings varied from occasion to occasion; this reflects their antenarrative character and prospective sensemaking. The logic on which interpretations are based does not remain constant throughout the research process. If at point of time A, the interpretation is based on logic a, it does not imply that at point of time B, the logic would also be a. Instead, it might be b, c, x, or y. This becomes obvious in comparing drawing 1 to 2 and 3, and drawings 2 and 3 to 4. The form of drawing 1 differs from drawings 2 and 3: it is not a circle, but two separate figures connected by an arrow. In a circle, there is a continuous and endless movement, which does not exist in drawing 1. Furthermore, drawing 4 is a linear composition of small figures which is usually read from left to right. It has a beginning, middle, and end, things absent in circles. Drawing 5 is distinguished from all the others by its form and structure. There is a circle which encompasses figures in no clear or strict order, and outside of the circle, there are two figures. One is a desk lamp in a balloon and the other is very difficult to make sense of.

The interesting point here is that all drawings still have something in common. They are all efforts to visualize the same phenomenon, the way that a story told by a leader circulates within an organization. All the drawings are, in one way or another, dynamic. They consist of arrows, wavy lines, somersaulting arrows, circles, question marks, and so on. Although their form and structure vary considerably, a common idea connects them together. At the moments when each of the drawings were made, we had no vision of what would be coming in the future, but the connecting idea provided the opportunity for prospective sensemaking. The embryonic ideas found in previous drawings had an influence (albeit we were unaware of the dynamic) on the following drawings, although the form and structure differed. This also reflects Boje's argument that antenarratives are travelers. They can morph their form and content as they travel from context to context.

CONCLUSIONS

This chapter examined drawings and sketches made during a research process in terms of their constituting an innovative style of writing. The drawings help to make sense not only of the analysis, but they also have a prospective dimension. Because drawings are not complete or definite at the moment of drawing (they are the embryos of emerging ideas and innovations), they are also future oriented in a sense that they illustrate something which has not yet emerged. Thus, drawings may function in a similar way to antenarratives. They appear as dispersive, incomplete, and fragmented during the research process, but they also provide guidelines for understanding the present condition of the research and are simultaneously signals of the future analysis.

REFERENCES

Aristotle. (1997). *Runousoppi* [*Poetics*. Finnish Edition]. Helsinki: Gaudeamus.

Aro, L. (1996). *Minä kylässä. Identiteettikertomus haastattelututkimuksen folklorena*. Helsinki: Suomalaisen Kirjallisuuden Seura.

Auvinen, T., & Sintonen, T. (2009). Storiosis in Finnish High-Tech Organization. Standing Conference for Management and Organization Inquiry (scMOI) Proceedings.

Boje, D. (1995). Stories of the storytelling organization: A postmodern analysis of Disney as "Tamara-land." *Academy of Management Journal, 38*(4).

———. (2001). *Narrative methods for organizational & communication research*. London: Sage.

———. (2008). *Storytelling organizations*. London: Sage.

Clifford, J. (1986). Introduction: Partial truths. In J. Clifford & G. E. Marcus (Eds.), *Writing culture: The poetics and politics of ethnography*. Berkeley: University of California Press.

Collier, J., Jr., & Collier, M. (1986). *Visual anthropology. Photography as a research method*. Albuquerque: University of New Mexico Press.

Comaroff, J., & Comaroff, J. (1992). *Ethnography and the historical imagination*. Boulder, CO: Westview Press.

Czarniawska, B. (1997). *Narrating the organization: Dramas of institutional identity*. Chicago: University of Chicago Press.

———. (2004). *Narratives in social science research*. London: Sage.

Eräsaari, L. (1995). *Kohtaamisia byrokraattisilla näyttämöillä*. Helsinki: Gaudeamus.

Fisher, W. R. (1994). Narrative rationality and the logic of scientific discourse. *Argumentation, 8.*

Hill, R. C., & Levenhagen, M. (1995). Metaphors and mental models sensemaking and sensegiving in innovative and entrepreneurial activities. *Journal of Management, 21*(6), 1057–1074.

Lévi-Strauss, C. (1963). *Structural anthropology*. Harmondsworth, UK: Penguin Books.

———. (1969). *The elementary structures of kinship*. Boston: Beacon Press.

Lyotard, J. F. (1984). *The postmodern condition: a report on knowledge*. Minneapolis: University of Minnesota Press.

Marcus, G. E., & Fisher, M. J. (1986). *Anthropology as cultural critique: An experimental moment in the human sciences*. Chicago: University of Chicago Press.

Mason, P. (1990). *Deconstructing America. Representations of the other*. London: Routledge.

Ricoeur, P. (1991a). Life in quest in narrative. In D. Wood (Ed.), *On Paul Ricoeur: Narrative and interpretation*. London: Routledge.

———. (1991b). *From text to action: Essays in hermeneutics, II*. Evanston, IL: Northwestern University Press.

———. (1992). *Oneself as another*. Chicago: University of Chicago Press.

———. (1994). Imagination in discourse and in action. In G. Robinson & J. Rundell, J. (Eds.), *Rethinking imagination: Culture and creativity*. London: Routledge.

Siirtola. H. (2007). *Interactive visualization of multidimensional data*. Dissertations in Interactive Technology, Number 7. Tampere, Finland: University of Tampere.

Sintonen, T., & Auvinen, T. (2009). Who is leading, leader or story? the power of stories to lead. *Tamara: Journal for Critical Organization Inquiry, 8*(8).

Weick, K. E. (2001). *Making sense of the organization*. Oxford: Blackwell.

12 Narratives
A Love Story

Anna Linda Musacchio Adorisio

1 NARRATIVE AND ANTENARRATIVES IN BOJE'S WORK

Narrative and antenarrative are key concepts in Boje's research on story-telling in organizations (Boje, 1991, 1995, 2001, 2008).

As Boje claims: "In organizations, storytelling is the preferred sense-making currency of human relationships among internal and external stakeholders" (Boje, 1991, p. 106) and the storytelling organization is a "collective storytelling system in which the performance of stories is a key part of members' sensemaking and a mean to allow them to supplement individual memories with institutional memory" (Boje, 1991, p. 106).

In organizations, Boje noticed, "people told their stories in bits and pieces, with excessive interruptions of story starts, with people talking over each other to share story fragments, and many aborted storytelling attempts" (Boje, 1991, p. 112–113), opening the path to the idea of multiple and competing voices, multiple stories, and multiple interlocutors.

In his 1995 article, Boje noticed that storytelling organizations could be seen as "pluralistic construction of multiplicity of stories, storytellers, and story performance events that are like Tamara[1] but are realized differently depending upon the stories in which one is participating" (Boje, 1995, p. 1000). Boje used the terms 'story' and 'storytelling' to refer to the complex, fragmented and nonlinear sensemaking performances occurring in orga-nizations. As he claimed in his 2001 book: "This fragmented, non linear, incoherent, collective, unplotted and improper storytelling, is what I mean by the term antenarrative" (Boje, 2001, p.1).

Antenarrative is thus a storytelling performance or a set of performances that do not hold the organization and the coherence of a narrative. Boje noticed how ante refers not only to the idea of anticipation (following the Latin *ante* as 'before') but also to the usage of ante as a stake, with the idea of a bet on the future course of events. Boje's attributed to antenarra-tives the nature of bets: antenarratives are never conclusive, but rather frag-mented and loosely constructed. They are polyphonic within a group but I would add also within an individual, who can provide different versions of the facts before getting (assuming that he ever gets) to a final version. In some cases elements of antenarratives can emerge as contradictions or as hints in a rather well-constructed narrative. I will provide examples of this from the accounts of bankers of a southwestern bank in the town of Las Cruces, New Mexico.

Boje's notion of narrative, however, does not correspond only to a well-constructed account but rather to a crystallized version of it for an entire group or for an individual. In this sense for Boje "to translate story into narrative is to impose counterfeit coherence and order to an otherwise fragmented and multi-layered experiences of desire" (Boje, 2001, p. 2).

This aspect represents in my view the core of Boje's elaboration on the notion of narrative and its novelty compared to the work of narratologists, whose work does not take into account the social and historical context in which the narrative is inscribed nor the distinctly subjective act of the telling.

The interesting aspect of Boje's narrative/antenarrative articulation stands in the entering of the dynamic and complex aspects that shape the narrative/antenarrative relations.

Narrative genres, Boje affirmed, are "encased in a linear, monological, framework, that has become representation, detached from living story (. . .) I take the radical position that retrospective sensemaking narratives renarrate experience into centripetal forces of heteroglossia, while ignoring the more centrifugal forces of story" (Boje, 2008, p. 190).

Storytelling organizations are the interplay of both centripetal and centrifugal forces as they are "an *and* relation between processes of narrating and storying and between narrative and story forms" (Boje, 2008, p. 8).

Such relation is a complex, dialogic relation for Boje. "My reference to emergent story (dispersion) in relation to control narrative (centering) is in its more dialogical manner than mere information processing model. Storytelling complexity does not obey hierarchic order" (Boje, 2008, p. 38).

And "strand of narrative and antenarrative are interwoven, raveling and deraveling, weaving and unweaving in families and Storytelling Organizations and in societal discourse" (Boje, 2008, p. 240).

Storying interpenetrates with linear narrative in organizations where "narrative control makes one way out of coherence, the only (approved), talked about way of sensemaking" (Boje, 2008, p. 19).

But as Boje continued: "Yet the officially narrated identity (of sameness), is always susceptible to some new (different) way of making sense of an organization, that can turn into some new complexity, envisioning some new strategic plot, or devise some way to transform a privileged way into a restoried way to make sense in a Storytelling Organization" (Boje, 2008, p. 20).

2   LINKING NARRATIVE AND ANTENARRATIVE TO COMMON SENSE AND EXPERIENCE

In this section I will revise the concept of narrative and antenarrative as conceptualized by Boje under a different light than the one proposed by

Boje: my interest is in the relationship that organizational members (but we can say individuals in general) entertain with the narrative or antenarrative that they constantly produce and in which they are daily immersed.

What I believe is important here is to stress how the role narratives play in providing meaning to reality is problematic for the individuals involved. Individuals in organizations use narratives and a language that is inevitably socially negotiated.

As argued by Volosinov: "The expression utterance is determined by the actual conditions of the given utterance—above all by its immediate social situation . . . the word is oriented toward an addressee . . . and in the absence of the real addressee, an addressee is presupposed" (Volosinov, 1973, p. 85).

The narrative utterance cannot be understood outside the context in which it is performed and to which it is in relation with, as expressed by Volosinov: "Orientation of the word toward the addressee has an extremely high significance. In point of fact, word is a two-sided act. It is determined equally by whose word it is and for whom it is meant. As word, it is precisely the product of the reciprocal relationship between speaker and listener, addresser and addressee. Each and every word expresses the 'one in relation to the other' . . . the immediate social situation and the broader social milieu wholly determine—and determine from within, so to speak—the structure of an utterance" (Volosinov, 1973, p. 86).

Whereas in the narratologists' work there is no reference to the social aspects that drive the emplotment into narrative, the work of Bakhtin and that of Gramsci explore the relation between language, ideology, and hegemony.

For Bakhtin the "Unitary language constitutes the theoretical expression of the historical processes of linguistic unification and centralization, an expression of the centripetal forces of language. A unitary language is not something given but is always in essence posited—and at every moment of its linguistic life it is opposed to the realities of heteroglossia" (Bakhtin, 1981, p. 270).

There is a constant movement of centrifugal and centripetal forces working at the utterance level: "Every concrete utterance of a speaking subject serves as a point where centrifugal as well as centripetal forces are brought to bear. The processes of centralization and decentralization, of unification and disunification, intersect in the utterance; the utterance not only answers the requirements of its own language as an individualized embodiment of a speech act, but it answers the requirements of heteroglossia as well; it is in fact an active participant in such speech diversity" (Bakhtin, 1981, p. 271).

Narratives for Boje tends to eliminate heteroglossia by imposing what Bakhtin would call a unitary language, or a "normative grammar" for Gramsci (Gramsci, 1985, p. 181). Such normative grammars are in continuous relationship with spontaneous grammars at both the individual and collective level. I see a parallel between Boje's concepts of narrative/antenarrative and the idea of normative/spontaneous grammars in Gramsci.

I am interested in how the stabilization of antenarratives into narratives (or in a similar way in their silencing) can depend on the strength that ties an individual to a certain identity that 'drives' certain versions of the facts rather than others; on the desire that such individual has to conform to the accounts performed by others; or on the 'official' version that is shared among a certain group to which the individual seeks to belong.

Using Jedlowski's notation on "common sense" and "experience" (Jedlowski, 1994), I believe that antenarratives tend to stabilize in the form of accounts of 'common sense' or, as an alternative, they can become resources for the personal elaboration of the 'experience' of the subject. They will move in one way or the other following the needs that the subject will have in a specific moment in emphasizing his belonging to a group or on the other hand to stress the specificity of his lived experience or his position regarding the events.

Common sense is for Jedlowski "what people take for granted within a certain culture or a certain social circle" (Jedlowski, 1994, p. 10), whereas experience is "the whole of what we live everyday and of the moments that, suddenly, make us question the sense of all this. In other words, it is the idea of a movement that repeatedly takes us away from the attitude of the common sense and faces us with a personal question of sense" (Jedlowski, 1994, p. 11).

The concept of common sense is particularly relevant for a discourse on narrative/antenarrative because it has to do with the individual need of belonging to a certain group, of his acknowledgment as a member of such a group. Hegemonic narratives are not created in a vacuum; they are sustained and fed by members of each community that oftentimes do not question the sense of them but rather rely on the emotional attachment that they produce.

If the world of common sense is that of the suppression of the doubt, it is not "stable nor homogenous" "from the life of a man, or a woman, and his/her belonging to a common sense there is a gap, the possibility of a différance" (p. 61).

3   EMPIRICAL RESEARCH IN A SOUTHWESTERN BANK

In this section I will provide examples coming from a study I performed in Las Cruces, New Mexico, from 2006 to 2008. I have interviewed bankers belonging to a bank that has undergone major changes in the past 20 years after being bought two times and being part of a large network now.

The interviewees can be divided in two different sets. The first set is that of the people that did belong to the community bank, the original group: the CEO, the CFO, and the vice president of the bank. These three people were the managing team of the bank for several years and together faced the transition into the two different acquisitions. Only one of them is still working for the bank. He still maintains his office in the tower where he cherishes the memories of a lifelong work experience.

The second set is that of managers of the latest acquiring bank that were not involved with the community bank prior to the acquisition of it through the first acquiring bank. Their age range is different and also their ties with the community are different. In the excerpts you will find in parenthesis after each excerpts symbols like A1, B1, C1, D2, E2. The letters correspond to the different interviewees and make it easier for the reader to identify them; the numbers refer to the belonging to the first set or second set (former community bank identified with 1 and large bank identified with 2).

I have made long unstructured interviews with both set, recorded materials, and transcribed materials for an overall effort of more than 200 hours including the preparation of the interviews, the actual recording, the transcriptions, and the editing.

The excerpts are the result of transcription of conversational storytelling. Sometimes you may find ( ) when the tape was not clear or . . . when people are pausing or when there is a jump to a different topic: what is possible in conversation may seem difficult to read in writing, so I ask the reader to make an effort in this sense. Between parentheses (( )) you may find nonverbal aspects that accompanied the storytelling, such as laughing or pondering. When a sentence is capitalized it means a higher volume of the voice, great emphasis provided by the interviewee.

I will propose an excerpt to start looking at the idea of narrative and common sense; in this case I asked the interviewees to sketch the origins of the community bank:

> Let's start at the beginning, this bank was chartered in 1905 and that was even before we were a state; the second, and before you leave you need to go up on the wall and look at all the presidents, there are pictures on the wall and the dates are up there, so if I tell you, if I miss something you go up there and verify, I think the second president of the bank was Galles and if you have been here long you have heard about Lee Galles, in Albuquerque, Lee Galles, Chrysler, Chevrolet, Cadillac, all that stuff, well their grandfather was the second president of this bank; the third or the fourth president of this bank was a man named Snow, he owned all the farm you know where Stahmann Farms is on Snow Road, and he was known as the "Alfalfa king" and it's all in that book. . . . (Metz, 1991) (A1)

As we can see, there is a constant reference in the excerpt to the community; the interviewee gives a chronological account of the first presidents of the bank and links them in their geographical and social context. He also mentions the 'book': it is the book of a historian who wrote an account of the bank from its beginning to the 1990s prior to the first acquisition. Already in this excerpt we can see how there is a tendency to relate to a common ground 'you have heard about' or 'you know where Stahmann Farm is' or to a crystallized narrative 'it's all in that book.' But at the same time the excerpt portrays spontaneous storytelling in the form and content to the narrative of the origin provided in the book:

> Strong and magnetic individuals have guided the bank since its creation. Nicolas Galles, Oscar Snow, H.B. Holt and William Sutherland are four of many who gave it direction and good judgment during its formative years. Frank O. Papen and a host of others have since guided it to even more impressive heights. (Metz, 1991, xi)

Or in a journal article on the celebration of the 90th anniversary of the bank:

> It started as a dream by a handful of local business leaders who saw the potential for a great future in a small community on the banks of the Rio Grande in southern New Mexico . . . the history of the institution is as fascinating as the region it serves. Its growth and development was the reflection of the contributions it made to the economic engine that has today made Las Cruces and Dona Ana County one of the fastest growing regions in the nation. . . . In 1951, an energetic young local businessmen who had come to Las Cruces to sell insurance in the early 1940s, acquired his first shares of stock in First National Bank. That man was Frank O. Papen, the man who has guided First National for nearly half of its years in existence to become the dynamic institution that it is today.

Both of these extracts can be assimilated to narratives, as they represent a crystallized version of the story of the beginning and the entering of Frank Papen, the man who guided the bank for more than 40 years.

In the spontaneous storytelling performed by the interviewees, the entering and the role of Frank are questioned and challenged:

> Frank Papen, who owned the management control of the bank, he hired Charles to come in and straighten that out and so a lot of the thing that transpire during that time that Charles come to work until he got sick and he was involved in a car accident and had a tragic end, really, but he is the guy that I really credit for having saved the bank a couple of times in that process because Frank was not a banker, and the book says it and also John probably would have told you that. (C1)

The sentence 'Frank was not a banker' is a sentence that is expressed by almost all the people we interviewed. They all credited him for being a people person, for having transformed the community of Las Cruces and modernized the town, but the 'Frank was not a banker' is a kind of a constant refrain, in the organizational storytelling I have witnessed.

Here are some examples of this refrain in both written and conversational storytelling.

> Frank Papen was not a banker. He didn't know banking laws and banking procedures. He was an insurance man and he knew insurance backwards and forwards. That's why he asked me to come in. He knew how to pick good people who knew banking, and therein lies his success. (Haner interview with Metz June 6, 1989)

And one of the interviewees:

In a lot of respect the executive vice-president does much more management than the president does, in some instance I know that was true when Frank Papen was the president and Charles was the executive vice-president, lot of people consider this sacrilegious to say about Frank Papen, but he was not a banker . . . he was a people person, he understood people and he just had the ability to gain people respect and confidence and I don't think he ever mistrusted anybody, oh that's extreme I am sure he did but he liked people. (B1)

Another interviewee:

> He was an external kind a guy and he was a product of his time, and that was the time when you know the sixties and the seventies until you know we went through that first wave of energy that first oil embargo 72–73 United States has a sort of predictor projections in terms of economics after the second world war we weren't having some of those wild kind of swings in the economy . . . so his old job was selling and he would, I don't know if it says anything in the book about it, but he would have admitted himself he would go down to the lower valley which was where he was from, the Anthony area and would sell loans to people, he would go and talk to this guy and collateral was not an issue to him, he just knew them, he knew that they were good old boys and Charles was the guy that had to manage all that because he knew the safety and soundness issues and Frank was an insurance agent and he sold insurances and he sold bank services in the way he sold insurances (C1).

'Frank was not a banker' is a refrain that, although challenging the myth of Frank, is nevertheless organized and petrified within the community and thus adhere in my view to a narrative rather than a story or antenarrative.

Along with the refrain of 'Frank was not a banker' there are a number of narratives that are shared by almost all the people interviewed, even the ones that did not belong directly to the bank. One of them is the "Anthony Story."

> One of the most interesting stories that I like to tell, I grew up in the South Valley, and I worked in Anthony, well originally when Mr. Papen

was putting his bank together the bank was on one side of the street and it was called First State Bank of Anthony, Texas and he bought that bank and changed the name on it to the First National Bank of Anthony and he built a huge beautiful building but what he didn't realized is that he got across the state line . . . Mr. Haner and Mr. Papen spent considerable time in Washington and they had them to change into First National Bank of Anthony, New Mexico and he changed to the First National Bank of Dona Ana county . . . HE WAS THE ONLY ONE TO EVER MOVE A BANK ACROSS THE STATE LINE AND CHANGE THE NAME OF THE BANK FIVE TIMES. (A1)

Here is the same story from different interviewees, and it must be noted that it is spontaneous storytelling. I did not ask for a recollection of the particular story:

(B1): John can tell you the story better and I don't know whether he did it or not, but he (Frank) acquired what was called First National Bank of Anthony, Texas.
   Linda: and he moved it across the state line . . .
   (B1): Right and nobody knows by this day how he got that done.
   Linda: and that was something he was really proud of . . .
   (B1): I don't know whether it was a matter of power or he just confused the hell out of people and ended up with what he wanted ((LAUGHS)) I don't know, but he was able to get things done, his attitude was if it need to be done we will find a way to get it done and that was his ( ) to go head and try.

Another account by a different interviewee:

Because when he bought that bank in Anthony, went down on a weekend talked with somebody in the bank and he got his buddy to build, they found some land and got his buddy to give a favorable bid on building that building and so they had the building built the way I remember the story I don't know if I am totally accurate on this, the way I remember the building was built and it suddenly occurred that the bank was not in New Mexico was in Texas and had to be moved and those days they had the ban on interstate banking, and so after several trips to Washington he and Charles Haner the guy I was talking about, Charles primarily because Charles knew all the players in Washington and he was a good friend of the Comptroller of the Currency at that time and they went back on several occasions and finally closed one eye and keep reading the statute and keep rereading them and finally found that there was a comma left out of one sentences that changed the meaning of a sentence, that allowed that bank to move over to the New Mexico, so they gave the approval and then they went back and cleaned the act and that's a true story and that would never happen today either. (C1)

There are a lot of stories around the tower and what is fascinating is that four out of five people interviewed spontaneously told us stories about the construction of it. We can easily affirm that the tower it is not only a feature of the Las Cruces landscape but its narrative is actually part of the collective memory of this community and survives in the orality.

Here is one of the interviewee's account:

> (leafing through the book) There's our tower. There's the tower downtown here, now the Wells Fargo tower, built in 1967. My understanding is that when they built the building it was going to be seven storey high and then Frank Papen was having a cocktail with the contractor and said what would it take to go up another three, so all the utilities, all that is on the seventh floor, where typically would be up on top, they had three more floors, that's what Ben and John have told me, the old facts. . . . (D2)

Another interviewee:

> And originally was going to be a seven story, well he wanted a ten story building and they couldn't make its feasibility work and so they finally settle to seven and as a side the economy was in a tank in the late sixties and they guy that was building it had another job that fell through and he had a bunch of crew that he needed to keep busy so he went to Frank and said I'll put the other three story of that building for 300000 I don't remember the number but significantly less it would have been had we contracted before because he was trying to keep his crew busy, so that's how it ended up to be a ten story building, if you go downtown and you go through that building today you would see that the air conditioning and all the mechanical is on the seventh floor and that's why, because it was already been topped out when they came to it. (C1)

What is interesting is that Frank's figure is equally recognized by the people that served at the bank but also by those that were part of the acquiring team (the second acquiring team, as I did not interview the first acquiring team).

We could conclude that all the excerpts proposed go in the sense of narrative and common sense, rather than in the sense of antenarrative and experience. The reconstruction of the past is that of a golden age, where:

> Mr. Papen considered every employee here part of his family, it was all a family atmosphere, everybody got along to a certain degree . . . and it's just like marriages, you don't go along with your husband all the

time, but in the end you are fine and so that's the way they ran the bank all those years, and everybody loved Mr. Papen, I don't know anybody who didn't love Mr. Papen, he was an icon. (A1)

And:

(A1) It was awesome! A lot of times we disagreed on a lot of things and especially in loans I would want to sell a loan and Ben and Tom would say no, we don't do this and we don't like this, do this and this and this, but we walked out of the door and we were all together we were a team, we never walked out and I never told a loan customer not, we were all a team and everybody sang the same song . . . and that's the way Mr. Papen wanted it . . . and we did that for 25–30 years in the bank.

There is a tendency towards narrative modes even when the dominant narratives are questioned such as in the excerpt that follows:

I will tell you, one of the traditions that had evolved was that before the bank opened and after we would review the rejected checks, after we finished that, we would go to the coffee shop and there was a lot of just general conversation we talked about things happening in the community, things that were happening in sports and happening in politics but you always ended up to some extends to things that were affecting the bank and that is not to say that we did not have more structured formalized management meetings, but a lot of the conversations, in the coffee shop had to do with banking and a lot of ideas evolved there, decisions that didn't require a lot of analysis so you made there those decisions, a pretty informal process. (B1)

And it becomes evident here, where even a rational explanation is provided for the challenging of the narrative:

See my background has been with the Federal Land bank and it was highly structured and the applications were very detailed and comprehensive and we had policies for everything so . . . to be honest I was never totally comfortable with the informal management decision making process but there was more than one time that I felt like we may be wasting time during those sessions at the coffee shop and I had more important things to do so I quit coming, well when I quit coming I found that I was going out of the loop so quickly . . . so I started to go back to the coffee shop ((laughs)). (B1)

Or here:

But I got a little bit more aggressive one year, I felt that if there was somebody that was not performing at the level . . . with their salary level, they need to work somewhere else and I made that recommendation. . . . (B1)

Where the contrast to the common sense is made explicit:

And when we were at meeting for a specific individual that has been working for the bank for some period of time and Frank Papen said "no, that person has been with us for a long time, we would keep that person. (B1)

And:

But over the years it became really obvious that our personnel costs were too high and it was having an adverse effect on profitability but the employees were members of Frank's family and if you have been more than ten years you had to screw up big time to get in trouble . . . the only way you could get fired from this bank was to get caught stealing or insult the boss family. (B1)

Introducing a new perspective:

People of Frank's generation, he was loyal to the people that got into the dance, but the survival of the business required some things that those people couldn't bring to the table and he still had loyalty to them and to be completely frank, Frank had a lot of struggle with that because my job was to make it work and sometimes you have to make some tough decisions that are inconsistent with that loyalty. (C1)

My question is whether also these last excerpts are just other narratives, rather than antenarrative story excerpts, following the distinction made clear by Boje and outlined in the previous sections. The management perspective's being just an alternative narrative to the patriarch narrative perspective.

CONCLUSIONS AND DISCUSSION

In this chapter I have revised the concepts of narrative and antenarrative as conceptualized by Boje in his work on organizations. The important aspect highlighted by Boje is the hegemonic role narratives play in organizational context and the importance of the search for antenarrative lines that are retraceable in an 'ante' state of affairs and in the dialogic multiplicity of stories always going on in organizations, at a centripetal as well as a centrifugal level. Centripetal forces can be associated to narrative lines whereas centrifugal forces can be associated with antenarrative fragments.

My interest stands in the language, in the expression that makes these forces visible, and I have used Bakhtin's concept of unitary language/heteroglossia, and Gramsci's normative/spontaneous grammars as a way to conceptualize this. I have then linked narrative and antenarrative to Jedlowski's notation on common sense and experience.

The question that rises is why in organizational contexts such as the one I have studied, there is an orientation towards narratives to be performed by each and every interviewee in a striving to adhere to a certain common sense and how even the story lines that challenge such common sense can nevertheless be assimilated to narratives rather than antenarratives.

NOTES

1. In Tamara, Los Angeles' longest running play, a dozen characters unfold their stories before a walking, sometimes running, audience (Boje, 2001, p. 4)

REFERENCES

Bakhtin, M. (1981). *The dialogic imagination: Four essays* (Michael Holquist, Ed.; Caryl Emerson & Michael Holquist, Trans.). Austin: University of Texas Press.

Boje, D. (1991). The storytelling organization: A study of story performance in an office supply firm. *Administrative Science Quarterly, 36*(1), 106–126.

———. (1995). Stories of the storytelling organization: A postmodern analysis of Disney as Tamara-Land. *Academy of Management Journal, 38*(4), 997–1035.

———. (2001). *Narrative methods for organizational and communication research.* London: Sage.

———. (2008). *Storytelling organizations.* London: Sage.

Gramsci, A. (1985). *Selections from the cultural writings.* London: Lawrence & Wishart.

Jedlowski, P. (1994). *Il Sapere dell'esperienza.* Milano: Il Saggiatore.

Metz, L. (1991). *Southern New Mexico empire: The First National Bank of Dona Ana County.* El Paso, TX: Mangan Books.

Volosinov, V. N. (1973). *Marxism and the philosophy of language* (L. Matejka & I. R. Titunik, Trans.). New York: Seminar Press.

Part III

Antenarratives and Organization Change

Introduction to Part III
Antenarratives and Organization Change

This introduction is due to Maurice Yolles and David Boje, who set out to not only overview the papers on organizational change and their mutual relationship in this part, but in doing so to set this into the context of complexity and chaos, and to show that there is a place where antenarrative theory can link with the sociological tradition of *lifeworld* and purposeful communications. This latter aspect also provides a modern addendum to the notions of Schutz and Luckmann (1974), and their interest in the knowledge content that arises with narrative that is relavent to organizational change

There is an intimate relationship between social change and culture, and this applies not only to societies, but to organizational socials too. As organizations develop, they usually form a dominant culture reflected in its predominant paradigm. However, sometimes important cultural divisions occur, for instance after a company takeover, or during the creation of a joint venture,; or even during a process of transformational change such as privatization where, as in the post-Soviet history of Yugoslavia, autonomous cultural components spontaneously compete for dominance after release from politically enforced submergence.

In such a fragmented arena, antenarratives replace the more usual apparently coherent narratives that both enrich complexity, and deplete the coherence of any semantic sedimentation that may have appeared to have arisen previously. In such cases the organization may be seen to become socially ill through analytical schizophrenia, creating mixed signals within its corporate body, and confusion and chaos that can lead to the running down and endangerment of organizational survival.

Understanding the complexity of organizations usually requires partitioning theory, that which enables complexity to in some way be analytically divided into digestible and relatable compartments. Ontological distinctions can offer one pathway, leading to alternative conceptual frames of reference that need to be relatively simple and thus distant from the complex detail that members of a collective are normally exposed to. As Cohen and Stewart indicated in their book *The Collapse of Chaos: discovering simplicity in a complex world* published in 1994, this occurs when the conceptual frame of reference is emergent. Emergence can collapse chaos and bring order to a human activity system that seems to be in random fluctuation. It is representative of a totality that cannot be disaggregated. To relate this to narrative theory, we distinguish between a thematic *lifeworld* and an associated *real-world* of a situation, the former being composed of communicative, and the latter, operative behaviors. In the lifeworld, the notion of emergence refers to the idea that mutual communicative interactions create systemic possibilities that allow narrative simplicity to emerge from antenarrative complexity.

Ontological and conceptual devices for creating greater simplicity and hence more understanding of complex lifeworld situations are well known. In the late 1950s, Talcott Parsons modeled complex social situations in terms of three ontologically distinct systems: culture, society, and personality, all interactively linked together within a place for communicative understanding called lifeworld. Schutz and Luckmann provided an epistemological exploration of the nature of lifeworld in their book *The Structures of the Lifeworld* published in the 1970s. Habermas and Luhmann individually further developed this tradition in the 1980s in their own distinct ways. Lifeworld involves a group of participants who interpret an action situation and together arrive at some agreement about it. Within it, the participants pursue their plans cooperatively on the basis of a shared definition of the situation. It is a place where purposeful communications are undertaken in a social environment, a global place where people and social collectives maintain their proprietary local worldviews and communicate with intention over a theme. In engaging in the lifeworld they create knowledge laden narratives. These arise from the worldviews and develop as part of communication exchange processes, each communicator with its own local narrative. Each locality has an epistemic content that enables it to maintain a capacity to project meanings and through interaction to satisfy the intention to create mutual local understanding that offer a potential for the formation of common agreements. However, the lifeworld is not always a nice and simple integrated and coherent place. Often it is fragmented, and communications operate through a collection of antenarratives. This is consistent with a lifeworld in which the localities are autonomous and maintain strict horizons of knowledge that are not accessible to other localities, often resulting in miscommunication.

Simple lifeworlds are necessarily related to simple situations. The situations can be defined and modeled according to the methods and tools which enable easy and direct explanation, and confident event prediction to occur. This must be a function of our ability to understand the situations, and an ability to find concepts and tools through which explanations that work can be provided. Heylighen (1996), in his consideration of the distinction between simple and complex, distinguishes between structure and dynamics. Structurally complex situations may be said to be independent of the processes by which information is encoded into fabricated chronicles, and decoded after narration. In complex situations, information is used to identify components that are arranged in some intricate difficult-to-understand pattern or structure. This limits the likelihood of acquiring information from thematic stories that is supposedly representative of situations. During this the process of encoding and decoding is semantically subjective, confused with antenarrative, and is unable to provide semantic representation of the whole situation. Dynamically complex situations occur when a large amount of effort is applied to identify the information content in a situation, and when the outcome of some process is difficult to predict from an identifiable initial state. Its definition can be differently elaborated on by harnessing the concepts of chaos and emergence. In this way, like the incoherence of the tuning up of an orchestra, antenarratives can assemble into a coherent structure providing partitions of whole stories. This has a reflection in modern day dynamic and complex enterprises, a condition that does not complement the deterministic wants and needs of corporate strategists.

This notion is fodder to **Steve King**, who in Chapter 13, "Survival Toolkit for Sociotechnical Project Complexity," examines the internal corporate environment to explore how organizations can become not only effective but viable (enabling them to maintain their integrity, identity and autonomy), and by connecting thematic stories with antenarratives in an attempt to make sense of what they perceive. Such attempts have a likelihood outcome, resulting in success only for the highly insightful explorer. The relationship between simple and complex is ultimately one of conceptual perspective. However, complexity is always revealed if one is able to drill down to more granular levels of detailed reality. Simple situations tend to relate to lower degrees of granularity, are reducible to a set of parts in simple causal relationships, and each part can be analyzed independently without necessarily relating it to the assembly as a whole. In complex situations, it is essential to relate the parts to the whole given that the whole is known, and there may be many causes that generate observed effects that may not occur in simple relationships. Some hold the view that complexity begets complexity. Cohen and Stewart refer to this as the principle of "conservation of complexity" that occurs when people expect complex situations to have complex causes. This simple cause-effect rule relationship is not often born out in practice. As we considered in previously, in certain circumstances amplification of disturbances to organizational order can occur with the result that simple causes can have fall-out consequences that are quite complex and lead to chaos. There is also the idea of antichaos, proposed by Stuart Kauffman. Here, complex causes produce simple effects indicating that complexity can diminish as well as increase. Extending this to the narrative, antenarrative processes may generate simple outcomes that can diminish complexity. Complexity can provide a harbor for chaos, and they are inseparable twins: "Now that science is looking, chaos seems to be everywhere" (Gleick, 1987: 5). Today, we are more frequently talking not of dynamic situations as being simple, but rather as being complex, and when we say this we are implicitly referring to the dynamics of chaos. In complex situations, the dynamic of chaos amplifies tiny differences hidden in the detail of the complexity, and enables the unexpected to become the predominant. The antenarratives that emerge from such situations are therefore not easily connected.

Gerhard Fink and **Maurice Yolles** in their Chapter 14, "Narratives, Paradigms, and Change," are interested in the relationship between simple normal and complex post-normal social situations through the paradigms that represent them. For them, paradigms are knowledge based with pragmatic extensions that enable meaningful narratives to develop and deliver perceived stories that are hopefully reflections of the nature of the patterns of knowledge held. In fragmented lifeworlds that are populated by antenarratives, this can be an unachievable aim. They develop a theory of paradigm change that encompasses both narrative and antenarrative processes. How change develops is then related to the relationships between these states of being, and the theory has in its elements the capacity to predict change. As part of this development, Fink and Yolles refer to corporate human activity systems that wish to survive. As such they need to maintain their behavioral stability. By this we might mean lifeworld or real-world behavioral stability, since one is normally a pre-requisite for the other, lifeworld communications being connected through intention to real-world operations. Both lifeworld and real-world stability are required, constituting separate but intensely interactive systems. To maintain stability this they must pass through a various stages of change. In the context of this book, like Luhmann (1995), we really interested in lifeworld behavior. The impact on such behavior includes turbulences from the environment that result in systemic perturbations, and these can make its communicative control process fail as its threshold of stability is reached. So in order to regain stability, the system learns to introduce lifeworld behavioral adjustments and consequently the likelihood of improved understanding. If stability still fails and a point of structural criticality exists that makes the structure susceptible to local change, then a different learning process occurs where the cognitive model is modified in an attempt to regain stability. The plurality of local changes taken together generate antenarratives that, for participants of the whole situation, contribute to semantic confusions.

In Chapter 15, entitled "Antenarratives of Change in Mexican Innovation Networks", **Enrique Campos-López, Alena Urdiales Kalinchuk**, and **Hilda Hernández** are interested in such turbulences, brought in current times through innovation. Seen only in terms of the development of new products and services, it is this that keeps competitive corporations buoyant, even if they also contribute to market disequilibrium and environmental crisis. Innovation affects diverse cultures and the social and political mechanisms that maintain them, as well as the narrative expressions that accompany them. Seeing situations in terms of their attendant complexity of unrelated problem limits the scope of understanding, and damages the holistic way in which situations may be perceived. Such problems can only be resolved through an integration of a set of fragmented narratives and the delivery of whole stories, a situation that centers on exploring the semantic distinctions in the tacit knowledges and their related attitudes that under-pin lifeworld expressions. Stacey (1993) is also concerned with chaos and organizational instability, when he asks why they cannot maintain consistency in their performance. By this he is referring to operative performance, but the question also applies to narrative performance. He argues that there are various reasons why instabilities can occur, and management incompetence and ignorance are two factors. However, even if these factors are addressed, organizations may still be prone to instability. The reason for this is that organizations are self-organizing bodies that operate with bounded instability far from equilibrium. According to Rosenhead (1998), the chaos paradigm of management may really be seen as a component of the complexity paradigm of management, and inherent to systems thinking. Under chaos, an organization displays behavior that is not predictable, even though it has certain regularities. In analyzing the work of Stacey, Rosenhead further indicates that chaos management theory, contrary to the rational paradigm, adopts the perspective that includes the following notions: (a) analysis loses its primacy, (b) contingency (cause and effect) loses its meaning, (c) long-term planning becomes impossible, (d) visions become illusions, (d) consensus and strong cultures become dangerous, and (e) statistical relationships become dubious. I n such circumstances, ordinary management fails, and there is a need to engage with extraordinary management, that engages with open-ended change.

It is such situations that are of interest to **Nicholas Snowden** in Chapter 16, entitled "Connecting Antenarrative and Narrative to Solving Organizational Problems", who explores such extraordinary situations through antenarrative thinking. Like extraordinary management, this is less structured than narrative thinking as well as being more creative, more evolutionary orientated, and challenges traditional ways of solving organizational problem situations. Improvisation is a byword in developing satisfying outcomes, but in extraordinary post-normal situations, and this needs to be structured across time.

In Chapter 17, **Kenneth Mølbjerg Jørgensen** is ever the genealogist tracing the representing, but doing it in living stories and in narrative and antenarrative writing. As the author suggests, "it is important to remember that the chapter proposes a resituated relationship of narrative and story and not that the hegemony of the duality of narrative and story is turned upside down in favor of story. BME voices are important in society and organizational life." The term 'living story' is inspired by Derrida, who argues that story has no borderlines (see Boje, 2008; see Jo Tyler in Chapter 7 who develops living story in her own way). Following Gary Saul Morson, Jørgensen looks at narrative as backshadowing that in our approach becomes an antenarrative of rationalistic, linear, progress. Instead of just making antenarrative future-oriented, Jørgensen theorizes that "antenarrative implies working with multiple pasts, presents, and futures." I must admit, my own way where narrative backshadow becomes refolded into a linear antenarrative foreshadow, without noticing the present, and all its sideshadows is changed by Jørgensen's move. Jacques Derrida looks at such narratives turned linear BME antenarratives as terroristic torture. For Mikhail Bakhtin such monological narratives are quite different from the dialogical story answerably present in once-occurrent Being. Jørgensen and I have written about ways narrative has been hegemonic to story in writings on business ethics Jørgensen develops living story as a chronotope (Bakhtin's relativity of timespace in the novel), as a relationship between nonlinear texts and their multiple sideshadow possibilities and their (ante-narrating) foreshadowing outcomes as they deconstruct and reconstruct other texts in different spaces and times in many stylistics (reports, letters, diaries, logbooks, accounts, minutes, budgets, as well as all that social-cyber media: websites, films, webcasts, etc.).

In Chapter 18, Daniel Dauber and Gerhard Fink tell us tales of merger and acquisition (M&A) survivors. They examine how antenarrative can be understood in the context of M&As and how they contribute to their research questions. Like Ardorisio's chapter 12, they provide stories of the aftermath of a bank that became acquired. They use antenarratives to introduce their interview partners. Dauber and Fink found that M&A survivors had different antenarratives. Some wanted to co-participate to shape the future and not just be shaped by how others shaped it for them. Living stories and fossilized BME narratives might become obsolete as M&A organizations assimilate or blend in different living stories. The tales of M&A survivors unfold their antenarrating in different insights into the strategies pursued to tame turbulent environments. The method used was to look at critical incidents of the present to sort out how the antenarrating connected present to future possibilities.

REFERENCES

Boje, D. (1991). The storytelling organization: A study of story performance in an office supply firm. *Administrative Science Quarterly*, 36(1), 106–126.

——. (1995). Stories of the storytelling organization: A postmodern analysis of Disney as Tamara-Land. *Academy of Management Journal*, 38(4), 997–1035.

——. (2001). *Narrative methods for organizational and communication research*. London: Sage.

——. (2008). *Storytelling Organizations*. London: Sage.

Cohen, J., Stewart, I., 1995, *The Collapse of Chaos*.Viking, Penguin Books, London.

Gleick, J., 1987, Chaos, Sphere Books Ltd., London

Heylighen, F., 1996 *Web Dictionary of Cybernetics and Systems*, www.cna.org/isaac/Glossb.htm#Complexity, accessed June 2005

Luhmann, N., 1995, *Social Systems*. Stanford University Press, California. Translated from the 1984 German edition.

Rosenhead, J., 1998, Complexity Theory and Management Practice, Human Nature Review. www.human-nature.com/science-as-culture/rosenhead.html, accessed 2003.

Stacey, R., 1993, *Managing Chaos*. Kogan Page Ltd., London.

13 Survival Toolkit for Sociotechnical Project Complexity

Steve King*

The enterprise landscape has multilayered interconnectedness and dynamic complexities that are increasingly hostile to corporate planners and technologists. Welcome to the complexity era.

In today's hyperconnected enterprise infrastructures, unpredictable network effects cascade through densely intertwined social and technology fabrics. With nonlinear complexity, small inputs and random 'noise' can precipitate large unpredictable results that are described (but not predicted with certainty) by chaos theory and complexity science (Barabasi, 2003; Bohm, 1984; Gleick, 2008; Hayles, 1991; Laughlin, 2006; Lorenz, 1996; Morin, 2008; Prigogine & Nicolis, 1989). Some key characteristics of complexity in the enterprise realm:

- Declining relevance of the *normal probability curve* as a guiding principle for planning, risk, and quality (Taleb, Goldstein, & Spitznagel, 2009).
- Decreasing effectiveness of classic *command-and-control* hierarchies
- Rapid rates of change that make *grand plans and large design specs* obsolete before they are complete
- Increasing value of *peer social networks* for goal setting and problem solving
- Delicate *interrelatedness* of many social, technical, business, financial, operational dimensions

For those who design business processes, software, and organizational structures, complexity is particularly daunting due to the persistent need to balance two oppositional forces: diversification and integration (Geirland, 1996; Regev & Wegmann, 2006; Weick & Sutcliffe, 2007).

1. *Integration.* The complexity era has a high rate of change that demands an integrated, unified response from the entire end-to-end enterprise. This requirement fuels the (decades-old) drive to standardize on centrally mandated processes, practices, and technologies across many functional silos. Integration requires standards, consolidation, and

orchestration at some level—operating systems, hardware, software, interfaces, networks—and often at many levels, including human aspects in the form of standard policies, procedures, business dictionaries, compliance/governance initiatives. Integration moves in the direction of sameness for infrastructure and capabilities.

2. *Diversification.* Complexity also creates an equally pressing need for the enterprise to preserve diversity, autonomy, and local independence of internal processes, technologies, best practices, and niche language/concept frameworks. Infrastructure diversity is increasingly nonoptional in highly unpredictable commercial environments where we never know for sure which solution path will succeed or fail.

Figure 13.1   Enterprises have an ongoing and daunting requirement to balance the oppositonal forces of integration and diversity.

High levels of integration, standardization, and consolidation create sameness that ultimately opens the door to cascading threats and reduced richness of innovation—diversity is the anecdote.

The simultaneous push towards orchestrated/unified systems vs. diversified/autonomous systems can be viewed as the interplay of powerful opposing *centripetal/centrifugal* (centering/decentering) forces that enterprises must resolve in their strategic planning and operational cultures. Some of the issues are technical—for instance, the benefits and pitfalls of data center consolidation that collapse previously autonomous IT resources into central facilities—but equally important are the social, organizational, and linguistic aspects. To achieve a balanced mix of standardized and diversified resources, there must be ongoing creative choreography of people, processes, policies, and technologies. Integration/diversity efforts hit enterprise staffs where they live, so this is a cognitive and cultural playing field.

IT'S ALL NOISE . . . IT'S ALL SIGNAL

Business and project planners are often seriously handicapped when approaching the divergent aspects of complexity because they have management culture baggage that represents projects and plans as simple goal-directed *beginning-middle-end* (BME) narratives and linear success stories that don't map well to spiraling nonlinear complexity scenarios.

Planners also have the tendency to polarize inputs, opinions, and management information as either 'relevant' or 'irrelevant' . . . that is, they *ignore informational noise*, even though it's a key aspect of complexity. Chris Marshall, a widely published enterprise model designer, writes about the status quo perspective on management information:

> Any data that does not directly support the decision [making process] is *noise*, which dilutes the impact of the relevant information and consumes management time in its interpretation. (Marshall, 2000)

This is a classic binary view of information that sees 'signal' as the central solution path and 'noise' as all the decentralized, unusual ideas and marginal opinions that must be excluded from corporate decision making. Noise-adverse decision making is analogous to quality management programs that attempt to relegate anomalies and errors to the outermost noisy fringes of the normal distribution curve, for example, Six Sigma, TQM, Ishikawa, and so on. This model may work on highly controlled plant floors but it's largely unworkable in complexity fabrics where 'rare' and anomalous events are increasingly normal (Taleb et al., 2009).

In the complexity era, it's dangerous to ignore noise at the fringes of social or operational distribution curves because noise is a critical aspect of complex, emergent systems. Innovations and solutions often spring from areas that at first appear to be undifferentiated noise. Ignore or underestimate noise and all its anomalous analogs and there is little hope of adapting to complex uncertainty and nonlinear change.

Simple linear success stories that ignore noise, complexity and uncertainty . . . these are the working tools of traditional planners who believe that goals should originate *top-down from experts* and senior executives in a hierarchy of company purpose that marginalizes diverse grassroots networks and peer-to-peer effects. Marshall sums up the widely held belief that goals and requirements are best crafted top-down:

> An enterprise is a purposeful system designed to create value, typically expressed in an abstract, high level vision statement, which is decomposed into increasingly concrete and detailed missions, goals and achievable objectives. (Marshall, 2000)

In contrast to this view, complex projects and business initiatives are more productive if traditional top-down, command-and-control methods are supplemented by bottom-up influences. The command hierarchy is not going away but it must be deployed in combination with peer structures and emergent networks. Complexity requires that managers 'think with the network' not (just) their golf partners.

Corporate planners often miss the opportunity to use bottom-up network effects, but the U.S. military has a long history of original thinking about distributed command-and-control structures. From a National War College paper:

> The Marine Corps' Sea Dragon initiative envisions a radically new, decentralized system of command and control. Hallmarks of this concept are command-by-influence through mission orders, reliance on the initiative of subordinates, based on local situational awareness, and more self-contained units capable of semi-autonomous action on a distributed battlefield. [Units] are less likely to be effective at learning and adapting to a chaotic environment when their behavior is governed by top-down rules. (Gore, 1996)

Organizations generally benefit from some sort of shared goals but rigid top-down purpose hierarchies tend to suppress the noisy bottom-up aspects of value creation that are hallmarks of the complexity era. According to Weick's requisite diversity philosophy: "People are better able to get complex assignments done when given more discretion within a framework of common values" (Geirland, 1996). Other examples:

- A provocative study in the consumer-goods industry found that companies reap a higher return on investment and better success rate when product innovations (and hence company direction) come 'bottom-up' from customers, and not from cloistered executives or R&D scientists (Shah, 2008).

- Cisco Systems became more competitive after radically decentralizing its management structure to allow strategic decision making in a large peer community of over 500 managers (McGirt, 2008).
- The Mozilla Firefox browser is a robust commercial product built by harnessing complex, emergent social network effects and peer network productivity (Bell, 2009).

In spite of all the interest in self-organizing emergence, complexity science, and chaos theory, mainstream corporate decision makers and engineers still privilege deterministic top-down hierarchical value systems and unitary root causes in a way that ignores the possibilities, threats, and opportunities found in operational noise, grassroots voices, and marginal influences that can rapidly go mainstream (Taleb et al., 2009; Weick & Sutcliffe, 2007).

THE SPIRAPLEX PARADIGM

Complex enterprise projects and initiatives are always somewhat unique but they have in common a pattern of *helical* (spirally intertwined) interactions among these aspects:

- top-down decision makers
- peer-to-peer social network influences
- heterogeneous technology platforms
- isolated functional teams and operational process silos
- orthogonal fields of domain expertise
- conflicting intracompany cultures

In many cases, project failures are caused by the cascading effects of technical blunders combined with poor communications between functional silos that have very different language and concept frameworks. To deal with spiraling, multilayered interactions between sociotechnical project aspects, project managers today need a new type of hybrid toolset that interweaves technology, business, and linguistic best practices.

> Language not only transfers knowledge, it also imparts consciousness and coherence. It brings detailed knowledge into being and contextualized it . . . Language is also a crucial instrument of self-discovery and self organization. (Leebaert, 1992)

In addition to the usual flow charts, functional decomposition, and entity diagrams, project models should include a strong component of story fabric and linguistic content that is developed and organized in lockstep with the conventional static and dynamic modeling methods (ERD, class diagrams, data flow charts, UML, etc.). Going forward, complexity will not be richly harvested and accommodated without a rich set of story models for every project and enterprise initiative.

To facilitate consulting work in complex enterprise environments, the author has coined the term 'spiraplex' to describe projects that contain a bewildering mix of cross-discipline dimensions. The spiraplex concept draws on:

- spiral (nonlinear, helical)
- plexus (network of interlaced parts)
- lexical (working unit of meaning)

To qualify as spiraplex, a project must contain a diversity of domain languages and conflicting best practices that congeal into a linguistic critical mass of confusion and project risk. In general, spiraplex projects are emergent nonlinear phenomena that are very hard to understand, master, and manage with a linear BME top-down mind-set.

Spiraplex infrastructure will not be easily tamed by any specific school of thought but there are some strategies that have emerged in the software engineering and organizational studies disciplines that can help us move away from outdated project and management thinking. The methods for dealing with dynamic enterprise complexity described in this writing draw on two bodies of seemingly unrelated knowledge:

1. *Antenarrative story analysis,* invented by David M. Boje for understanding and improving enterprise narratives, concept frameworks, and cultural belief systems
2. *Agile software development*, a software programming philosophy described by Eric Ambler, Robert Martin, and others

Both of these approaches have a natural affinity for chaotic complexity and rapid change. The intersection of antenarrative theory, Agile development, and complexity science is a space of immense richness and possibilities for solution cross-pollination.

ENTERPRISE STORYTELLING

Increasingly, enterprise thinkers are finding that business process/practice improvement requires attention to organizational 'stories' that guide how we view the world and how we work together. A search on Google for 'corporate storytelling' yields dozens of Web sites, consulting services, and news articles on the subject of story strategies for business.

At its best, organizational story analysis seeks to understand and improve the narratives, myths, histories, and underlying concept/belief systems that corporate culture is made of. David M. Boje's *'antenarrative'* version of story analysis is well suited to spiraplex enterprise projects and business initiatives. "My theory of storyability is that story turns event into experience, and shapes that into collective memory" (Boje, 2008, p. 194).

In the business and technology context, planning of project success paths requires the creation of viable project stories (conceptual paths) that everyone can understand and work from. In the antenarrative approach, story consultants acknowledge they can't fully know or control what will happen, so they allow language, concepts, and communications to be more speculative, emergent, and heuristic.

Traditional plans and projects proceed from one domain silo to the next in a rigid linear manner, for example, from research to engineering to testing to marketing to sales to support, with each specialist group doing their thing in relative isolation using their own compartmentalized concepts and language. Story analysis adapts to complexity by seeking solution paths that 'spiral' with nonlinear diversity through corporate resource silos via open-ended, forward-looking (prospective) project language, designs, and specifications (Boje, 1996, 2001a, 2008). Simple linear beginning-middle-end story paths are not suppressed, but BME thinking is greatly supplemented and subsumed in this approach.

Antenarrative-based story analysis and story cultivation from the Boje school offer enterprise project planners and designers a rich array of conceptual tools. Here is a small sampling:

Antenarrative. Future-oriented (tentative, experimental) language/concept constructions leading to working stories that can mature into formal innovations and creative productivity. Antenarratives can be seen as fragmented, pre-narrative verbal wagers on a possible future stable discourse. "Antenarrative, the pre-story is a bet that a coherent narrative or a multi-story dialogism will be forthcoming" (Boje, 2008, p. 198).

Dialectics. Story dialectics explore how enterprise actors internalize various managerial and social narrative structures, which can expose submerged cognitive oppositions and social/self identities that control how we express ourselves and think. Dialectics looks at how we define ourselves and our voices in self-reflexive ways. Our self-defined (often self-limiting) internal audience is engrained in each utterance we make. Unexamined internal identities contribute to narrow-minded polarized viewpoints and lockstep groupthink—which works against complex project efforts in many ways.

Dialogics. The interaction of many opinions, beliefs, and points of view in a productive tapestry of multivoiced (polyphonic) enterprise dialog. Top-down management styles and BME thinking repress all but the central managerial voice, a dangerous practice in the complexity era. Dialogic story analysis teases out the productive creativity found at the intersection of many different team voices, including opinions and knowledge that come from peer networks, grassroots user bases, and marginal or emerging areas of the extended enterprise.

> In business language, a dialogism is when people with different logics meet in the same time and place, and engage in something transcendental, on their differences, allowing for the possibility of something generative to happen, out of the explorations. (Boje, 2008, p. 22)

Chronotopes. A linguistic/conceptual fusion of time and space which forms a familiar inner venue where awareness and communication can take place. All fictional, journalistic, mythic, business, and technical stories rely on chronotopes to convey a tangible sense of time/place to readers. There are many chronotopic archetypes embedded in our cultural fabric. These underlying situational themes manifest as travel stories, fortress stories, epic hero stories, prison stories, and so on—all of which are conceptual building blocks for enterprise project discourse, it turns out.

Antenarrative story analysis encourages the creation and propagation of textual 'story fragments'—unfinished or premature linguistic constructions that are often the precursor to innovation and solutions. In combination with cross-discipline sensemaking dialogics, an antenarrative bet can be conceived in one enterprise silo . . . gestated in another . . . and matured to formal narrative in a third before cycling around again. In traditional enterprise planning and projects, story fragments and experimental concept frameworks are generally frowned upon and seen as noise. In story analysis they are grist for the complex solution mill.

Spiral story sensemaking allows antenarrative analysts to capture complex, dynamic enterprise content that goes beyond linear BME fairy tales. According to Boje:

> Antenarrative double spirals embed story fragments with context. The antenarrative double spiral also jettisons fragments as the intertextual antenarratives form a spiral that traverses time–space. Old story fragments get restoried or exchanged for different ones. (Boje, 2004b)
>
> The antenarrative double helix is continuous, it is unfinished and unfinalized at either end. The present keeps unfolding; the past keeps being restoried (or rehistoricized). An antenarrative is a storyteller's bet that a pre-story (an improper story) can change the system. Antenarratives are spun on a bet that they can change the meaning of past, present, or future to their audiences. (Boje, 2004b)

ENTER AGILE!

Although they come from seemingly different universes, antenarrative methods are remarkably similar to strategies for sociotechnical complexity that emerged independently in the Agile development community (Ambler, 2004; Martin & Augustine, 2005).

Agile is in response to a long history of large software development failures that wasted millions of dollars and years of effort (Leishman & Cook, 2002; Standish Group, 1995). After decades of horrendous software project losses, landmark studies in the 1990s forced the software industry to sober up and rethink its methods.

A 1995 DoD study on software spending found that 75% of military software projects were canceled midstream or never deployed (Leishman & Cook, 2002). In the commercial realm, a Standish Group study of over 8,000 commercial software projects found that only 16% of large projects were considered successful. This so-called Standish "Chaos Report" summed up the situation this way: "Software development projects are in chaos, and we can no longer imitate the three monkeys—hear no failures, see no failures, speak no failures" (Standish Group, 1995).

After witnessing a seemingly endless string of spectacular multimillion-dollar project failures, senior software developers got serious about alternative and creative practices that moved away from traditional linear, monolithic point-A-to-point-B project 'waterfall' paths. In 2001 this thinking became sufficiently coherent to enable an "Agile Manifesto" that laid out key ideas, which have since been refined and extended. The Agile continual test-and-adjust strategy draws on and refines earlier Spiral and Rapid Prototype development methods (Boehm, 2000).

- The best architectures, requirements, and designs emerge from self-organizing teams.
- Welcome changing requirements, even late in development. Agile processes harness change for the customer's competitive advantage.
- Business people and developers must work together daily throughout the project. —*www.Agilemanifesto.org*

To deal with ever-threatening issues of uncertainty and failure, Agile developers strive to fail faster, fail more often, but *fail forward*, that is, build failure into the plan and then get past it. Agile doesn't attempt to execute work in a single linear BME pass of design-build-test-run phases. Agile instead uses an iterative circling approach that executes many rapid passes of the development cycle, making continual adjustments to the design along the way. Agile iterates through design, planning, coding, and testing phases during the course of a project and does not necessarily do these steps in a linear BME order.

The Agile Manifesto presents a curiously social and organizational set of precepts coming as it does from a technical enclave. Agile developers combat failure by diving deep into multiple business and technical expertise silos looking for convergence and divergence of stakeholder views. Agile has a number of strategies for breaking down communication barriers in complex cross-functional projects. Plans can be based on dynamic collections of elicited *user stories* that software features must support (Martin, 2002).

THE GENERALIZING SPECIALIST

The Agile development paradigm was forged in the bellows of spiraplex-grade software projects. In this realm, Agile developers often play a pivotal, pan-discipline role, referred to as "generalizing specialist" (Ambler, 2004; Augustine, 2005; Carroll & Daughtrey, 2007), which requires a hybrid skill set that is deep in some specialized fields but also broad enough to span many diverse expertise domains coherently. As with antenarrative story analysts: Agile generalizing specialists are capable of explicit and tacit content transformations that cross multiple line-of-business, technical, functional, and cultural silos.

An Agile developer speaks each domain's business or technical language and serves as a touch point that facilitates productive dialogues among often antagonistic organizational stakeholders. This is critical for spiraplex contexts because diversity of goals, diversity of methods, and diversity of success paths are highly necessary if complexity is to be survived. Without the generalizing specialist role in the mix, there is no master specification, architecture, or project plan that can ensure success (Cockburn, 2001).

> It is the role of the architect to develop this vision together with the team and then keep up the flame. This is mainly a social task. The architect has to mediate between the different experts to help them find the best solution. The architecture has to be stable enough to provide a working backbone, yet flexible enough to adjust to changing requirements and to correct when it is found to be faulty. An architecture that doesn't change is a dead architecture and usually results in a dead project. (Coldewey, 2002)

When the Agile generalizing specialist is augmented with antenarrative knowledge, the result is a *spiraplex consultant* who has a supercharged skill set that is well suited to the challenges of hypercomplex projects. The spiraplex consultant extracts business cases, requirements, use case scenarios, and designs from diverse functional and cultural enterprise silos without imposing a top-down BME viewpoint. Consequently, the value of isolated domain experts and specialists is unlocked with an efficiency that is not possible with less hybrid approaches.

Although the spiraplex consultant role is just emerging, it's pretty clear that this skill set could uniquely prepare project managers and planners for the conflicting integrate/diversify influences and related centripetal/centrifugal forces at play in today's enterprise infrastructures.

The various cultural and functional silos in a complex enterprise project can be visualized by spiraplex consultants with the help of David M. Boje's Tamara "distributed theater stage" analogy. Tamara is a stage play that is performed simultaneously by actors in different rooms of a building so the audience can wander freely from room to room, experiencing the narrative in a highly fragmented, faceted, and chaotic manner (Boje, 2001b).

Using the Tamara model, the spiraplex consultant can operate as a uniquely heterogeneous sensemaker who has the ability to span complexity boundaries with simultaneously divergent story analysis across 'different rooms' of the project. Tamara 'story tracing' is a valuable dialogic tool for spiraplex consultant because enterprise projects have many Tamara qualities.

COGNITIVE BLOCKS AND FLIPS

Spiraplex projects benefit from numerous antenarrative-based insights and practices, particularly the content transformations (Boje, 2008) that take place when project language is allowed to morph from enterprise silo to silo via a mix of interspersed microcultural sensemaking modalities.

When working as a generalizing specialist consultant on complex, cross-departmental projects, the author has often witnessed a dialectical pattern of *cognitive blocks and flips* that limit the team's ability to span various helical aspects of the work.

A cognitive block is a project blind spot that occurs when team members don't have the linguistic bandwidth necessary for sampling viewpoints from outside their specialist silo. A cognitive flip takes place when a project worker flips from one domain perspective to another without conscious awareness of the flip. Examples from recent project ethnography:

- Team members who flip from top-down command-and-control responses to consensual peer-group decision making (social network) without self-awareness
- Flipping from impact assessment (risk planning) to opportunity assessment (sales and marketing)
- Flipping from horizontal matrix management to a vertical reporting org. chart structure

Flipping between silo perspectives can be triggered like a reflex by external or top-down narrative controls, in which case there will be a limited, stereotyped set of responses from each project worker.

Unexamined flipping and habitual blocking of concepts from outside the native domain are two common project behaviors that greatly reduce the likelihood that valuable contrasting/conflicting viewpoints can be socialized and harvested in complex projects. In spiraplex terms, cognitive flips and blocks greatly reduce a worker's ability to transform content/decisions/goals/values from one dimension of the project to another (e.g., from engineering spec to financial goals to human resource issues to supply chain metrics to environmental concerns and sustainability, etc.) (Barker, 2007).

Cognitive limitations are often associated with embedded, polarized self/group identities that infer correctness and completeness of a silo's cultural concept framework in a largely static and impervious manner (Boje, 2008, p. 19).

A skilled spiraplex consultant can use dialectic/dialogic spanning methods to interrogate oppositional language and identity patterns in each project silo, looking for marginalized signs of 'other stories' and other concept frameworks, for example, a marketing metric that is appropriated and buried in the financial language of an accounting report, or the rigid top-down conceptual model of a boss embedded unconsciously in the granular design work of an employee, and so on.

Cognitive aspects of project management can be addressed with the awareness that there are always other stories and other identities that make necessary contributions to the successful project solution and success path diversity. "Those generalized others survey our telling of a story, its contents, implications and the way we tell it" (Boje, 2008, p. 192).

Antenarrative spanning methods create a new set of dynamic, nonpolarized 'living project stories' that go beyond stale BME linear narratives, allowing project thinking to evolve in a complex emergent manner. One potential outcome of this approach is the formation of 'faceted communities of practice' that can rapidly interface with many different value chain components and concept frameworks, solving business and technical problems and defining accurate product requirements in a pluralistic manner that is free from outdated narrative controls and cognitive blind spots (Boje, 2001c; Lave & Wenger, 1991).

JUST-IN-TIME DESIGN: ACT, THEN THINK

Traditional technology projects start with a detailed design specification before the development work is executed. The 'spec' is then used as a highly deterministic beginning-middle-end (BME) roadmap that drives work throughout the linear steps of the project. This so-called 'waterfall' approach to project management is still widely used today in spite of its essential contribution to hugely expensive failures (Hibbs, Jewett, & Sullivan, 2009; Pfleeger & Atlee, 2006). When the nonlinear, bottom-up emergent, dialogic aspects of a project are ignored by BME waterfalls, negative effects include:

- Reduction of heuristic, experimental project team creativity
- Repression of free-form linguistic interplay among stakeholders and domain roles
- A very narrow solution space that lacks requisite complexity, serendipity, and external influences
- Lack of much needed nonlinear paths through project and solution

Waterfall fits our familiar, comfortable linear narratives about how work unfolds in a tidy, orderly manner, but it has a fundamental inability to adapt to real-world complexity and the nonlinear, recursive nature of spiraplex infrastructure. "So the question is: why is the [software project] failure rate so high? A large part of the blame can be traced to the widespread adoption of the Waterfall method" (Hibbs et al., 2009).

Waterfall design specs typically enact a linear *plan-before-acting* paradigm that dominates a project's conceptual framework. Waterfall's rigid unidirectional design disallows *strategy during implementation* efforts. BME waterfalls kill project-worker creativities and path diversity by drastically limiting think/act iteration and recursive possibilities (Cockburn, 2001; Ehin, 2008).

In Agile, the goal is lean design and 'just-in-time' planning, that is, do just enough front-end thinking to get some project action going . . . then, after results of the action are reviewed . . . do a bit more thinking . . . but not too much! In a nutshell: Thinking without acting is as bad as acting without thinking. A seminal Agile text by Highsmith uses the phrase 'barely sufficient' to convey this:

> I use the term "Agile Software Development Ecosystem" to describe a holistic environment that includes three interwoven components—a "chaordic" perspective, collaborative values and principles, and a *barely sufficient* methodology. . . . (Highsmith, 2002) [emphasis mine]

Traditional waterfall projects often generate hundreds or thousands of pages of BME specs that are supposed to guide a project safely from start to finish. But in reality, there are many holes, gaps, and fissures in this narrative. The BME spec exists not because it is a viable plan but because of the strong top-down cognitive influences it exerts on the project team, managers, and planners.

BME project specs can be seen more accurately as a sort of "architectural spectacle" (Boje, Rosile, Duran, & Luhman, 2004), apparently solid but made only of narrative fragments united by linguistic flourishes in an artificial cohesion that operates on project audiences in a theatrical sense. Spec as spectacle, indeed!

In projects run by Agile, antenarrative-aware spiraplex consultants, a more loosely defined 'living' spec is drawn from many different expert/function silos and evolved as action proceeds. The living spec can use textual methods that provide the project community with a chronotopic, dimensional, situated experience wherein all project milestones are considered and refined simultaneously in a relational network of diversely ordered sets. In this context, social sensemaking and decision making are centrifugal and centripetal—uniquely able to balance centralizing and decentering influences.

TEST, THEN *BUILD*

With the Agile 'test-first' best practice, heuristic acting-mixed-with-thinking occurs as developers build software test routines *before* there is any software code to test—this is quite the opposite of how software and other engineering tests are usually deployed *after* development in the old BME model. Test-first design is not a process of rigid front-end BME goal setting; rather, it is experienced-based 'refactoring' (refining) of a heuristic model. Hence, planning can paradoxically follow testing and building. Other related Agile methods:

- *Design patterns.* Even in complex spiraplex environments, there are recurring patterns that can be mapped and modeled. Software design patterns are very different from rigid functional specs because they give developers a sort of flexible roadmap that allows many different paths through the project landscape and many different interpretations of the 'best route' to success. Indeed, some popular design patterns are so flexible they have been used to create radically different applications.
- *Refactoring.* Refactoring is a key strategy for mixing up of thinking/acting with the aim of just-in-time design. According to noted Agile maven Martin Fowler, refactoring is the process of changing a software system so as to improve internal structure while not altering external functionality (Fowler & Beck, 1999). Refactoring is done incrementally and iteratively as the programmers experience the code base and interact with real-world users in situ.

When a spiraplex consultant engages all diverse project stakeholders in a communal backwards/forwards process of *act-then-think*, it creates a productively 'dissipative' effect that frees the project from the neurolinguistic constraints of waterfall BME narratives. This opens the door to the positive influences of chance occurrences, controlled serendipity, and novel solutions that come from noisy bottom-up sources of groundbreaking innovation.

SPIRAPLEX INTEGRATION

For the past couple of decades, system/application/data integration has been a major unfulfilled goal of corporate executives and technologists who are responsible for the end-to-end performance of extended supply/demand chains (Hohpe & Woolf, 2004; Putnik & Cunha, 2005). To achieve end-to-end enterprise process cohesion, integration must forge centrally agreed-on standards and policies that cut across functional silos, IT systems, specialist vocabularies, tacitly embedded work practices and knowledge, and so on.

> Integration is the driving force of this decade of IT (information technology) spending. As enterprises buy more and more packaged applications, it is estimated that the task of combining these application "silos" results in over 40 percent of the IT spending, even though the amount of code written for integration is significantly smaller than 40 percent. This is because integration projects tend to be one-of-a-kind, and complex to write. (Jhingran, Mattos, & Pirahesh, 2002)

In spite of massive investments in integration and interoperability of systems and software, and in spite of the huge effort expended on service-oriented architectures, meaningful integration eludes enterprises to a large degree even after 20 years of work. Meanwhile, the forces of complexity have introduced the centrifugal/decentering need for diversity and empowerment of local solutions that in many ways works against centrally mandated integration initiatives.

Based on the preliminary experiences of the author: by extending the Agile skill set with Dr. Boje's advanced linguistic, cognitive, and organizational story methods, the spiraplex mind-set could allow planners and designers to play more effectively on the enterprise integration playing field. Spiraplex consultants potentially have the unique ability to marshal the rich set of cross-discipline community interactions that are necessary if infrastructure projects are to span decentering and centering sociotechnical forces.

SPIRAPLEX RISK MANAGEMENT

Spiraplex methods can also potentially lead to better risk management by creating many alternative paths to project success, making enterprises less susceptible to 'black swan' failures that easily wipe out a single critical path (McKelvey, 1999; Perrow, 1984). Black swan events are qualitatively and quantitatively extreme, but they are inevitable in complex infrastructure, as is described in a *Harvard Business Review* article on business risk:

[In] a world of tame randomness, around two-thirds of changes should fall within certain limits (the–1 and +1 standard deviations) and that variations in excess of seven standard deviations are practically impossible. However, this is inapplicable in real life, where movements can exceed 10, 20, or sometimes even 30 standard deviations. Risk managers should avoid using methods and measures connected to standard deviation, such as regression models, R-squares, and betas. (Taleb et al., 2009)

Project managers need a new way of thinking about risk and uncertainty, a new way to generate probable and possible scenarios and planning stories, a new way to socialize and prepare for threats and opportunities. Clearly, today's threats and unforeseen events have major human aspects:

While hazards and their aftermath can be identified, risk depends on a complex interplay of a number of social variables, which are ultimately combined by human judgment. (Tsohou, Karyda, & Kokolakis, 2006)

Navare (2003) concisely describes the social nature of risk and crisis management: "Culture, structure, experience and legal compliance requirements converge at the point of crisis."

The spiraplex "agile + antenarrative" mentality is a potential advantage for risk management in several dimensions:

Social and organizational. Corporate risk management practices have traditionally been deployed with an eye to systems and processes, with little regard for subtle socio-organizational dimensions (Perrow, 2007; Sutton, 2006). Spiraplex thinking is equally versed in business, operational, technical, social, and cognitive concerns.

Process path diversity. Spiraplex consultants are always looking for serendipity and spiral path diversity in the emergent project noise fringe and grassroots voices of the value chain—today marginal, tomorrow mainstream. Emergent antenarrative story and restory exercises that can provide alternative path diversity through an uncertain probability landscape (Boje 2001a, 2004, 2008). Rich and diverse antenarrative-based scenario generation allows alternative processes, edge cases, and exception handling to be introduced into the process infrastructure.

Spiraplex consultants can think through possible threat/opportunity scenarios in vivid and highly situated chronotopic storyscapes (Boje, 2008). Chronotopic analysis can potentially help risk managers gain insights into black swan and nonstochastic, emergent events that plague our supposedly deterministic systems and financial markets on an ongoing basis.

Fail fast, fail forward. Spiraplex thinking expects that failure and anomalies will not stay outside the statistical process control bounds. Black swans are around every corner and the spiraplex outlook expects them (Talel, 2001, 2007). Because they are alive and by nature unpredictable, antenarrative-based risk management can help spiraplex project consultants achieve a mental posture that is poised and ready for the uncertainty and unexpected failures that spring naturally from complex, nonlinear, and nondeterministic enterprise environments.

AGILE ENERGY AND HORSE SENSE

Another aspect of Agile development is the 'pair programming' practice that creates an intimate software coding experience between two co-developers working in close proximity, often sharing a single computer and trading off tactical and strategic roles (think vs. act!). One of the partners does the hands-on keyboard 'code-cutting' while the other looks on and thinks ahead. Then they switch off.

Pairs can change partners periodically so that the entire group of programmers cycles through each area of the project. Agile pair programming is a strongly interactive, 'membrane-to-membrane' work experience that facilitates high-bandwidth body language and collaborative problem solving using all the rational and intuitive skills of the development team. (This is similar to air-traffic controllers working in pairs with four eyes and two brains on the radar screen in tandem.)

The intuitive real-time communications found in Agile pair programming has been described in shamanistic terms by David M. Boje as "energy sensemaking" (Boje, 2008) and by Grace Anne Rosile as "horse sensemaking" (Rosile, 1999). It is likely that energy management insights from the Rosile/Boje camp will greatly enhance pair programming productivity and work satisfaction.

On-site ethnography sessions are another project discipline that benefits from engagement of all communication channels: body language, facial microexpressions, and elicitation of terse linguistic constructions loaded with subtext and contextually activated signification. Spiraplex ethnography is greatly facilitated via high-energy 'group membrane' sensemaking and nonverbal horse-sense intuition on the part of consultants. When trained in antenarrative principles, spiraplex consultants can soak up a maximum amount of explicit and tacit knowledge as they cross back and forth between specialized enclaves interacting in real time and real space with all sorts of diverse and orthogonal collaborators.

In conclusion, complexity is not a hopeless situation if managers, designers, and planners use linguistic methods to intuitively weave success paths, project stories, and antenarrative fabrics from a mix of helical sociotechnical enterprise dimensions. It's the author's view that these methods will be viable in virtually any business or technology initiative that needs an alternative to heavy BME master plans and top-down design specs. Software projects are just one of a large range of commercial areas where the antenarrative-aware generalizing specialists can survive and thrive.

REFERENCES

Ambler, S. (2004). *The object primer: Agile modeling-driven development with UML 2.0*. Cambridge: Cambridge University Press.

Augustine, S. (2005). *Managing agile projects*. Englewood Cliffs, NJ: Prentice Hall.

Barabasi, A. (2003). *Linked: How everything is connected to everything else and what it means*. Cornwall: Plume.

Barker, T. (2007). Exploring the differences between accountants and marketers in terms of information sharing. *Marketing Intelligence & Planning*, 26(3), 316–329.

Bell, G. (2009). *Building social Web applications: Establishing community at the heart of your site*. Sebastopol, CA: O'Reilly Media.

Boehm, B. (2000). *Spiral development: Experience, principles, and refinements*. Pittsburgh: Carnegie Mellon University, Software Engineering Institute.

Bohm, D. (1984). *Causality and chance in modern physics*. New York: Routledge.

Boje, D. M. (1996). *Postmodern management and organization theory*. London: Sage.

———. (2001a). *Narrative methods for organizational communication research*. London: Sage.

———. (2001b). *Tamara Manifesto: Journal of Critical Postmodern Organization Science*, 1(1), 1, 15.

———. (2001c). Las Vegas striptease spectacles: Organization power over the body. *M@n@gement*, 4(3), 201–207.

———. (2004b) *Antenarrative Double Spiral Theory*. Retrieved June 1, 2010, from www.peaceaware.com/McD/pages/Antenarrative_Double_Helix.htm.

———. (2008). *Storytelling organizations*. London: Sage.

Boje, D. M., Rosile, G. A., Duran, R. A., & Luhman, J. T. (2004). Enron spectacles: A critical dramaturgical analysis. Organization Studies, 25(5), 751–774.

Carroll, S., & Daughtrey, T. (2007). *Fundamental concepts for the software quality engineering*. Milwaukee: American Society for Quality.

Cockburn, A. (2001). *Agile software development*. Reading, MA: Addison-Wesley.

Coldewey, J. (2002). *Together we stand; architecture is dead—long live the architect!* Workshop at OOPSLA Conference position paper, Seattle.

Fowler, M., & Beck, K. (1999). *Refactoring: Improving the design of existing code*. Reading, MA: Addison-Wesley.

Geirland, J. (1996). Complicate yourself. *Wired Digital*, 4.04, April.

Gleick, J. (2008). *Chaos: Making a new science*. New York: Penguin.

Gore, J. (1996). *Chaos, complexity and the military*. Washington , D.C.: National Defense University, National War College.

Hayles, N. K. (1991). *Chaos and order: Complex dynamics in literature and science*. Chicago: University of Chicago Press.

Hibbs, C., Jewett, S., & Sullivan, M. (2009). *The art of lean software development: A practical and incremental approach*. Sebastopol, CA: O'Reilly Media.

Highsmith, J. A. (2002). *Agile software development ecosystems* (p. xxxii). Reading, MA: Addison-Wesley.

Hohpe, G., & Woolf, B. (2004). *Enterprise integration patterns: Designing, building, and deploying messaging solutions.* Reading, MA: Addison-Wesley.

Jhingran, A. D., Mattos, N., & Pirahesh, H. (2002). Information integration: A research agenda. *IBM Systems Journal, 41*(4): 555–562.

Laughlin, R. (2006). *A different universe: Reinventing physics from the bottom down.* New York: Basic Books.

Lave, J., & Wenger, E. (1991). *Situated learning: Legitimate peripheral participation.* Cambridge: Cambridge University Press.

Leebaert, D. (1992). *Technology 2001: The future of computing and communications.* Boston: MIT Press.

Leishman, T. R., & Cook, D. A. (2002). Requirements risks can drown software projects. *CrossTalk—The Journal of Defense Software Engineering*, April.

Lorenz, E. N. (1996). *The essence of chaos.* Seattle: University of Washington Press.

Marshall, C. (2000). *Enterprise modeling with UML.* Reading, MA: Addison-Wesley.

Martin, R. (2002). *Agile software development, principles, patterns, and practices.* Englewood Cliffs, NJ: Prentice Hall.

Martin, R., & Augustine, S. (2005). *Managing Agile projects* . Englewood Cliffs, NJ: Prentice Hall.

McGirt, E. (2008). How Cisco's CEO John Chambers is turning the tech giant socialist. *Fast Company Magazine*, November.

McKelvey, B. (1999). Avoiding complexity catastrophe in coevolutionary pockets. *Organization Science, 10*, 294–321.

Morin, E. (2008). *On complexity (advances in systems theory, complexity, and the human sciences).* Cresskill, NJ: Hampton Press.

Navare, J. (2003). Process or behaviour: Which is the risk and which is to be managed? *Managerial Finance, 29* Iss: 5/6, pp. 6–19.

Perrow, C. (1984). *Normal accidents: Living with high-risk technologies.* New York: Basic Books.

———. (2007). *The next catastrophe: Reducing our vulnerabilities to natural, industrial, and terrorist disasters.* Princeton, NJ: Princeton University Press.

Pfleeger, S. L., & Atlee, J. M. (2006). *Software engineering: Theory and practice.* Englewood Cliffs, NJ: Prentice Hall.

Prigogine, I., & Nicolis, G. (1989). *Exploring complexity.* New York: W.H. Freeman.

Putnik, G., & Cunha, M. M. (2005). *Virtual enterprise integration: Technological and organizational perspectives.* Santa Fe: Idea Group Inc.

Regev, G., & Wegmann, A. (2006). *Business process flexibility: Weick's organizational theory to the rescue.* International Workshops on Business Process Modeling, Development and Support, June 5–6.

Rosile, G. A. (1999). *Discourse from the horse's mouth.* Language and Organizational Change Conference presentation, May 15, 1999, Columbus, Ohio State University.

Shah, S. K. (2008). *Innovation communities: A path from innovation to firm & market formation.* University of Illinois Working Paper #05–0107.

Standish Group (1995). *Standish group chaos report.* Boston: Chaos Knowledge Center.

Sutton, S. (2006). Extended-enterprise systems' impact on enterprise risk management. *Journal of Enterprise Information Management, 19*(1), 97–114.

Taleb, N.N. (2001). *Fooled by randomness: The hidden role of chance in the markets and in life.* New York: W. W. Norton & Company.

———. (2007). *The black swan: The impact of the highly improbable.* New York: Random House.

Taleb, N. N., Goldstein, D. G., & Spitznagel, M. W. (2009). The six mistakes executives make in risk management. *Harvard Business Review*, October.

Tsohou, A., Karyda, M., & Kokolakis, S. (2006). Formulating information systems risk management strategies through cultural theory. *Information Management & Computer Security, 14*(3), 198–217.

Weick, K., & Sutcliffe, K. (2007). *Managing the unexpected: Resilient performance in an age of uncertainty*. San Francisco: Jossey-Bass.

*For further information and to ask questions about antenarratives from the authors of this book, please go to Steve King's website storyorgs. com.

14 Narratives, Paradigms, and Change

Gerhard Fink and Maurice Yolles

1 INTRODUCTION

In attempts to explain different aspects of human behavior, distinct autonomous groups come together in niche areas to form constellations of theory, such as in organization theory, personality theory, and conflict theory. Each paradigm is itself a conceptual pattern of thought, ideology, and pragmatism that begins its life through the groups' appreciations of their apprehended epistemic truths. Any coherent autonomous durable group that has the ability to form a culture and develops both cognitive interests and purposes will form a paradigm, which lives through that group. Within it, ideological appreciations are formulated which guide the group operationally. These appreciations are meant as a somewhat reflective view of a situation, with both cognitive and evaluative aspects. Formulated systemically, appreciative systems (Vickers, 1965) are generalized versions of appreciations that allow paradigm holders to formulate goals and give accounts of a variety of situations.

This chapter is concerned with not only paradigms and narratives and how they change, but also with the stories that narratives are connected with. There is a fundamental connection between paradigms, narratives, and stories. Paradigms are knowledge based with pragmatic extensions that enable meaningful narratives to develop and deliver perceived stories that are hopefully reflections of the nature of the patterns of knowledge held. The connections between paradigm, narrative, and story, however, may not be simple and linear, and indeed may involve discontinuous breaks that distinguish each of these ontological distinctions one from another. The nature of the connections between these ontological parts is, however, beyond the purpose of this chapter, although insights can be found in Yolles (2007).

Paradigms exist through their set of belief-based propositions, which creates their conceptual form. When the beliefs are logically rationalized and systemized so that they coalesce figuratively (in the sense of Piaget, 1950; also see Duverger, 1972), they establish a phenomenal potential to explain experience. Then, they may be referred to as ideology. The ideological system of thought is manifested as narrative when the potential for experience is used to shape knowledge into story (Yolles, 2007). According to this view, paradigmatic narrative is ideological dogmatism when it not only facilitates the emergence of specific types of stories but also logically constrains what can become a story.

When in a given constellation of paradigms a plurality of them is interact, their stories ring out to contribute to a concerto of meanings. Where there is little semantic harmony, paradigm conflicts and wars develop (Casti, 1989; Chari, Kehoe, & McGrattan, 2009; Hatch & Cunliffe, 2006; Kuhn, 1970). In such conditions the narratives are connected with a cacophony of sound that demands recognition of the antenarrative nature of the constellation. For instance, in organization theory there have been calls for a return to an intellectual orthodoxy (Clegg, Hardy, Lawrence, & Nord, 2006, p. 44), whereas the rise of conflicting paradigms suggests the importance of the current antenarrative phase.

In this chapter we use the overall process of paradigm change to show how narratives change by processes of information drift and diffusion, differentiation, and complexification.

2   KUHN, PIAGET: FROM PARADIGM CRISIS TO TRANSFORMATION

According to Kuhn, a paradigm involves four dimensions of common thought: common symbolic generalizations; shared commitment to belief in particular models or views; shared values; and shared commitments of exemplars (concrete problem interventions). It is constituted as "the set of views that the members of a . . . community share" (Kuhn, 1970, p. 176). The then novel ideas of Kuhn (1970) on paradigmatic change have led to not only gentle criticism connected with the way paradigmatic incommensurability is dealt with (e.g., Budd & Hill, 2007) but also to the elaboration of notions about paradigm change (e.g., Fischer, 1992).

Kuhn (1970) argues that science passes from a *normal* mode through one of *crisis* and then to one of *revolution*. In essence the development of normal science embraces processes of continuous change in theory (Rauterberg, 2000). It operates in a thematic application domain and creates narratives and stories that support a dominant epistemology and allows for a unitary perspective for the construction of knowledge.

Revolutionary science refers to a transformative mode of paradigms and is connected with the idea of scientific revolutions. It tends to be limited to specific (thematic) subdivisions of a field of science that has passed through the prerequisite sense of crisis. The transformative mode arises when paradigms have poor operative intelligence (a term we shall return to shortly), that is, when observed phenomena, which are identified by some as 'problems,' cannot be properly explained by theories which are derived from the dominant paradigm. The revolutionary period results in confusion about what constitutes a problem, a solution, and a method. When the rationality of issues is replaced by emotionality, and they are settled not by logic, syllogism, and appeals to reason but rather by irrational factors like group affiliation, majority, or 'mob rule' (cf. Casti, 1989, p. 40), then antenarratives emerge and challenge the dominant paradigm, which is maintained by a 'power-rule.'

Beyond Kuhn, Ravetz (1999) and Funtowicz and Ravetz (1993) introduced the notion of *postnormal science*. That is the place for antenarratives to emerge, indicating a condition where situational facts are uncertain, values in dispute, stakes high, and decisions urgent (Ravetz, 1999, p. 3). In such situations defenders of challenged paradigms usually refer to 'paradox,' that is, a false dichotomy that can be supported by the dominant paradigm and thus should serve to silence the critics who apparently are incapable of logical thinking: the critics who deliver the antenarratives. For example, it is considered by some to be a paradoxical claim on corporations that they should assume corporate social responsibility and/or environmental responsibility, when they see that their primary task is to generate financial wealth and thereby make profits.

Because paradigms are dynamic, it should be possible to track their viability—those able to achieve a high level of operative intelligence and survive the four possible modes of existence: from normal to postnormal through to critical and further on to transformational science. Understanding and tracking such changes is feasible using the viable systems modeling approach adapted from Schwarz (1997).

3   PARADIGMS NARRATIVES AND STORIES

3.1   Seeing Narratives and Stories Ontologically Distinct

There is a fundamental ontological connection between paradigms, narratives, and stories (Yolles, 2007). The connection between them is not simple and linear, but a simple representation can be found in Figure 14.1. Paradigms are *existential*, dealing with meaning and knowledge and operating through cultural values and establishing a base for attitude; narratives are *noumenal* in that they are cognitive constructs that, using attitude, are able to plan for the pragmatic deployment of knowledge in the form of stories, the latter being observable phenomena and thus belonging to the *phenomenal* domain.

The ontological connections have both relatively simple and more complex names. In the next paragraphs, the connection between the noumenal and phenomenal domains is referred to as operative intelligence, and that between the existential domain and the operative domains is referred to as figurative intelligence, terms that originally derive from Piaget (1950). The terms 'figurative' and 'operative intelligence' can be used as a replacement for the more usual cybernetic terms of autopoiesis and autogenesis (see Yolles, 2009). Because these latter terms are normally associated with 'living systems,' these are also being referred to when assigning the notions of Piagetian intelligences. So what are these?

Whereas Maturana and Varela (1979) were responsible for the idea of autopoiesis, Piaget (1950) developed the idea of operative intelligence for his research into child development. He saw reality is a dynamic system of

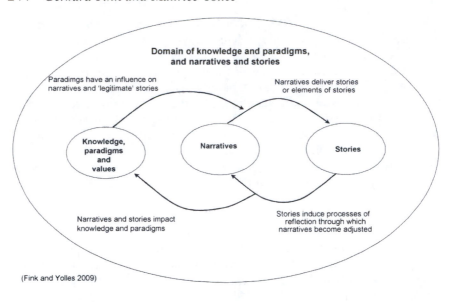

(Fink and Yolles 2009)

Figure 14.1   The ontological connection between paradigms, narratives and stories.

continuous change defined through transformation of information (Demetriou, Doise, & Van Lieshout, 1998), to enable it to be integrated into existing mental schemes, while enabling the specifics of any objects of attention to be taken into account. Whereas the transformations refer to any kind of change, they apply to states that refer to the condition in which a thing or person can be found between transformations. Operative intelligence is the active part of intelligence that is responsible for the representation and manipulation of the transformational aspects of reality, and it involves all actions that are undertaken so as to anticipate, follow, or recover these transformations. It frames how the world is understood, and it is contextually adaptive. According to Sternberg (1996), it operates through two functions: assimilation and accommodation. Assimilation refers to the active transformation of information that can be integrated into existing mental schemes in the form of *combination* with previous knowledge (Nonaka & Takeuchi, 1995), and accommodation refers to active transformation of mental schemes in a second-order learning process in the form of *internalization* of new principles (Nonaka & Takeuchi, 1995) for the referencing of individual interactions. Considering that *operative intelligence* can be constituted as a network of transformative processes, in Figure 14.1 it is this that allows narratives to become stories, so that good operative intelligence can result in efficacious stories.

Piaget also has used the notion of *figurative intelligence*, which is the static part of intelligence that derives contextual meaning from experiences involving operative intelligence. It involves any means of representation that may be used to maintain mental states that intervene between transformations. Now Piaget's notion of figurative intelligence can be adapted to become dynamic if one sees it as the creator of a figurative base that develops noumenally in any personality. This occurs through a dynamic process of sedimentation of cultural and epistemic beliefs that result in the figurative base, and so figurative intelligence can be elevated into a dynamic process equivalent to autogenesis that develops from a higher order set of principles by which operative intelligence is guided.

The narrative-story relationship, however, may not be properly maintained. Under certain conditions pathologies can arise in operative intelligence, resulting in an inability for stories to result efficaciously from narratives. This can sometimes result in story fragmentation more usual of antenarrative, and hence a misunderstanding may develop. The figurative connection between the paradigm and the operative couple of domains that links narrative with stories can also be subject to pathology, so that the efficacious delivery of narrative may, for instance, be poorly coupled to (or even uncoupled from) knowledge, meaning, or cultural values, and also may have no impact on the storytelling environment. More, the narratives may appear to be fragmented, and this may give the mistaken impression that antenarrative is in place. These narrative fragments may decay so that they neither deliver new stories nor become associated with living stories.

3.2   Seeing Narratives and Stories Ontologically Similar

Whereas in Figure 14.1 we considered narrative to be constituted as figurative in nature, delivering phenomenal story as part of its natural process, it is also possible to alter the frame of reference and hence the way in which we see their nature and connection.

In the model of Figure 14.1, narrative and story are analytically independent, the former being figurative and delivering phenomenal story; so that they are seen to be ontologically distinct and connected by a network of (autopoietic) processes. However, it is possible to change the frame of reference and see them as ontologically similar. This has been done in Figure 14.2, where they are also seen as having phenomenal autonomous observable states that are both connected with utterance and performance.

The model in Figure 14.2 hence allows us to draw personality into a narrative-story relationship. Here personality is both figurative and cognitive and thus information rich, whereas narrative and story are considered as observable phenomenal events that are connected with utterance and performance, and are both manifested from personality. The connection between narrative and story is now constituted as a 'structural couple' and illustrates the dynamic cycle between narratives and stories where they learn together through their history of associations. They also have a number of concepts attached. *Guidance:* Operative intelligence is guided by a network of principles based on paradigms, knowledge, and values. The principles related to expressing oneself are also often referred to as 'metanarratives.' Metanarratives guide individuals how to express their goals, intentions, and interests.

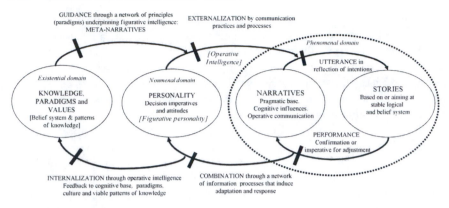

Figure 14.2   Dynamic model illustrating the cycle between narratives and stories.

Externalization in communication practices impacts the emergence of narratives as outcomes of decision-making processes or spontaneous reactions of individuals. It impacts the processes with which narratives are becoming stories, which could or by intention should have an influence on other individuals' or groups' intentions and actions. Narratives become observable phenomena in the form of *utterances*, some of which fit into existing stories (living stories) or turn into new stories. Ineffective utterances decay.

Any utterance that is manifested from personality, be it narrative or antenarrative and resulting in story or story fragment, can (or will) induce a *performance*-related assessment process, whether or not the representations fit the purpose. If they fit the purpose, the narrative and/or its story are confirmed in their desired effects, and they may reemphasize an existing paradigm. If they don't, adjustment is needed. That may take place in the form of *combination* of new experiences with previous knowledge and may influence the adaptation of figurative intelligence. If new combinations of knowledge prove to be operatively successful, then perhaps also the systems of values and paradigms will be adjusted in a higher order learning process: in this case *internalization* may lead to the adoption of a new paradigm.

The thick bars in Figure 14.2 indicate the possibility of pathologies, that is, that the efficacious nature of the respective network of processes is affected, inhibited, restrained, or do not function well, or alternatively they may be amplified beyond the intended needs of context. This has an impact on the relationship between the paradigm, personality, narrative, and story, so that any expected relationships may disappear, creating unexpected outcomes that affect observer perception and understanding.

4   UNDERSTANDING PARADIGMS

Whatever the frame of reference that explores the interconnection between paradigms, narratives, and stories, paradigms maintain a generic connection with narratives and stories.

Scientific theories normally arise from metaphors (Brown, 2003) that begin with literal everyday experiences, and are then mapped into a domain of application to enlarge and enhance an inquirer's understanding of it. They are converted into a theory. A constraint on the development of theory may be that the initial metaphor may not be sufficiently rich to adequately represent the application domain, resulting in bounded paradigms that limit descriptive and explanatory capability.

The dynamic process that viable paradigms and their narratives can pass through as they change is illustrated in Figure 14.3 and in Table 14.1 (adapted from Schwarz, 1997). It explains the cycle of change in terms of paradigmatic narratives for viable paradigms that are able to survive by transforming their natures, initially by developing through normal science, experiencing uncertainty, and moving into postnormal science, crisis, and hence to metamorphosis. During this process, nonviable paradigms and its postnarratives decay, whereas a viable paradigm will become complexified as it develops more attributes and explanatory power in its theory and transformation narratives.

Mode 1 can be described as the place for the equilibrium development of paradigms and hence their narratives. It is the relatively simple, parsimonious narrative mode created through epistemic imperatives that drive stories, which can maintain their own dynamic. Incremental changes enable the equilibrium to move slowly. However, they maintain inbuilt limitations driven by the ideological dogma and its values that create a paradigm. Thus, in organization theory a narrative plurality is conceived to be unable to account for the whole of a thematic *Reality* (Hatch & Cunliffe, 2006). This also appears to be the situation in other fields, for example, the thematic domain of personality research or in economics, where liberals are in dispute with Keynesians. Each schema operates as a distinct and unconnected narrative resulting in different storytelling. That leads to mode 2.

The *postnormal* or *mode 2* may be linked with antenarrative, where a constellation of different paradigms exist in an incoherent disjointed, discordant space. Mode 2 goes beyond the traditional assumptions that science is both certain and value-free. In addition to the application of routine techniques, judgment also becomes necessary. Karl E. Weick's article on 'Theory Construction as Disciplines Imagination' in the 1989 *Association of Management Review* special issue appears to represent a perfect match with Kuhn's ideas about the role of intuition, imagination, and receptivity to new ideas.

In contrast to the *normal*, the *postnormal* mode is concerned with complexity. It has interests that relate to uncertainty, assigned values, and a plurality of legitimately argued perspectives. These attributes are antenarrative in nature. A plural collective construction of multiple voices develops, each with a narrative fragment and none with an overarching conception of the story that is becoming (Boje, 2001). 'Feminist Organizational Theorizing,' 'Postcolonial Analyzes,' and 'Actor-Network Theory' are excellent examples provided by Calás and Smircich (1999).

Mode 3 is that of *crisis*, a crisis-narrative condition *(cri-narrative)* in which paradigmatic and nonparadigmatic narratives reflect the crisis that the

Table 14.1 Explanation of the Options for Paradigmatic Change and its Narratives

Mode of Narrative	Step	Movement towards evolution
Mode 1: Narrative	Stabile equilibrium	The paradigm and its narratives exist with a stable belief system and logical base, though during normal development the base may change its form (morphogenesis). Where there are too many distinct narratives with competing stories, equilibrium is lost.
Mode 2: Antenarrative (uncertainty drift)	Paradigmatic drift Tension development Tension increase and structural criticality	Antenarrative develops as dissipative processes are introduced and a constellation of conflicting paradigms result in a cacophony of voiced narratives. In a complex application domain, drift enables unexpressed potentials to be actualized. The drift takes the paradigm away from its stable position and gives rise to tensions between its ability to explain and predict, and questions about its methods in relation to observations.
Mode 3: Crisis narrative (Crisis)	Fluctuations	Asks the question "What next?"
		The tensions, following the tropic drift that moved the paradigm away from its stable narrative position, are leading it to structural criticality. If the paradigm loses robustness, fluctuations are amplified. Fluctuations occur internally, or in the environment as noise. Through amplification of fluctuations due to tensions following uncertainty drift, a discontinuity occurs in the causal sequence of events/behavior. This likely will be accompanied by debates about utility of the epistemological basis.
	6. Bifurcations	When bifurcations occur the paradigm is able to take a variety of possible paths. At this point three options are possible:
	7.1 type change: Paradigmatic death (post-narrative)	In type 7.1 change, paradigmatic death represents a process of disorganization, regression, or extinction of the paradigm, ultimately leading to the possible loss of group member carriers. This can be seen as the outcome of a catastrophe bifurcation.
	7.2 Type change	In 7.2 type change the process of change begins with "more of the same" small changes that maintain its current state but do not resolve issues. Complexification of the logical base and modes of practice can occur during a process of iteration. This may involve 'living stories' to emerge.
Mode 4: transformation-narrative (Transformation)	7.3 Type change	In 7.3 type change, metamorphosis occurs, leading to a new logical base of propositions that induce new forms of practice. This is referred to as morphogenic change, occurring through amplification and differentiation. It is a relational process that develops in the paradigm through positive and negative feedback, and integration, when the new cognitive base is manifested figuratively and pragmatically.

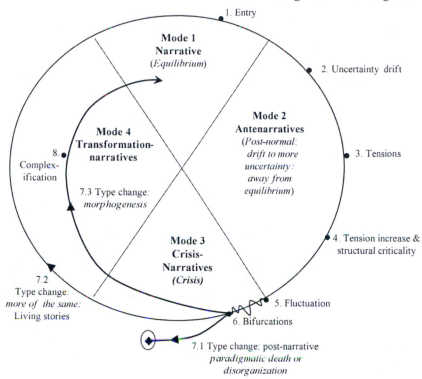

Figure 14.3 Four modes of paradigm change reflected in a cycle of narrative change.

paradigm is passing through. It is a boundary condition for transformation and a prerequisite for revolution (Kuhn, 1970). Anti-, counter-, or contra-stories may emerge to contrast paradigm-conforming stories. As the crisis deepens, narrative carriers commit themselves to some concrete proposal for reconstruction to a new framework. Where different frameworks exist, communication fails and loses its semantic content. Polarization develops, when members of the different camps become constrained by the boundaries of their competing paradigm (Hatch & Cunliffe, 2006). Crisis is closely related to the 'incredulity toward meta or master narratives—and to a continuing question of *how to write* legitimate knowledge' (Calás and Smirchich, 1989, p. 664). The current 'rigor vs. relevance' discussion reflects an unstable cognitive strategy that oscillates between the constraints of normal science and a search for a better frame of thought—one that might allow a novel integration of fragmentary representational structures that exist across a plurality of paradigms on a higher level of abstraction, differentiation, and integration (Fischer, 1992). It is here that new social ties, circles, and networks form and new virtual paradigms may rise.

In mode 4, the *transformative* mode, paradigmatic *transformation-narratives* are defined. It is there where new 'virtual paradigms' may arise or old paradigms may be reborn, perhaps with modest amendments, and become supported as full paradigms. Two forms of conceptual extension are possible:

(a) lateral, so as to be able to identify phenomena not previously known; or (b) transitive, where a higher level of theory (referred to as metatheory) than those known before arises that may be linked to a whole group of lower level theories without substantially changing any. A crystallization of support occurs when the emergence of a new cognitive consensus emerges (Fischer, 1992)

5   NARRATIVES DRIVING PARADIGM TRANSFORMATION

In our cycle of change we have said that paradigms pass through a transformational mode. The question may be asked, How does the shift from one mode to another develop?

The normal mode of a paradigm exists through its adoption of a normative epistemology, which lies at the basis of its formalized patterns of knowledge. This may be challenged with the development of doubt about its veracity (e.g., Meehl, 1997). Doubt becomes expressed in antenarratives, that is, utterances that deviate from what is perceived to be 'normal.' When a paradigm exists in normal mode and is repeatedly and persistently challenged in this way, the result can be a shift into a postnormal mode. It becomes unstable when opposing interests organize a culture shift from one state to another (Rummel, 1979). Such challenges can finally result in structural changes that lead to pragmatic adjustment when modes and mechanisms of practice alter.

Instability and conflict emerge when 'real-world' change occurs more rapidly than the ability a culture has to adjust; this creates a cultural lag. Cultural lag is constituted as the difference between what it and its narratives tell and what some segments of a culture consider ought to be. New challenges emerge in the form of antenarratives. In crisis, conflicting views find their expression in contra- or counternarratives, which together constitute a set of crisis narratives. If a sort of balance or equilibrium does not emerge between opposing interests, wants and costs, investments and rewards, capabilities and power, consent on a dominant paradigm is not possible. This leads to the onset of culture shock and cultural instability (Dahl, 2000) and the eventual development of new modes and means of practice. During this process, conflicts and relativisms are likely to arise, and the paradigm shifts into postnormal mode.

6   CONCLUSION

In this chapter we refer to the rise of the complexity view and the need of explicit examination of control and communication within organizational situations, with respect to the expectation that new theory might emerge.

It has been explained that there is a fundamental distinction between knowledge-based paradigms, narratives, and stories in any autonomous system, although the frames of reference that models their ontological interconnection can be altered. Understanding the connection between paradigms, narratives, and stories is fundamental to appreciating how stories develop into perceived focus of meaning or disappear into a cacophony of disparate semantics, and different frames of reference allow distinct modeling contexts. We have also shown that even by changing the frame of reference that allows one to explore the relationship between paradigms, narratives, and stories, for instance, by including variable personality into the model, we are still able to maintain stability in the story that we present about processes of change.

Predominant paradigms in human agency theory may go through a cycle from *normal* mode to *postnormal* mode, fall into *crisis*, and finally to one of *revolution*. This is consistent with their moving from paradigmatic narrative, to antenarrative, to crisis-narrative, and on to transformation-narrative mode. As a paradigm enters its antenarrative mode, the normal prevailing confirmatory mode approaches to theory must be considered to have lost their capability to make useful predications, something that is not always recognized by researchers. This leads to crisis (crisis-narrative mode), which may result in a conceptual revolution where extant theories are replaced or reborn. New sets and systems of classifications, emphasis on relations between events and occurrences rather than on substances, and new motivation-oriented theories might emerge that emphasize motivational aspects and address the concerns of groups of individuals with newly emphasized shared needs and desires. A metaview of phenomena and the ability to identify redundancies and variety in a system create views of patterns of change and capabilities to adapt to new challenges by self-organization.

Paradigms may die, when the predominant narrative mode continuously tends to fail with its applications to radically changing societal domains, or at least needs substantial transformation. Then, the emerging theories represent themselves through antenarrative in the constellation of paradigms that it exists within. In this sense, paradigmatic antenarrative constellations are concerned with complexity, and have interests in aspects which relate to uncertainty, assigned values, and a plurality of legitimately argued perspectives. They maintain their potential of returning to narrative.

In conclusion, we note that paradigms only exist through their holders who carry, define, and maintain them. Paradigms are maintained among others by the narratives and stories they produce. Durable paradigms may be seen as viable human-activity systems that are complex and adaptive and able to maintain a separate existence within the confines of their existential and other constraints. In essence, in this chapter we do not deal with such constraints.

REFERENCES

Boje, D. M. (2001). *Narrative methods for organizational and communication research*. London: Sage. also see http://cbae.nmsu.edu/dboje/papers/narrative_methods_intro.htm, accessed June 2008.

Brown, T. L. (2003). Making truth: Metaphor in science. University of Illinois Press, Champaign, IL.

Budd, J. M., & Hill, H. (2007). The cognitive and social lives of paradigms in information science. In *Proceedings of the Annual Conference of the Canadian Association for Information Science*, Ed. Clement Arsenault and Kimiz Dalkir,

11, McGill University, Montreal, Quebec. Retrieved January 2009, from http://www.cais-acsi.ca/proceedings/2007/budd_2007.pdf

Calás, M. B., & and Smircich, L. (1999). Past postmodernism? Reflections and tentative directions. *Academy of Management Review*, 24(4), 649–671.

Casti, J. L. (1989). *Paradigms lost*. London : Abacus.

Chari, V. V., Kehoe, P. J., & McGrattan, E. R. (2009). New Keynesian models: Not yet useful for policy analysis. *American Economic Journal: Macroeconomics*, 1(1), 242–266.

Clegg, S., Hardy, C., Lawrence, T., & Nord, W. (2006). *The Sage handbook of organization studies*. Sage, Thousand Oaks, CA, and London, UK. Retrieved June 1, 2010, from http://books.google.co.th/books?id=gJBOZ1a8u-4C

Dahl, S. (2000). *Communications and culture transformation: Cultural diversity, globalization and cultural convergence*. London: ECE. Retrieved June 1, 2010, from www.stephweb.com/capstone/1.htm

Demetriou, A., Doise, W., & Van Lieshout, C. F. M. (1998). *Life-span developmental psychology*. Chichester, UK: John Wiley & Sons.

Duverger, M., 1972, *The Study of Politics*. Thomas Nelson and Son, London. Originally published in 1968 as Sociologie Politique, Presses Universitaires de France, Paris.

Fischer, K. (1992). The social and cognitive dynamics of paradigmatic change: A scientometric approach. *Science in Context, 5*, 51–96.

Funtowicz, S. O., & Ravetz, R. (1993). Science for the post-normal age. *Futures*, 739–755, 25/7 September 1993.

Hatch, M. J., & Cunliffe, A. L. (2006). *Organization theory*. Oxford University Press, Oxford, UK.

Kuhn, S. T. (1970). *The structure of scientific revolutions*. Chicago: University of Chicago Press.

Maturana, H. R., & Varela, F. J. (1979). *Autopoiesis and cognition*. Boston: Boston Studies in the Philosophy of Science.

Meehl, P. E. (1997). The problem is epistemology, not statistics: Replace significance tests by confidence intervals and quantify accuracy of risky numeral predictions. In L. Harlow, S. Mulaik, Stanley, & J. Steiger (Eds.), *What if there were no significance tests?* (pp. 393–425).

Nonaka, I., & Takeuchi, H. (1995). *The knowledge-creating company*. New York: Oxford University Press.

Piaget, J. (1950). *The psychology of intelligence*. New York: Harcourt & Brace.

Rauterberg, G. W. M. (2000). How to characterize a research line for user-system interaction. *IPO Annual Progress Report, 35, 66*.

Ravetz, J. R. (1999). What is post-normal science? *Futures*, 31(7), 647–653.

Rummel, R. (1979). *Understanding conflict and war*. Beverly Hills, CA: Sage. Also see www.hawaii.edu/powerkills/CIP.CHAP8.HTM, retrieved February 2009.

Schwarz, E. (1997). *Summary of the main features of a holistic metamodel to interpret the emergence, the evolution and the functioning of viable self-organizing systems*. Retrieved January 2009 from www.autogenesis.ch/Res1997.html

Sternberg, R. J. (1996). *Cognitive psychology*. New York : Harcourt Brace College Publishers.

Vickers, G. (1965). *The art of judgement*. London: Chapman & Hall. (Reprinted 1983, Harper & Row, London)

Weick, K. E. (1989). Theory construction as discipline imagination. *Academy of Management Review, 14*(4), 516–531.

Yolles, M. I. (2007). The dynamics of narrative and antenarrative and their relation to story. *Journal of Organizational Change Management, 20*(1), 74–94.

———. (2009). Migrating personality theories part 1: Creating agentic trait psychology? *Kybernetes, 36*(6), 897–924.

15 Antenarratives of Change in Mexican Innovation Networks

Enrique Campos-López, Alena Urdiales-Kalinchuk, and Hilda G. Hernández

INNOVATING THE INNOVATION

To face the complexity and turbulence of the present times, many changes are on the way. One of them is 'innovating the innovation.'[1] This is one of the biggest changes brought by globalization, leaving behind the traditional linear models and considering innovation only as the generation of new products and services to keep firms competitive. The externalities and market failures partially induced by innovation are causes of the environmental crisis and social disequilibrium reinforced by contingencies spawned from their entangled relations.

To innovate is no longer a challenge imposed exclusively on the corporate world, firms, and scientific communities. It spreads to the social realm; regions and localities must regenerate their culture to build up new mechanisms, governance strengths, and new stories need to renew our reference frameworks. The effects of technological change are not only restricted to the economic realm; they affect the society and environment as the innovation process unfolds. Deep changes in language and communication patterns become one of the cultural consequences of innovation. Octavio Paz, the Mexican Nobel laureate, once wrote (Paz, 1994) that technological change shakes the language's tree, and words drain their blood, losing their significances. As words lose their accustomed meanings, symbols enter into crisis, a chaotic process takes place, and new narratives emerge. As ships surrounded by seagulls arriving to the desired port, innovations enter into the economy accompanied by flocks of new symbols. Novelty is not only in the new products but also in the new narratives that emerge as the innovation cycle unfolds.

COOPERATIVE INNOVATION AND NETWORKS

Innovation is moving beyond the material and technological change to face the challenges imposed by the global traumas. A key element of this 'innovating the innovation' trend is the surge of a myriad of interorganizational cooperative strategies for creating knowledge that are being catapulted into the social and economic context, via alliances, consortia, and, with an increasing importance, Cooperative Innovation Networks[2] (Gloor, 2006). The best examples are found in the information and communication technologies (ITC) and in the emergence of modern biotechnology (Powell, 2005).

Together with the networks motivated by technology, other cooperative strategies are nurtured; these are networks motivated by the threats accompanying the global traumas. These networks are becoming relevant between nations of the European Community (Cooke, 2003) and Canadian provinces (Gertler & Wolfe, 2002), and some emerging economies such as Brazil, are also experimenting. Their purposes are quite diverse: to be ready to cope with climatic contingencies, to link advanced science and technology to the problem of environmental resource sustainability, and to face the increasing health and security threats. For these networks, technology is not a *per se* objective, but a strategy within a problematic framework. They are created between firms, scientists, and governments, as in the triple-helix model, but also including other social innovation agents. Bifurcation in the innovation concepts is exploring new forms of perception, narrative, and representation of coming threats.

AN EPISTEMOLOGICAL CHALLENGE

There is an epistemological and cognitive challenge faced by every region in the world. The Brazilian Santos de Sousa (2009) writes about this challenge faced by the nations of the South, nonindustrialized countries that have to improve their cognitive capital and to develop their scientific and innovation capabilities, but through the lenses of a postmodern concept of innovation, in which natural sciences integrate into a common field with the humanities and with common sense. However, many southern hemisphere nations have meager resources for science and technology and insist on lineal and sequential innovation models based on the interplay between research and development (R&D) and the industrial activity, making it difficult to tackle the problematics emerging from their surviving and adaptation process.

An increasing need for a innovation comes from the strategies to cope with climate change (IPCC, 2007). Two main strategies are drawn: one is *mitigation*, aiming to reduce the emissions of greenhouse gases through technological innovation; the other is *adaptation*, promoting social practices that prevent some effects that will be unfolding in the coming years. In *mitigation*, the emphasis is on technology, new policies, and electricity networks; in *adaptation*, the challenge is a cultural transformation to equilibrate reactive behaviors with prevention through regional social networks.

In each strategy, innovation acquires different meanings and a different narrative. *Mitigation* focuses on the logic provided by the technology;

adaptation is a social construct emerging from a network of antenarratives, a new common sense, and renewed metaphors. One emerges from the high-tech labs and the other from the concerns of the social grassroots. Two paths to face complexity, two ways of social interaction and learning, two forms for creating, interpreting, and evaluating innovation policies. It is not a dilemma but instead a bifurcation, one including the other, both part of the social learning system, demanding a new epistemology similar to the double loop proposed by Chris Argyris for the organizational learning (Argyris & Schön, 1974), where improvement and innovation are reinforced by a learning-to-learn loop. The imperative is already here: to create a new awareness, comprehension, and systems thinking to understand the coming risks (Morgan, Fischhoff, Bostrom, & Atman, 2002; Sterman & Sweeney, 2007).

NARRATIVES AND POSTMODERN SCIENCE

A new epistemology must grow between scientific fields and the social domains. The challenge is to translate the global menaces into local actions, to integrate the several time perceptions, to include the social agents and capital, and to take into account the productivity of the traditional systems. Narratives should be closer to chaotic rhizomes (Deleuze & Guattari, 1987) than to the structured logic of scientific papers. Psychologist Jerome Bruner (1990) wrote about the two trends that have been shaping the development of the cognitive sciences, that is, technical innovation and social innovation. The technical conceives cognition as a data-processing process and the other trend as a construction of meanings. This dichotomy was artistically expressed by T. S. Eliot in his well-known verse.[3] Now it seems that we have to walk back, creating a new narrative about innovation, regenerating the common sense through a learning spiral that the same Eliot evoked in another of his poems.[4]

Empowered local and regional processes are needed to rescue and build their stories through a new participative thinking on messy issues. Cognitive psychologists recently discovered that there is a distributed collective intelligence improved by working in 'small world' networks (Goldstone & Janssen, 2005). A learning and innovation strategy has to be based in cooperative social networks (Castells, 2000) moving from the interest to the practice needed to create new orders of knowledge and innovation possibilities. Social networks can be a regional strategy useful as a feedback to reinforce local self-regulation and autopoiesis. Narrative must be present to expand the limitations of the scientific and technological discourse.

In the scenario drawn by Santos de Sousa, fusing the scientific discourse with narrative is an imperative. From the overlapping of natural sciences, humanities, and common sense will emerge new knowledge. The new epistemology has to be reflected into the market, society, and environment, giving birth to a new ecology where ethics coexists with creativity. Network learning becomes a Borgian Aleph, taking us, in the same trip, to the past, into our living story, and immersing us into the turbulent waters of the antenarrative searching for better futures. To achieve this systemic level of narrative, new forms of social interaction are needed, some intentional, others provided by the surprises and the synchronies needed for the social creativity.

A paradox of our time is that the emerging global traumas could only be punctuated[5] through the chaotic emergence of regional social networks. The old incremental policies can be disrupted through the virtuous circles nurtured within these chaotic networks. Social mechanisms make irreversible what is learned, build up a systemic perception, and induce cultural transformation. Networks imply a new narrative, closer to what David M. Boje (2001) calls antenarrative.[6] Metaphorically speaking, networks become the antenarratives, having been socially constructed specifically to perceive complexity and explore optional futures.

NETWORKS AND ANTENARRATIVE

Formation of collaborative social structures pursuing innovation is a process where adaptation predominates over design. The literature offer several approaches to interpret the incubation of these cooperative innovation strategies; one of the most powerful metaphor comes from the basic science. The theory proposed by Prigogine and Stengers (1984) for the thermodynamic of irreversible process is widely used as a metaphor to explain how complex social structures evolve. Larry D. Browning's case studies on ITC (Browning, Sætre, Stephens, & Sørnes, 2008) and the incubation of consortia (Browning, Beyer, & Shetler, 1995) use the full array of concepts—fluctuations, bifurcations, attractors, irreversibility, dissipative structures—offered by Prigogine's thermodynamic concepts.

The new innovation epistemology takes place in a complex domain requiring a continuous redrawing of its limits, beyond the corporate, science, and the market. New innovation concepts emerge from the messy regional issues linked to the global risks, a new concept of innovation that is not only a direct effect of a scientific or technological idea but one that emerges from the *pulling* effect of the regional problematics. This situation creates the need for new policies integrating R&D and innovation with environment, health, and education. Policies that not only pursue the transfer and adoption of advanced technologies, but also use networking to facilitate the development of new learning skills in the regional agents in order to allow them to perceive and to represent their problematics, and to create roadmaps with emerging scientific knowledge. These networks will be capable of inducing creativity and of exploring the long-term effects of the technical solutions. Networks as social processes are able to transform their stories into antenarratives, narratives, and scenarios. This is not easy to achieve, and requires new methodological approaches for the use of narrative methods for the making, communication, interpretation, and assessment of new policies (McCloskey, 1990; Roe, 1994).

INNOVATION IN MEXICO

Mexico faces all these transformational challenges. The country has considerable delays in perceiving innovation and to develop indigenous strengths to use innovation as a driver for regional progress. Until now the efforts were focused on the construction and maintenance of a science and technology system far from a postmodern concept. This pervasive fragmentation reflects on the internal organization of the policymaking institutions and on the R&D federal centers showing specialized emphasis provoking weak interactions with the innovation agents. Mexico has a fragmented set of stories as snapshots instead of a systemic view, mostly linear or cyclic narratives emerging from a process guided by a bureaucratic culture—stories guided by the parsimony of Occam's razor rather than the requisite variety proposed by Ross Ashby in his cybernetic theory (Ashby, 1964). This fragmentation is an impediment for perceiving and representing regional messy issues as opportunities for innovation. From the year 2002 a new science and technology law started to reduce this gap and promotes cooperation in R&D and innovation projects among regional organizations. Policymaking has been increasingly active in bringing new instruments.[7] Those promoting regional projects based on cooperative forms such as networks and alliances among regional or interregional agents are bringing more comprehensive approaches (OECD, 2009).

NETWORKS IN COAHUILA

Regional institutions, such as the Coahuila's Council for Science and Technology (COECYT), started to promote the formation of networks of interest on critical state issues such as water scarcity, climate change, housing, and renewable energy sources. Coahuila is a northern Mexican state comprised of regions facing different developmental cultural challenges: low-risk perception and awareness; loss of environmental resource sustainability; eroding competitiveness of small industries; poor cooperation and little solidarity among innovation agents; hierarchical communication. Each region has its own peculiarities on leadership styles, entrepreneurship, and social attitudes towards change.

Networks have been induced to bring together local agents—scientists, academics, entrepreneurs, government agents, members of NGOs, experts—interested in the selected issues. Members are encouraged to improve their skills for social interaction and communication, to expand their information base, to exchange experiences and stories, and to prepare, jointly, R&D proposals.

NETWORKS OF INTEREST

The first networks in Coahuila took the shape of "communities of interest" (Wenger, 2002). Members showed poor writing skills and networks battled to build up a collective narrative. With time, some weaknesses are diminishing and interest sustained.

Valuable lessons were obtained on the need to induce an early social integration and build individual skills for interacting in transcultural domains. The observations on the reluctance among the individuals and groups to construct their narratives were striking. The difficulty was to obtain individual stories, and to achieve collective narratives catalyzing group perception of their problematic domains. Voluntary networks facilitators, appointed by COECYT, led the process, but had limited time and experience, and were also responsible for the building up of network narrative and documentation. Some of these constraints were gradually reduced by conferences and training workshops.

With each network of interest focusing on a specific issue, interaction increased but in an intermittent way. Some (mining and ITCs) documented their stories as well-defined strategic planning; others were dominated by a cathartic explosion of oral stories. Three types of narrative contexts emerged: the sustainability issues, competitiveness in small enterprises, and the lack of motivation by scientists to participate beyond their specific scientific domains. Stories were dominated by thinking in terms of 'problem solving,' making problematization and dialogue difficult.

Initially, it was thought that networks would be structures able to write down sound proposals for ambitious projects and portfolios. After two experimental years, results showed that in order to enhance cooperation skills a preparatory step was needed.

SPORE AND THE NETWORKS OF PRACTICE

Experiences led in 2008 to the project "Incubation of Networks of Practice for Cooperative Innovation." Abbreviated 'Spore,' the project aims to explore, through experimental activities, how networks of practice could be formed and become capable tackling the issues, extracting problematics, and creating innovation options and scenarios. The meaning of *problematic* was taken from Russell Ackoff[8] (1981).

A strong emphasis is made to distinguish between problem and problematic, between problem solving and problematization. In each situation, stories and narratives are different. Participant groups unconsciously incline towards problem solving. Problems require solutions, whereas problematics are persistent situations needing management. Spore placed emphasis on what Michel Foucault (Pastor & Bernal, 2006) describes as problematization, requiring a change to the way of thinking about 'messy' situations. Stories and narrative are radically different between 'problem solving' and problematization. Narrative sensitizes stakeholders to the problematic.

Spore integrates methods and tools under the assumption that with proper interactions, networks will be capable of performing a learning process that was named by the team, Cycle Problematic-Innovation (CPI), described in Table 15.1. During this cycle, formed by four stages, various methods and tools were used to improve team attitudes. The desired group skills and individual behaviors emerge from the interaction in fields (Ba) and the application of different methods of inquiry, initial emphasis on abduction (Flach & Kakas, 2002) and induction, socialization, and collective action learning. CPI's design integrates ideas from action learning (Argyris, Putnam, & McClain Smith, 1985; Roth, 2000) models together with previous experiences from the authors (Campos-López & Urdiales-Kalinchuk, 2005).

Spore started presenting, in formal meetings, the concepts and approaches to be used through the CPIs. Then the several issues initiated their problematization step, followed by a more analytical and deductive stage where ideas for innovation were road mapped and outlined.

Within the problematization step, the basic methods are narrative, systems thinking, and action learning, as already mentioned. CPI resembles the organizational learning model presented by Ikujiro Nonaka (1995) known as SECI.[9] Narrative is constructed, causally analyzed, and then archetypes are identified and traced. Simplified, the sequence goes through seven steps: problematic profile; tacit knowledge; stories; antenarrative; narrative; archetypes; scenario.

Spore observes the network incubation process, how the relationships are created, how from those relationships a narrative network on the problematic emerges, and how it is transformed into a new knowledge, outlining possible innovation paths, potentially valuable to invigorate state programs with projects, portfolios, and policies. Antenarrative evolves from fragmented stories into a narrative, and later to logic proposals for science, technology, innovation, and policymaking.

These activities are performed in 'interaction fields' resembling the concept of Ba[10] as an environment where knowledge is shared, created, and utilized. Ba concepts were developed by Nonaka from ideas by the Japanese philosopher Kitaro Nishida (1990). Activities, including physical

Table 15.1   Cycle Problematic-Innovation

Conepts Compo- nents	CPI's Process			
	Phase 1 Problematiza- tion Problematic	Phase 2 Scenario: Business as Usual	Phase 3 Scenarios of Innovation	Phase 4 Communica- tion and Sensitization
Methods	• Antenarrative • Analysis • Systems Thinking	• Narrative • Scenarios • Systems Dynamics	• Experts • Opinions, Delphi • Scenarios • System Dynamics	• Policy Analysis • Evaluation • Case Studies
Interacting Fields Ba's	• Exercising • Originating	• Exercising • Dialoguing	• Systematizing • Dialoguing	• Systematizing • Exercising
Activities	• Interviews • Problematize • Workshops • Web	• Interviews • Problematize • Workshops • Web	• Surveys • Modeling • Information	• Interviews • Hearings • Documentation
Behaviors	• Curiosity • Trust • Search for Allies	• Cooperation • Security • Motivation	• Skills • Mastering • Security	• Enthusiasm • Pride • Satisfaction • Affect
Docu- ments	• Stories • Antenarrative • Narrative • Problematic	• Problematic • Archetypes • Causal Structures • Scenario	• Systemic Story • Road Maps • Scenarios • Antenarrative	• Case Study • Proposals

interaction (Sweeney & Meadows, 2008) induce cooperative and communicative attitudes within a dialogical environment. As CPI unfolds, interaction fields increase complexity and causal structures emerge to outline the
systems thinking models. Narrative is an effective platform to introduce
systems thinking tools. Beginning is the critical step where the cooperative
social behaviors are nurtured, stories start to show, and messy antenarrative appears.

NARRATIVE AND PROBLEMATIC

The problematics addressed emerged from an iterative process with existing networks of interest, through interviews, conversations, encounters,

workshops, and meetings. Five, shown in Table 15.2, were primarily selected to be taken through the CPI process. Stories and antenarratives collected in each network differ in many ways: diversity of voices and images; multiple agents with their mental and inference models; conflicts; skepticism over government plans; emotions; contexts; scientific information; time perception. Emotive memories play an integrative role, for example, the story of the first time a child heard of water scarcity and the entrepreneur being awarded with his first patent. Everything counts.

To move from antenarrative to narrative and then to go deeply into the problematic, several elements are considered: the domain, the concerns and critical behaviors, time horizon, agents involved, structural elements (variables), milestones, and contingencies.

ANTENARRATIVE, AWARENESS, ANALYSIS, AND ARCHETYPES

Stories around the problematics show diverse complexity. The best case is found in narratives on the depletion of La Laguna's aquifer. Attention had been focused on blaming the agriculture and dairy industries, and scarce mention was made of the deforestation of highlands where most of the water feeding the aquifer is captured. Problematization changed the persistent tautological thinking: 'If the aquifer is collapsing then let's stop extracting.' Several other facets started to appear, ending with a critical question always present: 'Why have an incurable way of thinking in the same way; are there no other forms to think about it?' People start to move out from thinking in circles to spiral thinking. In most of the incubated networks of practice, a similar conscience started to appear.

Through the construction of the antenarratives in most of the networks of practice, changes took place in how the groups perceive the core problematic: recognizing how the dominance of a problem-solving bias led to the distorting of complex situations into a collection of unconnected problems urging for immediate actions and partial solutions was an important finding, consistent with Boje's work.

A key observation is on the lack of a systemic conscience about the problematic, with groups unable to weave the prevailing fragmented images into a coherent representation, and with opening attitudes that constrained collaboration. An important step is integrating and presenting the narrative of the problematic to network members and asking them to create relations among their stories, helping to expand the limits of the individual perception and, eventually, to perceive a shared domain of interest that induces needed cooperation to start to outline the problematic.

Defensive attitudes must be identified and ameliorated from the outset. The inability to nurture a systemic consciousness about the problematic emerged as another key outcome. That is why problematization is so important as the starting step, challenging the traditional approaches to the problematics. Antenarrative can be considered as a valuable tool to incubate the initial polyphony of the inevitable initial chaos, and as the first individual strokes of a collective mural.

Spore adopted narrative as a central working method and for collective construct. From this perspective, each network becomes an inquiry system founded on a participation-based pragmatism (James, 1981), similar to what West Churchman identified as a Singerian inquiring system (Churchman, 1971).

As stated earlier, Spore fuses three approaches: action learning, narrative methods, and systems thinking (Meadows, 2008). Along the CPI some specific techniques and tools from these approaches are used, such as emulations and policy games (Duke & Geurts, 2004), providing effective communication patterns and metaphors that ease problematization. The concept of *simulacrum* and its role in postmodern culture (Baudrillard, 2006) are a key concept to be considered in network incubation.

Depending on the problematic, different narrative analytical methods are employed. Some are of general application; others could find uses in more complex narratives. For extracting causal structures, some methods reported by Boje[11] were used (Boje, 2001). Table 15.2 shows methods used in eliciting causal structure and then identifying the archetypes, also suggesting the other possible applications. Archetype[12] is a systems thinking tool used to interpret perceived behavior in terms of causal structures. Some of the archetypes that were extracted from the analysis of narratives are showed in the same table.

NETWORK INCUBATION AND LEARNING DISABILITIES

Two main interrelated learning processes take place in Spore. One is on performing the CPI and building up its narrative base; the other deals with the observation of this process, modeling it and obtaining the best practices. Emphasis is placed to identify the defensive routines practiced by the participants.

One of the first questions posed by the participants was: 'What is in Spore for me? Why is it worth spending my time on this and sharing something that I know?' As the project moves on, changes start to flourish. Defensive routines[13] ameliorate and a more intense, loose, and flexible interaction takes place. As in organizational learning theory (Argyris & Schön, 1974), individuals, being part of interorganizational networks, show similar defensive attitudes that inhibit cooperation and learning. Systems thinkers (Senge, 1990) have taken those 'defensive routines' and developed a set of 'learning disabilities,'[14] incidentally similar to the concept of attractors in Prigogine's theory.

When the networks—interest or practice—start to be formed, these learning disabilities dominate; then one goal of incubation is to dissolve

Table 15.2 Problematics, Narrative Methods, and Systems Archetypes

Problematics	Methods for Analysis •actually applied	Archetypes identified
Water and Conscience Weak social awareness, consciousness, and participation inhibit the sustainable management of water systems, provoking a fragmented perception far from the systemic approach that is needed.	Causality• Intertextuality Microstoria• Grand Story Deconstruction	•Tragedy of the Commons •Limits to Grow •Fixes that Fail •Shifting the Burden to the Intervenor •The Enemy is Out There •The Parable of the Boiled Frog
Sustainable Housing Climate change will affect health and well-being of low- income population. Housing is a critical element that has not been considered as an adaptation strategy.	Causality• Microstoria• Plot•	•Tragedy of the Commons •The Parable of the Boiled Frog
Dairy Goat System Regional Goat Dairy system is weak in: safety standards, collaboration, innovation, and marketing strategies. Situation erodes sustainability and competitiveness	Causality• Plot•	•Limits to Grow •The Delusion of Learning from Experience •The Myth of the Management Team
Small Metal Shops Small metal-mechanic firms lack a cooperation strategy to have a better negotiation position with large corporate clients There are many challenges that solved jointly could improve their competitiveness;, however, lack of trust is a systemic constraint.	Causality• Microstoria•	•Drift to Low Performance •Limits to Grow
Biotechnology and Solidarity In Coahuila there are many problematics needing innovation based on advance biotechnology. However, scientists are not very interested beyond their areas of interest. A lack of cooperation, isolated efforts, and innovation policies.	Causality• Plot•	Seeking the Wrong Goal

Table 15.3   Learning Disabilities in Incubating Networks

Learning Disability	Intensity
I Am My Position	5
The Enemy is Out There	4
The Illusion of Taking Charge	2
The Fixation on Events	4
The Parable of the Boiled Frog	3
The Delusion of Learning from Experience	4
The Myth of the Management Team	3

through the use of antenarrative, which is constructed from interviews and a blog; then in workshops antenarrative is deconstructed, creating a cooperative environment by using action learning initiatives (Sweeney & Meadows, 2008), and simulation games.[15] And intensive dialogue allowed the group to share their voices and improve the antenarrative. This is a learning process reinforced by dissolving disabilities. From observations and surveys from the networks participants, the most frequent and persistent learning disabilities are those shown in Table 15.3.

Disabilities for intraorganizational learning are also present in network incubation. Groups formed by individuals coming from a diversity of cultural contexts, organizational settings, and personal mind-sets show similar behaviors. Disabilities can be observed in how the stories are written, in the antenarratives, in the communication patterns, and in the behaviors shown in the learning fields (*Ba*). To dissolve these disabilities is a key initial task because networks are voluntary, short lived, and with the purpose to build a full narrative on how to cope with coming problematics.

POSTSCRIPT

Reducing the perception gap is critical for addressing critical regional issues. Networks, stories, antenarrative and narrative, systems thinking, and action learning are tools that can be fused to facilitate the incubation of networks, particularly in the problematization critical stage.

ACKNOWLEDGMENTS

Thanks are given to the networks members and coordinators for their participation. For invaluable support to the Consejo Estatal de Ciencia y

Tecnologia del Estado de Coahuila (COECYT) and Rosa Isela Martínez de los Santos, officer in charge of the Cooperative Innovation Networks.

The Incubation of Cooperative Innovation Networks is a project coordinated by CIATEJ with the support of the Fondo Mixto CONACYT-Coahuila.

NOTES

1. This expresión refers to the new approaches to innovation happening in the last two decades. From sequential models to networked and open innovation (Prahalad & Krishman, 2008).
2. According to Peter A. Gloor, a Collaborative Innovation Network (COIN) is a cyberteam of self-motivated people enabled by the Web to collaborate in achieving a common goal by sharing ideas, information, and work.
3. Where is the Life we have lost in living? / Where is the wisdom we have lost in knowledge? / Where is the knowledge we have lost in information? T. S. Eliot, *The Rock.*
4. We shall not cease from exploration, and the end of all our exploring will be to arrive where we started and know the place for the first time. T. S. Eliot, *The Four Quartets.*
5. *Punctuated equilibrium* is a theory about evolution that, instead of slow increments, argues that evolution proceeds through periods of small quasi-equilibrium steps, then interrupted in a nonlinear mode. It has been adopted as a metaphor to explain transformational process in fields such as economy, innovation, sociology, management (Gould, 2002).
6. David M. Boje describes 'antenarrative' as stories earlier to narrative. Story is an account of incidents and events, but narrative comes after and adds 'plot' and 'coherence.' Antenarrative as David M. Boje defined it is a 'bet on the future,' 'as before narrative linearity and stability sets in' and as a 'prospective sensemaking.' Boje propose three types antenarrative: sequential, cyclical and rhizomatic.
7. Closely related programs are Alianzas Estratégicas y Redes de Innovación (Strategic Alliances and Innovation Networks) by the National Council of Science and Technology (CONACYT) and Redes Temáticas de Investigación (Research Thematic Networks).
8. Russell Ackoff describes the French word *problematique* "as two or more interdependent problems" . . . "I call it mess."
9. According to Nonaka's SECI learning theory, there are four modes of knowledge conversion: Socialization (Empathizing), Externalization (Articulating), Combination (Connecting) and Internalization (Embodying). There are two types of knowledge: tacit and explicit.
10. According to Nonaka, the concept of *Ba* has some similarities with the concept of "communities of practice." Nonaka propose four types of *Ba*: Originating, Dialoguing, Systemizing, and Exercising.
11. David M. Boje describes 10 methods for narrative analysis: Deconstruction, grand narrative, microstoria, story network, intertextuality, causality, plot, and theme.
12. *Systems archetypes*: Common system structures that produce characteristic patterns of behavior. Donella H. Meadows mentions Tragedy of the Commons, Limits to Grow, Fixes that Fail, Success to the Successful, Escalation, Shifting the Burden to the Interventor, Fixes that Fail, Drift to Low Performance, Rule Beating, and Seeking the Wrong Goal.

13. Strive to be unilateral, minimize losing and maximize winning, minimize the expression of negative feelings, and be rational.
14. Peter M. Senge: I Am My Position, The Enemy Is Out There, The Illusion of Taking Charge, The Fixation on Events, The Parable of the Boiled Frog, The Delusion of Learning from Experience, and The Myth of the Management Team.
15. Through the workshops simulation games based on systems thinking and system dynamics were used. One of the most effective has been the Fish Banks Developer by Dennis L. Meadows.

REFERENCES

Ackoff, R. L. (1981). *Creating the corporate future*, New York: John Wiley & Sons.

Argyris, C., Putnam, R., & McClain Smith, D. (1985). *Action science*. San Francisco: Jossey-Bass.

Argyris, C., & Schön, D. A. (1974) *Theory in practice: Increasing professional effectiveness*. San Francisco: Jossey-Bass.

Ashby, W. R. (1964). *Introduction to cybernetics*. London: Routledge.

Baudrillard, J. (2006). *Simulacra and simulation*. Ann Arbor: University of Michigan Press.

Boje, D. M. (2001). *Narrative methods for organizational & communication research*. London: Sage.

Browning, L. D., Beyer, J. M., & Shetler, J. C. (1995). Building cooperation in a competitive industry: SEMATECH and the semiconductor industry. *Academy of Management Journal, 38*(1), 113–151.

Browning, L. D., Sætre, A. S., Stephens, K. K., & Sørnes, J.-O. (2008). *Information and communication technologies in action: Linking theory and narratives of practice*. New York: Routledge.

Bruner, J. (1990). *Acts of meaning*. Cambridge, MA: Harvard University Press.

Campos-López, E., & Urdiales-Kalinchuk, A. (2005). *El Arte de Iniciar: La innovación en el tiempo de las redes*. Report to the National Council of Science and Technology (CONACYT).

Castells, M. (2000). *The rise of the network society*. Blackwell Publishers.

Churchman, W. (1971). *The design of inquiring systems*: Basic Concepts of Systems and Organization. New York: Basic Books, Inc.

Cooke, P. (2003). *Strategies for regional innovation systems: Learning transfer and applications* (p. 1). Vienna: United Nations Industrial Development Organization.

Deleuze, G., & Guattari, F. (1987). *A thousand plateaus: Capitalism and schizophrenia*. Minneapolis: University of Minnesota Press.

De Sousa, S. B. (2009). *Una epistemología del sur: Le reinvención del conocimiento & la emancipación social*. Buenos Aires: Consejo Latinoamericano de Ciencias Sociales.

Duke, R. D., & Geurts, J. L. A. (2004). *Policy games for strategic management*. Amsterdam: Dutch University Press.

Flach, P. A., & Kakas, A. C. (Eds.). (2000). *Abduction and induction: Essays on their relation and integration*. Springer.

Gertler, M. S., & Wolfe, D. A. (Eds.). (2002). *Innovation and social learning: Institutional adaptation in an era of technological change*. New York: Palgrave Publishers.

Gloor, P. A. (2006). *Swarm creativity: Competitive advantage through collaborative innovation networks*. New York: Oxford University Press.

Goldstone, R. L., & Janssen, M. A. (2005). Computational models of collective behavior. *Trends in Cognitive Sciences, 9*(9), 424–430.

Gould, S. J. (2002). *The structure of evolutionary theory.* Cambridge, MA: Belknap Press of Harvard University Press.

Intergovernmental Panel on Climate Change (IPCC). (2007). *Climate change 2007—the physical science basis: Working Group I contribution to the Fourth Assessment Report of the IPCC.* Cambridge University Press.

James, W. (1981). *Pragmatism.* Indianapolis: Hackett Publishing Company.

McCloskey, D. N. (1990). *If you're so smart: The narrative of economic expertise.* Chicago: University of Chicago Press.

Meadows, D. H. (2008). *Thinking in systems,* White River Junction, VT: Chelsea Green Publishing Company.

Meadows, D. L. (2007). A brief and incomplete history of operational gaming in system dynamics. *System Dynamics Review, 23*(2–3), 199–203.

Morgan, M. G., Fischhoff, B., Bostrom, A., & Atman, C. J. (2002). *Risk communication: A mental models approach.* Cambridge: Cambridge University Press.

Nishida, K. (1990). *An inquiry into the good.* New Haven, CT: Yale University Press.

Nonaka, I, (1995). *The knowledge creating company.* Oxford University Press.

OECD. (2009). *Regional innovation in 15 Mexican states.* Policy brief, April.

Pastor, M. J., & Bernal, A. O. (2006). Michel Foucault: Un ejemplo de pensamiento postmoderno. *A Parte Rei, Revista de Filosofía,* 46, Julio.

Paz, O. (1994). *La casa de la presencia: Poesía e historia. obras completas.* Edición del Autor, p. 303. México, D.F.: Fondo de Cultura Económica.

Powell, W. W. (2005). Networks of innovators. In J. Fagerberg, D. C. Mowery, & R. R. Nelson (Eds.), *The Oxford handbook of innovation.* Oxford: Oxford University Press.

Prahalad, C. K., & Krishnan, M. S. (2008). *The new age of innovation.* New York: McGraw-Hill.

Prigogine, I., & Stengers, I. (1984). *Order out of chaos: Man's new dialogue with nature.* New York: Bantam Books.

Roe, E. (1994). *Narrative policy analysis.* Durham, NC, & London: Duke University Press.

Roth, G. (2000). *Car launch: The human side of managing change.* Oxford University Press.

Senge, P. M. (1990). *The fifth discipline: The art and practice of the learning organization.* New York: Doubleday.

Sterman, J. D., & Sweeney, L. B. (2007). Understanding public complacency about climate change: Adult's mental model of climate change violate conservation of matter. *Climate Change,* 3–4, 213–238.

Sweeney, L. B., & Meadows, D. L. (2008). *The systems thinking playbook: Exercises to stretch and build learning and systems thinking capabilities.* Sustainability Institute.

Wenger, E. (2002). *Cultivating communities of practice.* Boston: Harvard Business School Press.

16 Connecting Antenarrative and Narrative to Solving Organizational Problems

Nicholas Snowden

INTRODUCTION

This chapter explores the potential impact of the evolving theories relating to antenarrative, story, and narrative (as defined by Boje, 2008, p. 7) that challenge traditional ways of solving organizational problems. It considers how we can make use of the outputs of antenarrative processes, and how, in conjunction with more traditional narrative processes, the improved generation and selection of pragmatic, credible, and engaging solutions might be facilitated. The less structured, more creative contribution that antenarrative thinking can make to problem solving is investigated. Finally, the possibility of using story dispersion in conjunction with narrative coherence to improve the chances of 'guessing right' when we attempt to make decisions that impact on the future of our organizations is considered, along with implications for academics and practitioners.

In my work developing the leadership skills of prospective senior managers, the participants are regularly disturbed by the findings of numerous studies that reveal a feeble success rate for most organizational change efforts (Anonymous, 2008; Beer & Nohria, 2000; Kee & Newcomer, 2008). The irony is that many management-development courses prescribe a syllabus that privileges the same potentially flawed tools and techniques that would appear to have failed to provide solutions to the problems of the organizations in these depressing studies.

This suggests that our organizational problems are becoming increasingly complex, ill-structured, and resistant to existing problem-solving techniques (Gleick, 1987; Grossman, 2004; Handy, 1994). It would seem we need to challenge our 'rational' business processes, yet be pragmatic so as to connect and engage with organizations that, in attempting to act in their stakeholders' interests, move only cautiously toward adopting largely untried approaches to solution finding.

Barge (2004) identified a host of organizational problems which storytelling and narrative have been used to help resolve. Various studies have examined how narratives have been used to make sense of corporate life, being deployed to help sustain corporate cultures, to construct shared meaning, to socialize new members, to engage in strategic planning, and to manage organization and leadership change. However, he goes on to state:

> The problem with traditional narrative analysis is that it focuses on identifying a single story to characterize an organization and event, thus creating in Van Maanen's (1988) terminology a "realist" tale. (Barge 2004, p. 108)

Geiger and Antonacopoulou (2009, p. 411) go further, stating that organizational narratives can create inertia, and can be responsible for "... *creating self-reinforcing mechanisms and blind spots,*" thus preventing recognition of problems until, presumably, more severe symptoms begin to impact.

We should be concerned that, in the chaotic world described, the influences on our problems are increasingly numerous, ambiguous, vague, and dispersed. Therefore, decisions on how to move forward in our organizations (and indeed in our lives) are rarely clear cut, their outcomes are uncertain, and yet so much hangs on them.

So it seems there is a need to develop more sensitive and responsive processes that could help in these situations. For example, Goranson and Cardier (2007) investigated the role of narrative in determining the value of artificial intelligence; Bonabeau (2003), in reporting a study that suggests 45% of managers prefer to trust their instincts rather than facts and figures when making business decisions, made the point that various technological tools are being developed to assist in the generation of, and selection between, the vast number of options for managerial action. These technological fixes hold a great deal of promise, with rapidly growing computational power meaning that vast numbers of combinations of past events can be processed through the systems. However, they are inevitably based predominantly on retrospective, historical, linear thinking, as their decision data are based on inputted experience, that is, traditional narrative forms. Hayashi (2001) also takes the view that retrospection is dominant in our decision-making processes, reminding us that a reflexive approach is crucial to successful 'intuitive' decision taking.

So it would seem there is scope for antenarrative to contribute to the debate on how to improve our organizational responses to the problems of a complex, ever-changing business environment.

THE RATIONALE FOR LINKING ANTENARRATIVE, NARRATIVE, AND PROBLEM SOLVING

Humans naturally gravitate to narratives: Denning (2005) gives many reasons for the pervasiveness of narratives within organizations, such as the speed of communication, ease of remembering, ability to evade the corporate radar, economic value, and so on. Boje (2008, p. 4) notes how *"narratives shape our past events into experience using coherence to achieve believability,"* and sees all organizations as 'Storytelling Organizations'; Goranson and Cardier (2006, p. 2) imply that to create narrative is a *"driving imperative"* for our lives, as we seek to organize and position ourselves in relation to events and contexts.

Given the way narrative is embedded into social interaction, there is justification for its inclusion in a new problem-solving approach. But 'real-life' narratives are not as Aristotle would have them, that is, they are not ordered and complete with a beginning, middle, and end (BME); they are fragmented, interwoven, and complex (Boje, 2008). Gabriel (2000, p. 42) agrees, and defines *"proto-stories"* as fragments of a narrative before it is fully formed; he goes on to examine how a single additional 'snippet' of a story, be it fact or fiction, can then seed the crystallization of a full-blown version of a narrative, a version that could have been very different had a different snippet been added.

It could be argued that this fluid, churning, uncertain, chaotic nature of storying is at the heart of antenarrative: A new storytelling-based approach to problem solving should re-create this context and have some method of making sense of the 'soup' of antenarrative that is produced by the process.

Robertson (2001, p. 17) summarizes the work of a number of authors in describing problem solving as: *" . . . finding your way towards a goal. Sometimes the goal is easy to see and sometimes you will recognize it only when you see it."*

He sees the psychological study of problem solving as involving three key issues. First, how to mentally represent a given problem and what processes then come into play to solve it. Second, the extent to which we apply what we learn in one context to a different context. Third, understanding how we learn from experience of solving problems.

Potentially, radical Creative Problem Solving (CPS) techniques such as *'Wildest Ideas'* and *'Picture Stimulation'* (McFadzean 1998a, p. 58) could generate pre-story 'antes' (i.e., story snippets, fragments). Sense must then be made of them. Typically, we make sense through creating narrative: Czarniawska (1997, p. 78) recognizes this sensemaking and problem solving power, claiming that *"a story [narrative] consists of a plot comprising causally related episodes that culminate in a solution to a problem."* (Words in square brackets are mine, added to provide consistency with the terminology of antenarrative.)

However, antenarrative theory provides a further framework to enrich our understanding of the forces at work as we attempt to make sense of story fragments and, in doing so, helps to address the three issues that Robertson sees as central to problem solving, remembering of course that 'making sense' of a problem is not synonymous with solving it.

Brown (2005, in Brown, Denning, Groh, & Prusak) describes how Xerox field engineers successfully and naturally use story to generate solutions to ill-structured copier problems; he explains how they start from the known, that is, the data of the situation, and use this to stimulate memory of story fragments of previous incidents:

> All the time they walk around the machine, weaving this complex story [narrative], until finally they have a story [narrative] that can explain every piece of data about this complex machine. (Brown, 2005, p. 71, in Brown et al.)

This naturally occurring approach imitates the CPS approach described by Treffinger, Isaksen, and Stead-Dorval (2006) (see Figure 16.1), which shows the divergent thinking in antenarrative, followed by the convergent thinking that narrative encourages (Boje, 2008).

This model provides the building blocks for Isaksen's 'Creative Problem Solving Model' (see Figure 16.2) and informs a potential format for deploying CPS techniques to stimulate creation of antenarratives, followed by techniques to allow these antenarratives to coagulate into a range of potential future narratives.

Adapted by permission from Treffinger, Isaksen and Stead-Dorval (2006). Creative Problem Solving: An Introduction (4th edition).

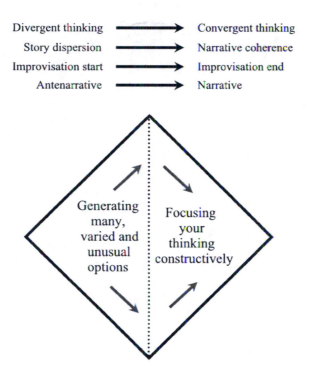

Figure 16.1   The building blocks of creative problem solving.

Adapted by permission from Isaksen (1988)

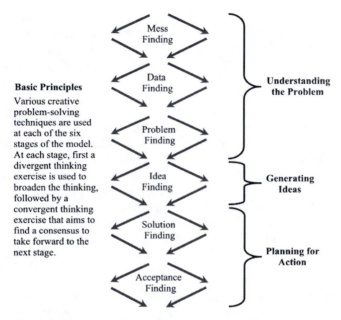

Figure 16.2   A creative problem solving model.

Shotter's work (1993, pp. 150–152) offers further insights into the linkage between narratives and managerial work: He argued that management is similar to authoring a conversation, and the managers' task is:

> . . . not one of choosing, but of generating, of generating a clear and adequate formulation of what the problem situation "is", of creating from incoherent and disorderly events a coherent structure within which both current activities and further possibilities can be given an intelligible place.

He goes on:

> . . . and of doing this, not alone, but in continual conversation with all the others who are involved. . . . To be justified in their authoring, the good manager must have a sharable linguistic formulation to already shared feelings, arising out of shared circumstances—and perhaps that this is best done through the use of metaphors rather than by reference to any already existing theories.

So a precedent exists for using antenarrative, story, and narrative in problem solving; in fact, we do it constantly.

GENERATING ANTENARRATIVE THROUGH CREATIVE PROBLEM SOLVING AND IMPROVISATION

Given that antenarrative has an important role to play in understanding and solving problems, it is vital that antenarrative content can be generated. Presumably, imagination and creative thinking are central to this. The book *Imaginization—the Art of Creative Management* (Morgan, 1993) opens with the famous quote from Albert Einstein:

> Imagination is more important than Knowledge. To raise new questions, new possibilities, to regard old problems from a new angle, requires creative imagination and marks real advance in science. (Morgan, 1993, p. i)

For this study, I have focused on the role of CPS techniques in general, and the influence of improvisation in particular. These methods have the capability to produce a rich crop of potential routes to potential solutions, although the key to resolving any specific problem is to make sense of these independent antenarrative fragments and stories through "*prospective sensemaking*" (Gioia & Mehra, 1996), as will be discussed later.

There are many ways to facilitate the generation of new ideas (for examples, see Adams, 1986; McFadzean, 1998a & b; Van Gundy, 1992).

In his 1998 essay, Weick explores the contribution that can be made to organizational analysis by adopting an improvisation mindset, taking jazz improvisation as an exemplar. He proposed a continuum of degree of improvisation (Weick, 1998, p. 544) that has resonance with the "*Creative Continuum*" (in McFadzean, 1998b, p. 4): Both continua imply that as the requirement to progress from incremental change to transformational change occurs, there is an increase in the requirement for imagination, concentration, and risk taking by those involved in the improvisation or CPS technique.

Other approaches to generating antenarrative could come from the arts (Shane, 1998). Arguably, filmmakers invent antenarrative in the form of key moments that are engineered to stick out like a sore thumb within the screenplay, and which stimulate the audience to think forwards through a range of potential futures that hinge on a seemingly innocuous event. They are invited to ask "Why was that important? What will happen now?" and importantly, to contemplate a range of possible outcomes. With the benefit of hindsight, the filmgoer can see how the story fragments fitted together (in the director's typically monological narrative).

Goranson and Cardier (2007) suggest that it is dissymmetry, incongruence, and conflict that capture the interest and imagination of an audience, presumably facilitating their mental transportation into the future possibilities antenarrated in the moment of the action.

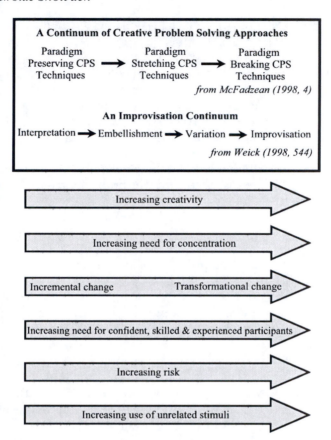

Figure 16.3   Comparing approaches to creative problem solving and improvisations.

Indeed, it could be argued that art in many forms is often concerned with condensing antenarrative into one compressed format or another (film, play, picture, book, etc.) to encourage observers to participate in contemplating the potential plots that may emerge from the fragments of story that they absorb from the performance or viewing. Paradigm-breaking CPS techniques (see Figure 16.3) use dissymmetry, incongruence, and conflict to assist in generating radically new ideas and new perspectives. That said, to make use of an antenarrative approach to problem solving, we must also be able to identify and collect the ante fragments when they occur—skills that can be learned (Boje, 2008).

So CPS techniques have a good deal in common with the practice of improvisation, and would seem appropriate for generating antenarrative. Many different narratives could be developed by storying the fragments produced. From these, it should be possible to evaluate and select some options for further development, while leaving others as potential seeds for yet more narrative routes; less suitable options need not necessarily be discarded, as "folding" of narrative (Goranson & Cardier, 2007) allows different narratives to be viable on many different levels, as explored in 'Tamara' sensemaking (Boje, 2008).

MAKING SENSE OF PROSPECTIVE SOLUTIONS

In his book *Sensemaking in Organizations* (1995, p. 13), Weick states that *"Sensemaking, however, is less about discovery than it is about invention."*

Gioia and Mehra in their review of the book argue that " ... *prospec tive sensemaking is aimed at creating meaningful opportunities in the future"* (1996, p. 1229).

So, to find solutions that work in practice, we must envision how our intervention will impact on the problem, and how that intervention will take place. Practically, the crop of envisioned routes and futures must be reduced to facilitate action.

Kotter and Schlesinger (1979, p. 113) point out that:

> No matter how good a job one does in selecting a change strategy and tactics, something unexpected will eventually occur during implementation. Only by carefully monitoring the process can one identify the unexpected in a timely fashion and react to it intelligently.

This implies that even as we make sense *forward*, we must also make sense in the *here and now*. Yet in his description of key properties of sensemaking methods, Weick (1995) argues that sensemaking is largely *retrospective* in nature, and highlights the importance of envisioning the future in a way that is sufficiently focused to provide a guiding, motivating symbol, yet is still flexible and malleable enough to morph into a format that fits the emerging environment.

Whereas there is more work to be done on how to make sense in problem solving, much has been written that can be applied to the topic: Bakhtin states that *"the fantastic in folklore is a realistic fantastic"* (1982, pp. 150–151), implying that solutions provided by storying and antenarratives must be believable to be effective. Indeed, Goranson and Cardier (2006) observed that the more resonant the narrative is with an audience's own situation, the more powerful the impact of the narrative. This has implications for any solution-selection mechanism used with antenarrative-based problem solving—any predictive narrative produced must 'fit' the organizational paradigm, that is, it must be believable if it is to provide motivation to act. This need not exclude a flexible, evolving solution that would perhaps fit with an antenarrative approach.

Ryle (1979) implies that in jazz improvisation, 'sense' is made via "paying heed" to the influences on the music being played, that is, looking partly in the present, partly in the past, and partly at an anticipated future to 'feel' how the improvisation will fit, that is, how well it will interact with the context it has come from, the context it is in now, and the context that it is involved with co-creating.

Weick (1998) noted that improvisation artists do not necessarily know where they are going with their music more than a few seconds ahead, but good improvisers are skillful in recognizing an opportunity to return to the original melody or theme. He goes on to argue that a jazz improvisation has to start from a recognizable base; for the improvisation to have perceived value, we need to know where we have improvised from, and have an understanding of the genre and context that the improvising is drawing on and is melding with, to justify where it finishes (although the end point may not even be clear until after it actually happens). The value of improvisations come from *"the pattern they make relative to a continuing set of constraints formed by melody"* (Weick, 1998), that is, good, entertaining, valuable improvisation is not simply a set of rambling, jumbled notes.

This seemingly innate desire to structure story around a theme (hence creating a narrative) is supported by Goranson and Cardier (2007), who noted that the value of any artificial intelligence (AI) system was judged by how closely the narrative it created integrated with the humans that used it—in other words, how well the AI narrative made sense in the context in which it was used.

Applying these views to the task of making sense of antenarratives generated through improvisation and CPS, it would seem that many authors argue we need a theme as a reference point for our solution-finding attempts. While this is not entirely consistent with antenarrative thinking, pragmatism suggests that generating story from antenarrative, and narrative from story, should not be a random activity. Gioia and Chittipeddi (1991, p. 442) recognize the importance and power of a CEO who provides an inspiring 'picture' of the potential future, a picture that is *"visionary and evocative"* but deliberately ambiguous: They point out that humans' understanding and subsequent actions are based on interpretation of information and events, but that uncertainty helps to create the conditions in which they will engage effectively with change programs.

A further contribution is made in the work by Gioia, Corley, and Fabbri (2002): They also suggest that we make sense of experience only through retrospection, that is, through the development of a narrative that fits the 'facts' after they have occurred. It implies we cannot make sense of experience unless traditional storytelling cognitive processes are used, be it consciously or subconsciously, and that forward sensemaking is an impossibility. Again, this creates conflict with the central theme of this chapter over the proposed use of antenarrative and story rather than narrative to help to predict the outcome of problem-solving activity.

However, they go on to posit that we deploy the 'future perfect tense' to explain and understand how to act *now* so as to create the future we desire.

We imagine ourselves in the future desired or anticipated state and, from that future position, look back at the decisions we should and could have made in the 'here and now' that would influence the achievement of the envisioned future. This is, in effect, using retrospective sensemaking as an enabler for the testing of the credibility of our vision, and of our strategies to influence its chances of becoming reality.

In organizations, if the vision is too far removed from the current perceptions of the organizational history, culture, and image, attempts to move toward that vision will not be taken seriously by stakeholders—however, we can, and do, reinterpret history within the limits that the organization will tolerate, to provide a narrative that acquiesces with the future we want to create (Gioia et al., 2002).

They make the point, however, that there is danger in this revisionist approach; first, the image of change may become more important than the substance of change, and second: *"Tampering with cherished and institutionalized stories is a recipe for failure"* (Gioia et al., 2002, p. 631).

It would seem that changing the interpretation of past events and situations and, indeed, reinterpretation of current actions as if they were in the past (i.e., in the future perfect tense) can be a credible approach to forward sensemaking. However, antenarrative theory implies the approach is potentially flawed, as imagining forward and then looking back cannot fully account for the vast array of chaotic changes and interactions both in and between the forces that will influence the realization of the imagined future. However, the approach explained by Gioia et al. (2002) does bring the prospect of a sifting, sorting, and selection mechanism that would permit a large number of storied routes toward a 'vision' (as we might expect from "Tamara sensemaking" [Boje, 2008]) to be whittled down to a manageable range of options. It could also provide a vehicle for checking the plausibility of the reinterpretations of the past.

Heath, Pearce, Shotter, and Taylor, et al. (2006) would argue that this process must involve meaningful, effectively moderated dialogue, due to its potential to *"inspire the unique and the creative."* This moderation may simply involve 'taking turns,' a technique effectively deployed by Hansen, Barry, Boje, & Hatch (2007).

Further rational-choice models could then be used to facilitate selection between narrative options produced. Polyphonically evaluating the narratives as they emerge via a moderated dialogue may engage stakeholders in the resolving of organizational problems more effectively than other (traditional) evaluation methods. This is similar to Systemic Story Creation (SSC) described by Cecchin (1987); the SSC technique is retrospective in nature as it looks back at what organizational members have said and attempts to deconstruct the narratives told, and then reconstructs a new narrative from new perspectives using the story fragments. However, it is possible to see the value of SSC in extending the same approach to look at prospective sensemaking, rather than making sense of the 'now' by reinterpreting the past.

It appears that a theoretical case can be made for linking antenarrative, narrative, and problem solving, and a credible methodology using existing creative thinking and sensemaking techniques can be developed. We must now consider how the approach might work in practice, and some academic issues that could impact on its validity.

ISSUES IN DEPLOYING THE APPROACH

True improvisation, as with true paradigm-breaking CPS techniques, requires a skill set and mind-set that are rare in organizations; to effectively use antenarrative-based improvisation and CPS techniques as a mechanism for solving problems, the organization concerned would need to be experienced and confident in the approaches being used, and trusting of all participants and facilitators involved; this is consistent with the very early findings of my own research in this area. The 'safer' the technique, the less creative it is, and the more individuals feel the need to 'interpret' rather than 'improvise' (Weick, 1998), with the result that the output is less likely to be valuable in dealing with significant change. As he puts it: *"As dependency on initial models increases, adaptation to more radical environmental change should decrease"* Weick (1998, p. 545).

This does, however, suggest that a model that can be customized to fit the degree of change that is required could be valuable.

Clearly the conditions under which antenarrative is generated, sifted, and ultimately refined into a future narrative are critical. Shotter, quoted in Barge (2004, p. 120), observed:

> [We] must both be able to 'follow' others in our talk entwined activities, and also, act and speak in ways that they can also 'follow'. To do this, to follow another person's utterances, and to grasp how they relate to their activities, we must actively adopt a responsively-expectant attitude toward them. Besides noting the reference of their utterances to the current context, their content, we must also note their point, the changes in that context toward which they 'gesture' in the future.

Weick (1998, p. 549) quotes Wruck and Jensen in saying that when a firm *"disseminates improvisation rights"* it tends to encourage *"flexible treatment of preplanned material."* This finding would support a management approach that gave internal stakeholders the skills and latitude to improvise the way they operate, provided they respect the organization's values and culture.

If management is to identify the end point for the problem-solving exercise, for example, a vision of what the solved problem would be, Gioia and Chittipeddi (1991) suggest this would need to be negotiated, socially constructed, dialectic, and deliberately ambiguous. In addition, Dertouzos

(1999, p. 31) describes creativity as requiring ". . . *a schizophrenic combination of rationality and insanity that is outside the ordinary experience.*" Barrett (1999) adds that to tap into the *"deepest levels of creativity"* in staff, managers must also satisfy their physical, emotional, mental, and spiritual needs.

These are difficult conditions to create under any circumstances, and this could be a barrier to the successful deployment of an antenarrative problem-solving approach.

IMPLICATIONS FOR PRACTITIONERS

Stories and antenarrative can be used to help organizations by broadening the range of potential influences on a problem that we consider as we try to find solutions.

However, we need to take care over the use of improvisation and CPS: Improvisation in art is valued aesthetically, often for being artificially challenging and different. In business, this is not necessarily true as economic value does not automatically stem from being different.

For the proposed approach to be successful, it should be dialogical and involve key stakeholders. Yet organizations would be understandably cautious about fully involving (for example) current key clients in the processes.

In a pilot 'scoping' exercise, an antenarrative–narrative intervention was greeted with some skepticism, but did generate a number of different perspectives: A leap of faith (and considerable development of the model) is required before the approach can be effectively trialed; it could be seen as trivializing the problem being tackled if users are not committed to the value of the tool or are mentally ill-equipped to use it.

There appears to be a case for antenarratology in a problem-solving intervention. Yet given that antenarrative and narrative arguably occupy opposite poles on a continuum of flexibility of storytelling, it is perhaps counterintuitive to bring them together in a tool that is aimed at attacking the problems brought by a chaotic world. However, it may offer a method to bridge the gap between the randomness of free-flowing antenarrative and the often inappropriate yet familiar and comfortable certainty of petrified narrative.

Practitioners must attend to the need to make sense of problems and solutions, and this is recognized as a communal activity. So what are the consequences for those who work alone, either through preference or necessity? Weick (1995), referring to Schön's work, points out that the environment in which sense is made is important, including obviously both physical and social environment.

Given that social interaction and dialogue are so important in evolving our future-orientated narratives, hegemony within and between those taking part in the discourse must be appropriate—indeed, who could judge this? Weick (1995) also says that sensemaking focuses *on* cues in the environment, and is focused *by* cues from the environment—there are so many cues, our sensitivity to these is an issue, as it is that our understanding of a situation continually shifts as new cues are noticed, rendering any intervention useless.

There are some important risks and ethical dilemmas for practitioners to consider with the approach. For example, the risk of the improvised 'narratives in progress' being taken seriously by the nonparticipants, and the ethical issues surrounding the likelihood that authors would invent and discuss 'fictional' characters that were recognizable as real individuals from the organization.

IMPLICATIONS FOR ACADEMICS

Given that this chapter draws in part on work that has used art as a model for business, we should sensibly pose questions relating to 'value.' Equating artistic value with organizational value is potentially misleading, but does raise some interesting points relating to what customers and stakeholders truly value.

It could be argued that the idea for creating a 'system' for enhancing problem solving is inconsistent with antenarrative principles—typically, a 'system' guides, confines, and restricts activities rather than encourages the new, unexpected, and unusual. There is an obvious issue in that much of the work on antenarrative could be seen to question the value of creating an organizational narrative, yet the latter is a key part of the proposed approach. Indeed, this raises the question, can we plan to deal with chaos at all, or is this an oxymoron? How to make sense in problem solving would appear to provide an interesting research site.

CONCLUSIONS

Antenarratology has a contribution to make to generating future-orientated narratives; the challenge is to harness this to improve our ability to solve ill-structured problems. Identifying a method by which we can select between narrative options is perhaps the most demanding aspect of the approach, not least as it requires a significantly improved understanding of future sensemaking.

However, it is an important step forward to recognize that any plan for the future must account for the shifting, morphing, and disruptive action of antenarrative, potentially forcing end goals, as well as strategies to achieve them, to radically change.

I would argue that it is human nature to continually envision a future state of being, and to imagine how that vision may or may not become reality as time passes. We continually revise our actions, and ultimately the envisioned goal, as events impact on its chances of realization. To abandon this would be counterproductive in problem solving, as there is much in traditional systems that works well—we emphasize obvious failures of these systems to cope with chaos, perhaps without giving due recognition to the successes; environments are not chaotic all the time, and less radical problem solving and sensemaking techniques give good value in stable situations (Czarniawska, 2004).

However, it is also human nature to seek improvement; we continue to misjudge what is going to happen in our lives, to overlook influences that come strongly into play, and to fail to account for unforeseen events. The key issue is by how much our 'guesstimates' are off target.

The approach explored here proposes an attempt to combine antenarrative and narrative in a problem-solving tool that reduces, not eliminates, errors: Antenarratology can offer more intelligence on prospective outcomes and influences, opening our eyes to possibilities and helping us to prepare for the unexpected, and deploying this through narrative gives us the ability to act. The need to account for nonlinear, spiral, rhizomic, complexity-sensitive problems is accepted, yet a vehicle that delivers solutions in a palatable, digestible, and credible form is also recognized. This makes story dispersion followed by narrative coherence a potentially attractive approach. Perhaps only as we develop our understanding of antenarrative and how to use it predicatively will we begin to learn how to interweave our organizational goals with the chaotic nature of life. It may then be possible to develop a new problem-solving intervention that allows antenarrative to continually influence how solutions evolve.

REFERENCES

Adams, J. L. (1986). *Conceptual blockbusting* (3rd ed.). Stanford, CA: Perseus Books.

Anonymous. (2008). Why is the failure rate for organisation change so high? *Management Services*, Winter, 10–18.

Bakhtin, M. M. (1982). *The dialogic imagination: Four essays by M. M. Bakhtin.* Edited by Michael Holquist. Austin: University of Texas Press.

Barge, J. K. (2004). Antenarrative and managerial practice. *Central States Speech Association, 55*(1), 106–128.

Barrett, R. (1999). Why the future belongs to values added companies. *Journal for Quality and Participation, 22*(1), 30–35.

Beer, M., & Nohria, N. (2000). The code of change. *Harvard Business Review*, May–June, 133–141.

Boje, D. M. (2008). *Storytelling organizations.* London: Sage.

Bonabeau, E. (2003). Don't trust your gut. *Harvard Business Review*, May, 116.

Brown, J. S. (2005). Narrative as a Knowledge Medium in Organizations. In J. S. Brown, S. Denning, K. Groh, & L. Prusak (Eds.), *Storytelling in organizations: Why storytelling is transforming 21st century organizations and management* (pp. 167–172). Burlington, MA: Elsevier Butterworth-Heinemann.

Cecchin, G. (1987). Hypothesizing, circularity, and neutrality revisited: An invitation to curiosity. *Family Process, Vol 26*, 405–413.

Czarniawska, B. (1997). *Narrating the organization. Dramas of institutional identity.* Chicago: University of Chicago Press.

———. (2004). *Narratives in social science research.* London: Sage.

Denning, S. (2005). Storytelling in organizations. In J. S. Brown, S. Denning, K. Groh, & L. Prusak (Eds.), *Storytelling in organizations: Why storytelling is transforming 21st century organizations and management* (pp. 167–172). Burlington, MA: Elsevier Butterworth-Heinemann.

Dertouzos, M. (1999). Four pillars of innovation. *Technology Review*, November–December, 31.

Gabriel, Y. (2000). *Storytelling in organisations—fact, fiction and fantasies.* Oxford: Oxford University Press.

Geiger, D, & Antonacopoulou, E. (2009). Narratives and organizational dynamics: Exploring blind spots and organizational inertia. *Journal of Applied Behavioral Science, 45*(3), 411.

Gioia, D., & Chittipeddi, K. (1991). Sensemaking and sensegiving in strategic change initiation. *Strategic Management Journal, 12*, 435–448.

Gioia, D., Corley, K., & Fabbri, T. (2002). Revising the past (while thinking in the future perfect tense). *Journal of Organizational Change Management, 15*(6), 622–634.

Gioia, D,, & Mehra, A. (1996). Book review of *Sensemaking in organizations. Academy of Management Review, 21*(4), 1226–1240.

Gleick, J. (1987). *Chaos: Making a new science.* New York: Penguin.

Goranson, H. T, & Cardier, B. (2007). *Scheherazade's will: Quantum narrative agency.* EchoStorm Worldwide, LLC, American Association of Artificial Intelligence, Menlo Park, California.

Grossman, L. (2004, October 11). Forward thinking. Retrieved November 22, 2009, from http://www.time.com/time/covers/1101041011/story.html

Handy, C. (1994). *The empty raincoat.* London: Random House.

Hansen, H., Barry, D., Boje, D. M., & Hatch, M. J. (2007). Truth or consequences: An improvised collective story construction. *Journal of Management Inquiry,16*(2), 112–127.

Hayashi, A. M. (2001). When to trust your gut. *Harvard Business Review*, 79, no. 2.

Heath, R. L, Pearce, W. B., Shotter, J., Taylor, J. R., et al. (2006). The processes of dialogue: Participation and legitimation. *Management Communication Quarterly*, February, 341–375.

Isaksen, S. G. (1988). Educational implications of creativity research: An updated rationale for creative learning. In K. Gronhaug & G. Kaufmann (Eds.), *Innovation: A cross disciplinary perspective* (pp. 167–203). Oslo: Norwegian University Press.

Kee, J. E., & Newcomer, K. N. (2008). Why do change efforts fail? *The Public Manager*, Fall, pp. 5–12.

Kotter, J. P., & Schlesinger, L. A. (1979). Choosing strategies for change. *Harvard Business Review*, March-April, 106–114.

McFadzean, E. S. (1998). Enhancing creative thinking within organisations. *Management Decision*, 309–315.

———. (1998a). *The creativity toolbox.* Milton Keynes, UK: TeamTalk Consulting Ltd.

———. (1998b). Enhancing creative thinking within organisations. *Management Decision*, Vol. 36, no. 5, pp. 309–315.

Morgan, G. (1993). *Imaginization—the art of creative management.* London: Sage.

Robertson, S. I. (2001). *Problem solving.* Hove, UK: Psychology Press.

Ryle, G. (1979). Improvisation. In G. Ryle (Ed.), *On thinking* (pp. 121–130). London: Blackwell.

Shane, C. (1998). The fine arts of corporate management. *Across the Board*, Vol. 36, iss. 4, pp. 7–8.

Shotter, J. (1993). *Conversational realities: Constructing life through language.* London: Sage.

Treffinger, D. J., Isaksen, S. G., & Stead-Dorval, K. B. (2006). *Creative problem solving: An introduction* (4th ed.). Waco, TX: Prufrock Press.

Van Gundy, A. B. (1992). *Idea power: Techniques and resources to unleash the creativity in your organisation.* New York: AMACOM.

Van Maanen, J. (1988). *Tales of the field: On writing ethnography.* Chicago: University of Chicago Press.

Weick, K. E. (1995). *Sensemaking in organizations.* London: Sage.

———. (1998). Introductory essay: Improvisation as a mindset for organizational analysis. Organization Science, 5, 543–555.

17 Antenarrative Writing
Tracing and Representing Living Stories

Kenneth Mølbjerg Jørgensen

INTRODUCTION

Antenarrative is defined as nonlinear, incoherent, collective, unplotted, and prenarrative speculation, a bet a proper narrative can be constituted (Boje, 2001, 2008). Antenarrative analysis is the analysis of stories " . . . that are too unconstructed and fragmented to be analyzed in traditional approaches" (Boje, 2001, p. 1). Story is before—'ante'—narrative. To emphasize story instead of narrative means to uphold the unfinished and open character of interpretations.

Antenarrative captures the attempt to free stories from linear beginning, middle, and end narratives (BME) (Boje & Durant, 2006). It implies working with open time through a process of what Morson calls *sideshadowing*, defined as a way of understanding and representing a plurality of possibilities (Morson, 1994, p. 117). Sideshadowing thus implies working with stories that are constantly living and becoming in the here and now. Further, it implies perceiving research practice as a complex storytelling practice in which the major challenge is to understand and somehow represent multiple possibilities.

The concept of living story is used to highlight the fact that the character of interpretations and experiences is always open, polyphonic, equivocal, dialogical, unfinished, and unresolved. Living story is used here to emphasize two points about the research process. The first is that living stories, and their manifestation in organizational texts, are seen as the results of complex chains of interactions, negotiations, and struggles between many different actors, groups, organizations, institutions, and so on.

What characterizes the research text is not unity but multiplicity. As such, the research process should be focused on mapping (e.g., Elden, 2001) how these different forces interactively created these texts, thus creating an *alternative memory of the text* (e.g., Foucault, 1984; Jørgensen, 2007). Foucault's power analysis genealogy is proposed as a method for deconstructing these texts. Genealogy allows the researcher to create new stories of the world by allowing her to deeply interrogate what J. Hillis Miller (2004) calls ghosts, and parasitical presences of language as noted later in the paper.

The second point is that, whereas organizational texts are the results of complex storytelling processes, the research process is itself a storytelling process in which the researcher's voice is always present. This voice is present in the choice of theoretical and methodological texts, in the co-construction of organizational texts, and in the interpretation and representation of these texts.

Sideshadowing, in other words, represents a major challenge to how research is organized and represented. An approach is advocated whereby the validity of storytelling—in terms of co-constructing, interpreting, and representation—is always called into question (e.g., Creswell & Miller, 2008, p. 126) by confronting dominant voices with inconsistencies, nuances, variations, contradictions, and other voices. Intentions are to disturb, shake, and possibly overthrow narrative BME voices with alternative interpretations of past, present, and future.

The paper is organized as follows. Firstly the characteristics of living story compared to conventional narrative are discussed. Secondly, the problem of exploring living stories is discussed and genealogical analysis is presented as a method for exploring living stories. Finally, the challenges of writing as storytelling are discussed.

LIVING STORY AND NARRATIVE

"Foreshadowing robs its present of its presentness," Morson argues, " . . . by lifting the veil on a predetermined future" (Morson, 1994, p. 117). In foreshadowing, the sequence of events is already given as the specific outcome of a linear sequence of events; or in other words as a part of a BME narrative.

Instead, Morson proposes sideshadowing as a way of working with multiple futures. Sideshadowing seeks to restore presentness to the present. We are not at the beginning, in the middle, or at the end of a story. Arendt notes, for example (1998, p. 177), that to act means taking an initiative, to begin, and to set things into motion. Actions, in other words, imply new beginnings. Simultaneously we are always also in the middle of things. But we are never at the end in the sense that only one future or one event is possible.

Sideshadowing conveys the sense that actual events might not have happened. There are always alternatives to what happened. What exists need not have existed. There were other possibilities. Sideshadowing is used to create a sense of that something else. It is called sideshadowing to denote that " . . . instead of casting a foreshadow from the future, it casts a shadow from the side, that is from the other possibilities. Along with an event, we see its alternatives; with each present, another possible present" (Morson, 1994, p. 118).

To break the linear relationship of foreshadowing and work with the multiple possibilities of sideshadowing, we need to reconsider the dominating chronotope in the organizational literature. Chronotope comes from Bakhtin's work and is used to denote the connectedness of temporal and spatial relationship in understanding and representing organizational texts (e.g., Bakhtin, 1981, pp. 84–85). Chronotopes are the centers for organizing events in the novel (e.g., Bakhtin, 1994, p. 187).

Bakhtin actually describes it as organizing the fundamental narrative events here. As noted later in the chapter, I distinguish between narrative and storytelling as two very different ways of organizing events. For the time being, I will stay a little with narrative, because it is the dominant and dominating space/time relationship in the organizational literature. The narrative chronotope is consistent with foreshadowing. Ricoeur has argued that " . . . time becomes human to the extent that it is articulated through a narrative mode, and narrative attains its full meaning when it becomes a condition of human existence" (Ricoeur, 1984, p. 52).

Ricoeur explores the relations between time and narrative through what he calls three moments of *mimesis*. What brings these moments together is the power of configuration, which is the result of the intermediary position between the two operations, which Ricoeur calls mimesis1 (pre-understanding) and mimesis3 (after-understanding), and which constitutes the two sides of mimesis2 (plot and understanding). Ricoeur thus conceptualizes the relations between time and narrative by showing the mediating role that emplotment has between the moment of practical experience, which goes before emplotment, and the moment of refiguration that follows it. We are following " . . . the destiny of a prefigured time that becomes a refigured time through the mediation of a configured time" (Ricoeur, 1984, p. 54).

Thus, according to Ricoeur, human time is historical: there is a *before* and an *after* with intimate relations between them. Bruner follows Ricoeur and notes that narrative segments time " . . . by the unfolding of crucial events—at least into beginnings, middles and ends" (Bruner ,1996, p. 136). The argument is that through narrative we place ourselves in time and create coherence, continuity, and order through an integration of past, present, and future (e.g., Clandinin & Connelly, 2000).

The suggestion is, in other words, that self is (re)created as plot on the basis of prenarrative structures and applied in words and actions. Self is intentional and transforms diverse events or incidents into a meaningful story. It draws together heterogeneous factors such as " . . . agents, goals, means, interactions, circumstances, unexpected results" (Ricoeur, 1984, p. 65; Chappell, Rhodes, Solomon, Tennant, & Yates, 2003, p. 45).

The narrative chronotope is thus the construction of plot and order. Czarniawska (1997, p. 11) argues that narrative is a very handy concept, where the attraction lies in its pragmatism rather than any ideological premises. Further, she notes that the narrative paradigm is based on narrative rationality where narrative replaces conventional models of formal rationality (Czarniawska, 1997, p. 22).

Narrative chronotope is thus consistent with foreshadowing by emphasizing linear coherence, causal relationships between past, present, and future, unity and order. For Derrida (2004), narrative implies closure of the text. He makes a sharp distinction between narrative and story. For Derrida, narrative is linked to the idea of rational progress, objective truth; it follows that it portrays time as a linear process.

Derrida, for example, speaks of narrative as a demand for truth, which implies the perception that texts have beginnings, middles and ends, borders and boundaries. Narrative is an attempt to monopolize truth. Derrida argues that the demand for narrative is to tell exactly what happened (Derrida, 2004, p. 72) and further that it demands an I capable of organizing a narrative sequence and telling the truth (2004, p. 81). By this token he argues that narrative is " . . . a violent instrument of torture" (2004, p. 78), which imprisons life in a linear sequence and in this way excludes and marginalizes other voices.

It could be argued that the perception of narrative as a "violent instrument of torture" is too simple and negative. Following Hull, it could be argued that it is embedded in Derrida's philosophical skepticism, which seems to reduce hundreds of years of philosophy to a metaphorics of unicity—that is " . . . as variations of single troubling theme" (Hull, 1994, p. 326). According to Hull, this is accomplished by " . . . reading such allegedly diverse thinkers as Plato, Aristotle, Kant and Heidegger as repeatedly suppressing the transgression of univocity language itself initiates but masks" (Hull, 1994, p. 326).

The significant point is, however, to highlight that narrative, by emphasizing unity and coherence across time and space, gives a privileged position to particular voices in foreshadowing the future and representing the past. By emphasizing plot and coherence, narrative genres are always enclosed in a solid and unshakable monological framework, according to Bakhtin (1973, p. 12). The dominating voice is the voice of the author, who draws on present-day accounts to construct a reasonable and convincing narrative of what has happened and what will happen, but in this process she excludes and marginalizes other voices.

The critique of narrative is not carried out in order to destroy narrative. Narrative genres are important for our culture and identity. The linear coherence of beginning, middle, and end is widely embedded in management and leadership concepts and models. The logic of causality embedded in a linear model is an extremely important tool for management and leadership. But the critique of narrative is necessary in order to resituate the relationship between narrative and story and create the basis for a more democratic relationship between the many different voices in language.

Jørgensen and Boje (Jørgensen & Boje, 2009) argued that narrative has been hegemonic about story in business ethics and proposes a resituated relationship between the two where they are on a more equal playing field. According to Jørgensen and Boje, this creates reflexivity in terms of continually questioning ethics which are understood as the truth and morality claims embedded in the way we speak and act. In other words, a resituated relationship between the two terms paves the way for a more innovative language that breaks with the highly conservative and stylized language of narrative.

It is in the spirit of a resituated relationship that living story is proposed. It implies a very different chronotope than narrative. In contrast to narrative, living story implies restoring presentness to understanding events in organizations. Living stories are thus 'local' (e.g., Jørgensen, 2002) in the sense that these stories are independently and contextually understood; they are independent because they have an identity of their own. This does not imply that living stories emerge in a vacuum. On the contrary, living stories are contingent on what came before and condition what comes after but they *become* in interaction between the many different forces present in any situation.

The relationship between events is not linear; any living story is just one of many possible occurrences in the moment and it moves in unpredictable directions. Stories are never finished, not necessarily whole, and remain alive in the here and now. As noted by Boje (2001, p. 18), stories float in a soup of bits and pieces of story fragments. They are never alone but live and breathe in a web of other stories and self-deconstruct with each telling.

The term 'living story' is inspired by Derrida, who argues that story has no borderlines. It is at once larger and smaller than itself. It is entangled in a play with other stories, is part of the other, makes the other part of itself, and so on, and it remains utterly different from what Derrida calls its homonym, narrative (Derrida, 2004, p. 82).

Living story implies an emphasis on pluralism. For Bakhtin, this pluralism is present in any utterance. He argues that there are two fundamentally different forces of language. The *centripetal forces of language* (1981, p. 270) are forces that according to Bakhtin seek to overcome *heteroglossia*—the condition that the word uttered in that place and that time will have a different meaning than under other conditions (Bakhtin, 1981, pp. 263, 428).

The centripetal forces seek to unite and bring order but they operate in the midst of heteroglossia (Bakhtin, 1981, pp. 271–272)—that is, in "a language" that is stratified into a multiplicity of languages: languages of social groups, professional languages, generic languages, languages of generations, and so on.

Heteroglossia is what ensures the dynamics and development of language. There are always *centrifugal forces* that ensure processes of decentralization and disunification alongside the verbal-ideological centralization and unification (Bakhtin, 1981, p. 272). According to Bakhtin, these centripetal and centrifugal forces intersect in the utterance. Order and disorder are, in other words, countervailing forces of language, which always exist side by side.

Plurality and many different voices are as such always embedded in living stories. They are affected by innumerable, conflicting wills and intentions, and this is actually why action, according to Arendt, almost never achieves its purpose. In other words, nobody is the author or producer of her own life story. Stories reveal an agent, but this agent is never the sole author or producer (Arendt, 1998, pp. 184–185).

In summation, living story operates with a much more complex notion of how temporal and spatial relationships are connected. Living story emerges interactively and spontaneously in everyday life setting. Life thus becomes more indeterminate, where serendipity, chance, and unfinalizability are prominent features of everyday life.

Next, I will describe a research process, genealogy, which works with living story chronotope and thus sideshadowing in order to explore, understand, and represent organizational texts.

EXPLORING LIVING STORIES

As noted, the concept of story implies the suspension of beginning, middles, and ends. Story is always before (ante) narrative and implies undecidability, unfinalizability, and nonlinearity. This implies that the organizational text and the interpretation of the text are always antenarrative.

Texts are where people's realities are recorded in time and space. History is manifested in the continuous construction, reconstruction, and modification of texts. Derrida argues that *"There is nothing outside of the text"* (there is no outside-text; *il n'y a pas de hors-texte*; Derrida, 1997, p. 158), where text means something much broader than the pages of a book and includes the politics and ethics of action, material conditions, and so on (Boje, 2001, p. 22).

These texts may have the character of language, words, concepts, documents, monuments, use objects, art works or musicals, sculptures, choreographies, architectures, and so on (Arendt, 1998, p. 184; Derrida, 1997, p. 9). That there is nothing outside of the text means simply that there is no essential referent or transcendental signified. Texts (representations) refer to other texts, which refer to other texts, and so on.

The living story chronotope implies that the relationship between texts is not a linear one but on the contrary that there are multiple possibilities and outcomes when texts deconstruct and reconstruct into other texts. This is one of the founding principles of genealogy. Foucault, for example, argues that genealogy " . . . entertains the claims to attention of local, discontinuous, disqualified and illegitimate knowledges . . . " (Foucault, 1980, p. 83). In contrast to totalitarian sciences, genealogy is called " . . . an insurrection of subjugated knowledges" (Foucault, 1980, p. 81).

The first kind of knowledge resurrected is historical content that was buried and disguised in formal systematization—that is, order, coherence, system, and so on (Foucault, 1980, pp. 81–82). Instead of looking at the text with this unifying order, Foucault suggests looking at texts as the results of many small forces with their own histories and identities and existing in their own specific contexts.

The second kind of resurrected knowledge is disqualified knowledge (Foucault, 1980, p. 82)—stories that were deemed illegitimate and excluded from analysis. These are the marginalized voices: the losers in the game— the stories that lost the battle and thereafter almost completely disappeared from the scene. These are the darker sides of history.

Foucault wishes to give a more appropriate pictures of the conditions and circumstances in which texts emerged, how they evolved into other texts and still other texts, and so on, through the revival of such knowledge. This process is neither logically coherent, nor is it the result of a rational process. Rather, it means that the text is the result of interactions between different people, circumstances, and chance.

Foucault uses genealogy to describe this process of writing history. Genealogy is inspired by Nietzsche's critical history (Elden, 2001, pp. 111–112; Nietzsche, 1997, p. 60) and adapted to the studies of the relations between power and knowledge (Gordon, 1980).

Foucault distinguishes between three uses of history: the *parodic, dissociative*, and *sacrificial* uses of history (Bauer, 1999, p. 62; Foucault, 1984, pp. 91–95; Jørgensen, 2007, pp. 71–74). These three uses of history are examples of sideshadowing in that each confronts dominant narratives of the present. Each use of history looks at these narratives as masks that, in privileging dominant voices, conceal or filter what occurred.

Genealogy—through these three uses of history—is designed to construct an alternative memory of what happened. Genealogy thereby shakes, disturbs, and possibly overthrows dominant and linear interpretations of the relations between events by offering more detailed complex and nuanced accounts of the circumstances in which events happened, thereby revealing new relationships between emerging texts.

The parodic use is directed against reality in opposing " . . . the theme of history as reminiscence or recognition" (Bauer, 1999, p. 61). The parodic seeks to get behind history and seeks to avoid being seduced by webs of narratives that conceal the emergence of texts in imagined truths and morality claims. These imagined truths and morality claims are embedded in narratives of heroes and scoundrels, rational explanations, romanticism, images, and so on. Genealogical analysis seeks to tear off such masks and map actual events in their correct chronological order, in the proper context, and with a proper description of who is involved and what part they play.

The dissociative use is directed against identity in opposing history as continuity or representative of tradition. The dissociative use of history thus contrasts identity as expressed in people's narratives (Chappell, Rhodes, Solomon, Tennant, & Yates 2003; Sfard & Prusak, 2005). Instead of a linear identity, the dissociative use of history demonstrates the complexities, the contradictions, and the paradoxes in relation to who people are and how they have become who they are in a way in which we are not allowed to forget the darker sides of our history.

Finally, the sacrificial use is directed against truth in opposing the traditional 'objective' historian (Bauer, 1999, p. 61). In Foucault's opinion, power is an indispensable part of this development. This implies that every statement with its inherent truth and morality claim is always questioned by relating it to those who spoke the statement, the relations they have, and the context and conditions under which the statement was produced.

The text, therefore, is anything but neutral, objective, or value free. It is saturated with passions, interests, and intentions and exists in a continuous struggle and confrontation with others' passions, interests, and intentions. Violence, blood, conflict, dominance, and slavery are embedded in the production of texts—not liberty, equality, or fraternity (see also Foucault, 1984, p. 96).

Genealogical history doesn't presume that history is logical or directed to improvement. Foucault notes that " . . . historical beginnings are lowly: not in the sense of modest or discreet steps of a dove, but derisive and ironic, capable of undoing every infatuation" (Foucault, 1984, p. 79). Power is considered as less glorious, more mundane, and it emerges from a complex set of small, petty, and ignoble power relations (Haugaard, 1997, p. 43).

Power is the consequence of local strategies, petty confrontations, and struggles. Genealogy seeks to write the history in a way in which it reveals the development of these 'storytelling games.' This includes asking questions like where they came from, how they evolved and changed, who were involved, and in what circumstances these kinds of stories were produced. Genealogy recognizes that actors have *descended* from many different places (Foucault, 1984, pp. 81–83; see also Jørgensen, 2007, pp. 66–67).

Furthermore, genealogy seeks to show how phenomena have *emerged* (Foucault, 1984) as a consequence of complex "storytelling games" involving many different actors in different positions and with different intentions. Emergence is linked with force and the purpose of an analysis of emergence is to delineate the interaction between different forces (Foucault, 1984, pp. 83–84). "No one is responsible in emergence, because it occurs in the interstice" (Foucault, 1984, p. 85). This implies that actions have to be viewed in interaction with particular material circumstances and other actors. Emergence is never finished and it does not lead in only one direction. Instead, it may evolve in multiple directions.

Genealogy explores and represents research organized according to the living story chronotope. Genealogy, in other words, searches for stories and displaces what Bauer calls " . . . universalized accounts of history and create counter narratives that reject and subvert the ideological presuppositions of enlightenment" (Bauer, 1999, p. 63).

Genealogy implies the attempt to suspend presumptions and prejudices about what happened. The argument is to approach events on their own terms—without narratively organizing them into a predetermined sequence of beginning, middle, and end. Instead, genealogy implies sideshadowing through the detailed analysis of how stories develop, evolve, and change; that is, how stories become part of other stories, make other stories part of themselves, and so on.

As noted by Jørgensen and Boje (2009), this requires a great collection of source material which might illuminate what takes place in different contexts and spaces and in different points in time. This source material should provide rich and varied accounts of the complex, nonlinear, and paradoxical course of history. This includes the collection of historical material (Foucault, 1995; e.g., Jørgensen, 2007, p. 56). This includes, for example, minutes from meetings, reports, letters, diaries, log books, accounts, budgets, and other historical material produced in specific historical circumstances.

These sources may be supplemented by other research methods such as tape recordings (e.g., Silverman & Jones, 1976), participant observation (e.g., Boje, 1991), and so on. In principle, these methods record interactions as they occur in the moment and are as such consistent with living story chronotope. Genealogical analysis may also include qualitative interviews with actors even if these interviews are retrospective and have a tendency to post-rationalize the sequences of events.

The answer to this problem is pragmatic. Interviews with actors are still relevant, because they are invaluable sources of memory. Further, it would be extremely difficult—and ethically and ontologically problematic—to interpret interactions without asking the actors who took part in these interactions.

Foucault uses archaeology in the first phase of genealogy. The simple organizing principles are chronology, actors, and space (Jørgensen, 2002; Jørgensen, 2007, p. 57). Foucault defines archaeology as a *noninterpretative discipline* and as a *systematic rewriting of history* (Foucault, 1995, pp. 138–140). The purpose of this 'noninterpretative' archaeological procedure is to open our eyes for new, complex, and varied interpretations of history and to allow history to emerge 'from below,' so to speak.

Genealogy, on the other hand, is the tactic by which archaeological descriptions are brought into play (Foucault, 1980, p. 85). It is constructed from rather detailed descriptions of what took place, who were involved, and in what circumstances events took place. Genealogy in this respect is the tactics for interpreting those events in terms of interests, intentions, and relations of power as key interpretive concepts for *mapping* out the political situation in a particular society or organization (e.g., Elden, 2001): " . . . it (power) is the name that one attributes to a complex strategical situation . . . " (Foucault, 1993, p. 334).

WRITING AS STORYTELLING

The genealogist suspends beginnings, middles, and ends and opens up space for alternative readings and interpretations of organizational texts.

Nonetheless, she creates her own account(s) from the bundles of texts that constitute the research object. Even if the genealogist stays firmly within these texts and the different voices she observes in them, her interpretations rely on her own theory of the emergence of the text; for example, narrative chronotope or living story chronotope.

In terms of writing, the researcher faces immense problems because her voice is multivoiced and has been affected—consciously and unconsciously—by many different situations, actors, circumstances, and chance during her lifetime. Her writing will always constitute violence because she will emphasize some things instead of others, she listens to some voices instead of others, she does choose to follow the inspiration from some authors instead of others, and she does choose to use certain methods instead of others, and so on.

The history of the production of the scientific text is in no way different from the history of the phenomena which constitute the research object. This text is also polyphonic, plural, dialogical, unfinished, and unresolved. It also contains parasitical and ghostly presences of other voices, other interpretations, other texts, and so on. The power or voice of the author (Foucault, 2002) is an essential and violent condition in research (see also Pritchard, Jones, & Stablein, 2004, p. 215).

In regard to the validity of storytelling, the approach has been to continually question validity. Traditionally, however, this has been described in terms of questioning the author's interpretations by clarifying from where the author speaks, thereby creating transparency in terms of how the author's text emerged.

In this framework, calling validity into question becomes a question of clarifying and describing the circumstances in which, for example, the research question was framed and evolved, how the choice of theoretical and methodological frameworks and procedures took place, who were involved in the process, how they were involved in this process, and evaluating how it affected the researcher's account (Creswell & Miller, 2008).

This section discusses questioning validity directly within the author's writing itself. This kind of reflexive writing is called for by the living story chronotope. I suggest that we can get some inspiration from Benjamin's storyteller and Morson's work on sideshadowing in learning how to write reflexively, thereby questioning validity of storytelling in another way.

To begin the discussion, Benjamin argues that the art of storytelling is coming to an end (Benjamin, 1999, p. 83). "It is as if something that seemed inalienable to us, the securest among our possessions, were taken away from us: the ability to exchange experiences" (1999, p. 83). For Benjamin, storytelling is deeply rooted in experience. This is not written experience, and it is not experience based on rational thinking. Instead, storytelling is based on experience passed on from mouth to mouth (1999, p. 86).

Storytelling is not a job for the voice alone. Rather, storytelling is derived naturally from practice in which word, soul, eye, and hand are brought into connection (1999, pp. 105–106). Storytellers are oriented towards the practical interests of life (1999, p. 86). A story contains in this respect something useful that may consist in a moral advice, some practical advice, or in a proverb or maxim. This is practical wisdom embedded in the fabric of real life. According to Benjamin, counsel " . . . woven into the fabric of real life is wisdom" (1999, p. 86).

The storyteller is as such a counterweight to the progression of modernity, which in Benjamin's view is brutal and destructive of tradition, wisdom, and thus storytelling. Instead of using stories to communicate, modernity's mode of communication is characterized by something completely different, namely, by what Benjamin denotes as information (Benjamin, 1999, p. 88). Information is consistent with Western narrative tradition in seeking to wring out the essence of stories (e.g., Jørgensen & Boje, 2009).

Benjamin notes that every morning brings us the news from the globe but we are poor in noteworthy stories (p. 89). These are being killed in the process of being explained. " . . . no event any longer comes to us without already being shot through with explanation" (Benjamin, 1999, p. 89). This represents a narrative taming, stiffening, and deadening of a living story (Jørgensen & Boje, 2010). Instead, " . . . half the art of storytelling is to keep a story free from explanation as one reproduces it" (Benjamin, 1999, p. 89).

This means that the connections between events in terms of cause–effect linkages are not spelled out. It is left for the reader to interpret things the way she understands them. As such, storytelling achieves amplitude that Western narrative lacks (Benjamin, 1999, p. 89). Storytelling is, in other words, a way of working with the multiple possibilities of sideshadowing.

It does so in a natural way by simply letting be the ambiguities, complexities, and paradoxes of language and contexts, thus allowing for continuous negotiation and modification and refinement of the possible meanings of the text and its relationship to other texts. But storytelling does not try to explain the meaning of the text according to a particular theoretical principle or some logic of rationality.

To take the case of power as an example, Foucault has argued that power in his framework is an analytics of power and not a theory of power (Foucault, 1978, p. 94). He suggests that we must understand power where power works in practice instead of being guided by a particular theoretical conception of power; for example, observable power, covert power, and the power to shape desires and beliefs (Lukes, 1974; see also Hardy & Leiba-O'Sullyvan, 1998). In contrast, Foucault offers an analytics of power, the genealogy, as a means of describing the multiple and subtle ways that power works and the multiple points at which power works.

It should be noted that storytelling by no means implies a return to non-interpretative archaeology from tactical interpretation of genealogy. The storytelling approach rather implies carefully organizing and relating texts to one another in order to give rich and varied accounts of what takes place in moments of becoming. Storytelling thus also implies selecting texts, giving priority to particular texts, relating texts to one another, guessing, imagining, using metaphors, symbolic descriptions and comparisons, and so on.

Some examples of the stylistics of storytelling are given in Morson's work on sideshadowing, particularly through an analysis of Dostoevsky's novels. "Sideshadowing endows the novel with a sense of the unexpected and the mysterious. Other possibilities threaten to erupt at any moment and cast their shadow over everything that actually happens," he notes (Morson, 1994, p. 120).

The chronicler often tells us what could have happened instead of what happened. She gives the readers 'too many facts,' including a lot of seemingly irrelevant details with no clear explanation (Morson, 1994, p. 121). The chronicler cannot decide on any single version of events even if she has talked to everyone. Morson notes that she instead reports rumors, doubts her best sources, and offers alternative possibilities: "some say," "others affirm," "it is absurd to suppose," "the papers were surely mistaken to say," "now everyone at the club believed with the utmost certainty," and so on (Morson, 1994, p. 121).

In summation, the storyteller is the modern narrator's nightmare. Instead of answers, she offers possibilities. Instead of certainty, she offers doubt. Instead of giving us truth, she offers tales, stories, rumors, jokes, and gossip. Instead of giving us one single plot, she offers several plots of which some are offered with no clear explanation or ending (e.g., Morson, 1994, pp. 126–127).

The art of storytelling is a balancing act in terms of keeping the readers on track while continually questioning this track and staying open to other possibilities. It is to tell the story while at the same time contradicting and resisting the story. Telling stories are to indicate beginnings, middles, and ends while at the same questioning these beginnings, middles, and ends, thus opening up for other interpretations of pasts, presents, and futures.

CONCLUSIONS

Antenarrative implies working with multiple pasts, presents, and futures. It requires that we work with the notion of sideshadowing in doing research. This chapter has argued for the use of living story chronotope as a less conservative and more reflexive and innovative way of working with organizational texts compared to narrative chronotope.

The chapter has argued that genealogical analysis can be seen as an example of a method that works with living story chronotope in its practice. Finally, the chapter has discussed how we can learn to write in a storytelling way where the validity of any narrative sequence of beginning, middle, and end is continually questioned from within the construction of the author's text itself.

It is important to remember that the chapter proposes a resituated relationship of narrative and story and not that the hegemony of the duality of narrative and story is turned upside down in favor of story. BME voices are important in society and organizational life. They are important in management and leadership concepts, economic models, and in terms of our culture and identity.

What the living story chronotope does is to open the field for alternative voices, thereby questioning the validity of narratives in order that our language and narratives lose their self-sufficient and narcissistic character and we become able to visualize other possibilities. The art of storytelling seeks to do just that. Thereby, the resituated relationship of narrative and story is first and foremost a reflexive relationship, where the two terms, narrative and story, benefit from each other. They are not necessarily hostile and opposed to each other.

REFERENCES

Arendt, H. (1998). *The human condition.* Chicago, London: University of Chicago Press.

Bakhtin, M. M. (1973). *Problems of Dostoevsky's poetics.* Ann Arbor, MI: Ardis.

———. (1981). *Dialogic imagination—Four essays.* Austin: University of Texas Press.

———. (1994). Aesthetic visualizing of time/space: The chronotope. In P. Morris (Ed.), *The Bakhtin reader: Selected writings of Bakhtin, Medvedev, Voloshinov* (pp. 180–187). London: Arnold.

Bauer, K. (1999). *Adornos Nietzschean narratives—Critiques of ideology, readings of Wagner.* Albany: State University of New York Press.

Benjamin, W. (1999). *Illuminations.* London: Pimlico.

Boje, D. M. (1991). The storytelling organization: A study of story performance in an office-supply firm. *Administrative Science Quarterly, 36*(1), 106–126.

———. (2001). *Narrative methods for organizational & communication research.* London, Thousand Oaks, CA, New Delhi: Sage.

———. (2008). *Storytelling organization.* London: Sage.

Boje, D. M., & Durant, R. A. (2006). Free stories! *Tamara Journal 5*(3), 19–37.

Chappell, C., Rhodes, C., Solomon, N., Tennant, M., & Yates, L. (2003). *Reconstructing the lifelong learner—Pedagogy and identity in individual, organizational and social change.* London, New York: RoutledgeFalmer.

Creswell, J. W. & Miller, D. L. (2000). Determining validity in qualitative inquiry. *Theory into Practice, 39*(3), 124–130.

Czarniawska, B. (1997). *Narrating the organization—Dramas of institutional identity.* Chicago: University of Chicago Press.

Derrida, J. (1997). *Of grammatology.* Baltimore: Johns Hopkins University Press.

———. (2004). Living on. In H. Bloom, P. D. Man, J. Derrida, G. Hartman, & J. H. Miller (Eds.), *Deconstruction and criticism* (pp. 62–142). London, New York: Continuum.

Elden, S. (2001). *Mapping the present—Heidegger, Foucault and the project of spatial history.* London: Continuum.

Foucault, M. (1978). *Seksualitetens Historie—Viljen til Viden* [The history of sexuality—Volume 1]. København: Rhodos.

Foucault, M. (1979). *Discipline and punish—The birth of the prison*. Harmondsworth, UK: Penguin.

———. (1980). Two lectures. In C. Gordon (Ed.), *Power/knowledge: Selected interviews and other writings by Michel Foucault* (pp. 78–108). New York: Pantheon Books.

———. (1984). Nietzsche, genealogy, history. In P. Rabinow (Ed.), *The Foucault reader* (pp. 76–100). New York: Pantheon.

———. (1993). Excerpts from *The history of sexuality: Volume 1: An introduction*. In J. Natoli & L. Hutcheon (Eds.), *A postmodern reader* (pp. 333–341). New York: State University of New York Press.

———. (1995). *The archaeology of knowledge*. London: Routledge.

———. (2002). What is an author? In J. Faubion (Ed.), *Aesthetics, method, and epistemology* (pp. 205-222). London; Penguin Books.

Gordon, C. (Ed.). (1980). *Power/knowledge: Selected interviews and other writings by Michel Foucault*. New York: Pantheon Books.

Hardy, C., & Leiba-O'Sullyvan, S. (1998). The power behind empowerment. *Human Relations, 51*(4), 451–483.

Haugaard, M. (1997). *The constitution of power—A theoretical analysis of power, knowledge and structure*. Manchester, UK: Manchester University Press.

Hull, R. (1994). Styling Nietzsche: A note on the genealogy of Derridean deconstruction. *Man and World, 27*, 325–333.

Jørgensen, K. M. (2002). The Meaning of local knowledges. *Scandinavian Journal of Management, 18*(1), 29–46.

———. (2007). *Power without glory—A genealogy of a management decision*. Copenhagen: Copenhagen Business School Press.

Jørgensen, K. M., & Boje, D. M. (2009). Genealogies of becoming—Antenarrative inquiry in organizations. *Tamara Journal for Critical Organization Inquiry, 8*(1), 32–47.

———. (2010). Resituating narrative and story in business ethics. *Business Ethics: A European Review, 18*(3).

Lukes, S. (1974). *Power—A radical view*. Basingstoke, UK: Macmillan.

Morson, G. S. (1994). *Narrative and freedom—The shadows of time*. New Haven, CT, and London: Yale University Press.

Nietzsche, F. (1994). On the genealogy of morality. In K. Ansell-Pearson (Ed.), *Cambridge texts in the history of political thought*. Cambridge: Cambridge University Press.

———. (1997). Untimely meditations. In D. Breazale (Ed.), *Cambridge texts in the history of philosophy*. Cambridge: Cambridge University Press.

Pritchard, C., Jones, D., & Stablein, R. (2004). Doing research in organizational discourse—The importance of researcher context. In D. Grant, C. Hardy, C. Oswick, & L. Putnam (Eds.), *The Sage handbook of organizational discourse* (pp. 213–236). London, Thousand Oaks, CA, New Delhi: Sage.

Ricouer, P. (1984). *Time and narrative* (Vol. 1). Chicago and London: University of Chicago Press.

Sfard, A., & Prusak, A. (2005). Telling identities—In search of an analytic tool for investigating learning as culturally shaped activity. *Educational Researcher, 34*(4), 14–22.

Silverman, D., & Jones, J. (1976). *Organizational work—The language of grading the grading of language*. London: Collier Macmillan.

18 Tales of Merger Survivors

Daniel Dauber and Gerhard Fink

1 INTRODUCTION

So far, little research has been undertaken to study motives and strategies of individuals who survived several mergers or acquisitions within the 'same' firm. This chapter analyzes tales of merger survivors in the largest Austrian bank, which within the last 15 years has gone through several mergers and acquisitions. The main research questions focus on:

1. *What are the main concerns of merger survivors?*
2. *What are the main strategies to survive M&As?*
3. *What are the motives behind these strategies, in order to stay with the organization?*

The chapter is structured as follows. First, we outline how antenarratives could be understood in the context of M&As and how they contribute to answer our research questions. Second, we provide a short summary of the history of AUT Bank, followed by a brief overview of the methods applied and our sample. Next, we use a selection of antenarratives to introduce our interview partners. Finally, we provide answers to our research questions and a summary.

2 ANTENARRATIVES IN MERGERS AND ACQUISITIONS

Each organization has its own history filled with narratives and stories that are told, lived, and carried by its members. Change processes, such as M&As, cause instabilities and create uncertainty about the present and the future of organizations. Existing living stories and narratives might become obsolete due to processes of organizational assimilation or integration, that is, blending of different narratives. This provides space for new collective stories that emerge from mergers or acquisitions.

As can be seen from Figure 18.1, individuals involved in such M&A processes are confronted with critical incidents (Parsons & Shils, 1962). This

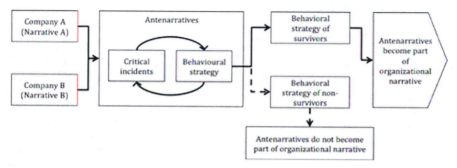

Figure 18.1   Blending of narratives in M&As.

is due to differences in organizational structure and culture, rules of behavior, leadership style, past and living stories, and so on. The larger the differences, the more 'critical' assimilation or integration processes may become, if the acquirer pursues an assimilation strategy where the organizational narrative of the acquired company becomes irrelevant. Acquired staff has to adjust. In reaction to critical incidents, individuals can set actions and implement 'new' behavioral strategies. Individuals tell antenarratives about the interplay of critical incidents and responsive behavior. Uncertainty about future development and tension between M&A partners result in culture shocks and critical remarks about frustrating experiences, and not yet in stories with a beginning, a middle, and an end.

It seems legitimate to assume that antenarratives of survivors differ from antenarratives of nonsurvivors. Influenced by their personal characteristics and motives, individuals become merger survivors or leave the organization as a reaction to critical incidents. Tales of merger survivors unfold antenarratives including critical remarks about incidents and provide insights into behavioral strategies pursued in turbulent times.

3   THE HISTORY OF AN AUSTRIAN BANK—A SERIES OF MERGERS AND ACQUISITIONS

AUT Bank, as it is known today, has run through a series of mergers and acquisitions within the last 19 years (see Figure 18.2).

In 1991, SPA Bank and LD Bank, both Austrian banks, decided to merge in order to found Austria's largest bank, leaving CDA Bank, which had been the market leader for years, in second place. Only six years later, AUT Bank bought all state-owned shares of CDA Bank, thus being transformed into AUT-CDA BANK, which had already developed a strong CEE-segment. Another three years later, the German GER GROUP took over Austria's largest domestic bank. AUT-CDA BANK got responsibility for the Austrian market as well as the CEE countries, where they had

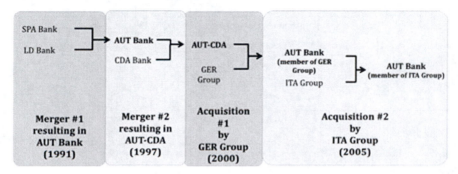

Figure 18.2   M&A history of AUT Bank.

developed reasonable competencies. This was also the first time that AUT-CDA BANK was owned by a foreign bank. More recently, the Italian ITA Group acquired GER GROUP. As a consequence, AUT Bank also turned into a member of the Italian bank group. The integration process was reinforced January 2009 and all of our interview partners are currently diving through a new wave of changes.

4   SAMPLE AND METHOD

We applied a qualitative research approach and opted for narrative interviews as our primary source for data collection. In order to be able to answer our research questions it was necessary to select representative storytellers that have run through several mergers and/or acquisitions.

As can be seen from Table 18.1, all interviewees entered today's AUT Bank before 1997 and still work there, thus were able to provide rich antenarratives and narratives on how to survive a series of M&As.

Following the principle of theoretical sampling, we interviewed men and women and decided to pick interview partners who started in different organizations before these mergers and acquisitions took place.

All interviews were recorded and transcribed. We used NVivo 8 in order to code the texts and to find answers to our research questions. All interviews were conducted in German, which is the mother tongue of the interviewees as wells as of the authors.

5   DIVERSE ANTENARRATIVES OF M&A SURVIVORS

In order to understand why certain individual strategies had been developed, it seems important to know a few details of the personal history of our interviewed merger survivors. By assuring the anonymity of our

Table 18.1   Sample for Narrative Interviews

Interviewee	Gender	Age	Started in the following organization	Works there since
'Financial Stability Seeker'	Male	49	LD Bank	1990
'Independent Thinker'	Male	55	SPA Bank	1989
'Job Hopper'	Female	45	SPA BankLD Bank	1989
'Recognized Expert'	Male	49	LD Bank	1989
Disappointed Survivor'	Male	58	LD Bank	1990
'Diversity Seeker'	Female	39	CDA Bank	1996
'Tactical Optimist'	Male	47	BA-IT (an affiliated IT company	2000

interviewees, we decided to give them nicknames that are related to their personal history and characteristic antenarratives of critical incidents that they experienced. This collection of antenarratives reflects a diversity of views among the interviewed persons.

The 'Financial Stability Seeker'

The most important issue mentioned by the 'Financial Stability Seeker' was the 'Golden Cage.' He stressed the importance of having a well-paid job. This was one of his strongest motives to stay with the organization. He got engaged in several organizational change projects, which helped him to survive. He teamed up with a power holder. Maintaining and developing a strong informal network was one of his strengths to survive such turbulent times. To him, the essential criterion was the willingness to shape the change processes together with others. These aspects are reflected in the following quote:

> *'FINANCIAL STABILITY SEEKER': In the company there is always a formal organization and a real one. The real one works through networks. This is also tacit information. If somebody is no longer in the network then he starts at zero hour when he comes back and suddenly disturbs [the network]. . . . my strength in the whole system is surely the network. . . . This is, in the meantime, after being in the organization for quite a long time, an asset, which I, if I change [taking a job in an other organization], would have to build up from scratch. Because*

there [another organization] I am Mr. Nobody. Here positive and negative networks exist, there are also some with which you do not like to be with, yes, this is beyond doubt, in the course of time, but it is an absolute asset, to know certain things. . . . This nearly gets a system-preserving function. . . . but also to extend with new networks, with new people. In order to connect them and generate value-added. There are some people in Germany or in Italy with which I keep in contact, mostly through e-mail or video conferences, where you do not know where in the organization they are located in truth: above, under or next [to me in the hierarchy].

The 'Independent Thinker'

For the 'Independent Thinker' it was important to do new and innovative things, and not being in charge of routine tasks. Whereas he referred to the importance of being close to the power holders, he never wanted to become a power holder by himself. He made critical remarks about the organizational policies, which induced him to say that he cannot be absolutely loyal to most power holders. Thus, he always tried to independently achieve goals important for the organization. After the takeover by the ITA Group, he decided to work in the headquarters in Italy, where he was surprised and shocked about the way Italian managers treated their subordinates. Although he suffered from a severe culture shock, he indicated that the work experience abroad helped him to develop a new network that now facilitates meeting his tasks for the bank:

'INDEPENDENT THINKER': . . . there were other things, one [person], I think, enrolled for holidays, because he wanted to go on holidays with his son who was going to have a special birthday. When [the son] had his birthday, his father's boss did not permit [the father] to take a few days off, only one day before [the vacations should have started he was informed about that]. He cried, a man, because his wife was of course yelling at him at home. And then he said ok. He continued and he was not allowed to go on holidays. So he asked [his boss] whether he could go home at least at 4pm and he [the boss] said: 'Yes'. And the next time he said: 'No. You need to stay until 9pm. There is something that needs to be done', which actually nobody needed. And he was down, because at home he had troubles with his wife and his kid [because of that] and his boss could not care less.

The following tale refers to another suffered 'culture shock':

'INDEPENDENT THINKER': One Monday I come to the office and people tell me: 'Look into the phone book'. I say: 'Pardon, what is this rubbish all about? I know my name, I know my phone number.'

'Look into the phone book.', and they [his colleagues] already grinned and played on my nerves and I say: 'Why?', and look into the phone book and saw that a new [organizational] structure was published in the phone book. There was no further information, neither given to me nor to the Italian colleagues. They [Italian managers] have put the new structure [on the intranet] and you could see in the phone book who your new boss was and to whom you report. . . . So, if you do this in Austria you would have a huge problem.

The 'Job Hopper'

The 'Job Hopper' took over several positions throughout the series of M&As of the Austrian Bank. She started in one of the branches of SPA Bank and later on attended the trainee program and worked in different divisions with different tasks. Due to her career within AUT Bank, the key for her to survive was coping with loss of power and quickly adjusting to new tasks. As far as her motives are concerned, she stressed that financial stability was an important factor. Due to the fact that she was almost professionally engaged in sports, she appreciated the job security offered by AUT Bank. To develop networks, she started to learn Italian:

'JOB HOPPER': I also can speak Italian since the time I work for the ITA Group. It was clear for me that I learn this language which is, so to speak the group language. This was not really necessary, but for me a big advantage, because [now] I can read and work with documents before they are provided in English. And of course, this is a step towards the colleagues that we have in Italy if I can talk in their language and can exchange e-mails in their language.

The 'Recognized Expert'

Building up competence in your field plays an important role, in order to survive M&As. This is especially true for the 'Recognized Expert.' Apart from being competent, he highlights that a certain fun factor is also necessary to be productive. He mentioned that his division was always a driver of change and responsible for the implementation of integration strategies. The 'Recognized Expert' is proud that his division always scores high in the annual employee survey that is taking place in AUT Bank since it was taken over by ITA Group. Due to their great results, they are frequently consulted by other divisions to give advice. This recognition and appreciation were a strong motivator for him to stay with the organization. Finally, he stresses the importance to cope with changes quickly and less emotionally:

'RECOGNIZED EXPERT': This, I call it 'moaning until you get ill' on a very high level, which happens from time to time, yes, this is

something, someone can get ill from, for himself getting ill, namely psychologically ill. But it [i.e., moaning] does not help. Yes. This means, the faster you develop your own strategy to think about the future and to say: 'Ok, there is change.' [the better it would be]. From my own experience I need to say that there are always new chances. It is not like all changes and all mergers [change your job] . . . , in most cases the job stays the same.

The 'Disappointed Survivor'

The 'Disappointed Survivor' started in another bank and changed to the LD Bank to boost his career. From today's point of view he looks back to this decision with mixed feelings. On the one hand he believes that his current position is lower than the one he would have right now in his former bank. On the other hand, he seems satisfied with what he could achieve, although still suffering a bit. He told us that the series of M&As has not changed a lot in his division, but in several other ones, for example, the sales department. The 'disappointed survivor' explained that there exists a clear distance to the top management which has less of an impact on his work. It is more the micro-cosmos, that is his division, which counts. Finally, he stressed that he is very proud of the old AUT Bank. For him it was an honor to work for the largest domestic bank. Today, he is disappointed that AUT Bank is owned by a foreign bank and is convinced that the best would be to leave AUT Bank as an independent Austrian bank. The following quote underlines the sorrow for an old narrative that got replaced:

'DISAPPOINTED SURVIVOR': . . . *from the size and the scope of the bank, the diversification, which had the old AUT Bank in the late 90s, covered a very, nearly everything and consisted of a certain foreign network. And in particular the next merger, I think in 2000 with CDA Bank, this would have been a wonderful, very great, huge, professional, national bank, just until the foreign headquarters came.*

The 'Diversity Seeker'

Like the 'Job Hopper,' the 'Diversity Seeker' worked in several parts of the organization and actively searched for new opportunities. She stressed that she likes her job, because it offers divers tasks and at the same time provides job security. Furthermore, she explained that her tasks have not changed dramatically throughout these M&As as her work is strongly focusing on national issues. However, she added that other divisions were more strongly affected by changes. Finally she indicated that people in top and middle management positions were more strongly affected by takeovers:

'DIVERSITY SEEKER': To simply survive was not a problem. Nobody was fired or advised to leave [the bank]. Of course, those persons who were in higher positions, because due to the merger the number of leader positions got cut in half ... [rather left the organization]. And of course these persons that already were in position [before the merger], did leave the house if they did not get the position [i.e., the same or better after one the merger]. ...

The 'Tactical Optimist'

The 'Tactical Optimist' provided us with several recommendations for surviving M&As, from a personal perspective as well as the perspective of a manager. For him it was important to be patient and not to be the first one to move into a new position as the first most likely faces severe difficulties. He stressed that it is necessary not to trust in rumors. Dazzlers walk around, tell how great they are, and feign particular knowledge of unofficial 'new processes.' Beware of false anticipatory obedience! For him it was important not to leave an old network and to be ready to extend it. The 'Tactical Optimist' is critical and misses an easily understandable strategy in the takeovers, at least by the ITA Group. Nevertheless, he is optimistic and tries to make the best out of it. His antenarrative about the change process was:

'TACTICAL OPTIMIST': There was no single [managed] change process. There was nothing of that kind. Nothing! This means, everyone who said that there needs to be a change project, was made irrelevant. The Italians distributed USB-sticks and a notepad as a present to symbolize the new structure. This was it. No events for employees. ... There was a speech of the CEOs as a web-podcast. This was it!

6 SIMILAR NARRATIVES OF M&A SURVIVORS THAT MIGHT BECOME A STORY

Within our sample of interviews we identified three major strategies, which were applied by most of our interviewees to survive the series of mergers and acquisitions.

6.1 'Better Shaping Change Than Being Changed'

Generally speaking, individuals in a merger can either try to shape the change they are running through, that is, become part of the process, or simply observe changes in their environment. Although patience was mentioned as a typical characteristic of merger survivors, this does not necessarily imply passivity.

Two different ways of shaping change have been reported: (1) Taking the position as a project leader and work outside the official hierarchy. (2) Participating in the operationalization of change strategies developed by the top management. The following quote describes the strategy of shaping change through projects, which have an impact on the organization:

> 'INDEPENDENT THINKER': *I have told that I always was the leader of integration. . . . This means, I always had, there was no option [to leave the organization], because I always formed part of what was actually always newly rebuilt. . . . and most often I created a job for myself or built up something. . . . I was always the team leader in teams, where you had, I do not know what I should do, except a keyword, so [he was told] Mr. 'INDEPENDENT THINKER' structure this. And then you start building structures and after half, three quarters of a year you hand it over, because then there starts the next one [the next project]. . . . We do not know anything but a vague idea. Search for people, structure this, [and get told] 'in two weeks I like to have a proposition'. After that we have about a year to do that. There was always something to be done. This is actually my strength, and fits my desire to get forward. I was always interested in that. . . . this way you always get in contact with things where others avoided to put their hands on, where they were afraid of burning their fingers.*

Another example describes how change was shaped within the organization:

> 'JOB HOPPER': *In the area of communication, there were different tasks throughout the years. Which have changed and have become bigger and this was a central issue if you look at the merger history. Because change management has, of course, always something to do with information and therefore you have never run out of work. . . . but you need to be prepared to take part in this change. . . . There were not many opportunities for participation. With respect to content: yes; with respect to structure: no. . . . In communication, due to the entry of ITA Group, there was a new approach, for the employees a totally new approach, called divisionalization . . . and the identity within the organization shall be strengthened within the divisions. I was responsible for the communication in the whole bank, the internal one. This means, you have to think about, what do the new divisions need from me on this new path. . . . With that I could test several communication channels. . . . Such opportunities and ways can be explored, if the framework changes and this is actually also an interesting job.*

According to these narratives it can be said that shaping change is limited to a certain extent and requires the willingness to take responsibility. No

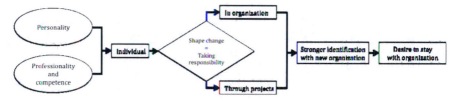

Figure 18.3 Building identification with new organization through active participation in change.

matter where change can be shaped by individuals, it helps them to find meaning in what they are doing and develop affiliation towards the new emerging structures. This seems to severely increase the willingness and the desire to stay with the merged or acquired organization as the new organization is partly reflecting the work of the merger survivors. These aspects are summarized in Figure 18.3.

6.2 Boundary Spanning

Boundary spanning refers to the development of informal networks across divisions within a company or organizations. Most interviewees stressed the importance of being part of a network. However, in times of mergers and acquisitions existing networks get either destroyed or less effective. The acquirer might be interested in eliminating them in order to reduce the strength of old power structures and pave the way for new ones. According to our interview partners, extending one's own network by getting in touch with members of the other organization is important. Individuals who are rather open to new experiences and more easily adjust to new situations are more likely to set boundary-spanning activities, thus have an increased chance of surviving in times of M&As.

> 'FINANCIAL STABILITY SEEKER': In the company there is always a formal organization and a real one. The real one works through networks. This is also tacit information. If somebody is no longer in the network then he starts at zero hour when he comes back and suddenly disturbs [the network]. . . . my strength in the whole system is surely the network. . . . This is, in the meantime, after being in the organization for quite a long time, an asset, which I, if I change [taking a job in another organization], would have to built up from scratch. Because there [another organization] I am Mr. Nobody. Here positive and negative networks exist, there are also some with which you do not like to be with, yes, this is beyond doubt, in the course of time, but it is an absolute asset, to know certain things. . . . This nearly gets a system-preserving function. . . . but also to extend with new networks, with

new people. In order to connect them and generate value-added. There are some people in Munich or in Milano with which I keep in contact, mostly through e-mail or video conferences, where you do not know where in the organization they are located in truth: above, under or next [to me in the hierarchy].

'TACTICAL OPTIMIST': During the merger, the network is of great importance. Namely the network in which you trusted before. You would be well advised during a merger, in times of a merger also to trust in it. Trust in networks stays constant.

'DISAPPOINTED SURVIVOR': . . . but if you know people at the top, from the Italian top-crew, then there is no difference [in communication paths]. You just have to dock with them. . . . So you actually have to build up new contacts with new decision makers, those who have power. . . . But you have to dock [with such people] and you need to know who actually is now in the center. This is not always visible from some charts, it is not that easy, but you experience it quite rapidly when you have been to meetings. There you have to pay attention.

'INDEPENDENT THINKER': [referring to a longer stay at the headquarter in Italy] . . . this I observe now, I made a lot of contacts, which actually help me right now.

'DISAPPOINTED SURVIVOR': So, you need to have the chance to get out of your division boundaries into the meetings, where also others are in, because otherwise you always stew in your own juice. This is it and it is very, very important.

6.3   'In the Shadow of Power' Strategy

The last strategy refers to individuals who team up with power holders or at least stay close to them, but at the same time are not considered being such power holders themselves:

'FINANCIAL STABILITY SEEKER': Implicitly, that I have not really planed as a strategy, was presumably the search or the development together with an important person in the organization was definitely also a strategy. Like with R. [a person] who at that time was on the up and up, also compared to the colleagues from SPA Bank, while 'colleague' is definitely an ambivalent term. For several years, I am doing the same right now as well again by not leaving the, by now, head of the resort . . . because I think, he still has upward potential and is, quasi, a support, a power basis. In terms of tandems.

'INDEPENDENT THINKER': This means, on the one hand, I had this desire to do new things, which always, logically, are new innovative things or secret ones or what ever takes place in the board of directors. This means, the desire to get forward always implicated

that I was very close to the chairman of the board. On the other hand, I dissociated myself from what happened there, like who will be put where, what kind of things will be turned to where or actually nearly immoral. . . . This means, I have never been absolutely close to him.

Instead or besides using a strong network, for example, boundary spanning, individuals benefit from power holders. Throughout the interviews it became clear that the desire to become a power holder themselves was not given. Very often middle and top management gets replaced in M&As. This was also true for AUT Bank. The threat of losing the job or being substituted was circumvented by this strategy and made individuals survive.

7 MOTIVES TO SURVIVE MERGERS AND ACQUISITIONS

The question that will be answered in this section is: 'Why should individuals be interested in continuing their work in a merged or acquired organization?' Based on our interviews, two aspects seemed to be crucial for almost all interviewees: job security and an interesting job.

7.1 Golden Cage

According to Schneider (2001), institutions serve the goal to reduce income insecurities, thus providing financial stability. This approach towards organizations is strongly reflected in our interviews. Nearly all interviewees highlighted the importance of tenure positions as one of the key motives to stay with the company. This policy existed until the merger of AUT Bank and CDA Bank for members who were over 35 years old and was called 'Definitivum.' This allowed individuals to stay with the organization until they retire, thus provided 100% job security guaranteed by law. The following quotes underline the importance of such a 'golden cage':

> 'FINANCIAL STABILITY SEEKER': *I think the financial strength is an essential aspect, the aspect of security which exists theoretically and legally.*
> 'INDEPENDENT THINKER': *There has to be mentioned one thing, you are sitting in AUT Bank, regarding your income you are like in a golden cage.*

The importance of having security was often related to age, indicating that elder people appreciate such security more than younger employees, due to the fact that older individuals have fewer chances on the job market than younger ones. This also seems to have a strong impact on whether people accept change more easily and are more willing to adopt new values, rules, and norms:

'FINANCIAL STABILITY SEEKER': But with increasing age, the question of changing the job now, to give up things which are financially profitable would be a difficult change. . . . So it is definitely a question of age.

'JOB HOPPER': But, as I said, I am 45, changing the job right now would mean that I maybe really earn more money within the next 2 or 3 years compared to here. But the way the industry now develops and in these times, this could change within 3 years. Then I do not have a job anymore and honestly speaking, a bird in the hand is worth two in the bush. So, for me, social security was also a factor.

7.2   Personal Interests: Fun-Factor and Diversity in Tasks

Besides financial issues, many interviewees stressed the importance of having an interesting job that inheres a certain 'fun factor' and provides opportunities for change in their job after mergers or acquisitions, that is, doing different tasks in one organization. These two aspects were also motives for staying with the organization as the following quotes illustrate:

'FINANCIAL STABILITY SEEKER': And it is somehow thrilling to experience that [i.e., organizational change] and survive within it.

'RECOGNIZED EXPERT': One of the most important, essential things is the fun-factor.

'JOB HOPPER': Such opportunities and ways [in testing and developing communication channels for the organization] can be explored, if the framework changes and this is actually also an interesting job.

To see and benefit from new opportunities and chances and the willingness to work in new environments was reflected by most of the interviewees. Some referred to cultural diversity as one factor of interest; others saw the chance to totally change the division within an organization that required different skills as an essential motive to stay with the company. Adaptability, flexibility, and openness to experience (as mentioned earlier) were truly facilitators:

'FINANCIAL STABILITY SEEKER': I have, like in a huge organization, absolutely new chances, new opportunities which are maybe even better than those compared to the primary organization [i.e., the organization before the merger or acquisition].

'JOB HOPPER': So, my working environment, as you find it in such a huge organization, if you take your chances, was not always the same.

'JOB HOPPER': Due to this career ['JOB HOPPER' worked in different divisions throughout the series of mergers and acquisitions], it

can be said, it is always possible, also in a merged organization, to find new additional interesting tasks.

'DIVERSITY SEEKER': . . . and the positive aspect of AUT Bank, also the reason why I am still here, I am in this organization since 13 years or so, is that you can always work in so many different divisions and areas, and having, so to speak, continuity with respect to employment law, that you can do something new every 3, 4, 5 years, if you want.

It has to be mentioned that these interests may not come as a surprise considering the personality of typical merger survivors. Individuals who are open to new experiences, who easily adapt and adjust to new situations will more likely search for new opportunities and chances in a newly formed organization and appreciate change to a certain extent.

8   CONCLUSION AND SUMMARY

This paper investigates in strategies, characteristics, and motives of individuals to survive turbulent times of change. Figure 18.4 graphically summarizes our main findings.

We present three different strategies that emerged out of the interviews. 'Shape the change' refers to the strategy where individuals develop an identity with the new organization due to the fact that they are given the chance

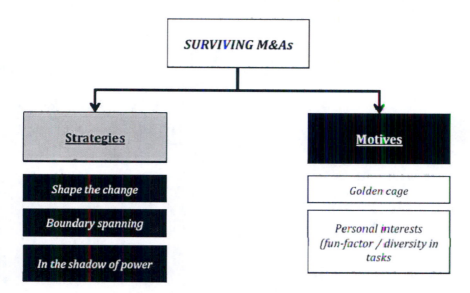

Figure 18.4   Summary of factors that have an impact on the survivability of individuals during M&As in critical incidents.

to participate in the change process, that is, form it in a way that seems appropriate for them. 'Boundary spanning' relates to the establishment of networks across divisions or organizations, what is of special importance in M&As. Interviewees stressed that this strategy facilitates communication within new structures and provides orientation and guidance. The third strategy, 'in the shadow of power,' describes individuals who team up with power holders, while not being power holders themselves. Individuals who follow this strategy benefit from their 'closeness' to the decision makers, but are not necessarily affected by restructuring efforts of an acquirer who may replace top and middle management.

Finally, two main reasons were found which explained why individuals desire to stay with an organization. The 'golden cage': organizations help to reduce income uncertainty. In the case of AUT Bank, tenure position was regulated legally, as long as it belonged to the saving banks sector. Having a lifetime job made it easier to cope with the fact that a relatively high-ranking employee may not advance further in their career, in particular, when a certain fun factor was linked to the current job, embracing a diversity of tasks and duties.

REFERENCES

Parsons, T., & Shils, E. (1962). Values, motives and system of action. In *Toward a general theory of action, Theoretical foundations for the social sciences* ed. Parsons, T. and Shils E., 47–234. Harvard University Press, Cambridge, Mass.

Schneider, D. (1995). *Allgemeine Betriebswirtschaftslehre. Band 1: Grundlagen*, 2. Auflage, Oldenburg Verlag, München, Wien.

Part IV
National and Globalizing Antenarratives

Introduction to Part IV
National and Globalizing Antenarratives

In Chapter 19, **Jeff Leinaweaver** tells us about the antenarrative dynamics that influence the identity process of becoming a global human. In this, he leverages the lens of the internationally adopted person to speak to the storytelling dynamics that influence global identity making, in general. Questions like, "Who are you?," "Where are you from?" pose problems for global humans such as the internationally adopted person. These are people constructed in-between multiple narrative identities and locations of self. Their storytelling crosses boundaries of culture, race, kinship, and otherness. They are caught in what Leinaweaver calls an eddy of stories that push, pull and buffet them about. Leinaweaver uses antenarrative inquiry to develop a critical antenarratology, a more critical storytelling, to get at the dynamics of narrative marginality. The contribution the chapter makes is demonstrating that all the living story web of relationship identities do not collapse into one cultural, racial, kinship, and/or citizenship narrative that comes with a BME arc. No story of the story, or narrative of the narratives will do. Marginality is too polysemic (too many meanings), too polyvocal (too many voices), too polydimensional (which is where holograms come in), too polylogical (too many logics), too poly-plotted (all those emplotments, how to choose), and too polychromic (too many temporality differences). The global collective storytelling dynamics of retro-narrative, living story webs of identity, and antenarratives of so many future possibilities makes for a fascinating study, but a strange life on the margins. Antenarrative is on the edges of the now, especially when its antenarrating going on for the very first time. There are those pregnant pauses where one stands on the edge of the abyss, contemplating how to storytell.

In Chapter 20, **Bill Smith** and I , look at antenarrating that hijacks some environmental rhetoric. We define antenarrative as a pack animal, always a part of a moving, shifting, changing assemblage. Antenarrative is all about movement, iterative rhythm and intra-play with material context that gives antenarrative its force and agency. As a genre of storytelling, antenarrative is more like a 'wave' and less like 'narrative,' which is more like a 'particle,' something stable, and stackable. When the term toxic began to couple with assets, some rather strange antenarrating occurred, developing into an assemblage antenarrative. Antenarrating is a kind of cascading rhetoric, making bets (antes) on the move, shaping the future yet to come. The intra-play of the toxic assets antenarrating from the materiality of the economic crisis and real estate market demise that ascribed mortgage backed obligations as a toxic scourge is quite telling. There is this morphing as the antenarrative cascade iteratively shapes and reshapes. It is an interesting assemblage, with antenarratives splitting off, joining and departing from other travelers. And the moving antenarrative assemblage has its weave with materiality, and with the narratives, and living stories. Like some rhizome virus, the imagery of toxic waste infected the host asset, becoming 'toxic asset.' It called to mind images of the super fund. This is more a moving trope than a set of contingent metaphors, and the moving trope antenarrates. How is it that toxic waste combines in assemblage with toxic assets? Smith and I, also view this as a spiral antenarrative. As the troubled assets become the great toxic assets, they further morph into dreams of super fund bailouts framed more toxic by administrators of the government. There was a spiral in the making, a whirlpool of sorts, gaining in speed and momentum resulting in public acceptance of government intervention and the residual of toxic assets.

Richard Herder, in Chapter 21, looks at more of these rhetorical antenarratives and brings *kairos* into the assemblage. Herder wants a rapprochement between antenarrative and *kairos*. Kairos is the rhetorical art of timing and location, making some actions more advantageous or decorous. The contribution he makes is to unpack the antenarrative aspect of ante as the bet, the wagering, that plays along a trajectory, a moving assemblage or spiral. His chapter takes us into the life of social movements, into the Coalition of Immokalee Workers struggle with Taco Bell. The farmworkers used *kairotic* storytelling practices to persuade this multinational corporation to changes it policies. It's all about the timing of the antenarrative practices. It's about doing something dialogical, not just opposing, but bringing into play something co-generative. Herder's chapter brings *kairos'* insights to antenarrative inquiry, and makes connections to the work of narrative economist Deirdre McCloskey and to the French thinker Michel de Certeau. And I greatly appreciated Herder's slant on my work on stylistic dialogism (bringing in other dialogisms of Bakhtin than just the polyphonic one, which is welcome always).

In Chapter 22, **Henri Savall, Véronique Zardet,** and **Michel Péron** present a new sort of storytelling theatre of organizations. Building on work of Bruno Latour (actor-network-theory) they develop an interactive-actor-polygon. My postscript gives you a wrap up, a way in which antenarrative inquiry can be more aligned with materiality, with timespacemaking, still ever on the move.

In my **Postscript,** I relate Chapter 22 to where I think antenarrative inquiry might be headed. It seems that there is some opportunity to bring some quantum physics to bear on discourse, to look at the intra-play of storytelling with timespacemattering. More of this in the next book.

19 Storytelling Narrative Marginality
On Becoming a Global Human

Jeff Leinaweaver

OVERVIEW

In society, we are often called upon to tell our stories of origin in everyday life. We are prompted to narrate the stories of our ethnic origins, where we grew up, details of our family, where our cultural loyalties lie, and who our ancestors were. Telling our ongoing story helps us make meaning of our daily experiences and provides the fuel for personal mythos, vocation, family, and overall sense of being in the world.

Over time, and through the various chapters of becoming, we are expected to narrate the story of why we are who we are. In answering and reanswering the question "What's your story?" we are perpetually tasked with honing the craft of reconstructing and situating our storylines. To manage how we show up in the world, we perform an intranarrative calculus. We game play and frame our storytelling in order to influence the coordinated management of meaning. We do so in a response to the biased nature of power and will embedded in the coherence of language (Foucault, 1984).

So, in this increasingly pluralistic world, what do people make when they tell the story or stories of being "born global"? How do people who were born global manage collective storytelling dynamics and influence how their story is told? What can be gleaned from this experience that provides new insights into the emergent nature of critical storytelling theory and the emerging notion of antenarrative inquiry (Boje, 2001, 2008)?

International adoption has emerged as one of those practices and experiences that births global people and creates the condition of narrative marginality. Internationally adopted people are born into a crossroad of stories. Internationally adopted people are specifically burdened with the task of coordinating the meaning of their narrative genealogy.

For an internationally adopted person, narrating one's origin story is not a simple task. Individuals must manage the in-between narratives of self that influence the boundary crossing between stories of nationality, culture, race, kinship, and otherness. As a result, internationally adopted people are caught in an eddy of stories that push, pull, and buffet their notions of narrative and origin of self. Within this context, simple questions such as "where are you from, who are you, what's your birthday, what's your cultural background?" do not elicit simple answers. Instead, these types of questions elicit a wrestling through of disclosure, conjecture, history, and spin based in part upon who's asking, why and how meaning should be reflexively framed within the situational, cultural, and narratological power dynamics at hand.

In my research on the narrative construction of international adoption identity, I used the lenses of antenarrative inquiry, critical storytelling (Boje, 2001), and the communication theory known as the Coordinated Management of Meaning (CMM; Leinaweaver, 2008; Pearce, 1989, 1994, 2005, 2007) to examine the various collective storytelling dynamics at play in conditions of narrative marginality. In this, I found an ongoing paradox around the storying of self, and how self is emplotted in relation to one's roots and the diffusion of self, culture, race, nationality, kinship, and otherness.

I approach my conversation on global identity development, and specifically international adoption identity, as a way to explore how a common question such as "what's your story" creates a narrative burden of self that is bound by a triadic tension of storytelling forces: retrospective narrative, living story narrative, and antenarrative (Boje, 2001, 2008). I hope to present new ways to view and use critical storytelling theory and antenarrative inquiry to unpack and understand the influence of collective storytelling dynamics on the globalizing nature of the human condition.

MULTIPHRENIA AND THE HEGEMONY OF NARRATIVE

Traditional storytelling often holds back the lived and ineffable experiences of life. Despite this, individuals are often required to situate an experience into a narrative arc that includes a beginning, middle, and end regardless of the inexpressible, murky, and embryonic aspects of meaning making. As Boje argues (2001), narrative and its form of retrospective storytelling are hegemonic and rule bound. Narrative reduces the flux and temporality of the human experience into a neat story. Story, therefore, becomes a distillate of life's messiness placed within a box with specific decisions of emplotment made to foreground certain aspects and background others. Emplotment is the active process of willing a story's disparate parts (such as actors, roles, themes, actions) and conditions (time and space) into one coherent narrative (Ricoeur 1984). Emplotment is the act of boxing up narrative. Emplotment is also an act of power and containment.

Gergen (1999) argues that because of globalization, postmodernism, and the technological birth of cyber identities (via social networking, e-mail, the Internet, mediated list serves, etc.), the traditional notions of a single coherent self and self-narrative are being eroded. Instead, people are becoming dynamically diffused, fragmented, and decentered into selves and stories of selves. As a result, the emplotment of singular narratives is becoming a complex juggling act within the greater context of storytelling our selves. This state of being is known as multiphrenia, where stories and selves can fall into conflict with the complexities and multiplicities of being and the hegemony of epic and singular narratives of self. My research leads me to argue that it is actually an inability to handle the collective storytelling dynamics of a postmodern self that leads to the condition of multiphrenia and exacerbates narrative marginality. Gergen (1999) calls this a saturation of the self, where people get caught up and drown in the churn between the paradoxical conflict between the traditional and the multiplicity of self.

As narrative marginals, and global people, I have found that internationally adopted people demonstrate a clustering of liminal identity stories that span race, culture, nationality, kinship, and "otherness" (Leinaweaver, 2008). As a result, the lived experience of international adoption overlaps and parallels with other narrative marginal individuals such as expatriates and their third-culture children (individuals born and raised as foreign nationals in one country and raised outside of their home country of origin), not to mention people such as intercountry refugees, immigrants, and those from complex blended multicultural families, and so on (Geertz, 1973; Leinaweaver, 2008).

The common denominator with all of these narrative streams is how each storied identity does not fit into any one cultural, racial, kinship, and/or citizenship narrative or box to which they have been exposed to or born into. Instead, these various narratives may fit comfortably on the edge and in the margins of all the narrative nodes as a dynamic and composite whole (Geertz, 1973; Lee, 2003; Masuoka, 1945, McCall & Simmons 1966). Yet, the narrative hegemony of modern society demands an easy-to-follow story arc with a beginning, middle, and end.

I argue that being born global, and specifically being internationally adopted, certainly falls into one of those multiphrenic experiences of being both difficult to narrate and a story of stories that is required to be told and emplotted in many different ways to many different inquirers. This is especially true in situational pressures where stigma and other stereotypes prevail. Accordingly, the international adoption story is not always singularly focused, linear, and rational with a beginning, middle, and end. This is a story of narrative marginality. Stories can be fragmented, liminal, chaotic, embryonic, and effervescent. Story can be polysemic (many-meaning), polyvocal (many voiced, or authored), and polychronic (temporal variability). The internationally adopted person has unique narrative burdens, as choices, that influence the poly-emplotment of story as a by-product of the various collective storytelling dynamics of retrospective narrative, living story narrative, and antenarrative.

ANTENARRATIVE AND COLLECTIVE STORYTELLING DYNAMICS

What if narrative cannot enforce its rules of order and the rationality of its storylines? Boje (2001) responds to this question with his propositional theory and concept of antenarrative. Antenarrative is a prospective coordination of coherence. Antenarrative is seen as a response and future bet to the crisis of narrative's hegemony. Narrative is a linear and controlled retrospective of story and its meaning. It is unidimensional with an imposed beginning, middle, and end, or formulaic narrative arc. Antenarrative eschews the narratological story. Antenarrative is speculative, polydimensional, and represents meaning making at the edges of the now and before a story is retrospectively spoken for the first time. Antenarrative resists narrative's control and the entropy of its deconstruction. Antenarrative holds the potential and mystery of meaning making.

Collective storytelling dynamics emerge as the interplay of four genres of storytelling: linear, retrospective narrative, living story narratives, and prospective antenarrative bets on the future (Boje, 2001, 2008). My research found that in conversation, narrative marginals were specifically tested upon their ability to manage (or not) collective storytelling dynamics (Leinaweaver, 2008).

The term 'antenarrative' is powerful because it names an experience of meaning making which may otherwise be characterized as something less than, illegitimate, or a pathology of some sort (Barge, 2004). Antenarrative not only names an experiential pattern of the human condition, but also

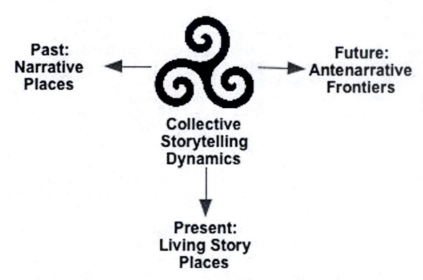

Figure 19.1   Collective storytelling dynamics—triadic storytelling.

exposes as a dynamic quality of antenarrative coherence making, such as multiphrenia. Naming antenarrative legitimizes its whereabouts as a conceptual force and flags itself on an epistemological map. I believe the power of antenarrative and the acts of antenarrative inquiry reside in being able to make the inchoate and ineffable story into something whole, credible, and witnessed.

As a dynamic, antenarrative sits in a yin/yang tension with narrative. It is its opposing doppelganger and resituates story in relationship to antenarrative's five principles: (1) antenarrative challenges narrative; it ups the ante by reframing what story means; (2) antenarrative is nascent, existing before story (narrative is memory of story); (3) antenarrative is freewheeling dialoguing, it is sensemaking; (4) antenarrative is nonlinear, fragmented, chaotic, cacophonous, and dualistic; it is polyvocal, polysemic, and polychronic; (5) antenarrative is in flux, living before plot has been agreed upon by the collective memory of storytelling (Boje, 2001).

I raise these issues because internationally adopted people and narrative marginals, in general, do not necessarily have stories that fit the typical narrative arc. Accordingly, I argue that these individuals have phantom episodes of narrative. Phantom episodes occupy missing data and unknown stories. They are missing links in the narrative DNA. As a result, these gaps in knowing are often smoothed over by way of assuming truths and other items found within typical retrospective narrative emplotment. Examples of this include internationally adopted people who have made up birthdates, locations, and guestimates of history; one person told me that she has no information, no ability to find any history, no baby pictures, no record of birth, and is often forced to tell people that she just is and was (Leinaweaver, 2008).

Accordingly, the individuals in my research emerged as being storytellers who were organically antenarrative, who have always had to up the ante of their storytelling in order to stay ahead of other people's narratives and their preexisting views of who they ought to be. As a form of game play, they learned to play with and cast about in their stories. One participant, who was Afro-Colombian and raised in a white Dutch family, said in response to not knowing anything in her background, or that of her brother (also Afro-Colombian, but not biologically connected), that they learned they could empower themselves by simply making up their stories on the fly. Mystery became a by-product of the phantom episodes, and the edge in the now-spective moment. As a result, they learned to use conjecture as a tool for antenarrative inquiry. One favorite way of beginning their antenarrative origin story was to begin by saying their white Dutch father had "magic balls" (Leinaweaver, 2008). They have unknowingly engaged in antenarrative inquiry in order to practice the destiny of their narrative DNA—in this case, as tricksters through the gaming of self through story.

THE INVASION OF COLLECTIVE STORYTELLING DYNAMICS

In storytelling, dominant cultural views demand allegiance to particular narratological ways of being and doing storytelling. This fuels narrative's hegemony. Outlying narratologies challenge the hegemony of the dominant culture's collective storytelling dynamics. Therefore, to be the primary narrator of a story is to become the person who holds a position of power over meaning making. The narrator controls the story's narratology, or how the story ought to be told.

Within this context, the narrator typically reinforces the social and cultural expectations of how stories (both fictional and nonfictional) are to be constructed, with an understanding there is a social price to be paid for telling the wrong story (Pearce, 1989). 'Official' narratives embolden the narrator(s) to take a position of power and inject social scripts into other subnarratives in order to sublimate the collective storytelling dynamics and own the coordinated coherence of meaning. These aggressive social scripts operate out of a preexistent socially constructed archetypal retrospective narrative. The ensuing narratological seesaw sets up the types of tensions narrative marginals must learn to navigate. These social scripts also become the bedrock for the person and/or subgroup's narrative genealogy.

The following example highlights the collective storytelling dynamics and afterlife of the impact other people's storytelling has had on an individual's ability to fully own and reflexively or prospectively tell the story of one's genesis and narrative genealogy (Leinaweaver, 2008, p. 93):

JENNIFER: *And so . . . as far as adoption stories that we were told or things that we were told about our adoptions, I think my parents, and I'm sure thousands of kids have had this happen to them, too you know, but were told things by others and the agencies or whatever in terms of making up these stories and that. . . . I look back on it now and I think they had a very negative impact on us.*

JEFF: *What were you told?*

JENNIFER: *We were told, you know, you came from Korea. You know your family, you know, couldn't keep you. We don't know why, you know. You came from a very poor country and you know they don't . . . they don't have a lot there and they thought your life would be better here. And, you know, maybe your mother was a prostitute. Maybe you would have grown up and been a maid, you know what I mean? So they painted this very dreary picture. You know what I mean of . . . and . . . and I can understand now in looking back, you know, what they were trying to do but I think from a . . . now, sort of how we look at things holistically in terms of how you present things, it might not have been the best thing.*

JENNIFER: *And now as an adult I look at it and I say well I wouldn't want to hear oh, your mother was a prostitute or you know what I mean? You know either you're lucky … it was that whole, you're lucky thing, you know what I mean? You were lucky you could be adopted and of course we love you and blah, blah, blah. You know what I mean? It was that whole making life here the rosy picture but life there, you know what I mean, is dark and glum as can be.*

Using a heuristic model from CMM known as the daisy model, I have used the daisy to pull out and highlight the many voices and narrators both heard and unheard in Jennifer's origin story. Each daisy petal represents a subsystem of selves, narratives, narratologies, and stories.

As the example shows, one's story of origin becomes susceptible to a multiplicity of dominant cultural narratives and archetypal scripts. As a result, narrative coherence is managed and distorted in coordinated frames, cultural twists, and romanticization of setting, motive, back story, plot, character casting, and so on. There is a "truthiness" to the truth, and as a result, telling truthful origin stories is not necessarily the point, or always

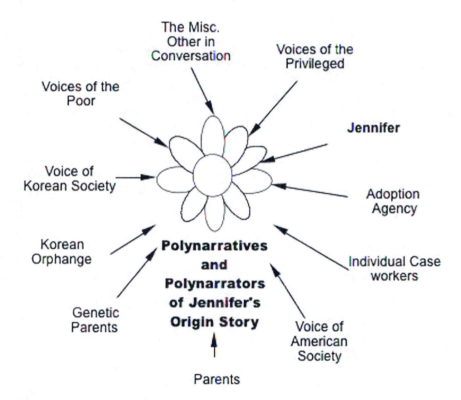

Figure 19.2 Jennifer's polynarratives and polynarrators.

an option. The story, as a made object, is what it is said to be within the situational context in which the story is told. There is a narratological oughtness to how the story should be told and made. There may also be a penalty for telling the wrong story, or differently than the official versions. Depending on who narrates, the primary identity of that story will pivot to the narrator's sense of position and level of power within the conversation (Pearce, 1989). Within this setting, the tension of being authored, as a made object, or authoring oneself becomes an emergent and subversive dynamic.

As a result, individuals in my research reported interpersonal and intercultural encounters in which they felt others engaged them on the basis of a preconceived script and a narrative expectation on how the conversation on origin and identity ought to unfold. In doing so, participants in my research reported they had learned to see and anticipate patterns within an unseen field of collective storytelling dynamics. In doing so, they have created a skill for being able to better navigate the sometimes murky waters of storytelling as strategic communication. One pattern that emerged in my research is something I call a Dead Snake (Leinaweaver, 2008). I refer to them as a dead snake based on a dialogic model from CMM (Pearce, 1989) that positions living dialogue and storytelling as an activity of turn taking that resembles a narrative serpent. I see the dead snake as a preexistent archetypal narrative script that gains life by dominating, taking over, or inserting itself into the narrative of a conversation. Another way to view this is from a genealogical view, whereby an interlocutor unknowingly accesses dominant social scripts as phantom strands of narrative DNA. The conversational DNA is then modified to accommodate these scripts of power and position.

The following is an example of an individual reflecting on the 'outing' of a dead snake and the blowback that occurs from when she takes control of the narrative and debunks power to tell the story differently:

JEFF: *So how do you manage conversations with others when they start inquiring about your adoption, and/or adoption in general; how do you kind of manage and coordinate this. You had mentioned previously about how people fight with you?*

JOAN: *Right.*

JEFF: *Is that your experience?*

JOAN: *Yes like this is . . . oh, you're adopted, an international case, so then they have this whole narrative that they attach to my adoption. So when I mentioned for instance that I had an intact family and that I was two and a half years and we had this village, which was its own little social system that doesn't fit their script. They don't want to hear it. Therefore they ask me can this really be true? Are you sure? Do you have proof? Because they don't want to believe it; it doesn't fit their narrative* (Leinaweaver, 2008, p. 129).

Dead snakes are made objects, micro-aggressions, zombie narratives, and narratological seeds. They are antenarrative by nature and in many ways resemble a linear antenarrative in that a script is also a 'line' in the angular zigzag of turn-by-turn storytelling. The following diagram depicts the story as it both unfolds in living turns as well as the dead snake elements that are poised as zombie antenarratives.

Internationally adopted people face the tension and challenge of authoring themselves versus being authored by others. International adoptee identity development is born dependent upon a narrative chain of custody to create and cast their narrative genealogy. International adoptees are given an 'authentic autobiography' as a 'real' origin story, when in actuality their roots are the embodied discourse of others, peppered with unknowns, mystery, and approximations about who they are and why they are who they are (Leinaweaver, 2008). Accordingly, the international adoption story is not an easy story to narrate.

As an example, internationally adopted people must often debate, spin, and parse the paradox of what 'real' means, as in real family or real culture, when people inquire about their origin. A driving factor behind this

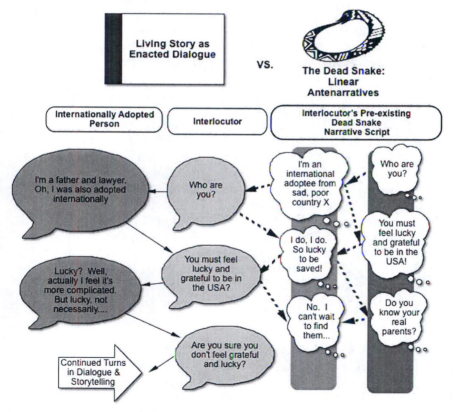

Figure 19.3 Dead snakes as linear antenarratives.

tension is how the notion of 'real' is socialized through story. In dominant, homogenizing cultures, such as 'white culture,' people may expect origin stories of real culture and real families by virtue of framing the meaning of real as that of being culturally contained, racially contained, or genetically contained in neat plug-and-play compartments (Lee, 2003; Volkman, 2005). As such, a qualifier such as 'international adoptee' or 'mixed-race' 'multicultural' family is made and used in society to subtly highlight not being the norm. For the internationally adopted person, they may not share the same neat qualifying narratologies and views. To them, real is relative, and their family may be their 'real' family and 'real' roots cultural template, despite the differences in meaning with the dominant culture's views of 'real.' They may also have 'real' loyalties to cultural stories that may be live-in contradiction to their appearance and/or fit with family. An example of this would be an adopted person from India living with their white family, whereby the inner narrative may have loyalties and reality stories of oneself as being white, yet externally being forced to tell and live out the story of their Indian physicality, and then being torn by loyalties to their Indian roots. The narratologies live in conflict and contribute to narrative marginality, and its spin. In conversation, questioning one's reality is not only a micro-aggression of narrative hegemony but may delegitimize, complicate, and create a chilling effect on how one learns to tell and reflect upon one's own genuine origin. It may also exacerbate the spin and liminality of various narratives. The lesson becomes that if you tell the story 'correctly,' all will be well. If you do not, there are stakes and risks involved in telling a story differently, or incorrectly. This is particularly entrenched in stories that emphasize or debunk stereotypes and stigmas.

My research with internationally adopted people shows that over time narrative marginals learn to become innovators of narrative, better able to spar by way of a tacit practice of antenarrative inquiry and conjecture. In turn, they have become cosmopolitan communicators and conversational leaders. By organically learning how to consciously emplot themselves in antenarrative storytelling, they have learned to intuitively ask themselves: Who's the primary narrator of my story? what kind of story is being made in our conversation together? how can I get ahead of this story in order to own my story and own the process of self-creation, design, and representation (Leinaweaver, 2008)? In other words, how do I most optimally own, coordinate, deconstruct, and manage the parts and the whole of self and selves? How can I become a storytelling martial artist?

TOOLS FOR ANTENARRATIVE INQUIRY: THE DIALOGIC WASHING MACHINE

In doing research on the complex identity stories of narrative marginality and people born global, I found there to be a great deal of tension in regards to how individuals reflected upon themselves as storytellers, and the afterlife of the stories told by them and about them. There was a palpable tension between stories lived versus stories told versus stories other people wanted to hear. These tensions in opposites fueled the spin of their narrative marginality and the framing of their narrative DNA.

To learn from narrative marginality as a condition, by-product, and indicator of collective storytelling dynamics, I worked with several heuristic models from CMM (Pearce, 1998) and used antenarrative inquiry as a form of critical storytelling (Boje, 2001, 2008) to deconstruct and develop new ways to unpack the genealogical map and capture identity stories on the move within a sea of narrative and antenarrative dynamics (Jørgensen & Boje, 2009).

Communication as storytelling is a two-sided phenomenon, meaning that the turns in dialogue are at some level a response to another turn in communication. To understand how people might become storytelling martial artists and overcome conditions such as stigma, racism, and so on, I found it important to visually understand and map the patterns of complexity found in storytelling. I didn't want to look through communication but rather to look at it in a more 3-D, or holographic, sense.

After my analysis and review for antenarrative stories (such as the linear antenarratives found in dead snake scripts), I found that a mandala of storytelling forces emerged as a critical tool and hermeneutic circle vis-à-vis Ricoeur's (1984) notion of emplotment. This allowed me to look at the dynamic geometry of storytelling.

If you were to look down into the open mouth of a washing machine, you might see an agitator working with and against the forces of the water and laundry. Like grist, the clothes are beaten, stretched, agitated, jumbled, bleached, sanitized, cleaned, and saturated with different types of dynamic forces. Now, imagine the same type of dynamic scenario occurring within a container of storytelling dynamics where narrative and antenarrative forces work to constrain, disrupt, and shape the discourse of storytelling as a medium for coordinating and managing meaning. I refer to these collective storytelling dynamics as the dialogic washing machine. I see the dialogic washing machine as a hermeneutic tool for antenarrative inquiry.

The dialogic washing machine spins as a sphere of identity and encompasses a lifeworld at both an individual and collective level. It is meant to represent an individual's storytelling consciousness and unconscious. This did not emerge as something that privileges narrative marginals, or those born global; rather, I saw this as a general depiction of the human condition and the triadic forces of storytelling (retrospective narrative storytelling, living story in the now, and prospective antenarrative story).

Within the mandala itself, the function of the storytelling bubble, as the agitator and hub, is to be the mouthpiece into and out of the sphere. As a mandala of collective storytelling dynamics, the dialogic washing machine is not to be seen as an exclusive tool for the interpretation of narrative marginality or international adoption identity. Rather, it is a hermeneutic to be used as a tool for critical analysis for both individual and organizational circumstances where there is a need to investigate storytelling from a more holistic and spatial understanding of the geometry of narrative.

The dialogic washing machine offers a systems level of awareness as to what people are constructing together through storytelling and how they make and manage (or are managed by) their various narratological identities. It is a gateway framework into finding and following strands of narrative DNA. This is key in relationship to the internationally adopted person, narrative marginal, or person born global whose cultural narratives and self-narratives are always in a turn-by-turn movement due to the narrative obligations of enacting one's self and the representation of one's identities across social worlds of intercultural complexity. Viewing storytelling as form of dynamic geometry, or from a place of spatiality, exposes a dynamic embeddedness that occurs as a result of being dynamically emplotted into narrative over the course of one's lifetime. I believe this implies that we, as human beings, can make better social worlds through the development of communicative resources, or rather learning to become a storytelling martial artist. One's 'success' could therefore be defined as how adept one is at coordinating and managing meaning to most skillfully represent one's internal sense of self vis-à-vis one's social worlds, cultural views, and personal identities. Oliver (1996) calls this developing a level of systemic eloquence. Accordingly, if one has a level of systemic eloquence, or virtuosity, as an antenarrative storyteller, one would be able to judge how one's ability to manage (or not) the resource of storytelling as a way to enhance communication and the quality of interpersonal relationships, sense of identity, and personal narrative.

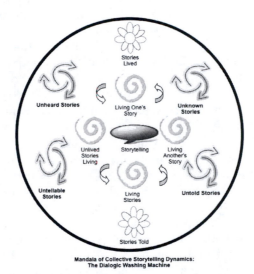

Figure 19.4   The dialogic washing machine.

Between the unidimensional and polydimensional dynamics of the dialogic washing machine, the mandala itself is also a sphere that acknowledges the shadow side of storytelling by naming the unspoken and unacknowledged elements of storytelling as active but tacit narrators of the storyteller's storytelling. This is similar to Hiles and Cermák's (2007) and Herman and Vervaeck's (2001) notions around narrative identity construction and identity positioning found within the interpersonal and situational tensions found around a specific constructed/constrained sjuzet (unbounded motifs of narrative) and fabula (or the historical or retrospectively bounded motifs of narrative). And whereas each person has his or her own dynamic sphere, in interpersonal and intercultural episodes of storytelling there is an overlapping of spheres, like a Venn diagram, between individuals, organizations, and/or cultures. It is indeed in this overlap where the coordination, conflict, and coherence of telling our story occurs.

I argue that the dialogic washing machine, as an interpretive and hermeneutic tool, offers a view of storytelling as a whirling dervish of antenarrative and narrative emplotment, whereby story is cast/recast, framed, interpreted, withheld, punctuated, spun, coordinated, managed, improvised, and ritualized. In my research (Leinaweaver, 2008), as a mandala of collective storytelling dynamics, the dialogic washing machine seemed to be driven by the constraints and linear emplotment of narrative devices such as a dead snake's use of labels and taxonomy to categorize, narratologize, and enforce power. Hiles and Cermák (2007) would frame this as identity positioning through narrative. I also found the dialogic washing machine exhibited various types of Bakhtinian (in Dentith, 1995) centripetal and centrifugal tensions that aimed to constrain or free up meaning making.

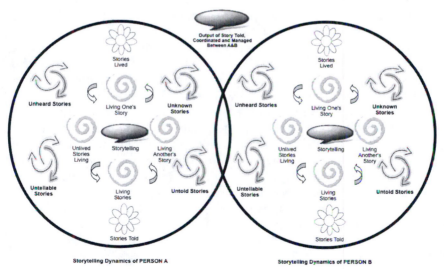

Figure 19.5   Venn diagram of collective storytelling dynamics.

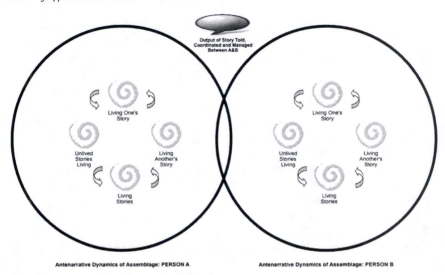

Figure 19.6   Venn diagram of collective storytelling dynamics.

Within the dialogic washing machine, I highlight four antenarrative dynamics that ultimately empower, constrain, influence, obscure, or repress storytelling in the living now of storytelling as well as an ante or bet for the future. The antenarrative dynamics are entitled Living Stories (LS), Living Another's Story (LAS), Living One's Story (LOS), and Unlived Stories Living (USL). These dynamics live in tension with each other, but are not exclusive of each other. They can exist as hybrids. They are antenarrative as they emerge and exist in the unfolding context of the situation at hand.

These four dynamics emerge out of the dynamic principles behind and between a story's narratological sjuzet (unbounded narrative and, in this case, antenarrative) and fabula (bounded narrative). These constructive, reconstructive, and deconstructive dynamics force out a story via a specific propositional frame and individualized emplotment. The sjuzet (ubounded narrative) influences how each person positions herself or himself in relation with the fabula (bounded historical narrative of a story).

So if one is expected to narrate a story to others, and manage an ongoing situational tension, what does one make when one tells the international adoption story? What are the narratological influences of others in the collective storytelling dynamics? How do we engage and deconstruct the afterlife of narrative's hegemony upon the storytelling of self? These are the questions that have emerged out of working with the dialogic washing machine. These are questions as genealogical tools for the generative and critical deconstruction of narrative DNA. The dialogic washing machine is a hermeneutic compass and tool to use as an antenarrative pickax and shovel in uncovering the dynamics and process of storying the self versus storied by others.

CONCLUSION

International adoption narratives hold the social scripts of others. It is in this mythos of pseudo-self and self-creation that orthodoxy of storytelling begins and the stakes in storytelling are shared and managed among a variety of other storytellers. These narrative artifacts become the living threads of an individual's storytelling consciousness, genealogy, and the bedrock of their narrative marginality. How one engages these strands of stories determines how one learns to pivot, frame, coordinate personal story within the triadic dynamics of retrospective narrative, now-spective living narrative, and prospective antenarrative (Boje, 2001, 2008).

The story of one's personal status quo is built in part by other narrators who operate as the primary narrators of one's life, both culturally and interpersonally. Within this narrative enmeshment, there is a power struggle for loyalty and obedience among stories and selves, and between the narrative margins of race, culture, nationality, kinship, and degree of otherness (Leinaweaver, 2008). Internationally adopted people are, in essence, global narrative marginals who are enmeshed in rootless webs *of* densely interwoven stories. Narrative marginality is the experience of being irrevocably caught between stories and selves (Leinaweaver, 2008).

In the growing population of individuals who are 'born global,' such as international adoptees, these people are often left flat-footed when facing the request to share and tell their root narrative of self. Questions such as "what's your story?" "who are you?" "where are you from?" raise more questions than answers and often lead to one being caught between stories and selves, cultures and races, kinship and nations. As narrative marginals, these people intuitively know that communication, as storytelling, is more than a linear transmission of information from one person to another. In fact, it is the linearity of transmission and narrative that causes problems. Instead, there is an emergent awareness around the ongoing dilemma of storying self, and how self is emplotted in relation to one's roots and the diffusion of culture, race, nationality, kinship, and 'otherness.' Storytelling is instead becoming a systems process out of which we make social worlds and global identities (Boje, 2001; Kegan, 1982; Pearce, 1989; Shotter, 1993, 2000).

As an act of freewheeling storytelling, antenarrative inquiry is becoming a way to stay ahead of the paradox and burden of narrative by way of creating new or imagined social realities and self-narratives at the edge of being that ultimately manage collective storytelling dynamics along with the dilemmas of narrative marginality. No longer is storytelling seen as a way to identify the objects, actions, and sequencing of events that occur in our lives in a process of retrospective sensemaking. Storytelling, through antenarrative inquiry, is a way of unboxing one's self and regaining power over self and one's narrative roots.

In order to re-see how a common question such as "what's your story?" creates a narrative burden, I approached this chapter's conversation on international adoption identity as a way to explore the world of narrative marginality, global identities, and collective storytelling dynamics I highlighted research on the narrative construction of identity that used the lenses of antenarrative, critical storytelling (Boje, 2001, 2008), and the communication theory known as the Coordinated Management of Meaning (CMM; Leinaweaver, 2008; Pearce, 1989) to examine the various collective storytelling dynamics at play in conditions of narrative marginality.

In addition, I presented a mandala of collective storytelling dynamics as a hermeneutic tool for individual and organizational storytelling. In doing so, I hope this offers a new approach to antenarrative inquiry. I also hope it creates new insights in empowered storytelling and advances the capacity for a type of martial artistry that transforms narrative marginality into a way of developing one's competitive edge as a communicator and global citizen. Clearly, it is important for organizations and scholars to begin to look at the multiplicity of the born global experience to better understand how antenarrative occurs as an organic outcome of this globalizing world. In so doing, practitioners and scholars of antenarrative inquiry may become better able to influence the capacity building of future leaders through new repertoires of antenarrative innovation and communication skills for a complex, interconnected world.

REFERENCES

Barge, J.L. (2004). Antenarrative and managerial practice. Communication studies, 55(1) 106+. Retrieved February 5, 2006, from Questia database: http://www.questia.com/PM.qst?a=o&d=5006805007

Boje, D. (2001). *Narrative methods for organizational & communication research.* London: Sage.

Boje, D. M. (2008). *Storytelling organizations.* London: Sage.

Dentith, S. (1995). *Bakhtinian thought: An introductory reader.* New York: Routledge.

Foucault, M. (1984). Nietzsche, Genealogy, History. In P. Rabinow (Ed.). *The Foucault Reader,* pp. 76–100. New York: Pantheon.

Geertz, C. (1973). *The interpretation of cultures.* New York: Basic Books.

Gergen, K. (1999). *An invitation to social construction.* London: Sage.

Herman, L., & Vervaeck, B. (2001). *Handbook of narrative analysis.* Lincoln: University of Nebraska Press.

Hiles, D. R., & Cermák, I. (2007). Narrative psychology. In C. Willig & W. Stainton-Rogers (Eds.), *Handbook of qualitative research in psychology.* London: Sage.

Kegan, R. (1982). *The evolving self: Problem and process in human development.* Cambridge, MA: Harvard University Press.

Jørgensen, K., & Boje, D. (2009). Genealogies of becoming—Antenarrative inquiry in organizations. *Tamara Journal for Critical Organizational Inquiry,* 8, 30–47.

Lee, R. M. (2003). The transracial adoption paradox: History, research, and counseling implications of cultural socialization. *The Counseling Psychologist,*
31(6), 711–744.

Leinaweaver, J. (2008). The coordinated management of a culturally diffused identity: Internationally adopted people and the narrative emplotment of self. Fielding Graduate University, Unpublished dissertation.

Masuoka, J. (1945). The hybrid and the social process. *Phylon,* 6(4), 327–336.

McCall, G., & Simmons, J. (1966). *Identities and interactions.* New York: Free
Press.

Oliver, C. (1996). Systemic eloquence. *Human Systems,* 7, 247–264.

Pearce, W. B. (1989). *Communication and the human condition.* Carbondale: University of Southern Illinois Press.

———. (1994). Interpersonal communication: Making social worlds. New York:
HarperCollins College Publisher.

———. (2005). The coordinated management of meaning. In W. Gudykunst (Ed.),
Theorizing about intercultural communication. Thousand Oaks, CA: Sage.

———. (2007). *Making of social worlds: a communication perspective.* Oxford,
UK: Blackwell Publishing.

Ricoeur, P. (1984). Time and Narrative—Volume 1. Chicago and London: University of Chicago Press.

Shotter, J. (1993). *Conversational realities: Constructing life through language.*
London: Sage.

Shotter, J. (2000). Inside dialogical realities: From an abstract-systematic to a par-
ticipatory-wholistic understanding of communication. *Southern Communication Journal,* 65, 119–132.

Volkman, T. (2005). Cultures of transnational adoption. Durham, NC: Duke University Press

20 The Rhetoric of Toxic Assets
An Antenarrative Analysis

William L. Smith and David M. Boje

INTRODUCTION

An antenarrative is a pack animal, always a part of a moving, shifting, changing assemblage. It is the movement, its iterative rhythm and intraplay with context, that gives it force and agency. As a genre of storytelling, antenarrative is more like a 'wave' and less like 'narrative,' which is more like a 'particle,' something stable, and stackable. It is just such an antenarrative assemblage and wave effect that shaped the economic landscape and its field of possibilities when 'toxic' became associated with 'assets.'

The *Wall Street Journal* headline read "Stench of Toxic Assets Lingers" and on June 11, 2009, this article was one of 55 articles the *Journal* had published in 2009 that included the term 'toxic assets.' In this article, Wessel (2009) questioned whether it was still necessary for the government to remove toxic assets from bank balance sheets in order to get credit flowing again. The seeming acceptance and related prevalence of the term 'toxic assets' as mainstream is of interest. Consider that prior to the inception of the TARP (Troubled Asset Relief Program), the term 'toxic assets' was only included in two *Wall Street Journal* articles. As the growing popularity and widespread acceptance of this term is increasing, an understanding is necessary.

There were 556 results for the term 'asset' on the Financial Accounting Standards Board (FASB) official Web site as of March, 15, 2010; yet a search for the term 'toxic asset' yielded no results. The accounting authority responsible for promulgating official accounting standards does not appear to recognize the popular term. However, as of March 15, 2010, there were approximately 343,000 results found on Google.

The toxic asset antenarrative quickly gained momentum in the public dialogue. According to Boje (2008, pp. 13–14):

> Forward-looking antenarratives are . . . able to change the future, to set changes and transformations in motion that have impact on the big picture. More accurately, antenarratives seem to bring about a future that would not otherwise be.

Antenarrating is a kind of storytelling that morphs as it cascades forward, re-forms its themes, and makes those terse little 'bets' (antes) on what the future might become. Antenarratives are in intraplay with all sorts of materiality, be it social interaction networks, tones and vibrations, gestures that move air and costume, marks on pages, or electronic signals on the Internet. Unlike the retrospective narratives, which can be catalogued and counted, the antenarratives are always in flight, splitting and merging with other antenarratives. The small 'bets' shape the future before any grand coherent petrified narrative is formed by ever expanding and narrowing the field of possibilities.

Living stories, the ones we live day-to-day, in the here and now, and are bridges between narrative past and antenarrative future. The three genres of storytelling (narrative, living story, and antenarrative) interweave, are all part of the moving assemblage (Boje, 2008). What is curious is how one becomes the other: an antenarrative comes to rest, stabilizes to become a narrative fossil. The living story does not know which way to turn, sometimes glancing past, other times prospecting some future out of a bit of emergence. In the populist venues, antenarratives and lots of folks' living story webs come up against some 'officially' legitimate (grand or smaller) narratives, as contenders reshape history, collective memory, and define possibilities.

The term 'toxic,' as it relates to waste, elicits visions of extremely hazardous material that should be contained at all costs in order to prevent a dangerous spread to the unsuspecting citizenry. Whenever there is an accident involving toxic materials, the public not only accepts but further expects government intervention to immediately contain the problem and thereby minimize the spread. After all, governmental entities such as the Environmental Protection Agency (EPA) are funded with taxpayer dollars. In fact, for fiscal year 2011 alone, the EPA discretionary budget request exceeds $10 billion. Accordingly, given the potential dangers inherent in toxic materials, the public abdicates monetary scrutiny to ensure public safety. As a result, the average citizens trust their government to act in the best interests of the governed.

The long-standing and accepted imagery of a toxic hazard served as the host for a toxic asset. Without the need for any substantive explanation or discourse, the perception is clear and public buy-in almost certain. The images of toxic hazard and toxic asset are clearly illustrated in Figure 20.1.

These images are terse, not a proper storytelling. They are nevertheless a part of tropes, about EPA and super funds, and all about the fear of death. These images are everywhere in the landscape, along the highways, as we follow trucks, in our industrial plants, symbols affixed to chemicals beneath the kitchen sink, or waiting on a shelf in the garage. It is these trope images that get appropriated, bound up in the themes of TARP discourse, hived off into storytelling, some of it about narrative past, others about living stories of people's lost mortgages, collapsing banks, and then there are

Figure 20.1   Toxic waste containers. Used by permission from Robert L. Steiner.

those rare geneses that form, the antenarratives. Just the word 'toxic' gets picked up and branded as part of the TARP, and this four-letter marker invites an unspoken antenarrative, as something akin to an EPA setting up a super fund to save us all from 'death.' Visual imagery can link ideas without any expressed rational connection much more easily than orality (Rose, 2001). Visual images discourage rhetorical argument and rational analysis because, as we are told from child to adult: 'seeing is believing.' And this is why TARP apologists link the unspoken images, and even unvisually executed images of 'toxic' to 'assets.'

BACKGROUND

Think of a major hazardous disaster such as Three Mile Island or Chernobyl and imagery of environmental cleanup comes to mind. Only qualified professionals donning specialized protective gear are able to come into contact with the toxic mess, as seen in Figure 20.2.

Gillian Rose (2001) looks at visual imagery as part of the discursive process. We see toxic environmental imagery, such as Figure 20.2, and begin to key in tropes that are easily reappropriated within the storytelling themes; the clear and present danger of the toxic spread and the need for containment.

Figure 20.2   Toxic waste professionals. David Crowley—Elmira FD. Used by permission from Brian Pratt.

There are numerous underlying factors that coalesce to form the complete image and related acceptance. First, the individuals charged with containment are qualified and possess the necessary expertise to properly clean up the toxic mess. Interestingly, the designation of 'qualified' is bestowed by the same groups or agencies that regulate such toxic substances; thus there is often no oversight or system of checks in place to question standard operating procedures (SOPs) and any ensuing problems when SOPs fail. And since the experts are trained and/or often employed by the same groups who established the SOPs in the first place, again there is minimal questioning of procedures or the status quo. The general public does not possess the knowledge or skills required in order to truly understand the problem, much less clean up the mess.

Second, these experts employ specialized equipment and protective wear necessary to safely come into contact with the hazardous material. Here again, the general public does not possess the necessary knowledge and equipment or have access to all the relevant information due to confidentiality, privacy rights, security needs, and so on, needed to clean up the mess. Third, toxic hazards typically are a public concern, and like epidemics, are too large to be dealt with by individuals. Thus the cleanup is abdicated to the government, whereby the spread of contamination is minimized at no direct cost to the public. Given the aforementioned, the government will employ the personnel and resources necessary to address the potentially lethal hazard, which is acceptable by the public.

With respect to assets, the connotation and usage of the term 'toxic' implies that those assets would have been dangerous for anyone to handle, even the experts. Further, the term 'toxic asset' implies the toxicity is inherent in the asset, not something actually caused by some of the same people now hiding behind this term. For example, something that was good and then went bad might be called spoiled or poisoned. But toxic seems to connote something hazardous from the start, without reference to any agency (human or otherwise) bringing about this dangerous state of toxicity.

Our thesis is that the government storytellers appropriated the term 'toxic' to imply a trope of associations (such as in Figures 20.1 and 20.2), weaving those collective memories (Boje, 2008) in between lines of orality and written texts, forming sometimes an antenarrative assemblage that becomes not only fortuitous 'antes' (bets on the future) but turns into something quite 'agential.' A storytelling that is agential has hardly been theorized, much less studied. Usually story is just dead form, stackable texts compared by some metric, sorted into this or that typology. When antenarrative is agential, it's a part of a rush, a cascade, even a spiral. It can also be a rather linear affair, or a repetitive cycle, or claim that one is there even if it is only an imaginary or illusory correlation of emplotment with context (Boje, 2001, 2008).

We think what we are noticing is more of a spiral than a line or (recurring) cycle. Rather than a fixed line or stages that bend and lock into a cycle, this is a spiral, one that veers out of control, becomes a vortex that at first has many possibilities, then tightens around the 'toxic asset' interpretative direction, and finally opens up again (Morson, 1994). These antenarratives are agendas that have coupling as their 'bets' and 'befores,' promising something more substantial as solutions go is right around the corner. There is not one but two spirals. One is the economy on a downward spiral that no one seems to be able to control. The other spiral is an invention, a solution, with EPA appeal, one that saves other assets from contamination; at least that is the 'ante.' There is urgency in both antenarratives of such force and agential appeal that rational discussion is precluded. There is no time to consider the issues, to talk of other possibilities, and opportunity costs are not assessed.

On September 20, 2008, then President George W. Bush, in a Rose Garden question-and-answer session with President Uribe of the Republic of Colombia, stated the following:

> I think most leaders would understand we need to get this done quickly and, you know, the cleaner the better. Yes, this is a big price tag because it's a big problem, Mike. I told our people I don't want to be timid in the face of a *significant problem* that will affect the *average citizen*. You know, some said, this is—we can *contain* this to just the financial community. In my judgment, based upon the advice of a lot of people who know how markets work, this wasn't going to be *contained* to just

the financial community. This problem could—would *spread* to the *average citizen*. (Emphasis added)

This statement was less than 24 hours after then Treasury Secretary Hank Paulson had just unveiled to America a new program called TARP, where he noted that the name was not official (Paulson, 2010). The 'program' resulted from a previous night closed meeting with Federal Reserve Chairman Ben Bernanke, SEC Chairman Chris Cox, and Treasury Secretary Hank Paulson in a lengthy and productive working session with congressional leaders. Paulson (2010) stated, "We began a substantive discussion on the need for a comprehensive approach to relieving the stresses on our financial institutions and markets."

Within 24 hours the 'troubled assets' term had changed to 'toxic assets' in the media. In the Associated Press headline "Bush team, Congress negotiate $700B bailout" posted on Saturday, September 20, 2008, at 11:12 pm ET, AP writers Julie Davis and Deb Riechmann stated, "The Bush administration asked Congress on Saturday for the power to buy $700 billion in toxic assets clogging the financial system and threatening the economy as negotiations began on the largest bailout since the Great Depression."

In further response to an ever-growing environment of financial uncertainty, the federal government enacted H.R. 1424: Emergency Economic Stabilization Act of 2008 in Public Law 110-343 to facilitate a bailout of the U.S. financial system and thereby stabilize the capital markets. This legislation bestowed upon the secretary of the Treasury authority to spend up to $700 billion to purchase "distressed assets" including collateralized debt obligations (CDOs), mortgage-backed securities (MBSs), and other categories of assets deemed as distressed, and further to make capital injections into any banks as he deemed necessary. The urgency of this legislation was clearly demonstrated by its rapid passage into law. On October 3, the House voted 263–171 to enact the bill into law. President Bush then signed the bill into the law known as the Economic Stabilization Act of 2008 within hours of its enactment and thus formally created the $700 billion TARP to purchase failing bank assets.

The speed of the events from proposals to House and Senate bills to enactment of law is almost unprecedented. Given the vast complexity of the subject matter and the seemingly apparent need for even a rudimentary understanding of the content, the obvious question is how could such complex subject matter be 'sold' by the administration in such a short time period. This question begs even further investigation given the lack of credibility ascribed to then President Bush. Immediate public buy-in was essential.

In his discussion of reframing a problem in order to influence a favorable result, Levine (2003, pp. 235–236) provided the following:

> Beware of exploitive professionals who frame their requests in misleading ways. Be especially on guard when they play to your fear of danger

and loss. The easiest way to assess the effects of a frame is to remove it. If you place a dark frame around a picture, all the colors appear lighter. . . . Without objectivity, you're a sitting duck.

By exploiting environmental rhetoric, the negative imagery ascribed to toxic assets can quickly and easily be sold to the public without the need for protracted explanations. The entangling antenarrative assemblage has both a generative (build the superfund) and an accelerating agential effect (do it before the downward spiral eats all the assets).

The unprecedented speed of government intervention was eerily tied to a previous crisis by former Secretary of Homeland Security Michael Chertoff. In a January 14, 2009, interview at the Council of Foreign Relations, Secretary Chertoff stated:

> I was going to begin by recalling a fair day in the middle of a September during my time in office when there was a *cataclysmic event*. And as a consequence of that event, there were really *profound changes* in the way the American government operated. The executive took some steps—excuse me—that were in the view of some an unprecedented exercise of power and there's criticism for that. The legislature moved some major legislation and there's a little bit of buyer's remorse about that. There were all kinds of legal issues that were thrown up. There were mistakes that were made. There were claims that there *wasn't enough transparency* about what was going on. And you probably think I'm talking about September 11th, 2001, but I'm actually talking about September 15th, 2008—the financial crisis—because in the wake of the financial crisis, the fettering of Lehman and the *cascading meltdown*, you saw much of the same kind of vigorous government action, and some of the same criticism of that action, that occurred on September 11th, 2001 when the World Trade Center physically fell down instead of *financially fell* down. (Emphasis added)

In sum, the average citizen could trust the government to protect the public from the financial crisis and thereby contain the spread of toxic assets. The government was best suited to 'fix' the problem. This is clearly illustrated in Figure 20.3.

Fixing the 'toxic' asset problem becomes part of not only an antenarrative view of the future, but sets the problem (its living story) into a passage point, where the present and future are connected. In short, the antenarrative spiral prompts a shaping of both present and future, as fixing the toxic mess. Dave Granlund's Figure 20.3 gives a storyteller's image of the key role played by the government through Treasury Secretary Tim Geithner's safe handling of the "Fed Toxic Assets Plan." It is as if it were a source of harm and hazard to the entire population. In just a few cartoon lines and tones, this antenarrative crafts a span between past, present, and future,

Figure 20.3   Toxic waste solution. Used by permission from Dave Granlund.

reimagining narrative, living story, in a few associations crafting an inevitable antenarrative future (or so it seems). The antenarrative is not complicated, yet not linear, and not fully coherent (something most narrativists demand all storytelling to be). It nevertheless averts the reader's attention, calling upon it to fill in the blanks, to carry it to another level of completion, as a wedding of EPA imagery with banking reality. This underlying foundation facilitated the rapid public 'buy-in' to the crafted narrative.

DISCUSSION

With the ever-growing popularity of the terms 'toxic assets' or 'troubled assets,' a definition of assets must first be provided. The Financial Accounting Standards Board (FASB) in Statement of Financial Accounting Concepts (SFAC) 6, Elements of Financial Statements, defines assets as: "Assets are probable future economic benefits obtained or controlled by a particular entity as a result of past transactions or events." This value concept is not unique to the United States. The International Accounting Standards Board (IASB), in its conceptual framework of accounting, defines an asset as: "An asset is a resource controlled by the enterprise as a result of past events and from which future economic benefits are expected to flow to the enterprise." In other words, assets have some value.

Further, the FASB also defined liabilities as: "Liabilities are probable future sacrifices of economic benefits arising from present obligations of a particular entity to transfer assets or provide services to other entities in the future as a result of past transactions or events." In other words, liabilities represent financial obligations that must be satisfied with assets. For example, the asset 'cash' is used to extinguish the credit card liability. Interestingly, by definition, an asset cannot have a negative value or be construed as toxic. At best an asset has some value and at worst an asset has no value or is worthless. It would be absurd to even consider an asset with a negative value.

Frequency Distributions

The toxic asset spiral can be observed as the increasing popularity of the term 'toxic asset' morphed from the scripted antenarrative framed by the administration. We considered the terms 'troubled assets' and 'toxic assets' included in public narratives. Accordingly, we utilized the LexisNexis Academic Universe to search these terms in (1) Major U.S. and world publications, (2) news wire services, (3) TV and radio broadcast transcripts, (4) Web publications, and (5) legal. Given the media spectacle surrounding the September 2008 introduction of the TARP, our search dates began January 1, 2008, and ended December 31, 2009. Whereas the following frequency distributions are not meant to provide any empirical inference, they nevertheless suggest anecdotally that these terms gained prominence and have now become entrenched in the media as the upward spiral emerged.

The toxic ante cascaded into rapid acceptance as the toxic asset mess and the dangers posed to the public financial system had to be contained by the administration, which scripted the narrative. Consider that the term 'toxic asset' was practically unheard of until the recent financial crisis but now appears commonplace in the present business vernacular. The following frequency distribution for toxic assets found in our search illustrates the sudden prevalence of the term around the introduction of the TARP. This can be seen in Figure 20.4.

To continue, the term 'troubled assets' was likewise not commonplace until the recent financial crisis and now it too appears in the present business vernacular. The following frequency distribution for troubled assets found in our search also illustrates the sudden prevalence of the term around the introduction of the TARP. This can be seen in Figure 20.5.

The terms 'toxic assets' and 'troubled assets' are now present in business vernacular. The spiral of sudden media popularity seemingly coincided with the timing of the TARP. And while the sheer volume of stories containing these terms has since subsided, their present acceptance and widespread use is forever etched in financial discourse. Figures 20.4 and 20.5 provide a simple chronology of the sudden popularity of the terms 'toxic

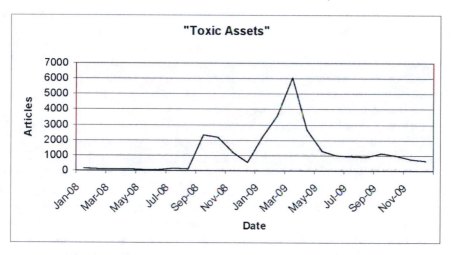

Figure 20.4　Articles that include toxic assets.

assets' and 'troubled assets,' whose genesis can be traced to the financial crisis antenarrative.

The crisis narrative framed by the administration required immediate acceptance and thus public buy-in; accordingly, providing transparent and lengthy explanations to inform the public may have slowed down the process and possibly derailed the TARP. Time was of the essence and the administration needed to quickly sell the scripted narrative. As a result, the toxic ante could legitimize to the public the need for swift and massive government action. The toxic assets that needed to be contained were nevertheless assets with some value. In fact, even if they had no value, were they truly toxic—and after all, what is toxic?

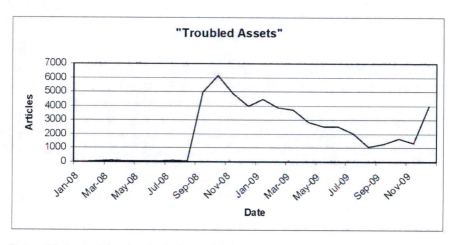

Figure 20.5　Articles that include troubled assets.

Interestingly, an understanding of these assets and the related toxic potential they posed to the financial system was seemingly not important. The assets most commonly referred to as toxic include collateralized debt obligations (CDOs) and mortgage-backed securities (MBSs). While there are other securities that may also be referred to as toxic, such as credit derivative swaps (CDSs), for illustrative purposes we will limit our discussion to the two most common as mentioned.

CDOs are simply packages or pools containing various loans bundled together in order to sell to investors. Rather than buy a specific loan, an investor will buy a share in a pool of loans. If the loans are collateralized, then each loan in the pool is backed by underlying collateral. In addition, the terms of the loans as well as the interest rates may vary accordingly. Thus, a bundle of collateralized loans could include short-term car loans and longer term business loans. While underlying collateral may contractually exist, some of the loans may actually default given the numerous original borrowers with different credit histories and the related credit risks involved. Further, the purpose of a bundled pool is to reduce the default risks. A few loans within the pool may go bad but the probability that all the loans will go bad is remote. The antenarrative scripted the TARP to purchase these toxic assets to prevent clogging the financial system. Rather than explaining some CDO pools may decline in value due to some bad loans, the toxic ante instead necessitated a $700 billion fund to immediately remove these toxic assets from the system and thereby contain their spread.

Next, MBSs are simply a group of mortgages originating from financial institutions that are subsequently bundled together. Similar to CDOs, packages or pools of mortgages are sold to investors. Rather than buy a specific mortgage an investor will buy a share in a pool of mortgage loans. Each mortgage in the pool is backed by underlying real estate serving as collateral. Like CDOs, the terms of the mortgage loans as well as the interest rates may vary accordingly. Also, similar to CDOs, some of the loans may actually default given the numerous original borrowers with different credit histories and related credit risks. The public was aware of the decline in real estate prices and the increase in foreclosures; however, there was still inherent value in the underlying real estate collateral. In other words, the loans were not all worthless because of real estate without any value. Yet, the antenarrative scripted the TARP to purchase these toxic assets caused by a weak real estate market. Toxic real estate would actually require real estate values beyond totally worthless. In fact, even if mortgages were in default, they were still secured by the underlying real estate collateral. As with CDOs, the toxic ante necessitated $700 billion to immediately remove these toxic assets from the system and thereby contain their spread.

In sum, while these assets deemed toxic may have diminished in value relative to the underlying securitization or pledged collateral, they nevertheless still had some inherent value. Recall that the definition of an asset can be thought of as something owned of value. Even if the value had been reduced to zero, we contend that the asset at worst may be worthless in value but certainly not toxic implying a negative value. The toxic ante has a negative implication requiring government intervention to quarantine and remove in order to prevent the spread of further contamination to other nontoxic assets. A toxic asset antenarrative ushered in the TARP interwoven in the downward spiral economy with the intervention fix creating the toxic asset spiral. Further, the toxicity has an indeterminate future destructive potential, one that invites a series of strange fixes (guarantees of executive bonus) within an assemblage of protections (save Wall Street at all costs). The parallel narrative of toxic assets to toxic waste is hazardous in the short run and beyond. We are left with more questions than answers. After the billions of TARP dollars are spent, the legacy of toxic assets remains engrained in our ever-changing narrative.

CONCLUSION

The defining moments in the trajectory of 'troubled asset' morphing into 'toxic asset' is embedded in the public's understanding of tropes of EPA super funds, as a way to address toxic waste, and protect the public from further contamination. In short, the administrative storytelling about TARP, and its amplification in the media, becomes a way the 'hazmat team' can reshape the future, and thereby change the course of history.

In this chapter we examined the recent financial crisis as presented by key government officials and the related response within the financial markets as the media stories unfolded. We further examined the expediency of legislation introduced as we contextualize the antecedent framing necessary to secure public buy-in. Key terms elucidated in our analysis include troubled assets; toxic assets; financial meltdown; and global financial crisis. Such inflammatory terminology may in fact serve to exacerbate fear and uncertainty throughout the public as confidence in the current financial system wanes. We thus consider the political rhetoric as we contextualize the framing of this crisis utilizing a narrative analysis. Our analysis suggests that antenarrative processes expedited agency, provoking unprecedented legislation that continues to shape future consequences.

The implications of our work can serve to elicit an explanation for the unprecedented and expeditious government intervention and relational understanding. We conclude that the antenarrative downward spiral of the economy was fitted with an antenarrative assemblage of 'toxic' and 'superfund' embedded meanings. These antenarrative spirals continue to intraplay. Their intraweaving is a strange sensemaking of the past, a way to change the sensemaking of living stories, and a prospective sensemaking with antenarrative momentum that becomes agential.

In this rhizomatic process, there is movement, force and counterforce, and generativity that ebbs and subsides. The agency of TARP and the antenarrative trajectory promises to tidy up an economic mess, to save investors and institutions from all toxic assets. No one stops to question the assemblage, whether an asset is actually toxic, or the instruments merely fraudulent. What if there is a different sideshadow, as Morson (1994) calls the one that is a spiral of possibility, where those perps are sent to jail. Future research can begin to come to terms with how antenarrative spirals operate, how they become primal agential forces, whirlwinds that shape futures, but are always more or less out of human control. We finally conclude with the need for further study and related extensions of our analysis.

REFERENCES

Boje, D. M. (2001). *Narrative methods for communication and organizational research*. London: Sage.
———. (2008). *Storytelling organizations*. London: Sage.
Bush, G. W. (2008, September). President Bush and President Uribe of the Republic of Colombia participate in joint press availability. Office of the Press Secretary. Retrieved March 14, 2010, from http://georgewbush-whitehouse.archives.gov/news/releases/2008/09
Chertoff, M. (2009, January). A conversation with Michael Chertoff. Council of Foreign Relations. Retrieved March 14, 2010, from http://www.cfr.org/publication/18251
Davis, J., & Riechmann, D. (2008, September). Bush team, Congress negotiate $700B bailout. Associated Press.
Environmental Protection Agency. (2010). *FY 2011 EPA budget in brief*. Retrieved March 14, 2010, from http://www.epa.gov/budget/2011/2011bib
Financial Accounting Standards Board. (2008). *Original pronouncements: Accounting standards*. Norwalk: CT, FASB.
H.R. 1424: Emergency Economic Stabilization Act of 2008, Govtrack.us. Retrieved January 9, 2009, from http://www.govtrack.us/congress/bill.xpd?bill=h110-1424
International Accounting Standards Board. (2006). *Conceptual framework*. Retrieved April 21, 2010, from http://www.iasplus.com/agenda/framework-b.htm
Levine, R. V. (2003). *The power of persuasion—How we're bought and sold*. Hoboken, NJ: John Wiley & Sons.
Morson, G. S. (1994). *Narrative and freedom: The shadows of time*. New Haven/London: Yale University Press.
Paulson, H. M. (2010). *On the brink*. New York: Business Plus.
Rose, G. (2001). *Visual methodologies: An introduction to the interpretation of visual materials*. London: Sage.
Wessel, D. (2009, June). Stench of toxic assets lingers. *The Wall Street Journal*, p. A2.

21 Well-Timed Stories
Rhetorical *Kairos* and Antenarrative Theory

Richard Herder

So how did a small band of immigrant workers pressure the largest fast-food company in the world to do something that could help transform these workers lives? NOW tells the David vs. Goliath story of a group of Florida tomato pickers that went toe to toe with a corporate giant and won. These workers fought an incredible four-year battle against Taco Bell and its parent company, Yum! Brands, to improve their working conditions and wages. Their success may have sparked a nationwide movement.

—David Brancaccio[1]

In this chapter I argue for a rapprochement between antenarrative and *kairos*, the rhetorical art of timing and location in relation to advantageous or decorous actions.[2] The benefit of such a move is that it allows us to provide a more comprehensive accounting of the speculative or 'wagering' dimension of antenarrative action by emphasizing how—by exploiting egregious gaps and contradictions in dominant narratives—marginalized storytellers can sometimes change the trajectory of organizations through time and space.[3] With this in mind, I begin by recounting highlights of an activist campaign, the Coalition of Immokalee Workers versus Taco Bell, in which a farmworkers coalition used *kairotic* storytelling techniques to convince a multinational corporation to reconfigure its purchasing policies. Following this I respond briefly to the critique of rhetoric put forward by Mikhail Bakhtin (an author whose work on dialogism has helped to shape Boje's views on antenarrative) and conduct a close reading of a key incident in the Taco Bell campaign. I conclude by weighing the benefits and limitations of a *kairotic* perspective for antenarrative theory and practice.

THE COALITION OF IMMOKALEE WORKERS' TACO BELL CAMPAIGN

The quotation at the start of this chapter is from a PBS television special about the CIW, a farmworkers' cooperative in Southwest Florida which, after a four-year battle, managed to convince Taco Bell Corporation and their parent company YUM! Brands to endorse their "Campaign for Fair Food" dedicated to improving wages and working conditions in commercial agriculture and to exposing instances of modern-day slavery.[4] How did the CIW, a group of perhaps two or three thousand immigrant farmworkers with, to say the least, modest financial and professional resources, manage to do this? In brief, they researched potential targets, held countless *encuentras* (open-ended, communal discussions) where they swapped stories and weighed their options, and they eventually settled on a plan to sponsor an anticorporate campaign to disclose how Taco Bell, a company which made millions selling Mexican fast food, had been quietly profiting from the oppression and enslavement of Hispanic and indigenous people in its organizational supply chain.[5] More to the point, they surveyed an organization, studied its narratives, identified potential weaknesses, and crafted stories designed to exploit the same. That is, the CIW made a storytelling wager; like the young King David, they gambled that by hitting a specific mark they could take down a more powerful foe.

Company executives were caught off guard by the accusations and complained they were being used as a 'stalking horse' in a conflict with growers.[6] Nonetheless, by the spring of 2005, the management team had had enough, and, in an agreement brokered through the Carter Center in Atlanta, agreed to all of the CIW's demands and called on other fast-food restaurants to do the same by endorsing the Campaign for Fair Food.[7] In subsequent years McDonald's, Burger King, Subway, and Whole Foods have signed onto the agreement.[8]

RAPPROCHEMENT: ANTENARRATIVE AND *KAIROS*

Antenarrative theory aims to account for the complexities of prenarrative speculation and is emphatically aligned with story rather than narrative. *Kairos* is traditionally thought of as referring to right timing and due measure in relation to rhetorical action. Moreover, both terms refer to ubiquitous communicative processes that elude precise definitions. In pre-Socratic rhetoric, *kairos* came to function as a sort of master term which, like *logos*, became difficult to pin down. At various times it has been taken to refer to 'profit,' 'moderation,' 'timing,' 'due measure,' and sensibilities about 'public decorum.'[9] Boje's work on antenarrative theory stays within a narrower range. Still, he discusses the concept in relation to a wide array of applied situations and theoretical concepts including storytelling speculation, stylistic strategy stories, and plurivocality. These last three categories, I maintain, constitute important points of intersection between *kairos* and antenarrative and highlight the similarities between the two. This is not to say the concepts are synonymous, only that they overlap in significant ways which, if explored, could advance theory and practice by providing a more detailed and nuanced accounting of how antenarrative speculation might influence the trajectory of organizational narratives while, at the same time, avoiding narrative subversion.

Storytelling Speculation

Boje defines the 'ante' portion of antenarrative as having to do with gambling, poker stakes, and horse racing.[10] In offering this definition he acknowledges his debt to Karl Weick's notions of retrospective and prospective sensemaking and to Alfred Schutz's concept of "coming to be."[11] Both authors evince an interest in how past experiences serve to shape expectations about the future.[12] Two aspects of Boje's analysis on storytelling speculation are of direct relevance to the relationship of antenarrative and *kairos*, the first being that both terms refer to intentional action as opposed to mechanical motion. The distinction is important because, as Kenneth Burke noted, "a billiard ball is neither moral nor immoral . . . it can only move or be moved."[13] That is, to the degree that antenarrative speculation has to do with intentional human action it will always have an ethical dimension. In antenarrative, however, moral agency is more clouded than it is in traditional accounts of *kairotic* action. This is because in antenarrative there is actually an entire swarm of speculative story strategies emerging at any given time. Any one or all of these stories are likely to employ *kairos,* but the sort of *kairotic* communicative action I am most interested in requires cooperative and decisive action that can be evaluated from an ethical perspective as a single action.

Even more important, antenarrative storytelling, like *kairotic* action, is 'chronotopic.'[14] Boje borrows the term from Bakhtin's concept of the 'chronotope'—the indissoluble intersection of space and time—in order to describe how speculative storytelling wagers might disrupt the future trajectory of narrative strategies.[15] What I want to notice here is that both antenarrative and *kairotic* actions disrupt chronotopic strategies. Put another way, they operate as challenges to what Deirdre McCloskey has called the "gnomic present"—the sense of time and authority invoked by the present tense use of the verb 'to be.'[16] Milton Friedman provided a memorable example of this rhetorical strategy with his famous line "The social responsibility of business *is* to increase its profits."[17] The word 'is' in this sentence serves to link corporate profitability (and ethics) to the supposedly pristine and eternal principles of liberal economics.[18] For the French thinker Michel de Certeau, *kairos* and the related concept of *métis* (cleverness) are the two indispensable factors in any effort to disrupt strategies of this sort that come to dominate time and space. Moreover, de Certeau treats any such disruptions as storytelling tactics where narrators use fragments of the past to break through a sedimented present tense. When successful, these techniques constitute the 'triumph of place over time' and open 'multiple paths of the future.'[19] This is not to say the techniques are simple. In de Certeau's analyses one encounters a mélange of actions where story and rhetoric, cleverness and *kairos*, time and space can become impossibly tangled—constituting a nest of difficulties that can frustrate theorists, but which storytelling 'pedestrians' often manage to negotiate in nimble ways on a daily basis in order to 'continually turn to their own ends forces alien to them.'[20]

Significantly, de Certeau's analysis goes a step beyond Boje's description of antenarrative storytelling by describing two types of tactical, storied resistance to sedimented narrative strategies. The first is a type of dispersed, plurivocal micro-resistance that serves "to introduce Brownian movement into the system."[21] This is the mode of action in the "walking rhetorics" of de Certeau's famous chapter Walking in the City where pedestrians learn to improvise new paths as readily as "Charlie Chaplin multiplies the possibilities of his cane."[22] In this mode of tactical resistance, change occurs gradually over extended time as logics of resistance 'insinuate' themselves into dominant strategies in such a way that the powerful come to believe the new ideas were a result of their own reflection.[23]

De Certeau labels the second set of tactics 'Storytime,' described as the tactical uses of accumulated memories to produce sudden interruptions in the 'equilibria' of time and space.[24] It is in this context (that is, in the carefully planned disruptions of status quo strategies) where *kairos* intersects most obviously with the 'ante' portion of antenarrative theory. Antenarrative may be unfinished, plurivocal, and speculative, but to the degree that it resembles 'a wager made on a horse,' it can also be decisive.[25] In de Certeau's chapter on Storytime one gets a sense of what the sort of wagering Boje has in mind might look like in applied practice. Two elements of the chapter are of special importance: patience and efficiency. Taken together they recall Deborah Hawhee's argument that at the intersection of kairos with *métis*, "*chronos* measures duration where *kairos* marks force."[26] Put another way, in *kairotic* storytime, narrators must often bide their time waiting for an appropriate moment when the accumulated force of memory stands the greatest chance of mounting a 'coup.'[27] As this implies, *kairotic* storytime tactics operate on the assumption that if one waits long enough, dominant strategies will always reveal a weakness—some gap in the armor that affords story a fleeting but significant opportunity. When storytellers exploit these opportunities proficiently—that is, when they hit the necessary mark at the right time—sudden inversions of attitudes and expectations become possible. "The structure of the miracle has a similar form."[28]

If I am reading Boje correctly, his conception of antenarrative, speculation, resembles de Certeau's model of Brownian motion, but sidesteps the more decisive action of the story-time wager. This does not mean he has avoided becoming entangled with *kairos*. This is because, quite simply, *kairos* is ubiquitous. In any discussion of speculative storytelling practices it is unavoidable. This becomes apparent when one looks at two examples from Boje's recent work on antenarrative storytelling. The first is his description of the "Rabelaisian purge . . . a grotesque method using laughter to degrade, debase, and descend and then to renew, rejuvenate, and redeem."[29] We can find an example of this sort of storytelling action in Bakhtin's essay on games playing in the works of François Rabelais where he describes the corpulent, corrupt Judge Bridlegoose, who renders decisions by casting dice.[30] By presenting a laughable but, in several respects, deadly accurate parody of a corrupt medieval judge, Rabelais 'clears the bench,' so to speak, to allow his audience to imagine a different sort of justice that shares in the integrity of living story and encourages legitimate speculation about future trajectories. Rabelais's description of the judge counts as a type of micro-resistance because the narrator presents no immediate demand for action and because the incident is but one of many related inversions in a carnivalesque tableau. At the same time, the parody counts as *kairotic* as it provides a clever and (for medieval audiences) readily recognizable caricature of a dishonest judge. Boje comes closer to de Certeau's *kairotic* story-time tactics in passages on 'polyphonic story strategies' and 'strategy narrative forensics,' where he describes a plurivocal and investigative process bearing a striking resemblance to the radically democratic strategy development sessions of the CIW.[31] What's more, as happened with the CIW, in Boje's description members of the organization participate on an egalitarian basis in an investigative process where they "look in between the lines for clues of omission."[32] The limitation of the analysis is that the investigation never draws to a point of decision, and one lacks a sense of the 'ante.' The analysis is not wrong. In truth, it strikes me as an important accounting of the sort of unrestricted discourse one would hope to see in organizations that take storytelling seriously. That said, from a *kairotic* perspective it is incomplete. The participants survey the field, but never place a bet on any one horse.

Stylistic Strategy Stories

Boje defines "stylistic story strategies" as the "juxtaposition of varied styles for image management."[33] He goes on to provide the example of McDonald's Corporation and its coining of the word 'McStyle' to describe its development of a variety of architectural styles in keeping with the aesthetic sensibilities of French culture. Two aspects of this explanation are important to an understanding of the relationship of antenarrative and *kairos*. First, once again, in this passage Boje's direct concern is with describing strategies of control. That is, he is discussing the centripetal side of Bakhtinian dialogism. Second, in this passage he carries the discussion to territory in which rhetoricians feel at home. For a discipline still struggling to recover from a hostile reduction to 'mere style' during the Middle Ages, the relationship of style and organizational strategies can appear self-evident.[34] Manipulation through ornamentation? You have our attention. Once again, though, a *kairotic* perspective demands a more expanded view of the practices in question. 'McStyle' is undoubtedly strategic, but so are the many other elements of style one encounters in organizational discourse from the cut of a CEO's suit to the clever turns of phrase one overhears at a holiday cocktail party. McStyle is not only about strategic manipulation through ornamentation; it is about maintaining a credible and appealing public face in keeping with the ethical and aesthetic sensibilities of the *zeitgeist.*

It is not difficult to find relevant examples from classical and contemporary rhetoric studies regarding the strategic dimensions of decorum. John Poulakos makes clear decorum figured prominently in early, sophistic notions of *kairos.*[35] By the time of Cicero, decorum (*to prepon*) had acquired a more disciplinary sense and was understood as "the universal rule in oratory as in life . . . to consider propriety."[36] One of the most influential accounts of decorum in contemporary rhetoric is Robert Hariman's description of the disciplinary dimensions of style in the court of Emperor Haile Selassie.[37] McCloskey carries the discussion of style into the realm of economics, and in so doing she provides a bridge to storytelling and organizational studies by positing "a rhetoric of stories will watch the words closely."[38] And Bruce Turpin follows McCloskey's lead by providing a detailed accounting of the role of decorum in the primary works of Adam Smith and Milton Friedman.[39] Turpin's work is especially important in this context because, by documenting how the language of praise and blame serves a disciplinary function in liberal economies, he suggests a role for *kairotic* resistance. Business executives are unlikely to change behaviors simply because they have been praised or blamed in public. Success depends on an artistic matching of insults, commendations, and public deeds.

Plurivocality

For Boje, antenarrative is about "the Tamara of storytelling" and about "the plurivocal interpretation of stories in a distributed and historically contextualized meaning network."[40] He borrows the basic idea from a stage play in which the story unfolds before a walking audience capable of tracing aspects of the dramatic action from a variety of angles. In Tamara storytelling, as with Heidegger's description of *aletheia* and William James's account of pragmatism, all observation and narration is situated and idiosyncratic.[41] For his part, Boje emphasizes the plebian circulation of living stories in opposition to managerial monological narration. In doing this he aligns himself with Bakhtinian dialogism—the contest between centrifugal heteroglossia and the centripetal force of homogenizing authority.[42] And it is at this point where any efforts to reconcile *kairos* and antenarrative theory are most likely to founder. This is primarily because Bakhtin, for reasons I will discuss in more detail shortly, perceived rhetoric as aligned with dialectic and centripetal authority.

For now, what I want to stress is that *kairos*, like antenarrative, has plebian credentials. This is because, as de Certeau explains, *kairos* (along with its near twin *métis*) are fundamental elements of a tradition of storied resistance that can be traced back as far as the pre-Socratic mythical figure of Corax (alternatively, a raven or the mythical founder of rhetoric).[43] Corax and his student Tisias, as de Certeau notes, are remembered for teaching people how to make the "weaker argument the better."[44] Critics of rhetoric such as Plato viewed this sort of thinking as corrosive to social order and as providing tacit justifications for arguments about a fickle and dyspeptic public prone to falling under the spell of articulate, self-serving rhetors.[45] When we look beyond Athens, however, it becomes immediately apparent that the ideas about social and argumentative inversion Plato found so frightening are ubiquitous themes in world literature. The Native American tales about the tricks of Kokopelli, and European 'fairy tales' like *The Emperor's New Clothes* and *Cinderella*, which feature dramatic social reversals, are hardly exceptional.[46] The techniques of Corax and other calculating storytellers of his kind have remained important in any context where people develop an interest in challenging "the exorbitant claim that *a certain kind* of production (real enough, but not the only kind) can set out to produce history by 'informing' the whole of a country."[47] To summarize, *kairos*, in at least one prominent strand of its complex history, shares the plebian and plurivocal sensibilities of antenarrative.[48]

Moreover, the plurivocality theme suggests yet one more striking similarity between *kairotic* and antenarrative practices: embodied intuition. For Boje, story and antenarrative are held out as living, local, and fully embodied. The latter is a theme that emerges in his more recent work, perhaps in response to Grace Ann Rosile's description of 'horse sense'—defined roughly as "body to body energy connections."[49] Especially in the passages of *Storytelling Organization* where Boje references these sorts of intuitive, embodied sensibilities about storytelling one finds intriguing parallels to classical conceptions of rhetorical *kairos*. The iconoclastic rhetorics of Corax, of the Sophists, and of the pedestrians who traverse de Certeau's urban landscapes all participate in what Deborah Hawhee has called a set of 'bodily arts.' In each case iconoclastic rhetors act on intuitive sensibilities that are difficult to articulate but which are born of long and intimate association with context.[50]

Several important themes converge in this last analysis, making it possible to recognize the relationship of speculation, decorum, and plurivocality in *kairotic* resistance. No one knows more than the servants how forks, plates, and dinner guests must be arranged for any given occasion in the master's house. When afforded this level of intimacy, those who have been effectively erased as subjects from dominant narratives are in a position to present testimonies about their experience of material discipline which, if recounted in a timely and compelling manner, stand a good chance of tripping up the powerful when they least expect it.

At this juncture one might wonder why—if *kairos* and antenarrative share such striking similarities—there has not been a long-standing conversation between rhetoric and management studies on the subject. The primary reason, I contend, is that, generally speaking, *kairos* is about winning. And winning requires closure. In so doing, it imposes plot and narrative coherence onto the flow of storied experience. The risk in such a process is that living stories will be swallowed up into monovocal and authoritative narratives. All *kairotic* action demands some degree of closure. This is a necessary condition of any formal wager. One places a chip on a particular spot and risks winning or losing. As I noted earlier, the 'story-time' *kairotic* action I have in mind raises the stakes by including cooperative betting in which an entire community casts its lot as one. His own definition of antenarrative aside, Boje would be justified in having reservations about the legitimacy of this sort of storytelling speculation. To understand why this is so will require a brief consideration of Bakhtin's objection to rhetoric.

BAKHTIN AND RHETORIC

The great value of the novel, Bakhtin believed, was that it could absorb the epic while the epic could not absorb the novel and retain its integrity as a genre.[51] In rejecting rhetoric as an aspect of dialogism he aimed to insure that it would not swallow up dialogism in the same manner that epic fossilized the living dynamism of early myths. His concerns were justified. As John Murphy has argued, rhetoric studies has had to learn to face the obvious: "Mikhail Bakhtin did not like rhetoric," and this was not due to ignorance or misapprehension.[52] Bakhtin understood "rhetoric shares blood with the novel," but this provided him with all the more reason to insist on treating dialogism as a "radically distinct" mode of discourse.[53] Given his familiarity with classical and medieval rhetoric, he felt justified in shifting the burden of proof. In effect, if rhetoric was to be allowed entry into the house of dialogism, it must be on a case-by-case basis and only then on the condition it explain why its tools would not serve to domesticate living stories and homogenize the future.[54] I hear echoes of these objections in Boje's summation of dialogism where he writes it is "neither dialogue . . . nor dialectics . . . this is quite definite."[55] I suggest honoring these sentiments. "Good fences make good neighbors."[56] Rather than attempting some sort of disingenuous move to 'defang' rhetoric or patronize dialogism, I think it is better to debate the issues straight up and present a case for why, in any given situation, other disciplines ought to pay attention to aspects of rhetoric—and more precisely—why antenarrative might be able to accommodate *kairos* without compromising the integrity of living stories.

In sum, by placing *kairos* and antenarrative in conversation with one another, one can provide a more complete accounting of three dimensions of antenarrative action: speculation, stylistics, and polyvocality. However, it remains to be seen how these dynamics play out in the applied context of the CIW's Taco Bell campaign and, more importantly, how a storytelling organization might utilize *kairotic* tactics while retaining the plurivocal integrity of living story.

KAIROS AND STORY TIME IN THE TACO BELL CAMPAIGN

The history of the CIW is undeniably gripping. A coalition of primarily Mexican, Guatemalan, and Haitian migrant laborers from a small town in South Florida, working in conjunction with an informal collection of student and church-based organizations, conducts independent investigations into modern-day slavery and then uses the results to call the world's largest purveyor of fast food to account.[57] No doubt, a primary reason the story has garnered the attention of journalists and audiences around the globe is that it presents an anachronistic moral conundrum.[58] Never mind that there were likely more slaves being trafficked around the globe in 2009 than there were in 1809;[59] the presence of people laboring at gunpoint on commercial farms only a short drive from the million-dollar condominiums of Naples or Miami Beach disrupts popular narratives about human progress and freedom and raises important questions about the ethical relationship of management and periphery. That is, were the slaves in Immokalee part of the Taco Bell "system"? Even if one concludes they were not, does this mean the company had no moral obligation to address their situation? More to the point, in their Taco Bell campaign the CIW worked these ambiguities to their own advantage and, in the process, provided memorable examples of how antenarrative storytelling speculation can incorporate decisive *kairotic* tactics without sacrificing its living, dynamic integrity. In what follows I develop this latter theme in relation to three incidents from the CIW campaign: their communal planning strategies; their decision to highlight the evangelicalism of CEO David Novak; and their staging of events in the neighborhoods where members of the management team lived with their families.

Plurivocal Strategy Development

The CIW was founded in the mid-1990s following an incident on a hot summer day when a young farmworker was beaten nearly to death after asking his supervisor if he could leave the field to get a drink of water.[60] The group struggled for several years to convince Florida growers to increase wages and improve working conditions.[61] By 1999 they had begun to look for alternative ways to air their grievances and in their research ran across an article in the industry publication *The Packer* describing Taco Bell Corporation as a major purchaser of tomatoes from commercial farms in the Immokalee area.[62] The coalition was struck by the irony of Mexican laborers picking vegetables for a company trading on Mexican culture and, as I explained earlier, began to hold prolonged, radically open community discussions where they worked out the strategies for the campaign. In the end, they developed a plan that appeared hopelessly quixotic. They decided to make a series of cross-country journeys to Taco Bell's corporate head-quarters in Irvine, California, where they hoped to present their case to the management team in person. Their demands were modest. They asked the company to pay one penny more per pound for tomatoes with the extra money bypassing the supply chain and being paid directly to tomato pickers. The CIW proposal would, in effect, double the wages for workers who had not seen a raise since the mid-1970s.[63]

Of course, the most dramatic aspect of the campaign involved allegations of slavery. By drawing attention to the secretive, daily dehumanization of workers on some commercial farms in Florida, the coalition prompted a portion of the public to begin to associate Taco Bell with slavery. The company management team felt blindsided by the CIW's claim that they were profiting from modern-day slavery. In fact, Jonathan Blum, CEO of Taco Bell at the start of the campaign, has never wavered on his claim that management was entirely unaware of human trafficking activities in Florida agriculture.[64] Of course, to say they were ignorant is not the same as saying they had no ethical responsibility. Nevertheless, Blum's claim is credible. The slavery operations in question operated on remote farms in the Florida Everglades, nearly 2,000 miles distant from the corporate offices. More-over, management was insulated from the situation by multiple layers of contractual agreements and legal precedents. Viewed from these remote distances, the slaves of south Florida became ciphers on the corporate led-gers—embodied instances of the corporation's "terministic screen."[65]

The crucial factor to notice in this context is how the CIW's actions resemble de Certeau's accounting of *kairotic* story-time, tactics. The cam-paign constitutes a "whodunit form in which the past, by coming back, overturns an established hierarchical order: '*He* must be the murder, then!'"[66] In more straightforward terms, all of the elements of the form are present. A marginalized group of people waits patiently for an opportune moment to use accumulated memory in order to upset a hierarchy that had, for all practical purposes, forgotten they existed. In this sense the Taco Bell campaign constitutes a paradigm example of 'pedestrians' learn-ing to channel the force of 'rambling, wily everyday stories' in order to upset a hostile present and to affect the future trajectory of an organization through time and space.[67]

PUBLIC DECORUM

Midway through the Taco Bell campaign, the company was purchased by Yum! Brands, the world's largest fast-food corporation. Soon after, Taco Bell moved its corporate offices to the YUM! corporate headquarters in Louisville, Kentucky. The move had several important implications for the campaign; one of the most important, it turned out, was that they gained more direct access to YUM! Brands CEO David Novak. In 2004, Novak, who is an evangelical Christian, was a featured participant in a panel discussion at a corporate leadership conference named, memorably, the "Lead Like Jesus Celebration."[68] The coalition and its allies did not have to do a great deal of research to figure out that Mr. Novak, whether he recognized it or not, was highly vulnerable to charges of religious hypocrisy.

The theme of the Lead like Jesus conference provided the coalition with an opportunity to highlight a dramatic incongruity in ethical performance with great specificity. In the fall of 2004, political columnist Sarah Posner wrote a blog posting entitled *Leading like Jesus* that the CIW later featured on its Web site.[69] In the posting, Posner highlights an apparent contradiction between Novak's participation in the conference and YUM! Brands' corporate policies. She begins by asking, "So how, exactly, does Novak lead like Jesus? Let's take a look." She then goes on to contrast Novak's $8.8 million annual salary with the 'poverty level' wages of the farmworkers and asks why he would take an obdurate stand against an organization fighting slavery, but pull company ads immediately when he received complaints about their placement on the racy evening soap opera *Desperate Housewives*. "That leadership must be A-OK with Jesus," Posner concluded, "just like involuntary servitude is good for the company's bottom line. But fictional depictions of sex, murder, and dysfunctional families? Unacceptable."[70] In effect, Posner helped the CIW make an argument that Novak could not claim to be a devout Christian business leader on the one hand and a profit-driven CEO willing even to overlook instances of modern-day slavery on the other.

Because Novak was participating in a religious event, he was fully exposed to criticism, and on one of the most pernicious and troubling of issues—chattel slavery. Two centuries earlier, a group of pious Christian abolitionists in England helped bring an end to the highly profitable slave trade in the British Empire by arguing the practice—no matter how much money it generated—was fundamentally un-Christian.[71] Mr. Novak fared no better against the modern-day abolitionists of the CIW than many 19th century business people did when confronted by people like William Wilberforce. Posner built a case for Novak's hypocrisy, but the coalition had been leveling the same sorts of accusations at public protest events. For anyone familiar with Christianity and Western history, the contradiction between Novak's religious stance and modern-day agricultural slavery is likely to appear self-evident. But that is the point. The language of praise and blame requires a leverage point in popular sentiment—among those things that have come to pass for common sense. Moreover, if activists are to exploit these sorts of contradictions between corporate practices and popular attitudes, they must be able to level an accusation at the proper time and in the proper manner so as to achieve maximum effect. Put another way, by identifying and exploiting Novak's 'Achilles' heel,' the farm workers of the CIW demonstrated their mastery of antenarrative action and of time-honored *kairotic* tactics.

Going Local and Plurivocal

Because Louisville, Kentucky, is a deeply religious community and a hub of action for the Presbyterian Church USA, the coalition had little difficulty gaining the cooperation of a few progressively minded church leaders and seminarians in identifying local churches and schools where they could make presentations about working conditions in Florida agriculture.[72] The great benefit of the strategy was that it allowed the CIW to take their campaign to the very neighborhoods where company employees lived with their families.[73] Executives of multinational corporations are not accustomed to fielding questions at the church fish fry, the family dinner table, or the local country club about their company's stance on human slavery. We can probably never know for sure how often these sorts of discomfiting conversations actually took place. Regardless, the strategy forced Jonathan Blum and other members of the YUM! management team to shift their perspective on the Taco Bell campaign from the corporate 'we' to the personal 'I.' By the spring of 2005, the CIW was, in effect, asking executives to explain—before their friends and families—how they were *not* profiting from the misery of others.

As I explained earlier, both antenarrative and *kairos* have plebian histories. They can be wild, impious, dissonant, and difficult to control. And in the CIW's neighbor-to-neighbor strategies in Louisville it becomes difficult if not impossible to disentangle the two practices. Moreover, Boje provides an uncanny description of the tactical logic of the campaign when he writes:

> The implication of the "story turn" is that the important interaction among storytellers is at the local level. At the local level, telling is communicative interaction in ways that are self-organizing emergent processes. However, there is still "story control" going on . . . There is a merger without the imposition of narrative control from the top (or center), such as by a managerial list group.[74]

It was this sort of local, improvised but *kairotic* storytelling that was on display in the neighborhoods of Louisville in the closing months of the Taco Bell campaign. Obviously, the tactics were embedded within a larger campaign strategy, but that strategy was plurivocal and participatory from beginning to end.

CONCLUSION

I have argued for a rapprochement between antenarrative and rhetorical *kairos* on the grounds that a careful melding of the two can provide a richer, more nuanced accounting of the speculative, future-oriented dimension of antenarrative theory and practice. Boje's description of antenarrative is similar to *kairotic* rhetorical tactics in its approach to storytelling speculation and the disciplinary dimensions of localized stylistic sensibilities, and in its focus on plurivocal communication. One finds support for this view in de Certeau's comprehensive and rhetorically grounded accounting of how 'pedestrians' have historically used storytelling tactics to disrupt and reorient the trajectories of narrative strategies. My description of *kairotic* antenarratives follows his analysis closely by assuming that storytellers must possess an intuitive understanding of local conditions in order to be able to capitalize on fleeting opportunities and brief openings in dominant narrative strategies.

This is not to say that storytellers ever act alone or, more precisely, that storytelling could ever be truly 'monovocal.' To the contrary, storytellers hone their *kairotic*, antenarrative abilities in localized conversations with their friends, neighbors, customers, and managers. But they are not restricted to this level. Sometimes storytellers rise up and speak, with legitimacy, for their communities in order to open novel pathways to the future.

As I have argued throughout, antenarrative and *kairos* are inextricably linked at a fundamental level, and yet a conscious merger of the two in tactical 'story-time' action presents significant risks. The trick lies in finding ways of preventing temporary 'plot' formations from solidifying into homogeneous, centripetal order. Boje argues our only genuine hope for arresting these gestures is to "make the political economies of strategy more visible."[75] He is right, of course, but I contend this line of argument leads directly to the wily techniques of *kairos*—a felicitous tradition for antenarrative wagers. If the colonizing, centrifugal force of narrative constitutes a serious threat to the vibrancy of story, then it seems prudent that when—through *kairotic*, storied action—a group is able to force narrative powers to lay their 'cards face up on the table,' one would be remiss not to examine them.[76] As Murphy has observed, in situations such as those we can imagine that perhaps "Lighting his cigarette with a laugh, leaning back in his chair, Bakhtin might well reflect upon the accuracy of his observations. After all, if rhetoricians can use his words, then the centrifugal force of language is beyond even his imaginings."[77]

NOTES

1. David Brancaccio, *The Battle Fields: The Coalition of Immokalee Workers vs. Taco Bell* (Public Broadcasting Service, 27 May 2005).
2. Gregory Mason, "In Praise of Kairos in the Arts: Critical Time, East and West," in *Rhetoric and Kairos: Essays in History, Theory, and Praxis*, ed. Phillip Sipiora and James S. Baumlin (Albany, NY: State University of New York Press, 2002), p. 199; Wolfgang G. Müller, "Style," in *Encyclopedia of Rhetoric*, ed. Thomas O. Sloane (New York: Oxford University Press, 2001), pp. 745–757.
3. I develop these ideas in greater detail in my ongoing PhD dissertation work on the rhetoric of anticorporate protest. My work in this area is indebted to M. Lane Bruner's studies on strategies of remembrance. M. Lane Bruner,

Strategies of Remembrance: The Rhetorical Dimensions of Identity Construction (Columbia, SC: University of South Carolina Press, 2002).

4. David Brancaccio, *The Battle Fields*; "Campaign Analysis: CIW Campaign for Fair Food & SFA 'Dine with Dignity' Food Service Campaign," sfalliance. org, August 2009, http://www.sfalliance.org/.

5. John Bowe provides a comprehensive and compelling account of the early days of the Taco Bell campaign in the first chapter of his book *Nobodies*. John Bowe, *Nobodies: Modern American Slave Labor and the Dark Side of the New Global Economy* (New York: Random House, 2007), pp. 1–78.

6. David Goetz, "Tomato campaign will march to Yum: Farmworkers protest wages, conditions," *Louisville Courier-Cournal*, February 27, 2005.

7. Amy Bennett Williams, "Whole Foods Agrees to Pay Immokalee Tomato Workers More," *Fort Myers News Press*, September 9, 2008; "Student/ Farmworker Alliance," March 1, 2008, http://www.sfalliance.org/.

8. Williams, "Whole Foods"; John Lantigua, "McDonald's Agrees to Increase Pay for Workers Who Harvest Its Tomatoes," *Palm Beach Post*, April 10, 2007, http://www.palmbeachpost.com/business/content/business/ epaper/2007/04/10/m1a_tomatoes_0410.html; Andrew Martin, "Burger King Grants Raise to Pickers," *New York Times*, May 24, 2008; "Subway to Pay More for Tomatoes," *Miami Herald*, December 2, 2008.

9. Phillip Sipiora, "Introduction: The Ancient Concept of Kairos," in *Rhetoric and Kairos* (Albany, NY: State University of New York Press, 2002), p. 1.

10. David M. Boje, *Narrative Methods* (London: Sage, 2001), p. 1.

11. Ibid., pp. 3 and 119.

12. Alfred Schutz, *Reflections on the Problem of Relevance* (Yale University Press, 1970), p. 39; Karl E. Weick, *Sensemaking in Organizations* (London: Sage, 1995), p. 25.

13. Kenneth Burke, *A Grammar of Motives* (New York: Prentice-Hall, 1945), p. 136.

14. David M. Boje, *Storytelling Organization* (Thousand Oaks, CA: Sage, 2008), pp. 138–154.

15. Ibid., pp. 13–14, 75–96, and 138–154.

16. Deirdre N. McCloskey, *The Rhetoric of Economics* (Madison, WI: University of Wisconsin Press, 1998), p. 11.

17. Milton Friedman, "The Social Responsibility of Business Is to Increase its Profits," *New York Times Magazine*, September 13, 1970, p. 32.

18. Frederic Jameson provides an alternative perspective on the freezing of time in his description of postmodernism as the emergence of a digitally synchronized and politically apathetic perpetual present tense. Frederic Jameson, "Postmodernism and Consumer Society," in *The Anti-Aesthetic: Essays on Postmodern Culture* (New York: The New York Press, 1983), pp. 111–125.

19. Michel de Certeau, Michel, *The Practice of Everyday Life* (Berkeley, CA: University of California Press, 1984), p. 36.

20. Ibid., p. xix.

21. Ibid., p. xx.

22. Ibid., pp. 100 and 98.

23. Ibid., p. xi.

24. Ibid., pp. 77–84.

25. Boje, *Narrative Methods*, p. 2.

26. Deborah Hawhee, *Bodily Arts: Rhetoric and Athletics in Ancient Greece* (Austin, TX: University of Texas Press, 2005), p. 66.

27. de Certeau, Michel, *The Practice of Everyday Life*, p. 85.

28. Ibid.

29. Boje, *Storytelling Organization*, p. 152.

30. Mikhail M. Bakhtin, "The Role of Games in Rabelais," *Yale French Studies,, 41* (1968). 131–132.
31. Boje, *Storytelling Organization*, p. 104.
32. Ibid., pp. 99 & 102.
33. Ibid., p. 123.
34. Müller, "Style," p. 748.
35. John Poulakos, "Toward a Sophistic Definition of Rhetoric," *Philosophy & Rhetoric*, 16(1) (1983), p. 41.
36. Cicero, *Orator*, trans. Hubbell, H. M. (Cambridge, MA: Harvard University Press, 1962), p. 359.
37. Robert Hariman, "Decorum, Power, and the Courtly Style," *Quarterly Journal of Speech*, 78(2) (1992), p. 149.
38. Deirdre McCloskey, *If You're So Smart: The Narrative of Economic Expertise* (Chicago: University of Chicago Press, 1992), p. 61.
39. Paul Bruce Turpin, "Liberal Political Economy and Justice: Character and Decorum in the Economic Arguments of Adam Smith and Milton Friedman" (University of Southern California, 2005).
40. Boje, *Narrative Methods*, p. 4.
41. Boje, *Narrative Methods*, p. 4; Martin Heidegger, *Basic Writings*, ed. David Farrell Krell (London: Taylor & Francis, 1978), pp. 293–294; James, William, *Pragmatism*, ed. Kublick, Bruce (Indianapolis: Hackett Publishing Co., 1981), p. 25. In the latter I am thinking particularly of James's account of a variety of perspectives on the sighting of a squirrel and of the squirrel's sighting of its human observers!
42. Boje, *Storytelling Organization*, p. 22.
43. Janet M. Atwill, *Rhetoric Reclaimed: Aristotle and the Liberal Arts Tradition* (Ithaca, NY: Cornell University Press, 1998); Debra Hawhee, *Bodily Arts*; Stephen Olbrys-Gencarella, "The Myth of Rhetoric: Korax and the Art of Pollution," *Rhetoric Society Quarterly*, 37(3) (2007), pp. 251–273.
44. De Certeau, Michel, *The Practice of Everyday Life*, p. 38.
45. George A. Kennedy, *A New History of Classical Rhetoric* (Princeton, NJ: Princeton University Press, 1994); Plato, *Gorgias* (New York: Oxford University Press, 1998).
46. Ekkehart Malotki, *Kokopelli: The Making of an Icon* (Lincoln: University of Nebraska Press, 2004).
47. De Certeau, Michel, *The Practice of Everyday Life*, p. 167.
48. Ibid., p. v. See de Certeau's dedication "To the ordinary man [sic]" in *The Practice of Everyday Life* ,where he lauds a "common hero, an ubiquitous character . . . very ancient . . . the murmuring voice of societies [who now act in opposition to] a mobile language of computations and rationalities that belong to no one."
49. Boje, *Storytelling Organization*, p. 18.
50. Hawhee, *Bodily Arts*, p. 70.
51. Mikhail M. Bakhtin, "Epic and Novel: Toward a Methodology for the Study of the Novel," in *The Dialogic Imagination: Four Essays by M. M. Bakhtin* (Austin: University of Texas Press, 1981), pp. 3–40.
52. Murphy is but one of several authors, including Mary Frances Hopkins, M. Lane Bruner, and James Jasinski, who have, to varying degrees, appropriated the analytic tools of Bakhtin's dialogism for use in rhetoric studies. M. Lane Bruner, "Carnivalesque Protest and the Humorless State," *Text & Performance Quarterly*, 25(2) (2005), 136–155; Mary Frances Hopkins, "The Rhetoric of Heteroglossia in Flannery O'Connor's Wise Blood," *Quarterly Journal of Speech*, 75(2) (1989), 198–211; John M. Murphy, "Mikhail Bakhtin and the Rhetorical Tradition," Quarterly Journal of Speech, 87(3)

(2001), 259; James Jasinski, "Heteroglossia, Polyphony, and The Federalist Papers," *RSQ: Rhetoric Society Quarterly,* 27(1) (1997), pp. 23–46.

53. Murphy, p. 275.
54. Bakhtin, Mikhail M., *The Dialogic Imagination: Four Essays* (Austin: University of Texas Press, 2004), passim.
55. Boje, *Storytelling Organization,* p. 72.
56. Robert Frost, *The Poetry of Robert Frost* (Holt Paperbacks, 2002), p. 36.
57. Bowe, *Nobodies,* pp. 1–78.
58. Duncan Campbell, "Taco's Tomato Pickers on Slave Wages," *The Guardian,* March 17, 2003; David Crary, "Human Trafficking in U.S. Poses Elusive Target for Coalition Trying to Combat It" (AP World Stream, October 30, 2005); "Modern Forms of Slavery in Industrialized Countries," *International Labour Organization,* May 11, 2005, http://www.ilo.org; "Slave Traders Jailed for 12 Years," *Sydney Morning Herald,* November 21, 2002.
59. Kevin Bales, *Ending Slavery: How We Free Today's Slaves* (Berkeley: University of California Press, 2007), pp. 10–19; Kevin Bales, Laurel E. Fletcher, and Eric Stover, "Hidden Slaves: Forced Labor in the United States," *Berkeley Journal of International Law,* 23(47) (2005), pp. 47–48.
60. Bowe, *Nobodies,* p. 27.
61. "The Taco Bell Boycott—A Short History," *The Witherspoon Society,* February 18, 2004, http://www.witherspoonsociety.org/2004/taco_bell_background.htm.
62. Bowe, p. 51.
63. Eric Schlosser, "A Side Order of Human Rights," *The New York Times,* April 6, 2005.
64. Jonathan Blum, "Testimony of Jonathan Blum - Chief Public Affairs Officer, Senior Vice President, YUM! Brands, Inc. to the Senate Committee on Health, Education, Labor, and Pensions: Hearing on Ending Abuses and Improving Working Conditions for Tomato Workers." Committee on Health, Education, Labor, and Pensions: United States Senate, 2008.
65. Kenneth Burke, "Terministic Screens," in *Language as Symbolic Action: Essays on Life, Literature, and Method* (Berkeley, California: University of California Press, 1966), 44-62.
66. de Certeau, Michel, *The Practice of Everyday Life,* p. 85.
67. Ibid., p. 89.
68. Bill Wolfe, "Seminar Will Stress Christ-Centered Leadership: 4,000 Expected at Southeast Church," *The Courier-Journal,* November 17, 2004.
69. "New Article Slams Yum Brands, Yum CEO David Novak!," Coalition of Immokalee Workers, 2005, http://www.ciw-online.org/2004-05news.html.
70. Sarah Posner, "Leading Like Jesus," Campaign for Labor Rights, December 13, 2004, http://www.clrlabor.org.
71. Neta C. Crawford, *Arguments and Change in World Politics: Ethics, Decolonization, and Humanitarian Intervention* (Cambridge: Cambridge University Press, 2002), p. 174. As Crawford explains, in the 18th and 19th centuries, Christianity became "the primary table on which to represent slavery and judge arguments about it."
72. Evan Silverstein,"Faith-Based Symposium Will Link MLK's Dream with Farmworkers' Hopes: January Event in Florida to Feature Biblical Reflection on Poverty, Justice and Human Rights." PCUSA News, December 17, 2004. Evan Silverstein,"Walking the Walk: Presbyterians Join Tomato Pickers in 8-mile Protest March." PCUSA News, March 2, 2004.
73. Elly Leary, "Immokalee Workers Take Down Taco Bell." *Monthly Review* 57, no. 5 (2005).
74. Boje, *Storytelling Organization,* p. 193.

75. David M. Boje, *Narrative Methods* (London: Sage, 2001), p. 118.
76. Kenneth Burke, "The Rhetoric of Hitler's Battle," in *Readings in Rhetorical Criticism* (New York: Vintage, 2005), p. 189.
77. Murphy, "Mikhail Bakhtin and the Rhetorical Tradition," p. 277.

REFERENCES

Atwill, J. M. (1998). *Rhetoric reclaimed: Aristotle and the liberal arts tradition.* Ithaca, NY: Cornell University Press.

Bakhtin, M. M. (1968). The role of games in Rabelais. *Yale French Studies, 41,* 124–132.

———. (1981). Epic and novel: Toward a methodology for the study of the novel. In *The dialogic imagination: Four essays by M. M. Bakhtin* (pp. 3-40). Austin: University of Texas Press.

———. (2004). *The dialogic imagination: Four essays.* Austin: University of Texas Press.

Bales, K. (2007). *Ending slavery: How we free today's slaves.* Berkeley: University of California Press.

Bales, K., Fletcher, L. E., & Stover, E. (2005). Hidden slaves: Forced labor in the United States. *Berkeley Journal of International Law, 23*(47).

Blum, Jonathan. Testimony of Jonathan Blum-chief public affairs officer, senior vice president, YUM! Brands, Inc. to the Senate Committee on Health, Education, Labor, and Pensions: Hearing on Ending Abuses and Improving Working Conditions for Tomato Workers. Committee on Health, Education, Labor, and Pensions: United States Senate, 2008.

Boje, D. M. (2001). *Narrative methods for organizational and communication research.* London: Sage.

———. (2008). *Storytelling organization.* Thousand Oaks, CA: Sage.

Bowe, J. (2007). *Nobodies: Modern American slave labor and the dark side of the new global economy.* New York: Random House.

Brancaccio, D. (2005, May 27). *The battle fields: The coalition of Immokalee workers vs. Taco Bell.* Public Broadcasting Service.

Bruner, M. L. (2002). *Strategies of remembrance: The rhetorical dimensions of identity construction.* Columbia, SC: University of South Carolina Press.

———. (2005). Carnivalesque protest and the humorless state. *Text & Performance Quarterly, 25*(2), 136–155.

Burke, K. (1945). *A grammar of motives.* New York: Prentice Hall.

———. (1966). Terministic screens. In *Language as symbolic action: Essays on life, literature, and method* (pp. 44–62). Berkeley: University of California Press.

———. (2005). The rhetoric of Hitler's battle. In *Readings in rhetorical criticism* (pp. 188–202). New York: Vintage.

Campaign Analysis: CIW Campaign for Fair Food & SFA "Dine with Dignity" Food Service Campaign. (2009). Retrieved August 2009 from http://www.sfalliance.org

Campbell, D. (2003, March 17). Taco's tomato pickers on slave wages. *The Guardian.* Retrieved June 1, 2010, from http://www.guardian.co.uk/world/2003/mar/17/usa.duncancampbell

Cicero. *Orator.* (1962). H. M. Hubbell, Trans. Cambridge, MA: Harvard University Press.

Crary, D. (2005, October 30). Human trafficking in U.S. poses elusive target for coalition trying to combat it. *AP World Stream.* Retrieved June 1, 2010, from http://www.highbeam.com/doc/1P1-114786043.html

Crawford, N. C. (2002). *Arguments and change in world politics: Ethics, decolonization, and humanitarian intervention.* Cambridge: Cambridge University Press.

De Certeau, Michel. (1984). *The practice of everyday life.* Berkeley: University of California Press.

Friedman, M. (1970, September 13). The social responsibility of business is to increase its profits. *New York Times Magazine.*

Goetz, D. (2005, February 27). Tomato campaign will march to Yum: Farmworkers protest wages, conditions. *Louisville Courier-Journal.*

Hariman, R. (1992). Decorum, power, and the courtly style. *Quarterly Journal of Speech 78*(2), 149.

Hawhee, D. (2005). *Bodily arts: Rhetoric and athletics in ancient Greece.* Austin: University of Texas Press.

Heidegger, M. (1978). *Basic writings.* D. F. Krell, Ed. London: Taylor & Francis.

Hopkins, M. F. (1989). The rhetoric of heteroglossia in Flannery O'Connor's *Wise blood. Quarterly Journal of Speech, 75*(2), 198–211.

James, W. (1981). *Pragmatism.* B. Kublick, Ed. Indianapolis: Hackett Publishing Co.

Jameson, F. (1983). Postmodernism and consumer society. In *The anti-aesthetic: Essays on postmodern culture* (pp. 111–125). New York: The New York Press.

Jasinski, J. (1997). Heteroglossia, polyphony, and the Federalist Papers. *RSQ: Rhetoric Society Quarterly, 27*(1), 23–46.

Kennedy, G. A. (1994). *A new history of classical rhetoric.* Princeton, NJ: Princeton University Press.

Lantigua, J. (2007, April 10). McDonald's agrees to increase pay for workers who harvest its tomatoes. *Palm Beach Post.*

Leary, Elly. Immokalee workers take down Taco Bell. *Monthly Review 57*, no. 5 (2005).

Malotki, E. (2004). *Kokopelli: The making of an icon.* Lincoln: University of Nebraska Press.

Martin, A. (2008, May 24). Burger King grants raise to pickers. *New York Times.*

Mason, G. (2002). In praise of *kairos* in the arts: Critical time, East and West. In P. Sipiora & J. S. Baumlin (Eds.), *Rhetoric and kairos: Essays in history, theory, and praxis* (pp. 199–210). Albany: State University of New York Press.

McCloskey, D. (1992). *If you're so smart: The narrative of economic expertise.* Chicago: University of Chicago Press.

———. (1998). *The rhetoric of economics.* Madison: University of Wisconsin Press.

Modern forms of slavery in industrialized countries. (2005). International Labour Organization. Retrieved June 1, 2010, from http://www.ilo.org

Müller, W. J. (2001). Style. In T. O. Sloane (Ed.), *Encyclopedia of rhetoric* (pp. 745–757). New York: Oxford University Press.

Murphy, J. M. (2001). Mikhail Bakhtin and the rhetorical tradition. *Quarterly Journal of Speech, 87*(3), 259–277.

New article slams Yum Brands, Yum CEO David Novak! (2005). Coalition of Immokalee Workers. Retrieved June 1, 2010, from http://www.ciw-online.org/2004-05news.html

Olbrys-Gencarella, S. (2007). The myth of rhetoric: Korax and the art of pollution. *Rhetoric Society Quarterly, 37*(3), 251–273.

Plato. *Gorgias.* (1998). New York: Oxford University Press.

Posner, S. (2004). Leading like Jesus. Campaign for Labor Rights. Retrieved June 1, 2010, from http://www.clrlabor.org

Poulakos, J. (1983). Toward a sophistic definition of rhetoric. *Philosophy & Rhetoric, 16*(1), 35–48.

Schlosser, E. (2005, April 6). A side order of human rights. *The New York Times.*

Schutz, A. (1970). *Reflections on the problem of relevance.* New Haven, CT: Yale University Press.

Silverstein, Evan. Faith-based symposium will link MLK's dream with farmworkers' hopes: January event in Florida to feature biblical reflection on poverty, justice and human rights." PCUSA News, December 17, 2004.

———. Walking the walk: Presbyterians join tomato pickers in 8-mile protest march. PCUSA News, March 2, 2004.

Sipiora, P. (2002). Introduction: The ancient concept of kairos. In P. Sipiora & J. S. Baumlin (Eds.), *Rhetoric and kairos: Essays in history, theory, and praxis* (pp. 1–22). Albany: State University of New York Press.

Slave traders jailed for 12 years. (2002, November 21). *Sydney Morning Herald.*

Student/farmworker alliance. (2008). Retrieved June 1, 2010, from http://www.sfalliance.org

Subway to pay more for tomatoes. (2008, December 2). *Miami Herald.*

The Taco Bell boycott—A short history. (2004). The Witherspoon Society Retrieved June 1, 2010, from http://www.witherspoonsociety.org/2004/taco_bell_background.htm

Turpin, P. B. (2005). Liberal political economy and justice: Character and decorum in the economic arguments of Adam Smith and Milton Friedman. Dissertation, University of Southern California.

Weick, K. E. (1995). *Sensemaking in organizations.* London: Sage.

Williams, A. B. (2008, September 9). Whole Foods agrees to pay Immokalee tomato workers more. *Fort Myers News Press.*

Wolfe, B. (2004, November 17). Seminar will stress Christ-centered leadership: 4,000 expected at southeast church. *The Courier-Journal.*

22 The Evolutive and Interactive Actor Polygon in the Theater of Organizations

Henri Savall, Véronique Zardet, and Michel Péron

1 THEATRICS AND MANAGEMENT

An organization is a theatre where numerous plays are staged, with multiple actors and stage directors. These different individuals perform intermingled roles based on intricate scenarios (Péron & Savall, 2007). Every management situation, like every dramatic composition, constitutes a conflictual system made up of conflict zones and cooperation zones to which are correlated visible and hidden cost performance. To expose dysfunctions, their consequences and then their deeper causes, referred to as root-causes, allows to lift the veil from taboos and non-dits (the unexpressed) (Savall, 1986).

1.1 Enterprises As Playhouses

An enterprise is a social space made up of complex relationships. It can be equated with a playhouse insofar as it constitutes a forum, a meeting place for open discussions of conflicting points of view, of antagonistic ideologies, in order to better handle the company operations and ensure its performance.

A deliberate strategic change process was conceptualized and implemented in companies and organizations of various sizes with a view to improving their social and economic performance on a long-term basis and ensure their sustainability. The Socio-Economic Approach to Management (SEAM) is set up in companies and organizations according to a socioeconomic intervention process (Savall, 1974–1975, 1978b, 1979, Savall, Zardet & Bonner, 2000, 1979, Savall & Zardet, 1987, Buono & Savall, 2007). The first phase consists in making a socio-economic diagnosis based on semiguided interviews carried out with numerous categories of actors in order to list the dysfunctions pertaining to their professional life and assess the resultant hidden costs. The findings of the socio-economic diagnosis are presented in two stages at a few weeks' interval: first a mirror effect in front of the actors interviewed, out of which may come an unexpected transformation of power, into shared governance, but also emanates the cogenerated (stakeholders and intervention-researchers) new script (intervention project; Boje & Rosile, 2003, Péron & Péron, 2003). Then in a second stage, intervener-researchers give their expert opinion. It typically includes the non-dits, that is, dysfunctions not mentioned overtly by the actors but made explicit by the external intervener with regard to his/her own observation, analysis, or interpretation. The socio-economic intervention is carried out in accordance with a methodology referred to as intervention-research (Savall & Zardet, 1984, 2004) implemented by intervener-researchers or by professional consultants trained to apply the method. We'll subsequently use the generic term 'external intervener' to designate either category of actor-researcher or professional consultant.

In the course of the change process, things get more complex as two different plays are being concurrently performed: the first corresponds to the usual activities of the company, to its specific trade. This play rarely evolves. Its cast is stable; improvisation opportunities are scarce (Girin, 1989). The second is the theater of change which corresponds to a new script dealing with survival development and sustainable metamorphosis, a managerial concern as legitimate and undisputable as day-to-day operations. Indeed, change is no longer an exceptional phenomenon but a company's permanent need in a globalized world.

Unfortunately, company actors are not good at dealing with this second script. The same actors are acting out the two scripts nearly at the same time. They can prove to be excellent players with regard to the day-to-day operation of their firm, but very poor ones when dealing with the new requirements of the script of change. The theater of change is not properly managed: there are no appropriate premises, nor convenient settings, the props have not been taken care of. The acting is not clearly defined in the scenario of change and the actors themselves are doubtful about the efficiency of the new casting and the new stage directions. In sum, company actors do not know how to effectively organize the theater of change.

External interveners have their part to play in both structures even though they predominantly intervene in the script of change when they strive to teach actors how to define, circumscribe, and interpret their roles, how to negotiate and eventually reach a consensus, how to deal with and remedy conflicts and strained relationships.

Should not this be the case, the actor who is used to play in situation comedies and does not feel at ease when (if) suddenly asked to perform in highly emotional scenarios tends more or less consciously to turn a blind eye to the latter. Typically, once the seamy sides of a scenario are voluntarily ignored or no remedy is offered, tragedy will take pride of place. In fact, training for change is no common occurrence. Structured in-house training programs do not include courses on how to train for change. No business schools train company actors to effectively cope with scripts of change. How can we expect to get first-class performers in the field?

1.2 Emotion and the Anthropological Spectrum

Emotion holds an important place in socio-economic management. Clandestine or inhibited in traditional management, it is recognized and enhanced in socioeconomic management. It represents at the same time a source, a means, and an end, a finality, a source of personal and professional satisfaction. Emotion is multifaceted—physiological, psychological, sociological, financial. Financial emotion gives utterance to the essential quest for autonomy and dignity by company actors. This multiplicity of assessment criteria encompassed by socio-economic management can be summed up in the anthropological spectrum (cf. Figure 22.1), which graphically presents the performance criteria in professional activity like any cultural or performance activity at the theater. Such an analysis avoids resorting to the traditional but mutilating separation of interacting categories: physiology, psychology, sociology, and economics.

The socio-economic value thus acquires many dimensions: financial (value added), sets of operating rules, philosophical, ethical, political, emotional criteria (Savall & Zardet, 1999b). Anyone can then draw a kind of balance bearing on those criteria as a whole, with economics representing but one relevant dimension among others. On the contrary, the countless supporters of classic mathematical modelization, based on a narrow conception of economic rationality, tend to reject the other dimensions into the dark regions of irrationality.

In qualimetrics modelization (Savall & Zardet, 2004), the qualitative form permits restoring the diversity which is intrinsic to the complex object studied in management or social science. It also allows explicitly to clarify the profound meaning of the knowledge thus produced, its nuances, and its

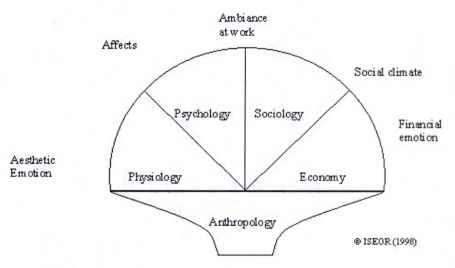

Figure 22.1   The anthropological spectrum.

limits. The quantitative form offers measurement indicators that support meaning, reduce subjectivity, channel emotions, and facilitate aggregating and comparing the different components of the studied object. The monetary analysis, as for it, helps translating the financial impact of dysfunctions into hidden costs or loss of value added. There is no static hierarchy of knowledge; the interaction between qualitative, quantitative, and financial phenomena is vital: Qualimetrics is a dynamic process.

The qualimetrics approach mobilizes three principles: generic contingency, contradictory intersubjectivity, and cognitive interactivity. The three principles should be kept in mind when considering the dialogic nature of many business situations. Company actors, when involved in the interactive polygon of actors, are consciously or unconsciously responding to them. The generic contingency principle, while recognizing the operational specificities of organizations, postulates the existence of invariants that constitute generic rules embodying core knowledge that possesses a certain degree of stability and universality. It avoids company actors having to grope their way on to the enterprise stage. It can be applied to stagecraft which has to comply with some reproducible rules and approaches as in the case of stage directions written into the script of the play by the playwright.

The contradictory intersubjectivity is a technique for creating consensus based on the subjective perceptions of different actors, in order to create more objective grounds for working together. It obviously applies to any dialogic situation and helps company actors or stage actors better internalize their respective roles through this learning and socialization process.

The cognitive interactivity principle is an interactive process (between intervener-researchers and company actors) of knowledge production through successive feedback loops, with the steadfast goal of increasing the value of significant information processed by scientific work. External interveners, when acting as directors in a playhouse or consultants within a company, benefit from this process to round off their proposals to the actors or the management. As David M. Boje puts it (Boje, preface to Savall & Zardet, 2004) "Qualimetrics traces the way in which numbers torture, fragment, abbreviate and invent stories. Qualimetrics sets many alternative stories against the dominant narrative of the firm, and in this way intervention researchers and participants coproduce an antenarrative, one bridging qualitative and quantitative practices" (Boje & Rosile, 2003).

David M. Boje and Grace Ann Rosile (2003) invite us to explore the theatrical aspects of socioe-conomic intervention and socio-economic management. Although the scenario is not written, it has the characteristics of a play. Thus the socioe-conomic diagnosis objective is to look for the organization, by reproducing samples of this metascript in the mirror effect (see section 2). The term 'metascript' was coined by Henri Savall and later endorsed by David M. Boje. It points to the first draft of a fundamental but unfinished scenario which constitutes a shared platform on which rest the different scenarios followed by the actors, working individually or in teams, marked out by the observable behaviors stemming from them. The starting point, that of the socioe-conomic diagnosis, is then to write and translate the metascript which discloses oppressions, conflicts, formal powers, and micro-powers concealed from all the actors. The metascript of the organization is indeed scattered between the numerous authors of fragmented scripts diluted throughout the organization. The plot and the dialogs are embodied in the individual and organizational narrative strategies (Barry & Elmes, 1997). The external interveners are trained to retranscribe these discourses, the verbatim script of the organization (Boje & Rosile, 2003).

The characters taking part in the script of change are numerous: internal actors or those external to the organization, that is, customers, suppliers, competitors. and institutions: that is to say, stakeholders as a whole. One specificity also rests with the multiplicity of roles, for in enterprises, actors are often players and spectators at the same time. The characters attend their own show, the company manager playing the part of director and organizer. Internal actors, alternately producers and internal customers, are thus simultaneously inside and outside the company. The absence of barriers, of separation between the roles of spectators and actors, leads to a collaborative conception of the play. The quality of the representation depends as much on the quality of the audience as on that of the players. The actors have a lot of leeway to play their roles from the metascript. When they wander from it, it creates dysfunctions and hidden costs. However, contrary to what happens with the classical theater, the author of the scenario does not stand alone. One can thus observe a multiplicity of scenarios, of directors, and, in the case of a few players, several roles assumed at the same time. They may play the parts of information providers, coproducers of knowledge, coappraisers of the intervention progress, research partners, and final users of knowledge.

Another noticeable difference: Unlike players who strictly stick to the scenario, in management structures the discipline is far less rigorous. The multiplicity of the parts played by actors and spectators implicitly and ambiguously mix up players and the audience. Sometime customers are witnesses or even actors, as it is the case with service activities where producers and customers are face-to-face. It is a common occurrence in catering institutions, bank agencies, postal services, domestic help. This specificity results in the simultaneous and concomitant satisfaction of customer-spectators and actor-producers if the performance is up to the mark. The multiplicity and variety of physiological, psychological, sociological, and economic criteria (cf. Figure 22.1) which could be considered as contradictory are reinterpreted in the light of socioe-conomic analysis, each one per se constituting a source of dysfunction and hence of hidden costs.

A play hinges around a more or less severe conflict, embedded in a plot. In the theater of managerial situations, conflicts are many-sided, and the psychological dimension important (Savall & Zardet, 2006). Buried-away facts, feelings, and thoughts, non-dits such as taboos or hard-to-drive-out subconscious conflicts, are brought to light.

1.3 Static and Dynamic Analysis: The Evolutive and Interactive Actor Polygon

Let us take a closer look at the script of change. In fact if some companies have at their disposal efficient scripts and efficient actors for their daily activity, they rarely have an explicit and structured script to initiate change operations. If it cannot be denied that the usual activity scenario contains underlying sources of conflict, that of change is packed with them. The external intervener can, indeed, intervene by proposing some improvements to the script of daily activity, by advising the company to modify its distribution to ensure a rotation of its actors. However, he/she invests himself/herself in the script of change as a matter of priority, when helping the actors clarify their conflicts, express them, deal with them, monitor them without ever attempting to avoid them. The word 'conflict' can be construed in different ways. We posit that behind this term feature all the discrepancies, divergences, controversies, antagonisms, and more generally emotional tensions and their origins. Indeed, on thinking it over, if we situate ourselves in a context of articulation between the management of the conscious and the working of the unconscious, in the midst of all these realities a dynamic conflict between different but interactive entities is continually kept going (Savall & Vallée, 2000), especially when power relationship issues are involved. Interplay, interactivity, and interconnection are words often mentioned in dynamic analysis.

Indeed, a product is rarely made or an activity seldom exercised solo without the assistance or participation of others. Any kind of activity carried out by two or by several individuals automatically requires some sort of negotiation which permanently testifies to an underlying chronic state of conflict. Typically conflicting issues are constantly to be addressed in enterprises and organizations as well as on stage.

The current trend, frequently observed in the Western world, in favor of a consensus between protagonists on the social stage consists in ignoring the non-dits, which tends to annoy and bring conflicts. And yet once the non-dit is clearly identified and accepted by the actors, to get something off one's chest is seen as beneficial for oneself and for the other company actors.

The same dialectics or problematics come into play at five levels in conflict analysis:

- The individual and all his/her intrapsychical determinants
- The teams and all their members
- The company or the organization and its subdivisions
- The activity sector and other business branches of the same type and all the companies sharing the same activity
- The societal or macroscopic level and all its activity sectors and regrouping entities or institution (Savall & Vallée, 2000).

An isomorphic phenomenon links these different levels of analysis because there is no critical difference between inframicroscopic and macroscopic levels, contrary to generally accepted ideas. Conflicts, when accepted, experienced, and monitored, are generative of progress and of socioe-conomic values. They make transformation possible. Resorting to the evolutive and interactive actor polygon is illuminating when it comes to understanding and improving the script of change.

Actors A and B (Figure 22.1), when alone on the stage, do not tell the same thing to each other than when C is present (Figure 22.2) or C and D (Figure 22.3), or C, D, and E (Figure 22.4). Thus, in order to advance in the studying of conflict or the solution of problems, it is necessary to alternate scenes with 2, 3, 4, 5 characters . . . by setting up flexible polygons which, through successive iterations, will enable the external intervener to extract as much information as possible in order to react and respond pertinently. The external intervener should constantly keep in mind that he/she is going to encounter in the polygons company actors with different backgrounds linked to different living stories and whose expectations may be poles apart.

In the socio-economic intervention process, the socio-economic diagnosis is followed by the socio-economic project phase, which consists, in accordance with a participative method, in working out some socio-economic innovation proposals aimed at sustainably reducing dysfunctions. A focus group is thus set up, steered by the CEO in the case of horizontal projects or by a department head if it concerns a vertical one.

By metaphorically using the word 'polygon,' we intend to insist on its usual definition in classical geometry as a simply connected plane region bounded by straight-line segments (its sides) in infinite number, which means there is no rigidity factor implied, as opposed to linear chains of cause and effects which are deterministic in essence. Inviting additional participants to join in prevents the organization from confining itself to the univocal, monologic narrative, which tends to kill any initiative. We should underscore at this point that our referring to a polygon of actors does not

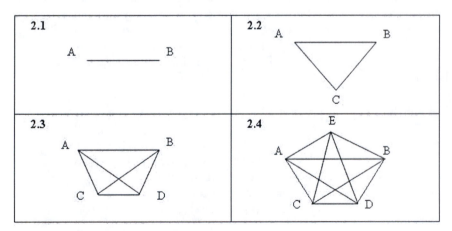

Figure 22.2   The interactive and evolutive actor polygon.

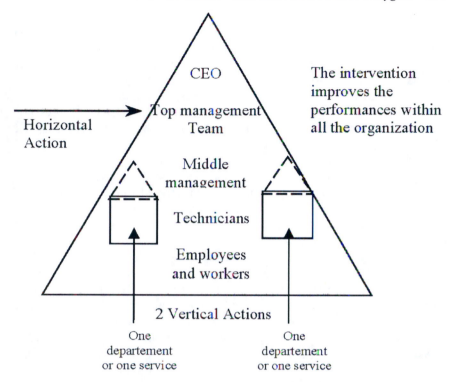

Figure 22.3 The HORIVERT process. CEO = Chief Executive Officer.

mean that we ignore the nonhuman elements in the environment of company actors or stage actors composed of 'itinerant' or movable objects not unlike props in theaters. We'll expatiate further on this point, when studying the notion of assemblage, taken as a number of things or persons assembled together. Interestingly, pronounced differently, the word points to a three-dimensional work of art that combines various objects into an integrated whole.

Participants to the focus group organize themselves in variously structured polygons on the stage of the theater of change:

- A face-to-face meeting is organized at the end of each session, between the project manager and the external intervener (Figure 22.1)
- A subgroup including, in addition to the project manager and the external intervener, one or two line managers close to the project manager
- A plenary group including the subgroup and the other supervisors in the department with supervisors from surrounding departments
- Focus groups led by members of the plenary group and including shop-floor workers

Alternating these polygons is key to successful dynamics. Additionally, the stage play is prepared in the wings by such and such actors who are to be on stage a few hours or a few days after. The role of the external intervener is specific: he/she can be compared with an assistant director—at the director's side—more particularly in charge of advising the latter on the steering of the change process. However, he/she does not take part in the actual performance in the place of a company actor and does not step onto the stage. Learning how to control his/her frustration, he/she does not draw his/her satisfaction from any direct interaction with the actors but from the acting out of the players he/she contributes to improve and from the loud applause of the audience. He/she helps constructing different, richer scenarios from multiple narratives by combining numerous original scripts. He/she may contribute to turn a complete failure, a theatrical 'flop,' into a high-performance enterprise, a box-office success (Péron & Savall, 2007).

Typically, the new script requires the inclusion of change activities in the scenario of the company's available resources. It helps spotting the numerous actors chasing after any sort of work because they have long been unemployed. Players who fail to get any proper contract and are confined to walk-on parts become disenchanted. They keep complaining but are ready to perform any other role, provided it is tactfully proposed. When leading roles are always given to the same actors, the others, who keep getting supporting parts, are bound to quit. Such a system generates and fuels dysfunctions and hidden costs, that is, a destruction of actual or potential value added. The competency grid that intervener-researchers strive to establish in the course of their interventions enables them to suggest changes in the distribution of roles among company actors. The redistribution may happen to coincide with the actual desires of the latter. The ISEOR deems it advisable to rotate company actors so as to avoid humdrum. Interestingly, resorting to competency grids helps interveners spot those that may feel out of place in a given employment. The compatibility of internal actors with the responsibilities attributed to them by the management enhances the credibility of the company in the eyes of the stakeholders (Péron & Savall, 2007). Additionally, implementing this method is a surefire way of decreasing company actors' resistance to change because putting people together is to change routine.

Besides, the external intervener is also an actor of change as far as he/she brings his/her additional contribution to the play. It is important that he/she should exempt himself/herself from the illusion that once immersed among the company actors, his/her own expertise would suffice to change things. He/she should always be in a position to see things differently, an advantage he/she is bound to lose when the involvement (immersion) is too strong and distancing inadequate. There are, so to speak, many summits in a polygon on which the external intervener must position himself/herself to get different representations of the polygonal region. By choosing the appropriate geopolitical position for observing the interplay of actors and by alternating these positions, they create a dynamic field as a generator of signs, facts, and information. Increasing the multiplicity of the images collected improves the quality and significance of collected information in perfect compliance with the contradictory principle intersubjectivity mentioned earlier. ISEOR intervener-researchers and consultants are advised to take their distance from the scenario that is unfolding under their eyes during their interventions so as to attain a better contextual understanding of relationships among company actors. One should proceed stage by stage: Each time the external intervener implants various ideas, he/she takes the time needed for his/her contribution to be accepted by the actors. The intervener's positioning is similar to that of the therapist (Savall & Vallée, 2000).

The actors, as individuals, evolve along with the scenario; thus conflicts are progressively brought to light and dealt with partly in the wings, partly on stage. The situations encountered in change management can be compared with a play whose scenario is rarely predetermined. It is vague and imprecise. Indeed, the search for clever solutions by a carefully chosen polygon of hierarchical actors favors creativity on the way. What is conceived together through cooperation stands a greater chance of being implemented. The actors again find a legitimate status in the conception of working methods they have been dispossessed of by the TFW virus (Taylor, Fayol, Weber) of the classical organization school (Savall, 1974–1975; Savall & Zardet, 2005). This virus imposes the hyperspecialization of functions and workstations, the separation of conceptualization and realization together with the depersonalization of work.

According to the socio-economic theory, the dynamics of organizational innovations is impulsed by the concatenation of actor polygons. One interactive polygon of actors designs the project; a second partly different polygon decides to implement it; a third, partly different still, brings it into play. Silence, that is, the non-dits (the unsaid), finds its place in those multiple settings. The role of the external intervener is to express it and construe its significance on behalf of the actors.

To implement a project requires considering the human and nonhuman elements at one's disposal. We have so far discussed the ins and outs of our evolutive interactive polygon of actors. It implies some strong interconnection, some reciprocal and mutual action and reaction during various meetings as for company actors and during rehearsals for stage actors, a clear departure from any monological framework. We have underlined the ISEOR avoidance of linear plotline considered as detrimental to the dynamics of change. Similarly physical working conditions and technical conditions and work constraints are also the object of a nonlinear assemblage approach, to take up Bruno Latour's concept (Latour, 2005). The assemblage of the materiality (layout of the rooms, computer systems, office equipment, Web access, etc.) may change over time, may be differently experienced by people, may announce some strategic changes within the company. In sum, it may, in a surreptitious sort of way, point to some kind of evolution in the workplace positively or negatively felt by company actors.

All the assemblages within the organization are different if one thinks in terms of structure. Improper assemblages may cause dysfunctions. ISEOR integrated training manuals progressively worked out during the interventions are key to ensure the coordination of the materiality and the actors all together and the proper connection with or adjustment to the materiality on the part or the users. In fact, the prop assemblage is meant to change along with the actor assemblage. This is how training with a view to better comprehend the significance of the plasticity of different assemblages is carried out together with a definite insistence on the advantages of multi-skilling when it comes to dealing with fast-developing techniques such as in the health sector. As was exactly the case with the actor polygons, each time you enter or suppress a new element in an assemblage you create a new assemblage. You change the scene, the stage setting, and the props, which may no longer fall nicely into place. You have to reconstruct the system. Excess or deficiency in such or such assemblages is bound to create dysfunctions if not conveniently dealt with. Repositioning an actor or a flip chart, all things being equal, is not meaningless. A cluttered desk or a clean table does not bring the same message across but we are not actually sensitized to the fact. Taking for granted that any assemblage of materials is appropriate for any given assemblage is wrong. Assemblages are context related. If you modify the casting without attending to the props, you are doing nonqualimetric interventions. Maintenance or renovation of the material or intangible objects (internal regulations, technical procedures) that make up an organization clearly exemplifies the change factor in assemblages. In socio-economic approach to management (SEAM), periodical cleanup is an efficiency factor and one of the major sources of reduced dysfunctions and hidden costs.

2 NON-DIT AND DELIBERATE PROACTIVE CHANGE STRATEGY

The socio-economic intervention method identifies three axes or forces related to the dynamics of change (Figure 22.4):

- The problem solution axis includes four phases which may look classical in management interventions: diagnosis, project, implementation, evaluation. Nevertheless, the concrete methods put into practice at each stage comprise some specificities. We shall enlarge upon those pertaining to the diagnosis and project phases.
- The management-tool axis points to the setting up of simple tools held in common through collaborative training, with the top management and the managerial staff, at first.

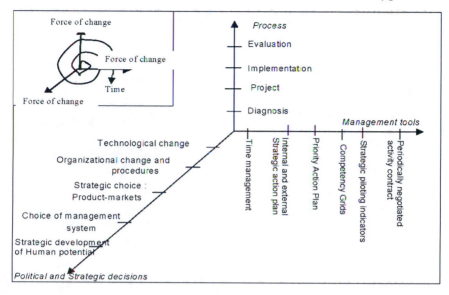

Figure 22.4   Synopsis of the three dynamic forces of change.

- Finally, the political and strategic decisions axis represents the energy, the determination, the will, the implication evinced by the top management and the managerial staff concerning the change process with regard to the making and implementation of decisions, while relying on the progressive engagement of other categories of actors.

Company organization charts often reflect a geometrical approach to space, playing with horizontal and vertical dynamics at the same time. The line of intersection and the direction of arrows give a glimpse at the constant interplay or confrontational interacting graphically represented in our interactive and evolutive polygons.

Embedding the change process according to the socio-economic intervention method requires some specific space restructuration referred to as the Horivert model (cf. Figure 22.3). One horizontal action and two vertical actions are simultaneously carried out (cf. Figure 22.5) so that the change process implies at the same time the top management, the managerial staff, and in two or three pilot sectors, the personnel at large.

At the theater, spectators should not be limited to viewing a single part of the stage but should rather be given the possibility of varying their angle of vision. Similarly the horizontal process, to be effective, must be applied throughout the enterprise. A stage director worth his/her salt should never be tempted to block the stage, as the phrase goes. The interactive and evolutive polygons of actors do not only symbolize the polyphony of management but also its ubiquity because the Greek root of the word points to a figure with many angles, calling to mind the "Tamaraesque simultaneous and fragmented multiplicity of theatre" (Boje & Rosile, 2003).

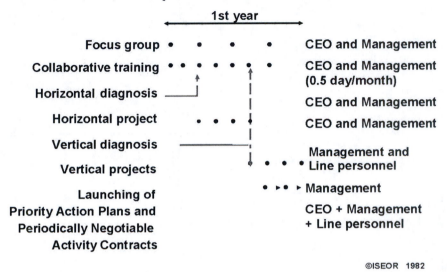

©ISEOR 1982

Figure 22.5   Chronology of change.

2.1 The Non-Dit in the Change Process

The socio-economic diagnosis aims to take stock of dysfunctions and to measure their economic consequences, referred to as hidden costs. The role of the semiguided interviews is critical. It allows various categories of actors to freely express themselves with regard to their exposure to dysfunctions in their professional activities. These semiguided interviews have two specific functions: a technical function helping to identify concrete dysfunctions and a psychological function facilitating listening and opening up, especially with regard to the unavoidable litigations encountered in one's professional life (Guillaume, 1989; Savall, 1978a).

The results of the socio-economic diagnosis are presented, stage by stage, to all the interviewees, so as to obtain a 'mirror effect,' by provoking a culture shock through two mechanisms: the deliberate omission of the organization strong points (for dysfunctions only are released in front of the interviewees) and the use of economic and financial terminology which calls the actors' attention to the utilization of economic resources. Indeed, hidden costs show that a substantial amount of economic resources is insidiously spent to remedy chronic dysfunctions, instead of being earmarked for value-added creation beneficial to others. The mirror effect is not limited to the verbatim reproduction of field-note quotes in front of actors. It has a strong social impact when the audience is eventually confronted by the external intervener's opinion, which is of course open to debate.

In fact, the second part of the socio-economic diagnosis, referred to as the expert opinion, puts forward the conclusions or rather the intimate conviction of the external intervener, researcher, or consultant. It enables the intervener to take some distance vis-à-vis the company actors (Matheu,

1986). The expert opinion is presented several weeks later than the mirror effect, first to the CEO, then to the management of the organization. This time interval makes it possible to think over the mirror-effect findings, and consider the dysfunctions listed by the actors, before the intervener delivers his/her expert opinion. The expert opinion is seen as more relevant and energizing when the resulting knowledge is not imparted too soon and not before the dust has settled. Time, of course, plays its part in the necessary distancing. The expert opinion is an additional tool in the socio-economic diagnosis evaluation process. It makes it possible for the intervener to clarify his/her own representation of what the company actors do not wish or do not dare to express (Savall & Zardet, 1999a). It is aimed at obtaining a consolidated validation of dysfunctions through alterations in the representations of 'reality' deeply ingrained in the minds of the company actors. In theatrical performance, silence plays a significant role as it brings to light the structures of the unspoken (Péron & Péron-Bois, 2006). In the business world, unvoiced comments are part and parcel of the script. External interveners should become experts at decoding the unsaid.

The expert opinion is worked out according to the contradictory inter-subjectivity principle explained earlier (Savall & Zardet, 1995). It enables the actors to double-check that their comments have been listened to, noted down, retranscribed, and not twisted, whatever their origin. The consensus/trust relationship is, therefore, a prerequisite for efficiently decoding the unexpressed, because it favors the attentive listening necessary to get a better grasp of what the intervener meant. This is achieved through the mirror effect and the debate it sparks off. Indeed, the confidence of company actors in external interveners is rather weak at the inception of the change process. It subsequently develops thanks to the strict compliance with deontological rules on their part and thanks to the distance they manage to keep in their relationship with the company. The external intervener progressively shifts from the role of methodologist to that of mediator to end up as a therapist to a lesser extent (Arnaud, 1996). Once the non-dits are presented, this triple role of methodologist, mediator, and therapist is alternately or jointly assumed. Thus in the 'swing-wing' polygon (cf. Figure 22.2), where the external intervener is present, the latter plays the part of a methodologist, by recalling the principles of an efficient solution to troubleshoot dysfunctions; then the part of a mediator by helping the other actors in the polygon to express themselves, to listen to one another, to develop cooperation among actors to build a teamwork spirit, and to reformulate one another's statements; and finally the part of a therapist by facilitating the expression of the unsaid and by making a diagnosis on the likely origins of the organization difficulties. To round off his/her intervention, he/she opens up new tracks to design root solutions together with the company actors.

The remedial treatment to the dysfunction disease is defined in a collaborative manner to facilitate its acceptance by the actors in charge of bringing it into play. It is common knowledge that doctors meet the same problems with their patients, when the latter do not scrupulously follow the prescribed treatment (Savall & Fière, 2007).

2.2 Significance of Non-Dits

The unexpressed observations brought to light are restored to their former 'between-the-lines' position among the actors' verbatim statements. This may be useful to increase cooperation but may also be detrimental to it. Taboo dysfunctions, once spotted, always mean something and can be seen as sources of value added if properly handled. To read between the lines may save the external consultant a number of problems. But if he/she failed to do so and does not understand the implicit message, it may become an important source of dysfunctions.

In the dynamics of evolutive and interactive actor polygons, the dichotomy between meaningful and meaningless non-dits is often observed, alternately creating progressive and regressive spirals. A progressive spiral is defined as a continuous process of cumulative improvement. The 'swing-wing' geometry of the polygons (cf. Figure 22.2) is essential because it renders possible the progressive emergence of company actors' verbalization through successive warm-ups and mutual encouragements, with the assistance of the external intervener. The cognitive interactivity principle comes into play when a verbal exchange of opinions between two or several actors generates some form of knowledge, a new awareness of original individualized knowledge (Savall & Zardet, 1996).

CONCLUSION

According to the socio-economic theory of organizations, the theater of change, in which all companies and organizations operate today, is an animated stage on which multiple actors interact, in compliance with poorly structured and rather obscure scenarios. Emotion plays a critical role in the success of these dramatic compositions in their different configurations: physiological, psychological, sociological, economic. One specificity consists in the multiplicity of roles and statuses: The actors are spectators; the external intervener takes the part of assistant director, without ever substituting for the actors. The 'swing-wing' scenes follow one another and alternate, favoring the successive warm-ups of the actors, thanks to these interactive and evolutive polygons aimed at increasing cognitive interactivity, a cornerstone of an effective and efficient teamwork. The non-dits hold an important place in such scenarios, indeed even in the denouement of the plot: tell, not to tell, intervene, let go. These are constant choices for all the actors. Indeed, in an ambiguous way, along with pathogenic non-dits, one can find reassuring, even indispensable, non-dits with regard to cohabitation and cooperation, a source of sustainable socioeconomic performance.

The theatrical analogy seems particularly relevant. It allows to better understand the respective parts played by company actors at different levels and the way they tend to respond to change. Various scenarios eventually emerge and roles can be modified or redefined through a dynamic process of innovation and a teamwork approach akin to organizational theatrics, which leaves some space to improvisation. Such a conception of intervention research by combining "artistic" approaches with the rigorous socio-economic method makes it possible to reconcile management as a science and as an art, an achievement which cannot but secure the pleasure which should stem from any human activity.

REFERENCES

Arnaud, G. (1996). What observation strategy for researchers in management. *Revue Sciences de Gestion, Economies et Sociétés, 22*, 235–264.

Barry, D., & Elmes, M. (1997). Strategy retold: Toward a narrative view of strategic discourse. *Academy of Management Review, 22*(2), 429–452.

Boje, D. (2004). Qualimetrics contributions to research methodology. In preface to H. Savall & V. Zardet, *Recherche en sciences de gestion: Approche qualimétrique. Observer l'objet complexe*. Paris: Economica.

Boje D., & Rosile, G. A. (2003). Theatrics of SEAM. *Journal of Organizational Change Management, 16*(1), 21–32.

Buono, A. F., & Savall, H. (Eds.) (2007). *Socio-economic intervention in organizations: The intervener-researcher and the SEAM approach to organizational analysis*. Charlotte, NC: Information Age Publishing.

Girin, J. (1989). Methodological opportunism in organizational management researches. *Journée d'étude*. La recherche-action en action et en question AFCET. Collège de Systémique, Ecole Centrale de Paris.

Guillaume, Y. (1989). Experimental research on hospital management. *Contributions of socio-economic analysis and psycho-social analysis* Doctoral thesis in management sciences, under the supervision of Véronique Zardet, Université de Lyon.

Latour, B. (2007). *Re-assembling the social*. New York: Oxford University Press.

Matheu, M. (1986). Distant familiarity. *Revue Gérer et comprendre*. Paris: Annales des Mines.

Moisdon, J. C. (1984). Management research and intervention. *Revue française de Gestion, 22*, 61–73.

Péron, M., & Péron-Bois, M. (2006). Quiet everybody action. *Revue Sciences de Gestion-Management Sciences-Ciencias de Gestión, 55*, 17–27.

Péron, M., & Péron M. (2003). Postmodernism and the socio-economic approach to organizations. *Journal of Organizational Change Management, 16*(1), 49–55.

Péron, M., & Savall, H. (2007). Raising the curtain on business operation theatrics. *Revue Sciences de Gestion—Management Sciences—Ciencias de gestión, 53*, 85–102.

Savall, H. (1974–1975). *Enrichir le travail humain, l'évaluation économique*. Preface by Jacques Delors, Dunod, Paris; translated into English (1981): *Work and people, the economic evaluation of job enrichment*, preface by H. I. Ansoff, Oxford University Press, New York; new edition (2010), preface by Anthony Buono, Information Age Publishing, Charlotte, NC.

————. (1978a). The psychological dimension of socio-economic analysis. *Bulletin de Psychologie*, 344, pp. 443–448.

————. (1978b). *A method for a socio-economic diagnosis of the enterprise.* Conférence IAE de Nice. Revue Française de Gestion, 22, pp. 96–108.

————. (1979). *Reconstructing the enterprise: Socio-economic analysis of working conditions.* Prefaced by François Perroux, Dunod, Paris, France.

————. (1986). Quality control of qualitative, quantitative and financial information obtained from organization actors. ISEOR-FNEGE-CNRS, Conference on Fundamental Methodology in Management Sciences.

Savall, H., & Fière, D. (2007). *Analogies between medical research and intervention research in management.* International Conference co-sponsored by ISEOR—Academy of Management (Research Methods Division), Lyon, France.

Savall, H. & Vallée, M. (2000). The conflict-cooperation creative alternation. Psycho-Analysis and Management Institute Conference, Paris.

Savall, H., & Zardet, V. (1984). *Tested-out socio-economic management tools: Cross-fertilization of information systems and organizational behaviors.* AFCET Conference, Paris.

————. (1987). *Mastering hidden costs and performances: The periodically negotiable activity contract.* Economica, 5th edition 2010; translated into English (2008): *Mastering hidden costs and socio-economic performance*, IAP, Charlotte, NC.

————. (1995). *Strategic engineering of the reed, flexible and rooted.* Economica, 2nd edition 2005.

————. (1996). Intervention research and cognitive interactivity. *Revue Internationale de Systémique*, vol 10, n 1–2, 157–189.

————. (1999a). The evolution of company actors' dependency vis-à-vis chronic dysfunctions within their organization. Psycho-analysis and Management Institute Conference, Lyon, published in a collective work, *Psycho-analysis, management and dependence within organizations* (2001).

————. (1999b). Multidimensional management decision as foundation of management sciences. *Contribution to the collective work in honor of Jacques Lebraty.* Presses Universitaires de Nice.

————. (2004). *Research in management science: Qualimetric approach. Observing the complex object.* Preface by David M. Boje, Economica; translated into English (2010, in print), IAP, Charlotte, NC.

————. (2005). *Tetranormalization: Challenges and dynamics.* Paris: Economica.

————. (2006). The emergence of hidden psycho-sociological micro-theories in socio-economic theory. Psycho-Analysis and Management Institute Conference, Lyon, France.

Savall, H., Zardet, V., & Bonnet, M. (2000). *Releasing the untapped potential of enterprises through socio-economic management.* ILO-BIT; 2nd edition 2008; published in English, French, and Spanish.

Postscript

An Antenarrative Theory of Socioeconomic in Intervention Research

David M. Boje

INTRODUCTION

This postscript was written after the book was mostly assembled. I had an opportunity to invite my French colleagues to contribute that closing chapter of the handbook. Grace Ann Rosile and I have been traveling to France each year to learn the Socio-Economic Approach to Management (SEAM). As you know from reading this book, published by Routledge, 'antenarrative' is defined as a 'prestory' (ante) or a 'bet' (ante) that some anticipated transformation will ensue (Boje, 2001). Antenarratives are frequently found in planning, strategy, foretelling market directions, and innovation. Antenarratives are waves; narratives are particles—objects, dead pastness texts. The issue I want to explore is how antenarratives shape the future in various approaches to 'research intervention' (IR) and 'action research' (AR).

In 1973 an accountant and economist named Henri Savall submitted his dissertation. He chose as his inspiration the work of Germán Bernácer (1883–1965), who in 1922 predicted the stock market crash of 1927, and did it 14 years before Keynes thought about it. Bernácer sent his ideas to over 20 economists but they only ignored his predictions. Finally, after the crash, Robertson (1940) wrote how Bernácer's theory was used by Keynes, and later Keynes had at least verbally in 1936 acknowledged it.

Savall reflected on his dissertation, and decided that management and organization needed more dynamic concepts, and set out to invent SEAM. At the time, the sociotechnical paradigms were getting off the ground (Eric Trist, Fred Emery, some later work by Lou Davis, and many others joined in). Henri decided that social and technical were being dualized, and this was bad enough, but also separated artificially from economics, accounting, and other fine disciplines such as ethics. Savall told me on June 17, 2010, at 11 a.m., "Performance is not the result of putting together resources (things); it's the result of dynamic historical movement."

And it was then, as he does every year for the past 11 years of our relationship, that he pulled out a concept of SEAM that I had not heard before. A seventh tool on the B-Axis, one that is not in any of his books with Zardet, Bonnet, or Péron. Its initials are EIAP.

As Savall put it, an enterprise "may produce high performance or many dysfunctions in [the] action polygon, even with all quality actors, it depends on the [material-actor] assemblage."

I had been sharing my new ideas on assemblages after studying the work of Latour (2005), Bennett (2010), and Barad (2007), not to mention Morson (1994) and, of course, Deleuze and Guattari (1987).

I explained that a network is not the same as an assemblage. I want the students at Lyon 3 and at CTU to understand these differences, so they can do an 'onto-story' (Bennett, 2010, pp. 3–4).

ON THE DIFFERENCES OF NETWORKS AND ASSEMBLAGES

1. An assemblage is migrative, itinerant, in movement whereas a network is ties, connections that recur, that pattern being more stable.
2. The network is social, but the assemblage is human plus nonhuman actants, agents, agencies.
3. The assemblage is more loosely coupled whereas networks are more tightly coupled (one of Weick's concepts, loose and tight coupling).
4. An assemblage is more about frames for arranging and sorting stuff that are existent in the history of the actants. A network has one frame, often imposed by the observer.
5. Agency is not just human, but the configurative assemblage of materiality has energy, what Bennett (2010) calls 'vibrant energy.'
6. The trace of each entity gives us an onto-story, a speculative one, crafted by an observer, who looks at the assemblage (Bennett, 2010, pp. 3–4).
7. We are so used to seeing only social networks; we do not notice the props, the staging of assemblages illuminating characters.
8. What Barad (2007) calls 'agential realism' is the intra-activity of materiality and discourse, and she never uses the word 'interaction' because that does not get at the exchanges, the mutuality of what is moving between, and in between, such an assemblage.

It occurred to me to do an onto-story experiment. I looked around to see what assemblages were present in the once-occurrent moment of being (as Bakhtin puts it). In onto-story, one notices the material objects that are found together, but have been part of quite different assemblages, and are now in a new one, together. For Bakhtin (1981) this would be stylistics, one that is dialogical, the styles of materiality conversing with one another. For Latour (2005, pp. 88–93) it's a reassemblage of the social, one that has materiality, that the (recent) social constructionists banished from the scene. 'Social construction' has become "a *synonym* for the real' and now when one says 'social construction' they mean, no reality exists at all"

(Latour, 2005, p. 89). This would not match up to Berger and Luckmann's (1966, p. 27) much more material conditions of everyday reality in social construction, where objectivity intraplayed with subjectivity, but did not disappear completely in the reification process: "The temporal structure of everyday life confronts me as a facticity with which I must reckon, that is, with which I must try to synchronize my own projects."

Back to my storytelling: I looked at the tables moved together, at the three chairs in which Henri Savall, Michele Péron, and I were to sit, and at the two flip charts repositioned for our meeting. Yes, it's an assemblage, but not an interesting one, I kept noticing. On the table we each had some material objects.

In front of me, I had placed my usual black composition notebook, and a pen I had crafted in my blacksmith shop, using an anvil and 3-pound hammer and some jigs I made.

In front of Henri was a more elegant notebook, a pen, and eventually a cell phone.

In front of Michele was a tablet, a pen, and his case to hold his glasses, and inside the case a yellow cloth.

I kept noticing. Henri and Michele were each wearing glasses.

"Our assemblages are different," I observed. "I had the laser surgery, and I do not need to wear glasses anymore."

"Michele," I continued, "has a case for his glasses, but you, Henri, must keep wearing yours, or they might get scratched. And Michele has that cloth so he can keep his lenses clean."

They stared at me and started to get it, so I pushed on. "We all have these taken for granted assemblage of materials that we take for granted, and yet we work quite closely with each assemblage. And this could be a new theory of change. When we have an excess or deficiency in our assemblage, we have dysfunctions. We do not have the right assemblage for the situation."

I had explained my theory of Aristotle earlier in the week, at a meeting on Saturday at ISEOR. There is, in book II of the virtue ethics book, a definition of virtue ethics that is about finding the intermediate path in a situation, where it is neither a deficiency nor an excess. Henri had told me at dinner that night that he has been studying Aristotle and sees what I mean by a convergence with SEAM.

It has to do with Aristotle's (350 BCE) idea that in virtue ethics we can learn a habit and learn to change habits that we have. In French there is the word 'habitude.' There is an habituation of actions, and that to me is what differentiates action research approaches from Savall's intervention research.

Aristotle (350 BCE) says, "We cannot find a process complete in form at any time . . . for if locomotion is a process from one place to another, it includes locomotions differing in form—flying, walking, jumping and so on . . . *Hence it is not complete at every time* . . . a process, it would seem, is not complete at every time; and the many [constituent] processes are incomplete, and differ in form, since the place from which and the place to which make the form of a process [and different processes] begin and end in different places" (Book x, Chapter 4). The key components of Aristotle's theory of locomotion seem, to me, to parallel Latour's ideas on what interaction is not. Aristotle's key points about locomotion:

- Processes are parts of larger processes
- No process is complete at every time
- Constituent processes are not complete
- Locomotion includes processes in *different forms*
- Locomotion links past, present, and future

For Latour (2005, pp. 199–202), there are five problems overlooked in 'interactions.'

1. Interactions are NOT Isotopic (not same place)
2. Interactions are NOT Synchronic (not same time)
3. Interactions are NOT Synoptic (not same optic)
4. Interactions are NOT Homogeneous (not same agencies)
5. Interactions are NOT Isobaric (not same pressures)

We had joked about it. I declared at the Saturday ISEOR seminar, "There is no action in action research." Michele replied, "I would like permission to use that line." Indeed, I had been studying what went wrong with AR since Kurt Lewin's Field Theory (see book on Kurt Lewin edited by Dorwin Cartwright, 1951). Lewin argued that the physical (materiality) aspects of individuals, groups, and organizations needed to be observed and studied, and then the psychological force fields of locomotion sorted out.

Boje: "I am trying to sort it out, this difference of AR and IR, and I think it has to do with very different theories of action. I see lots of talk about action in AR, but the projects don't seem to study action, or materiality. As Latour tells it, social science has a theory that has no materiality. When one says social construction these days, it means 'it does not exist.' And that is why he is so keen on assemblages. Not just him but Jane Bennett. And also Karen Barad (2007).There is no materiality in AR."

And "there is no research in action research," we all said together.

But surely there is research and action in action research. It's just that it's quite different from what we take to be action and research in intervention research.

If IR is not based on social construction epistemology, then what is it based on? To me the answer lies in the differences between networks that are just social and the assemblages that are much more than that.

Take, for example, the major dysfunctions that SEAM begins with in doing a diagnosis. The assemblages relate well to the SEAM dysfunctions (adapted from Savall, Zardet, & Bonnet, 2008).

1. **Working Conditions** is an assemblage of tools for the job, material resources that change and get changes over time, and this is a new theory of change. Certainly the old job design work by Davis and Taylor (1972), in the sociotechnical movement, was all about changing the assemblage of materiality in relation to that of social groups most effective for getting work done.

2. **Work Organization** is a materiality assemblage and a social network in a state of activity and the frames of this are in dialogic relation, as the discourse and the materiality and humanity get together. The work organization is about doing assemblages. When Cortez and later Onate invaded Mexico and then New Mexico, they have all sorts of assemblages. We know this from the supply records. There are big forges in the expectation of finding silver and gold deposits. The soldiers had their own small forges and tools, to make horseshoe nails, because without them the army does not go very far, not in rocky terrain. Blacksmith assemblages of tools and even hunks of iron were necessary in the organization of a conquest, and empire being constructed. Not only gold- and silversmiths, and ones making horseshoes, but ones to make swords, a very specialized assemblage of tools and techniques and materials.

3. **3Cs Communication**, Coordination, & Cooperation—Each one has a materiality and the materiality changes in the succession of something as simple (but it's really complex) as reading Aristotle (350 BCE), making notes in a notebook with my blacksmith pen, then typing them up into slides and connecting to a digital projector and watching the image appear on the screen, as Latour (2005) jokes, looking at the half-asleep students process it more slowly in their brains. The materiality, the substance changes in the communication, and look at all the materiality that must cooperate, and be coordinated. There are many tools and technologies in the 3Cs.

4. **Time Management**—The times are different throughout the assemblage. Short, medium, and long term; linear, cycles, and spirals, or more rhizomatic assemblages. When an entity migrates from one assemblage to another, then both (former and the target one) have changed. They are different than before. We cannot just delegate to someone if they don't have the assemblage to handle it. That will not save any time. They need infrastructure to bring care, and to have effectivity (efficacy).

5. **Training**—How do you simplify your life? You reassemble, let go of stuff that requires all that maintenance time and energy. You have to apprentice to learn an assemblage. In blacksmithing, hammering is not simple, how to use tongs, how hot to heat the iron, when to apply more oxygen to the coal, and a vat of oil or water to temper the steel. To develop good habits, virtuous ones, requires training, apprenticeships, and lots of time to experiment on the same sort of

piece, and to make many of the same pieces. Make a strap of 100 hinges, and the last 20 or so are pretty good. Make just one, and it's a mess. How can you be a process consultant if you don't attend to the materiality of assemblages? Humans are materiality, and their bodies are in intraplay with all sorts of corporeality and materiality. That all takes training to get the habitudes that are most effective, most virtuous.

6. **Strategic Implementation**—Move an organization from one assemblage to another by just changing its sign, from barbershop to stylist. Merger is a combining of assemblages, and spinning off is separating out entities of an assemblage that are duplicative, or replicative. There are innovative assemblages of software, and hardware, and people, and ones less so. Accounting is an assemblage of accounts, and audits look closely at assemblages. A business plan is an assemblage of ideas, spreadsheets, and some kind of storyline. I wonder if people who lack feel for the materiality of the enterprise can craft these sorts of strategic implementations.

It was at this point in the meeting that Savall began drawing on the flip chart, and associating with the ideas I had shared about the materiality assemblages on our tables, and the implications of assemblages in an assessment of dysfunctions.

EIAP Evolutive Interactive Actors Polygon. This is the seventh tool, and the basis for qualimetric intervention research (QIR), and a difference with nonqualimetric intervention research (non-QIR).

Savall talked as he wrote on the flip chart. I forget if it was in French or English. It was not his native Spanish. He asked, writing in English, "Is 'evolutive' the right word." I said, "I think it's a better word than 'evolution'; let's keep it." Savall continues, "By evolutive, I mean a change that has many differences, a disruption." "That would be in between evolution and revolution," I thought, and later shared this. So 'evolutive' is a new word, at least new in English.

Actors A and B have a meeting at 10:45. And both arrive on time. The meeting lasts till 10:55, which was the current time at ISEOR. B leaves. Then actor C takes a meeting with actor A, from 10:55 to 11:15. Savall demonstrates this by approaching the door, and pretending to be B, who leaves, and C, who now enters.

A says things to C, in AC, that were not the same as what was said to B, in AB. Actors and what they say changes at every moment, constantly. You cannot interpret the meaning of the quotes if you do not trace and know the kind of assemblage, the times. In training effective professional behaviors in management, you need to explain what is happening, and know the assemblages in order to deal with the conflicts.

In my notebook, I wrote "Tamara." This is a reference to the 1995 article on Disney as Tamara-land, the theory that the storytelling is going on simultaneously in many rooms of an organization, and actors, coming into a room from other rooms, can view and hear the same story, but walk out with very different meanings. Why? Because they have been part of a different assemblage, up to that point.

"Why the word 'polygon'?" I asked, adding, "I get the part about evolutive interactive actors." I explain how it relates to Tamara-theatrics, how many different combinations just a dozen people in 10 rooms can have, when it comes to storytelling.

Savall: "There is a relation between these ideas [assemblage & EIAP] and theatrics. From 10:45 to 10:55 is Act I, and from 10:55 to 11:15 is Act II. And the acts make up a scene, and there are other scenes. Is this a good play or a bad play, the props are not appropriate, or they are. This is the reason for many dysfunctions and lack of value-added. To answer your question the polygon is a circle with an infinite number of sides. The circle is an illusion." In short, the differences, the diffractions are what can be noticed in the assemblages.

Savall: "If you disturb (derange) the actors without attending to the props, you are doing non-qualimetric IR. When you shared with us your observations about the cloth in Michele's glass case that was qualimetric event."

To demonstrate, Savall asked Michele if he could have the cloth for an experiment. Michele at first guarded the cloth, not getting the context. When Michele handed over the cloth, removing it carefully from his glasses case, Henri put it in the middle, equidistant from each of them, and declared, "This is resource sharing, and it's a change in the assemblages, and the creation of a new assemblage between us."

David: "When did you come up with this new tool?" It was in 1987.

Savall: "When you start a meeting too fast, such as before the key actors are all present, then it's bad play of theatre. Better to go slow in the first five minutes, so the missing key actors can arrive. There is no credibility to speak important matters when they are not in the room. Slow down the meeting and let all the actors arrive. This in relation to assemblage of things, the props in theatre and the intervener, then is a sort of stage director, with co-stage direction by the leader of the meeting. The [intervention] rule is the actors play the play, not [consultants] play instead of the actors."

Michele: "The stage director recommends the people, props, the kinds of gestures. The stage director adds these stage directions in the margin of the script."

David: "There is also the blocking of the stage. You can tell the novice, who does not know how to use the stage. In blocking the action comes stage left, or stage right, and key actions are center stage. Blocking sets out the movement that occurs as actors and props move in assemblages scene by scene, act by act."

Savall: "There are two key principles. First principle: interaction to create knowledge is not static. Second principle: comprehend the theatrics, the assemblages of actors, the movement of actors between scenes."

It was my turn to share on the flip chart. I decided to share with them, for the first time, the four types of antenarratives that I had been studying.

I put the word 'PAST' on one side and the word 'FUTURE' on the other.

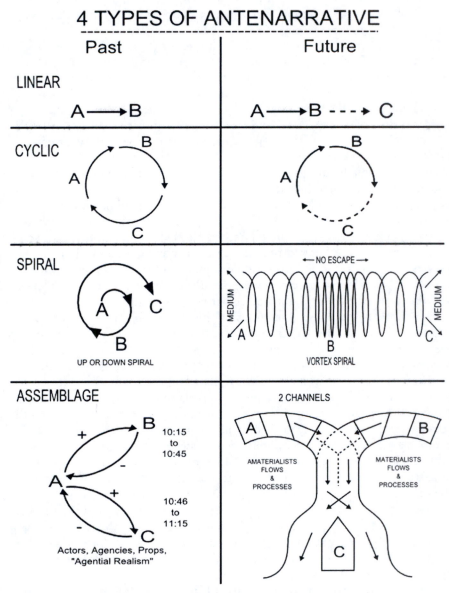

Figure P.1   Four types of antenarratives (figure by David Boje, prepared with the help of Rakesh Mittal, used by permission).

Under that I listed Linear A → B under PAST, and again, A → B under FUTURE. In linear antenarrative, we expect the past to repeat. We use retrospective sensemaking, thinking that this will happen exactly as before. It's a form of future perfect sensemaking. It does not work, but it's very popular in strategic planning.

I wrote Cyclic, and under PAST a circle with three arrows, labeled A, B, and C. And the same drawing under FUTURE. There is this idea that a cycle we recognize in the past will repeat itself in the future. It's a sort of bent line. It may work a bit better than linear thinking, but not much. Diedre McCloskey says that economists often use such cycle models, and they don't predict the future of the stock market. And in management we have organization life cycles, and in marketing product life cycles. It helps, but only a little with predicting the future.

Next is Spiral. Under PAST I drew the beginnings of a cycle with A → B, but then C veers out of that orbit, and becomes either a downward or upward spiral. Under Future I drew a horizontal spiral, a vortex, which resembled a spring, loose at each end, but tightly wound in the middle. As Morson (1993) argues, when you enter or leave a vortex, the forces are not so strong, but in the middle there are few degrees of movement. We can begin to notice when we are in a spiral.

Finally, I have been playing with the idea of assemblage. And under 'PAST' I wrote the A → B and the A → C sequencing of meetings in rooms of Tamara. Under FUTURE< the props that are actants, the actors who are actants, the scene blocking, stage directions, agential storytelling, and timespacemattering, as a summary of the generativity of ideas from our meeting this day.

In sum, perhaps action research (AR) is focused more on social networks, while Qualimetric Intervention Research (QIR) if focused more on the intraplay of assemblages and networks, and on the theatrics. As a self-proclaimed 'materialist' I want to develop what for Latour (2005) is an actor-network-theory approach to social construction, one that reassembles the social, including the 'vibrant materiality' (Bennett, 2010) conditions of what Barad (2007) calls 'agential realism' and its intraplay with storytelling that shapes the future of organizations. Storytelling can be agential, and implicated with and through materiality.

REFERENCES

Aristotle. (1985). *Nicomachean Ethics*. Terence Irwin, Trans. Indianapolis/Cambridge: Indianapolis Publishing Company. (*Nicomachean Ethics* was first written 350 BCE)

Bakhtin, M. (1981). *The dialogic imagination*. M. Holquist, Ed.; C. Emerson & M. Holquist, Trans. Austin: University of Texas Press.

Barad, K. (2007). *Meeting the universe halfway: Quantum physics and the entanglement of matter and meaning*. Durham/London: Duke University Press.

Bennett, J. (2010). *Vibrant matter: A political ecology of things*. Durham/London: Duke University Press.

Berger, P. L., & Luckmann, T. (1966). *The social construction of reality: A treatise in the sociology of knowledge*. New York: Anchor Books.

Boje, D. M. 2001. Narrative Methods for Organizaitonal and Communication Research. London: Sage.

Davis, L. E., & Taylor, J. C. (1972). The design of jobs: Selected readings. New York: Penguin Press.

Deleuze, G., & Guattari, F. (1987). *A thousand plateaus: Capitalism and schizophrenia* (B. Massumi, Trans.). Minneapolis: University of Minneapolis Press.

Latour, B. (2005). *Reassembling the social: An introduction to actor-network-theory*. Oxford/New York: Oxford University Press.

Lewin, K. (1951) *Field theory* in social science; selected theoretical papers. D. Cartwright (ed.). New York: Harper & Row.

Morson, G. S. 1993. Narrative and Freedom: The Shadows of Time. Conn: Yale University Press.

———. (1994). *Narrative and freedom: The shadows of time*. New Haven/London: Yale University Press.

Robertson, D. S. (1940). A Spanish contribution to the theory of 'fluctuations.' *Economicia, 7*(25), 50–65.

Savall, H., Zardet, V., & Bonnet, M. (2008). *Releasing the untapped potential of enterprises through socio-economic management*. Geneva, Switzerland: ILO (International Labour Office) Bureau of Employers' Activities.

Contributors

Mário Aquino Alves is Associate Professor of Organization Theory and Nonprofit Management at the Escola de Administração de Empresas da Fundação Getulio Vargas (FGV-EAESP), in São Paulo, Brazil. In recent years he has studied organization discourse and narratives. His current research interests include the impact of social movements in corporate strategy and in policy making.

Tommi Auvinen, Licentiate (business and economics), is PhD Student of Leadership and Management at the University of Jyväskylä, Finland. His areas of specialization are storytelling and leadership, and human resource management.

David M. Boje is a Bill Daniels Ethics Fellow, former Bank of America Endowed Professorship (awarded September 2006–2010), and past Arthur Owens Professorship in Business Administration (June 2003–June 2006) in the Management Department, New Mexico State University. His focus is on study of ethics, critical theory ethics, feminism, agential materialism, and storytelling and antenarratives in organizations. Professor Boje is described by his peers as an international scholar in the areas of narrative, storytelling, postmodern theory & critical storytelling ethics. He has published 17 books and 125 articles. Latest books Storytelling Organizations (Sage), and Critical Theory Ethics in Business (Info-age Press).

Enrique Campos-López, Ph. D. in Chemistry from the National University of México (UNAM, 1970). Founder and director of several Mexican research institutions related with technology, natural resources, systems and environmental management. Professor and invited scientist in Mexican and foreign institutions, Consultant for international organizations in industrial management, science and technology, information systems and training. Dr. Campos-López has being distinguished by the Mexican Government with National Award in Chemistry. At the present time is a Researcher in the CIATEJ (Guadalajara, Jalisco, Mexico), an R&D and innovation Center, part of the National Council of Science and Technology (CONACYT), where he is leading projects on innovation networks and cooperative research.

Darren Dalcher is Professor of Software Project Management at Middlesex University and Director of the National Centre for Project Management. He has been named by the Association for Project Management as one of the top 10 "movers and shapers" in project management and has also been voted Project Magazine's Academic of the Year for his contribution in "integrating and weaving academic work with practice". Following industrial and consultancy experience in managing IT projects, Professor Dalcher gained his PhD in Software Engineering from King's College, University of London. In 1992, he founded and has continued as chair of the Forensics Working Group of the IEEE Technical Committee on the Engineering of Computer-Based Systems, an international group of academic and industrial participants formed to share information and develop expertise in project and system failure and recovery. He has written over 150 papers and book chapters on project management and software engineering. He is Editor-in-Chief of *Software Process Improvement and Practice,* an international journal focusing on capability, maturity, growth and improvement; editor of a major new book series, *Advances in Project Management*, which synthesises leading edge knowledge, skills, insights and reflections in project and programme management and of a new companion series, Fundamentals of Project Management, which provides the essential grounding in the key areas of project management. He is a Fellow of the Association for Project Management and the British Computer Society, and a Member of the Project Management Institute, the Academy of Management, the Institute for Electrical and Electronics Engineers, and the Association for Computing Machinery. He is a Chartered IT Practitioner.

Daniel Dauber is a PhD candidate at the Vienna University of Economics and Business (WU). From 2007 to 2009, he had been research and teaching assistant at the Department of European Affairs (WU). His doctoral thesis focuses on hybridization in mergers and acquisitions. Since 2008, he is a member of the 'Merger & Acquisition Division' of the EuroMed Research Business Institute. His major research interests are International Business and Management, Organisational Change and Organisational Behaviour.

Clarinda Dir has worked for a non-profit for the last 25 years, currently as a Project Manager, and is an adjunct faculty member at the University of Central Missouri teaching Teams, Systems, and Organizational Behavior. Her research interests focus on the application of social behaviors, norms and theology to management strategy.

Lynette Drevin is a lecturer in Computer Science and Information Systems at North-West University, Potchefstroom, South Africa. She has authored and co-authored a number of conference and journal papers on the topics of security education, ethical issues in Information Technology (IT) and narratives in Information Systems (IS). She has been a member of IFIP WG 11.8 (Security Education) since 1995 and has acted as secretary of this working group for a number of years. She is a member of the Computer Society of South Africa (CSSA), the South African Institute for Computer Scientists and Information Technologists (SAICSIT) and the Association for Computing Machinery (ACM). Her research interests include information security awareness and education, ethics in IT, as well as the use of narratives in the investigation of Information System successes and failures.

Kim Economides is Director of the Legal Issues Centre and Professor of Law at the University of Otago in New Zealand (2009–). Previously, Professor of Legal Ethics and a former Head of Exeter Law School (1999–2004). Before joining Exeter University in 1979 he was a researcher on the Florence Access to Justice Project based at the European University Institute in Italy. He co-directed the ESRC-funded Access to Justice in Rural Britain Project (1983–1987) and from 1993–95 was seconded as Education Secretary to the Lord Chancellor's Advisory Committee on Legal Education & Conduct (ACLEC). He was Founding General Editor of the international journal *Legal Ethics* (1998–2008) and chaired the Board of Trustees of the Hamlyn Trust (2004–09). In 2006 he was appointed Specialist Adviser to the Joint Parliamentary Committee on the Draft Legal Services Bill, now the Legal Services Act 2007. He has held visiting positions at universities in Japan and Australia.

Gerhard Fink is retired Jean Monnet Professor. During 2002–2009 he was Director of the doctoral programs at WU (Vienna University of Economics and Business), Austria. He was the Director of the Research Institute for European Affairs during 1997–2003. He can refer to about 230 publications in learned journals and authored or (co-) edited about 15 books. In 2005, he was Guest Editor of the Academy of Management Executive. He is Associate Editor of the *European Journal of International Management* and Co-editor of the *European Journal of Cross-Cultural Competence and Management*. His research interests are in intercultural management, international business, business strategies and organisational change in the European market(s).

Barbara Fryzel, an economist by training with the diplomas from the University of Economics in Krakow (MSc in Corporate Finance) and the Jagiellonian University (PhD in Economics, Management Sciences), is an associate professor of management at the Jagiellonian University.

She was an Honorary Research Fellow at the University College London in 2006-2008 and is the laureate of the fellowship program of the Foundation for Polish Science. During her commercial career she co-operated with many international businesses including British Petroleum Plc or Royal Ahold, performing various operational roles including Commercial Manager, Associate Director Professional Consultancy and working for corporate clients investing in Central and Eastern Europe. Key publications include co-edited "The Role of Large Enterprises in Democracy and Society", B. Fryzel and P. H. Dembinski (eds), Palgrave Macmillan, 2010. She specializes in corporate social responsibility.

Kevin Grant, is a pioneer in the emerging field of spiritual leadership and developing spiritual community within organizations. He is a widely published author and a sought after lecturer and keynote speaker. Dr. Grant teaches leadership, corporate finance, and organizational behavior at leading colleges and graduate schools in California. His consulting clients include Fortune 500 and international non-profit organizations.

With a cross-industry perspective from the private to the public firm, he has brought his leadership style and insights to key leaders. Dr. Grant's career spans industries, serving as a treasurer of the second largest IT firm in the world, to CFO of privately held firms, and chief of staff of a prestigious philanthropic Foundation. His work has spanned from workouts and turn-arounds to mergers and acquisitions. In recent years, he has focused on his research in the field of leadership—primarily in the underserved field of spiritual leadership in the workplace. His extensive research and study has revealed practical tools that today's leaders need for effective and sustainable growth and opportunity. Raised in the third world cultures of Saudi Arabia, India and Pakistan, Dr. Grant is particularly acute to the international markets and the need for leaders that span cultures. His work comes from personal experiences within the workplace, and living in third world cultures.

His academic experience revolves around teaching and providing workshops on leadership and finance, earning degrees in MBA entrepreneurial finance and PhD in Organizational Leadership. Kevin continues to write and publish on subjects such as compassionate leadership, how to lead imperfect people and create an environment of forgiveness

Richard Herder is an assistant professor of speech communication at Southwest Minnesota State University. He is currently ABD in the PHD program in public communication, rhetorical studies track, at Georgia State University in Atlanta, Georgia. He is interested in anti-corporate campaigns and his work draws upon resources in rhetoric, critical theory, and organizational studies.

Hilda G. Hernández holds a PhD in Sociology and is professor at the School of Sociology and Political Sciences of the Universidad Autónoma de Coahuila in Torreón, México. Her research deals with the culture of participation of social actors in the management of Laguna water system and related education issues. She coordinates a cooperative innovation network of agents interested in exploring cooperation and social learning as ingredientes for the sustainable use of water resources in La Laguna (México). With the participation of university students, she is building-up a regional archive of water news, testimonies and narratives.

Yue Cai-Hillon is an assistant professor at the University of Central Missouri teaching strategic management and management consulting. Prior to entering academia, Yue worked as a software developer. Although it was a short lived career, the experience allowed her to personally experience the disjointed relationships of the grand narratives and antenarratives between the individuals and the organizations. Since then, she has worked closely with Professor David M. Boje in the field of critical management and storytelling organizations. She has published articles, book chapters, and conference proceedings on the interpretation of strategy changes through storytelling, organization discourse, management consulting, and organization social consciousness. Her future research interests are strategy changes beyond text, global industrialization and responsibilities, management consulting, and action learning beyond lectures, cases, and simulations.

Steve King is a veteran management consultant, technologist and social media architect with 20 years of hands-on experience in the areas of organizational project design, knowledge management, software development and industry analysis, including strategic work for Cisco, Intel, HP, Dell, Motorola, IBM, Microsoft and McGraw-Hill. King has published over 150 articles and papers for an international audience of business and technology professionals.

Jeff Leinaweaver, PhD—Institute for Social Innovation, Fielding Graduate University. Jeff Leinaweaver is a fellow with the Institute for Social Innovation at Fielding Graduate University. As a fellow, he studies and explores the social construction of narrative identity, narrative marginality, antenarrative inquiry and how cross-cultural communication affects the use of self. He also works with the World Café foundation on topics related to social change, sustainability and storytelling. In addition, he is an organizational and leadership consultant working in the areas of sustainability and global diversity. He has a PhD in human and organizational systems and is a certified coach and global professional in human resources (GPHR).

Sergio Luis Seloti Jr., has a Bachelor´s degree in Business Administration from Universidade Presbiteriana Mackenzie and a MSc in Business Administration from Escola de Administração de Empresas da Fundação Getulio Vargas (FGV-EAESP). Specializing in Business Strategy, he has researched the formation of Strategic Alliances and the Sensemaking process between executives at big coporations through Storytelling. He is currently a professor at Impacta Technological University in Brazil as well as the managing partner at Influire, a consulting firm focused on strategic solutions.

Kenneth Mølbjerg Jørgensen, Ph.D., is Associate Professor at The Department of Education, Learning and Philosophy at Aalborg University in Denmark. He does research and teaches within power, language, ethics and identity in relation to management, education and learning. Kenneth has authored and co-authored numerous books, book chapters and journal articles. Recent authored and co-authored books and articles are "Power without Glory—A Genealogy of a Management Decision" published by CBS Press, "Human Resource Development—A Critical Text" published by Sage and "Resituating Narrative and Story in Business Ethics" published in *Business Ethics: A European Perspective.*

Anna Linda Musacchio Adorisio, is a post-doctoral fellow at the Gothenburg Research Institute, University of Gothenburg, Sweden. She holds a Ph.D in Communication Studies from the University of Lugano, Switzerland. Prior to Sweden, she has conducted research in Switzerland, U.S.A. and Italy. She studies storytelling in banking institutions.

Majella O'Leary is a Senior Lecturer in Organization Studies at the University of Exeter, UK. Prior to moving to Exeter in 2002, she worked for five years as a Lecturer in Management at the National University of Ireland, Cork. Majella's takes a broadly critical approach to her research and is interested in the cultural, political and ethical aspects of work and organizing. Majella has built up a strong reputation in the area of research methods and in particular, organizational storytelling and she has used organizational storytelling as a way of understanding organizational issues in the newspaper, legal, and financial industries and in particular in understanding moral and financial scandals. Majella's work has been published in journals including *Human Relations* (where it received a best paper award), *Journal of Management Inquiry, Journal of Business Ethics, European Journal of Business Ethics and Legal Ethics.*

Michel Péron, is emeritus professor at the University of Paris 3 Sorbonne Nouvelle. He is a researcher at the ISEOR and the CERVEPAS; His research interests lie in cross-cultural management, corporate ethics and the history of economic ideas.

Grace Ann Rosile, PhD, associate professor of management at New Mexico State University, studies organizational storytelling, ethics, pedagogy, and academic integrity. "Storying" integrity led to her 2005 Center for Academic Integrity national award. On two boards (Journal of Management Education, and Standing Conference on Management and Organization Inquiry), she has articles in the *Journal of Applied Behavioral Science, Management Communication Quarterly, Organization Studies, Ephemera, Journal of Management Inquiry, Journal of Management Education, Journal of Organizational Change Management*, and *Communication Research*. She created training in embodied leadership, teamwork, and communication using structured experiences with horses called "Horse Sense At Work" (www.horsenseatwork.com).

Henri Savall, is professor of management at the University of Jean Moulin Lyon 3, IAE Business School. He is the founder and director of the ISEOR research center. He created in 1973 the Socio-Economic Approach to Management which is based on a critical theory of traditional economic and management sciences. This theory has been experimented in a variety of companies and organizations across countries and continents, based on his seminal book "Work and People" first published in English in 1981.

Frits Schipper, studied physics and philosophy. He did his Phd in philosophy with a dissertation on the epistemology and philosophy of mathematics of Husserl and Carnap (in Dutch). After his Phd he became lecturer in the philosophy of science at the VU University Amsterdam. Currently, he coordinates a masters program in the philosophy of management and organization (M&O) at this university. Being a member of two research groups (dep. of philosophy and dep. of economics VU), his research is on philosophical issues in connection with M&O; among special areas of interest are creativity and rationality, (corporate) governance, epistemology and knowledge management, philosophy and practice. Presentations of research, inter alia, in Barcelona, Boston, Helsinki, Kopenhagen, Las Vegas, London, Lyon, München, Namen, Oxford, Philadelphia, Oxford, Washington DC. He is a member of the Executive Editorial Board of the journal *Philosophy of Management* and chairman of the Vanwoodman Society.

Teppo Sintonen, PhD (business and economics) and PhD (sociology), is Adjunct Professor of Leadership and Management at the University of Jyväskylä, Finland. His research and writing projects and publications have addressed ethnicity, identity, leadership, the concept of culture—all approached from a narrative/storytelling and qualitatitive methodology informed, construtionist perspective. He has taught courses concerning for example narrative research methods and diversity management.

William L. Smith is an Assistant Professor of Accounting and Information Systems at New Mexico State University. He is a licensed CPA and business consultant. His current research interests include analysis of financial disclosures, rhetoric and storytelling, decision making, and critical theory in financial accounting. He is published in academic journals that include *Qualitative Research in Accounting & Management, Organizational Research Methods, Behaviour & Information Technology*, and *TAMARA Journal of Critical Organization Inquiry*.

Nicholas Snowden is a lecturer in management, and a business trainer. Having started working life in the agricultural industry, he gained an MBA at Henley Management College, focusing on Creative problem-solving techniques. He is currently completing a PhD in Management at Hull University Business School, examining the role of story and antenarrative in problem-solving. He lives in Beverley, England, with his wife and young family.

Jawad Syed is a senior lecturer in human resource management at Kent Business School, University of Kent, UK. His main academic interests include gender and diversity in organizations, international HRM and organizational knowledge. Dr Syed has widely written on issues related to business and HRM including his articles in the International Journal of Human Resource Management, Asia Pacific Journal of Management, Human Resource Management Journal, Human Resource Management Review, Management Learning, Women's Studies International Forum, and Gender, Work and Organization. In August 2010, Dr Syed co-founded and became a member of the first Working Group of the South Asian Academy of Management (SAAM), a professional association for scholars dedicated to creating and disseminating knowledge about management and organizations in South Asia.

Jo A. Tyler, Ed.D. is Assistant Professor at Pennsylvania State University, Harrisburg, where she teaches in the M.Ed. program in Training and Development. Prior to joining Penn State, Jo was a corporate practitioner in multinational environments for 25 years, beginning at Hewlett-Packard, and most recently as vice president of organization and management development at Armstrong World Industries. In addition to her work at Penn State, she consults with organizations interested in the influence and interplay of their stories, storytelling and organizational narratives, and provides customized workshops on a range of topics. She has published articles and book chapters on storytelling and listening in organizational settings, as well as on other topics related to organizational development. She can be reached at jat235@psu.edu.

Alena Urdiales-Kalinchuk, is an Industrial Engineer with 15 years of experiences as a consultant and trainer for Mexican organizations on systems thinking, organizational learning and team building. She has being research consultant in the design and implementation of projects on incubation of cooperative innovation networks and communities of practice where she has being applying concepts such as participative action learning, narrative, and systems tools. Presently she lives in Guadalajara being part of an interdisciplinary team doing research on the formation of innovation networks among the members of fruit supply chains of the West part of Mexico.

Diane Walker. I have had a life-long fascination with schooling, most recently culminating with a dissertation on a pedagogy of critical happiness, and the implications for teaching and learning. I've expressed critical happiness as those qualities by which people experience and understand pleasure, delight, contentment, optimism, joy, creativity, flow, satisfaction, and other similar qualifications in their subjective well-being. I am interested in the multi-dimensional connections amongst disciplines—particularly science, math, and literacy—and in how relationships between people contribute to greater happiness in teaching and learning, to the creation of a socially just world, and to education and the significance of life.

Maurice Yolles is professor emeritus in Management Systems at Liverpool John Moores University. His doctorate, completed two decades ago, was in mathematical social theory, in particular the formal dynamics of peace and conflict. He has published 2 research books with a third in preparation, and more than 200 papers. He heads the Centre for the Creation of Coherent Change and Knowledge, which runs courses and does research into transformational change. Within this context, he has also been involved in, and run, a number of international research and development projects for the EU and in Asia. He is the editor of *Journal of Organisational Transformation and Social Change*.

Véronique Zardet, is professor of management at the University of Jean Moulin Lyon 3, IAE Business School and co-director of the ISEOR research center. In 2001, she received the Rossi award from the Academy of Moral and Political Sciences (Institut de France) for her work on the integration of social variables into business strategy. Her research is focused on the conduct of strategic change and the improvement of socio-economic performance in companies and public services.

Index

Page numbers in *italics* denotes a table/diagram